Historicis
and the

ALSO BY PATRICK J. CHARLES

*The Second Amendment: The Intent and Its Interpretation
by the States and the Supreme Court* (McFarland, 2009)

Historicism, Originalism and the Constitution

The Use and Abuse of the Past in American Jurisprudence

Patrick J. Charles

McFarland & Company, Inc., Publishers
Jefferson, North Carolina

LIBRARY OF CONGRESS CATALOGUING-IN-PUBLICATION DATA

Charles, Patrick J., author.
    Historicism, originalism and the constitution : the use and abuse
of the past in American jurisprudence / Patrick J. Charles.
        p.   cm.
    Includes bibliographical references and index.

    ISBN 978-0-7864-7931-3 (softcover : acid free paper) ∞
    ISBN 978-1-4766-1515-8 (ebook)

    1. Constitutional law—United States—Interpretation and
construction.   2. Constitutional history—United States.
3. Firearms—Law and legislation—United States—History.
4. Citizenship—United States—History.   5. United States.
Constitution. 2nd Amendment.   6. United States.
Constitution. 14th Amendment.   I. Title.
    KF4552.C43 2014
    342.73'001—dc23   2014009418

BRITISH LIBRARY CATALOGUING DATA ARE AVAILABLE

Cover images © iStockphoto/Thinkstock

Printed in the United States of America

McFarland & Company, Inc., Publishers
   Box 611, Jefferson, North Carolina 28640
      www.mcfarlandpub.com

In remembrance of coach and mentor Thomas Metcalfe.

Table of Contents

Acknowledgments

As I finalized this manuscript, one the most influential men in my life passed away—Thomas Metcalfe. It is to his memory that this book is dedicated. For six of my formative years, Thomas Metcalfe (and his family) was a daily fixture in my life, teaching me the game of football, and, in the process, instilling the virtues of honor, integrity, loyalty, courage, commitment, and humility, as well as teaching the importance of teamwork, friendship, and family. Perhaps by fate, the passing of Thomas Metcalfe came at a time when I was reflecting on my own past; particularly what events and people have led me down this current path. I can unequivocally say that Thomas Metcalfe played an important part. For over fifty years Thomas Metcalfe instructed and inspired young men in the game of football. This included his sons, Ron Metcalfe and Randy Metcalfe, who were my coaches at James Whitcomb Riley High School, in South Bend, Indiana. During this later period, Thomas Metcalfe volunteered his services. He was not paid, but taught because of a tireless devotion to the game of football and serving the community.

I did not know it at the time it was all happening, but the teachings of Thomas Metcalfe and his family have had a lasting impact on my life, particularly in my service to the community. Thomas Metcalfe joined the Navy in World War II, and I would go on to enlist in the Marine Corps. Not surprisingly, much of what I learned in the Marines was an extended education of my time with the Metcalfe family. The same virtues of honor, integrity, loyalty, courage, commitment, and humility, as well as the importance of teamwork, friendship, and family rang true. I even remember the last time I was fortunate to be alongside Thomas Metcalfe. I had finished my five-year enlistment with the Marine Corps, was attending the George Washington University, and decided to spend the summer volunteering at football workouts. Living in Washington, D.C., at the time, I could have spent my summer working on Capitol Hill or at some political non-profit. However, I wanted to give back to the South Bend community, the Riley football program, and the Metcalfe family that had given so much to me. It was time and effort well spent, for not only was I able to spend time mentoring the next generation, but I was also able to show my gratitude to the Metcalfe family for placing me on the right path.

It is a path that eventually led me to graduate with a bachelor of arts in history and international affairs from the George Washington University, and a juris doctor from Cleveland-Marshall College of Law, both of which have proven instrumental to the writing of this book. And given that this is a book about history in law, I am indebted to a number of historians and legal professionals for their friendship, mentorship, guidance, and support. First, I owe a debt of gratitude to the faculty of the Cleveland-Marshall College of Law for its continuing support, especially David F. Forte, Kevin F. O'Neill, and Steven H. Steinglass. Since those formative years in legal training, I have been fortunate to work with or receive advice from other legal professionals who have been gracious in their time, including Richard L. Aynes, Josh Blackman, Joseph Blocher, Nora V. Demleitner, Garrett Epps, Ranjit Hakim, Calvin H. Johnson, Suzanne Loose, Darrell A.H. Miller, Francine Radford, Michael Rappaport, Reggie Robinson, Rachel E. Rosenbloom, David Rubenstein, Mike Sacks, Michael A. Scaperlanda, Peter H. Schuck, Lawrence Solum, Juliet Stumpf, and Geoffrey Wyatt.

The support and advice given by a number of historians has been equally, if not more, gracious. In addition to continuing support from the Department of History at the George Washington University, I have been fortunate to learn from a number of historians who specialize in a variety of fields, ranging from social history to intellectual history. This includes Adele Alexander, David Armitage, Muriel Atkin, Nemata Blyden, James S. Cockburn (deceased), Saul Cornell, Thomas Y. Davies, Paul Finkelman, Tim Harris, Peter Hoffer, Woody Holton, James Horton, Stanley N. Katz, Erin Rahne Kidwell, David Thomas Konig, Nathan Kozuskanich, Edward G. Lengel, Robert E. Mensel, William O'Reilly, William Pencak, J.G.A. Pocock, Jack N. Rakove, Lois G. Schwoerer, Quentin Skinner, Mary Thompson, Tess Webber, and Judy Weiss. To anyone I may have left out, I apologize for the oversight.

And of course I am appreciative of the continued support from friends and family. Since I published *The Second Amendment: The Intent and Its Interpretation by the States and the Supreme Court* (McFarland, 2009), a number of people have come and gone. I have reconnected with friends I had not seen since I was a Marine embassy guard protecting the United States Consulate in Shanghai, China. I also regained a person that I loved dearly and unconditionally, only to lose that person once again. There have been large additions to my life, such as an extended military family with Air Force Special Operations Command and the 352nd Special Operations Group. But with this gain comes loss such as when, on August 6, 2011, thirty-one special operations forces were shot down in a CH-47 Chinook in Wardak Province, Afghanistan. Then there have been brand new family additions such as three nephews born in 2013. Certainly, I could continue to provide examples as to how much has changed in the past four years. In some instances the change was positive, in some negative, and in others reflective. But no matter the outcome, I have come to appreciate those friends and family who have unconditionally loved, respected, and supported me. While they may not all agree with the propositions set forth in this book or even some of the decisions I have made in my life, they have been there when needed and continue to do their utmost to fulfill their promises. I will continue to do the same.

Last but not least, I want to acknowledge Annwen Elizabeth Evans Bates for editing the majority of the manuscript. One of the challenges in writing a book on history, originalism and the Constitution is making it palatable for general readers. This was a goal I hoped to accomplish, and undoubtedly Annwen's edits aided in this endeavor.

Preface

The use of history in law is a time-honored tradition. Well before the Constitution's ratification, the Greek muse Clio was invoked to support legal rationales, arguments and theories. Whether it is a historical event, tradition or custom is negligible, for each has been drawn upon, at one time or another, to provide a moral and philosophical guide to the law's development. Today the use of history in law is more prominent than ever with the rise of originalism. As to what constitutes originalism differs depending upon who is asked. Some view originalism as the use of historical sources to discern the meaning or intentions of the Constitution. Others perceive the task of originalism to be more complex. To these individuals, originalism is less about history and more about defining legal meaning at a particular point in time.

But no matter one's definition of originalism, the unabashed truth is originalism invokes history, calling upon Clio, to define the contours of the Constitution. The question this book hopes to answer, among others, is the legitimacy of this pursuit. Do originalist methodologies produce historically accurate results? If originalist methodologies do not produce accurate results, how is originalism's invocation of the past a legitimate form of constitutional interpretation? Are originalists correct in claiming originalism has always existed in one form or another? Were the founding generation's greatest legal minds thoroughgoing originalists as some originalists claim? If the founders were not originalists, how did late eighteenth-century legal minds invoke history when interpreting the law? Does the founding generation's view of history in law even matter and should it guide the present?

It is by seeking the answers to these questions that one learns originalism has not always existed, nor is originalism the embodiment as to how the founding generation interpreted the Constitution. Late eighteenth-century jurists did not employ history in law in a manner that resembles originalism in any of its forms. The reality—whether proponents of originalism want to admit it or not—is originalism is a modern-day legal theory that employs historical sources as a means to interpret the Constitution. Still, despite originalism being a modern legal theory, one may argue it is the best means in an imperfect world and leads us closer to restoring the framers' Constitution than any other legal theory. This is essentially the core of originalism as a legitimate legal theory. But it is difficult for originalism to claim legitimacy when its use of historical sources leads to ahistorical results. To be clear, the underlying problem with originalism is it runs counter to what the employment of accepted historical methodologies provides.

Therefore, what this book proposes is a different approach to history in law. It is what I refer to as historical guideposts. It respects historical methodologies, places text and events in total historical context, is honest about what the record does and does not provide, mitigates judicial mythmaking, and advances history as more of a guide to the law than a strict outcome determinative tool. The historical guidepost approach is not one and the same with originalism or other historically based approaches to interpreting the Constitution, for the historical guidepost approach first and foremost relies on the employment of historical methodologies to interpret the Constitution. It is only after a legitimate historical foundation has been established that legal methodologies and reasoning may be employed. The historical guidepost approach is also different given it does not seek to strip the judiciary of its independence. Instead, the historical guidepost approach operates on the presumption that the past and the present are not the same, nor can they ever be. Thus, there will be instances where the dead hand of the past is merely a consideration to weigh along with others. There will also be instances where the past should have no bearing on the present given the consequences that would result.

Seeing that historical methodologies are the gravitas of the historical guidepost approach, it will receive criticism from a variety of interpretational theorists. Those who subscribe to living constitutionalism or reject any historically based approach to constitutional interpretation will argue it is nonsensical to bind the present by the dead hand of the past. But criticisms like this, which seek to completely discard history as an interpretive tool, essentially undo the Constitution itself. For hundreds of years, history has played a vital role when interpreting the Constitution, meaning most of today's constitutional jurisprudence is rooted in history in some form or another, whether opponents of history in law want to admit it or not.

Those who subscribe to originalism or other historically based methods of constitutional interpretation will also criticize the historical guidepost approach, but on different grounds. Given the historical guidepost approach stresses employing historical methodologies before legal methodologies, claims of "history office law"—inquiring into the meaning of the Constitution, yet neglecting the distinctive aspects of the legal task at hand—will be common-place. However, "history office law" criticisms fail for two reasons. First, when legal commentators complain of "history office law" it is nothing short of a hypocritical double standard. It remains unclear why it is acceptable for the legal community to make claims about history through the employment of ad hoc legal methodologies, yet it is unacceptable for historians to make claims about the law, at a particular point in time, by employing historical methodologies. Second, and more important, it is difficult for any historically based approach to constitutional interpretation to claim legitimacy when the resulting historical narrative lacks objectivity or is inaccurate. This is not to say each and every historical narrative provided by members of the legal community is without objectivity and accuracy. There are a number of historically conscious legal commentators who employ historical methodologies properly and hold true to what the evidentiary record does and does not provide. But more often than not these legal commentators are the exception to the majority of "law office" historians.

In conclusion, the point of this book is to address the problems associated with history in law, and provide workable solutions that allow the legal community to answer the constitutional questions of today, all the while respecting the historical record in the process. For more than a century, historians and legal professionals have debated what role, if any, history should serve when interpreting the Constitution. While there is general agreement history serves an important role, historians and legal professionals remain divided over how the dead hand of the past should be applied to the present. Hopefully, this book offers the solution or, at a minimum, facilitates a deeper discussion as to what role history should play in constitutional jurisprudence.

1

History in Law's Dilemma: A Dialogue on History's Role in Constitutional Interpretation

History is a blessing and a curse when it comes to constitutional interpretation. On the one hand, history is a blessing because the evidentiary record can provide jurists insight into the Constitution's origins, drafting, ratification, and understanding. This history in turn is weighed, compared, and contrasted with modern issues, ideas, beliefs, and fears. It creates both a personal and societal connection with our forbearers, which at times blossoms into a form of nationalism. But the use of history for constitutional interpretation is also a curse. The dead hand of the past can be subjectively employed as a means to either impede societal progress or advance an interpretational philosophy. With so much at stake it is not surprising that the use of history to interpret the Constitution has been the subject of great debate for over a century.

The United States of today is nothing like what our forbearers envisoned or witnessed develop during the late eighteenth and early nineteenth century. At that time, social mobility and economic opportunities were limited.[1] The nation was agriculturally driven and most people were uneducated.[2] Furthermore, the majority of the population lived great distances from cities, urban centers or coastal towns. As St. George Tucker aptly described the period, America was different from previous republics, like Athens and Rome, in that it consisted of "an agricultural people, dispersed over immense territory ... whose population does not amount to one able bodied militia man for each mile square."[3] This situation no longer presents itself today, as the overwhelming majority resides in cities and urban areas, with only a small portion of the population working in agriculture. So, in considering the dialogical relationship between history and the Constitution, it is worth noting a number of

5

late eighteenth-century political considerations, such as a minimalist interna-tional footprint,[4] the American people's distrust of standing armies,[5] and a policy of avoiding foreign conflicts.[6]

Seeing that the United States of today no longer resembles its late eighteenth-century form, it is no wonder that historians criticize the impor-tation of the past for use in the present. But even before the Constitution's ratification, it was commonplace for lawyers and jurists to invoke history as a means to interpret the law. It is a tradition that continues to this day when the legal community invokes either the intentions, meaning or understanding of a respective constitutional provisions. This includes the United States Supreme Court. In a 1938 article titled *Constitutional History and Constitutional Law,* Julius Goebel, Jr., criticized the Court's "historical approach" to incorporating the Bill of Rights to the states through the Fourteenth Amendment's Due Process Clause. Goebel, a legal history professor at Columbia Law School, expressed disfavor with the Court's picking and choosing of history.[7] He argued if the Court found it prudent to incorporate a few English common law traditions, it must import "all facets of the matter examined."[8] On its face, Goebel's criticism was meant to be satirical, for he felt a rigid historical approach would be "proceeding along paths trodeen by the long procession of long dead judges of long dead kings."[9] But it is interesting that Goebel's crit-icism still applies today. The fact of the matter is, the selective importation of the past for the present remains problematic in terms of historical accuracy and constitutional objectivity. For when the legal community picks and chooses historical evidence to adjudicate constitutional questions it is a dis-service to the past. Furthermore, it shrouds the legal problems and issues of today under the disguise of history.

Seventy years after Goebel's article, historians, legal scholars, lawyers, and jurists are still debating the proper role, if any, history should play in consti-tutional jurisprudence, with no consensus in view. Today proponents of an historical approach are often self-labeled originalists. They believe historical sources provide the judiciary with an honest and unbiased approach to inter-preting the Constitution.[10] Originalists come in different forms. There are those who subscribe to original intent, or interpreting the Constitution through the intentions of the people who drafted and ratified it.[11] Then there are original meaning or understanding proponents who are closely aligned with textualists, but in an ad hoc historical form.[12] Often termed new origi-nalists, they call for constitutional interpretation based upon what a "reason-able speaker of English would have attached" to the words, phrases, and sentences at the time a constitutional provision was adopted.[13] There is also strand of originalism referred to as semantic originalism, which is similar to new originalism with the caveat that it rejects the expected application of text. In its place, semantic originalism asks the broader question as to how a prospective constitutional phrase would have been understood by the era that adopted it.[14] Lastly, there is original methods originalism, which elicits meaning by referencing to the interpretive rules existing at the time the constitutional provision was adopted.[15] In line with both original intent and original meaning originalists, original method originalism proponents assert Founding Era interpretive rules predominantly relied upon intentionalism and textualism.[16]

What we today refer to as originalism—the use of historical sources to guide or facilitate constitutional interpretation—is not revolution in legal theory, but an evolution. Again, even before the ratification of the Constitution it was common for late eighteenth-century lawyers and jurists to invoke history when interpreting the law. But in the twentieth century the use of history for constitutional interpretation assumed many forms, including historicism,[17] intentionalism,[18] interpretivist history,[19] law office history,[20] historical narrative,[21] etc.[22] Where originalism separates itself from these approaches is the extent to which the historical record is employed.[23] As Paul W. Kahn aptly describes it, originalists view "political time" as a "past to be preserved."[24] And in some ways originalism runs parallel to mythicism because it "understands the present life of the citizen to be a representation of the past," which in turn undervalues the current political order.[25]

Originalists are also unique in that they advocate most constitutional cases or controversies can be adjudicated through some combination of textualism and intentionalism. This claim is denounced by most legal historians.[26] As Saul Cornell has pointed out on numerous occasions, the varieties of interpretation that can be found in any historical era are numerous, with the framing era proving no different.[27] Certainly not every interpretation can be deemed reasonable nor can an objective historian accept each and every viewpoint as correct.[28] The fact remains that *any* historical conclusion must be based on substantially and intimately related evidence, and not merely an assemblage of data which provides a plausible interpretation to the twenty-first century reader.[29] In many instances it is difficult for even the most seasoned historian to answer questions of the past, let alone legal scholars, lawyers, and jurists who may be unfamiliar with the intricacies of a particular historical era or event.

Originalists counter the critiques of Cornell and other historians by claiming history and originalism are not one in the same. They take particular issue when historians make accusations of or comparisons to "law office history," i.e., the selection and manipulation of historical data favorable to a predisposed legal position. To originalists, their legal theory merely employs historical sources as a means to retain constitutional integrity, and thus must be treated as separate from the work of professional historians.[30] In the words of Associate Supreme Court Justice Antonin Scalia, originalism works because historical sources provide the "*best means available* in an imperfect world."[31] To state it another way, originalism is perceived by its proponents as "less subjective, and intrud[ing] much less upon the democratic process" because it rests on a "reasoned analysis rather than a variety of vague ethico-political First Principles whose combined conclusion can be found to point in any direction the judges favor."[32]

This "less subjective" and "reasoned analysis" claim has been the subject of heated debate for over three decades.[33] Historian William M. Wiecek has gone so far as to label originalism a "dangerous delusion" seeing that "knowledge even of the facts of the past is imperfect at best."[34] Likewise, historian Robert W. Gordon has criticized originalism as having to "pick and choose our way among the relics, polish some of them up quite a bit, and leave others quietly to rest at the bottom of the sea."[35] And despite these methodological inconsistencies being continuously pointed out, the perception among historians is that originalists have made little, if any, effort to modify and improve their approach.[36] Instead originalists turn defensive and claim historians are overstepping their scholarly expertise by committing "history office law," i.e., inquiring into the meaning of the Constitution, yet neglecting the distinctive aspects of the legal task at hand. In other words, originalists argue historians are not trained lawyers. Therefore, historians misunderstand the purpose of originalism given that they focus on concerns of history rather than law.[37]

With originalists making the accusation of "history office law" and historians returning the favor with claims of "law office history," the dispute over history for constitutional interpretation has become an interdisciplinary turf war. In defense of historians, originalists fail to acknowledge it is the historian's function to preserve the past from distortion in the present. Whenever and wherever historical objectivity and accuracy are discarded, the historian sees it as their duty to correct the record. For historians to ignore these distortions is to allow myth to consume our past for use in the present.[38] Furthermore, it is inconsequential for originalists to cite "history office law" as a legitimate argument, especially when constitutional historians are not aloof to the adversarial system or how lawyers are trained. Unless originalists can point to something more, some ethical or functionality problem with historians educating legal professionals about poor historical paradigms,[39] claims of "history office law" are more nominal than real. It would mean that historical context is of little importance in understanding our past, when it is the bedrock of all history, especially intellectual history, which serves as a cornerstone of constitutional history.[40]

Again, originalism is only one of many historical approaches currently employed by the legal community. Not every employment of history to define or adjudicate the law qualifies. Just because a scholar, lawyer or jurist relies on tradition or a discussion of the past for legal interpretation does not mean said scholar, lawyer or jurist is employing originalism or must be categorized as some form of an originalist.[41] But whatever approach to history in law is assumed, there is a consensus among historians that the sum of historical facts should be honestly marshaled.[42]

This is not to say historians are immune to letting their political predispositions or political preferences consume intellectual integrity.[43] This is a criticism that originalists frequently utilize to question whether historical methodologies are truly better. Cases of intellectual dishonesty by historians have been extremely rare, however. Yet originalists remain skeptical on the grounds that constitutional historians are perceived as being unfamiliar with how the law operates. This critique is completely without merit. Constitutional historians are not naïve to assume legal scholars and lawyers will always adhere to universally accepted historical paradigms or exhibit watertight historical knowledge. Furthermore, historians understand the legal and historical communities do not maintain the same professional goal.[44] While the historian must do their best to seek a neutral observation of the past and an honest account about what the record does and does not provide,[45] it is not the duty of the legal scholars and lawyers to be neutral, nor has it ever been improper for them to infer conclusions with minuscule evidence.[46] If anything legal scholars and lawyers are anti-historians, for most of their training and purpose is to characterize evidence in a way that supports position "X" or "Y." To be clear, legal scholars and lawyers see it as their duty to take a stand on difficult historical questions that historians are often ethically forbidden from answering.

Yet despite all the methodological and intellectual disagreements, historians have generally been in accord with the legal community on the most important point—history has a role to play in constitutional interpretation. For instance in 1963, historian Paul L. Murphy accused the Supreme Court of committing a number of "law office history" violations.[47] He wrote historians could do little to change the Court's "methodology of legal decision making."[48] Still, Murphy felt historians should view the challenge to educate the Court as "a unique and exciting one." So long as historians furnished "complementary modern architectural materials," wrote Murphy, the Court would "not have to rely upon scrap lumber, salvage bricks, and raw stones" when adjudicating constitutional cases and controversies from a historical standpoint.[49] Thus, one might categorize Murphy as both a historical realist and idealist.

As a realist, he believed the Court would never "cease to be criticized when its decisions rely upon historical evidence for points of law." However, the idealist in Murphy hoped the Court's history would be improved by historians providing "the most accurate, thoroughly documented, and impeccable history [they are] capable of producing."[50]

Two years later, Alfred H. Kelly wrote an influential article more critical than Murphy's, concluding that the Supreme Court's "self-assumed role as a constitutional historian, has been, if not a naked king, no better than a very ragged one."[51] He found the Court's practice of "law office history" particularly worrisome, seeing that "by quoting history, the Court made history, since what it declared history to be was frequently more important than what history might actually have been."[52] Kelly's dissenting view is one that continues to this day, i.e., legal professionals ask questions of the past that the past cannot provide.[53] Surprisingly, in spite of all the historical consequences that can result from poor judicial history, Kelly did not call for the abandonment of history when interpreting the Constitution. He understood the "nature of the judicial process" was "too close to that of history-writing for the Court to ever abandon" the practice entirely.[54] Therefore, he proposed that the legal academy seek a "more sophisticated and restrained approach to the use of history."[55] Just what this approach should look like is unknown, given Kelly did not provide a framework. He only warned it was improper to "use and abuse" history to advance a judicial philosophy.[56]

Even Julius Goebel, Jr., who was highly critical of any historical approach in 1938, later came to the conclusion that "history is of direct and specific utility" to interpreting the law. Up to that point in time, the use of history was limited "by an inquiry into what the law was or has been" to find a solution to "present perplexities sought."[57] But by 1944 the status quo had changed. History had become a greater guiding influence on the judiciary. As a result, Goebel felt compelled to remind historians of their moral obligations and the importance of intellectual objectivity:

> Where such an historian, therefore, undertakes to speak of the past, since it is something a future court may need and use, he assumes a responsibility not lightly to be dismissed. This is a moral obligation the implications of which are far-reaching, for not only must the judge put trust in his word, but the parties litigant whose rights are whose fortunes will be affected by it. Once it is accepted and woven into the fabric of precedent, it becomes something upon which still others will place reliance. This obligation is of a different order than any imposed by the self-discipline of scholars in the field of political and economic history.... No man's rights are affected by their mistakes of facts or their misrepresentations of data.... But a historian of the law must be mindful of the especial fealty which he owes.[58]

Here Goebel placed the burden on historians to guide the legal community. It is an approach that Alfred L. Brophy has recently characterized as "applied legal history" or "deeply researched, serious scholarship that is motivated by, engages with, or speaks to contemporary issues." It is history that highlights "past injustices or demonstrates alternative intellectual traditions."[59] Of course, the legal backdrop of today is something that Murphy, Kelly or Goebel would have never imagined. They could not have foreseen a situation where any number of their law professor colleagues or students proclaimed themselves to be their historical equal. Yet this is the backdrop of the law today as originalism has entrenched itself into constitutional thought. In a sense, members of the legal community have embraced the attitude that historical facts are facts no matter who writes about them.[60] Those who support this line of thinking have valid point so long as all the facts are honestly marshaled and placed in the right order.[61] But the legal community must also acknowledge that this line of thinking extinguishes any claims of "history office law" as hypocritical. It cuts against common sense and reason if the legal community finds it acceptable to opine on what the historical record provides, yet criticize constitutional historians for conducting the same interdisciplinary practice in reverse.

From the perspective of historians, the legal community has yet to improve upon the "law office history" problems of the early to mid twentieth century. The use of history for constitutional interpretation is still perceived as intellectually dishonest and in conflict with historical objectivity.[62] It is a criticism that will continue until the legal community understands the virtue and importance of total historical context.[63] Overall, the point to be made is the legal community has much to learn from the intellectual history debates of years past. Certainly, intellectual history methodologies are in continual flux (as is the law), but this is not because the discipline is in disrepute. It has gradually improved to achieve a better and workable understanding of our past.

Perhaps one mid twentieth century intellectual historian the legal community should turn to is Goebel. After accepting the use of history for constitutional interpretation, Goebel sought to educate the legal community that the "writing of history requires maximum effort in the discovery of evidence and the utmost candor in presentation, for in no other way can the interest of truth be served."[64] He hoped to teach his legal colleagues that a true understanding and reflection of American constitutional history required more than a focus on the years of 1787 to 1791. Its development preceded those dates and involved much more than evidence "relevant to the statutory and constitutional provisions."[65] Thus, to Goebel, a true constitutional reflection required an understanding of the moral, philosophical, and intellectual development of the Anglo-American common law, especially its relationship to written constitutions, including its evolving character towards advancing liberty, not restraining it by the dead hand of the past.[66]

As its stands today, it cannot be said that the legal community at large is adhering to Goebel's recommendations. History is often treated as no better than a subcontractor or ideological tool to advance one's predisposed conclusion.[67] In some instances the conclusion will coincide with what a proper historical inquiry reveals. Even a broken clock is correct twice a day. But in most instances the conclusion does not reflect what the historical record provides and is in serious conflict with other accounts. It can lead generations to believe a false or mythical account of history is true, when it is not. Herein is the ultimate consequence of using and abusing history to interpret the Constitution. When a court of law proclaims history "X" or "Y" to be true, it props up the belief that it is legitimate history. As any first year law student knows, the first lesson is that precedent is more persuasive than secondary sources. Whether the secondary source is the legislative record, legal dictionary, legal treatise or law review article, precedent is the foremost guidepost by which the judiciary decides cases and controversies. And when it is Supreme Court precedent, there is no higher source from which to argue, to include the Court's historical pronouncements.

Therefore, whether the judiciary wants to acknowledge it or not, it is the only branch of government with the power to declare history. By selecting history "X" or "Y" as true, the judiciary forms a thought police that litigants must follow and work with in future cases and controversies.[68] It also leads generations of people to believe a selected constitutional history is true, which can result in even poorer historical constructs and myths. As historian David Thomas Konig aptly describes it:

> When [myths are] given constitutional status, these invented traditions become norms, and they reinforce popular beliefs.... Put bluntly, once a court uses the past as a foundation for an opinion, the court redefines the meaning of the past and gives a new, expanded use for that past to a court with a much broader jurisdiction—the court of public opinion, whose black letter law is the dreaded conventional wisdom. When judges re-write history, they give it legitimacy that serves their needs and the needs of the regime they lead. That is, historical argument, when employed to give a decision more constitutional authority, confers social and political constitutive authority.[69]

In short, poor historical paradigms can have dire consequences in both law and history. Not only can the selection of history "X" or "Y" affect constitutional jurisprudence for generations to come, but it can also affect the

American people's understanding of their past. Therefore, maintaining historical accuracy is something that not only historians should care about. It is also important that the legal community make the attempt to adhere to historical accuracy or at least marshal it honestly.[70] The question moving forward is whether history can be employed responsibly and accurately in the process.[71]

It is at this juncture that historians and the legal community seemingly diverge as to how the historical record should be employed. The divide raises a series of methodological questions. From a legal perspective, the questions raised include: is the historical approach to constitutional interpretation consistent with the framers' intent in drafting and ratifying the Constitution? Did the framers intend to bind the problems of the future with the dead hand of the past? How did the founding generation and eighteenth-century jurists employ history to adjudicate constitutional issues? And for historians, the questions are mostly the same, with the caveat as to whether the past can be applied without disparaging it or rewriting it for future generations.

The answers to these questions are central to settling the history-law divide, but they are even more important from a legitimacy standpoint. That is, constitutional legitimacy depends upon accuracy and predictability—a fact to which most jurists are well attuned. But each jurist places a different value on the use of history to adjudicate constitutional cases and controversies. Take for example the nine justices on the United States Supreme Court. Some of the justices rely more on evolving and growing jurisprudence, some rely on the purposes and consequences of a particular outcome, while others give substantial weight to text and history. Each philosophy has its caveats, including a variety of subparts dependent upon the case or controversy before the Court. But in terms of invoking history, for most of the Court's history the standard operating procedure was to employ historical evidence as a means to support an interpretation more so than to control it. In other words, the dead hand of the past was more of a guide and used sparingly to dictate precedent.[72]

A great place to start is the seminal case *McCulloch v. Maryland,* in which Chief Justice John Marshall and the Supreme Court ruled the Second Bank of the United States was a constitutional exercise of federal power.[73] In writing what has become one of the most important constitutional opinions in American jurisprudence, Marshall said little about the framers' intentions in drafting the Necessary and Proper Clause.[74] He also did not resort to any dictionaries or eighteenth-century sources to define "necessary" or "proper." Instead, Marshall viewed the Constitution as a flexible document that permitted Congress to exercise a "choice of means" when adopting legislation for an "appropriate" end.[75] Marshall elaborated on this point.

[The Necessary and Proper Clause] is made in a constitution intended to endure for ages to come, and consequently, to be adapted to the various crises of human affairs. To have prescribed the means by which government should, in all future time, execute its powers, would have been to change, entirely, the character of the instrument, and give it the properties of a legal code. It would have been an unwise attempt to provide, by immutable rules, for exigencies which, if foreseen at all, must have been seen dimly, and which can be best provided for as they occur.[76]

McCulloch was not the first instance that the Marshall Court coined the flexible "choice of means" doctrine. Writing fourteen years earlier, in *United States v. Fisher,* Marshall invoked the doctrine to uphold the constitutionality of a federal bankruptcy statute.[77] Marshall wrote, "Congress must possess the choice of means, and must be empowered to use any means which are in fact conducive to the exercise of a power granted by the constitution."[78] Here again, Marshall did not invoke history, but instead proclaimed a common Federalist view of the Constitution. To late eighteenth- and early nineteenth-century Federalists, the Constitution was not a stagnant document intended to be limited by the "properties of the legal code,"[79] nor was it bound by the public debates and editorials from 1787 to 1791, or some form of *ad hoc* public understanding through dictionaries. Just as the American Republic was growing, evolving, and changing, Marshall understood the Constitution would as well, to advance the public interest and welfare of the United States.

Associate Justice James Iredell expressed the same opinion years earlier. At first blush, during the 1788 North Carolina Ratification Convention, Iredell asserted Congress "can have no right to exercise any power but what is contained" in the Constitution. He added: "Negative words, in my opinion, could make the matter no plainer than it was before.... Those rights which are unalienable are not alienated. They still remain with the great body of the people."[80] However, after sitting on the Supreme Court bench for nine years—making the time to reflect on the Constitution as a working document—Iredell changed his view.[81] By 1799 Iredell admitted his 1788 statement was made with "personal conviction" and "well founded" at the time, but now thought it to be an "erroneous opinion."[82] Iredell elaborated:

It is vain to make any law unless some sanction be [added] to it, to prevent or punish its violation. A law without it might be the equivalent to a good moral sermon, but bad members of society would be as little influenced by one as the other. It is, therefore, necessary and proper, for instance, under the constitution of the United States, to secure the effects of all laws which impose a duty on some particular persons, by providing some penalty or punishment if they disobey. The authority to provide such is conveyed in the following general words in the constitution, at the end of the objects of legislation particularly specified:

"To make all laws which shall be necessary and proper for carrying into executing the foregoing powers and all other powers vested by this constitution in the government of the United States, or in any department or offices thereof." A penalty alone would not in every case be sufficient, for the offender might be rich and disregard it, or poor, though a willful offender, and unable to pay it. A fine, therefore, will not always answer the purpose, but imprisonment must be in many cases added, though a wise and humane legislature will always dispense with this, where the importance of the case does not require it. But if it does from the very nature of the punishment, it becomes a *criminal,* and not a *civil* offence....

What is necessary and proper in a time of confusion and general disorder, would not, perhaps be necessary and proper in a time of tranquility and order. These are considerations of policy not questions of law, and upon which the legislature is bound to decide according to its real opinion of the necessity and propriety of any act particularly in contemplation. It is, however, alleged, that the necessity and propriety of passing collateral laws for the support of others, is confined to cases where the powers are delegated, and does not extend to cases which have a reference to general danger only. The words are general, "for carrying into execution the special powers previously enumerated, and all other powers vested by the constitution in the government of the United States, or any department or officer thereof." If, therefore, there be anything necessary and proper for carrying into execution any or all of those powers, I presume that may be constitutionally enacted.[83]

In recent decades, a number of constitutional scholars have dissected the origins of the Necessary and Proper Clause to include Marshall's "choice of means" doctrine. Was Marshall's view based on textualism, a personal understanding of the Constitution, or was he influenced by leading Federalists?[84] Surprisingly, the historical evidence points to impeached and forgotten Pennsylvania Judge Alexander Addison.[85] Before ever assuming his position as Chief Justice, Marshall was introduced to the writings of Addison through his mentor and friend George Washington. And after reading Addison's charge to the grand jury entitled *Liberty of the Speech and Press,*[86] Marshall wrote to Washington that Addison's analysis was "well written" and hoped that "other publications on the same subject could be more generally read ... to make some impression on the mass of the people."[87]

Addison's analysis of the Necessary and Proper Clause was rather influential in Federalist circles. This fact alone, however, does not sufficiently explain why Marshall adopted it. There were greater forces at play, particularly how Marshall witnessed Jeffersonian Republicans use their partisan agenda to impeach Federalist judges, which included the likes of Alexander Addison.[88] The threat this posed on the maintenance of an independent judiciary was well known.[89] And in 1805, when Supreme Court Associate Justice Samuel Chase was in the midst of his own impeachment proceedings, also at the hands of Jeffersonian Republicans, Marshall wrote the proceedings were "sufficient to alarm the friends of a pure & of course independent judiciary."[90]

The notable historical point here is that the Marshall Court would not succumb to political pressure to rewrite the Constitution as one political party or interpretational theory would have it.[91] For the Court to truly be independent, Marshall knew it must be able to interpret the Constitution according to its spirit and principles, as well as its text. Indeed, sometimes constitutional interpretation required a turn to history, but this was uncommon leading up to the mid nineteenth century.[92] History was just one of many tools employed when interpreting and deciphering the law.

Returning to often forgotten Alexander Addison, in a letter addressed to a "young gentleman" about to "enter the Office of the Judge," Addison recommended a number of sources to both the legal scholar and honest professional:

> Great part of your time, then ought to be devoted to revising, extending, and fixing deeply in your mind, your past learning. A careful study of the Greek and Latin Classics, will assist greatly to form a just taste. The English Essays of the Spectator, &c. will give you a relish for the beauties of our own language. Attention to the Mathematics, will improve and strengthen your faculty of reasoning. The study of Natural History and Philosophy, will form your heart to virtue. History will instruct you in the character of Man, and the ways of Providence. I know no book more deserving your attention than the Bible; you will find in it more useful maxims, than in any other work.
>
> Read *good* books rather than *many* books. Your reading may be various, without being desultory or promiscuous, and it ought always to be attentive. Divide your time systematically, and carefully pursue the system you adopt. The morning, for instance may be employed with the Classics, ancient and modern; the forenoon with Law; and the afternoon and evening, with Science, History, &c.... The study of Moral Philosophy, especially the morality of the New Testament, is of the utmost consequence to a Lawyer—for the first qualification for that profession, is to be an honest man.[93]

Here, Addison clearly points to history as being useful, but as a moral and philosophical guide, not an outcome determinative tool. As will be discussed in the next chapter, such an approach was common among founding era jurists. History was employed to discuss the path of the law rather than bind the present.[94] There are indeed a minority of cases where history was employed to extract legal principles.[95] However, even in these instances, a number of factors controlled how the historical record was applied.

An instructive example as to the factors an eighteenth-century legal mind would consider when interpreting legal text can be found in Josiah Quincy, Jr.'s *The Law Commonplace Book.* Quincy, a prominent Boston attorney, considered four factors when deciphering the meaning of statutes. This included (1) what the common law was before the law in question; (2) the "Mischief" or "Defect" that common law did not provide for; (3) the remedy appointed to "Cure the D[is]ease" of the state; and (4) the "true Reason" and "Remedy" behind the legislation.[96] To the contemporary legal mind, these four factors may confuse and seemingly contradict one another. For one, why would a jurist even look into the "true Reason" of the law when the text of the statute is available to control interpretation? The answer is simple—legislators often drafted a law with the purpose of being vague so that its words would change meaning over time. It is for this reason that eighteenth-century jurists considered a turn to history in some form or another. But this still does not answer how history was thought best employed.

Today, those who subscribe to originalism propose the use of dictionaries or original meaning to determine the scope of legal language.[97] In the late eighteenth century, however, Quincy wrote how the historical inquiry can be complicated:

> When we talk of Meaning + Intention of (such) Laws, we ought to distinguish between the Meaning + Intention of those that were the chief Promoters of them, + the Meaning + Intention of those who only gave their Consent to the passing Them. As to the former, I make no Question, but it was their Intention to oblige etc.... tho' they durst not declare their Meaning [and] Intention in express words, because it w[ould] either have thrown out their Bill, or have occasion'd the inserting some express words against what they intended: They therefore chose to draw up their Bill in a dubious Sort of Expression, that after they had got it pass'd into a Law, they might make the most of it in the Execution.[98]

Quincy's words are still applicable for anyone wishing to decode the text of the Constitution. Historians, scholars, lawyers, and jurists alike can all attest to a number of dubious expressions that leave much unanswered in terms of meaning or scope. In many cases, the debates and subsequent state ratifying conventions do not help. Words, phrases, and provisions are discussed in terms of generality rather than defined. And in some cases there are competing interpretations based purely on politics, creating an objectivity dilemma. This in turn leads us to conduct a thorough historical analysis, which can have its own objectivity concerns since we are all prone to overlay our own distinctions onto the past.[99]

Again, most originalists would advocate for such analysis to be textually guided in order to advance the cause of objectivity and legitimacy.[100] In contrast, the intellectual historian knows such an inquiry can hinder our understanding of the Constitution's larger purpose.[101] The fact remains that the Constitution was guided by a number of legal and social influences to include the common law, the law of nations or natural law, custom, and the lessons learned from events like the American Revolution, contemporaneous State constitutions, the failed Articles of Confederation, and a number of rebellions.[102] Although this type of inquiry is denounced by some originalists, decoding the meaning of any respective constitutional provision requires familiarization with a number of influences.[103]

Who is to say the inclusion of general constitutional terms was not intentional as, in Quincy's words, to "make the most of it in the Execution?" Consider the First Amendment's Press Clause as an example. Within the founding generation there was general agreement that the "liberty of the press" was a "palladium of liberty" crucial for establishing and maintaining a republican form of government.[104] Still, this fact does not answer the scope question. There was disagreement among the drafters and ratifiers as to what the "liberty of the press" embodied. Some viewed it as protecting all publications and printers, and others just decent and candid ones.[105] Further, what should we make of seditious libel? By 1798 a number of pamphlets and editorials denounced seditious libel as a violation of the liberty of the press, yet up to that point in Anglo-American jurisprudence it had never been declared so.[106]

All and all the point worth making is a powerful one: historical analysis—this being a highly objective engagement with historical analysis—is difficult, and the interpretational errors that can result warrant serious consideration. It is troubling that originalists admit this deficiency, but dismiss it as a minor issue. For instance, Antonin Scalia admits there is "plenty of room for disagreement" as to what a respective provision's "original meaning was, and even more as to how that original meaning applies to the situation before the court."[107] At the same time, Scalia finds such "difficulties and uncertainties of determining original meaning" defensible because originalism allegedly answers more questions than any other approach.[108]

Few will disagree with Scalia that history is a persuasive tool in shaping our jurisprudence. Even Seventh Circuit Court of Appeals Judge Richard Posner, a dissenting voice on originalism, agrees that the law is the "most historically oriented," "backward-looking," and "past-dependent" of professions.[109] Yet Posner questions whether it is wise for jurists to shape jurisprudence on originalist principles. While admitting originalism seems to virtuously curb "judicial discretion by adopting a mechanical method of interpretation, one essentially lexicographical and algorithmic rather than historicist," Posner argues originalism is nothing more than a cloak for conservative judges to "forge an historical pedigree for their preferred positions in order to deflect charges of judicial creativity."[110] This is not to say Posner outright dismisses history as a judicial tool. "There is no problem with judges using history," writes Posner, "when there is a consensus among professional historians."[111]

Associate Supreme Court Justice Stephen Breyer is of a similar opinion. He queries, "If the Court is to decide major constitutional questions on the basis of history, then why not ask nine historians, rather than nine judges, to provide these answers?"[112] Breyer understands originalists perceive themselves to be providing "answers to difficult constitutional questions by proceeding objectively, almost mechanically, to examine past historical fact." The goal being such an "objective approach" will most adequately determine the "framers' detailed intentions," which will in turn allow the Court to "build and maintain continued public support for its decisions."[113]

Breyer, however, foresees many problems with such a rigid historical approach. For one, history can fail to provide "specific objective directions." The legal question may be so narrow that any relevant or sufficient historical material will be difficult to find. And this is not even considering whether the historical evidence is substantially and intimately related to the drafting, framing, and ratifying of the Constitution.[114] In sum, the objective dilemma presented is historical assumptions are often packaged and sold as historical fact. There are just questions of the past that history cannot definitively or objectively answer. And rearranging historical pieces of evidence to support position "X" or "Y" may seem like a more objective approach to constitutional interpretation to non-historians, but it actually undermines the judiciary's ultimate goal of accuracy, and therefore legitimacy.

There is also the matter of assuming jurists are the equivalent of professional historians. If a pure historical approach is the most objective, jurists must be trained and equipped to accept or reject pieces of historical evidence.[115] This is not an easy task when litigants, accompanied by amicus briefs, are advancing a myriad of views on the same historical issue, event or subject. Judge J. Harvie Wilkinson III, another dissenter to originalism, has been rather outspoken about this dilemma. "Judges are neither trained nor equipped to conduct this type of inquiry," writes Wilkinson. It is "anything but constraining" for judges to answer historical questions with which "skilled historians spend lifetimes grappling." Of course, Wilkinson does not completely foreclose the use of history for constitutional interpretation. It is only originalism, as currently constituted, that is problematic. As he puts it, unless judges operate "in a system set up for historical inquiry," the judge must "play amateur historian to gain access to the often inconclusive historical evidence." The result is an objectivity failure because "matching up distant eras is a treacherous business," especially when "those who lived in different centuries inhabit very different worlds."[116]

In response to these judicial criticisms, originalists cling to the belief that the role of historian is manageable, especially legal and constitutional history. Michael Rappaport, for instance, dismisses outright the notion that historians are "better at understanding the history relevant to the original meaning." Because historians are not "normally trained as lawyers and they often look at the history from a non-legal perspective," they are led "astray when attempting to understand the original meaning." If anything, writes Rappaport, legal professionals are better equipped than historians because they have "a legal perspective and can bring that approach to analyzing the history."[117]

Rappaport's opinion is clearly in line with Scalia, who believes originalism provides jurists with common sense answers to the most controversial questions. Scalia concedes history can be difficult, but nevertheless asserts the historical record most often produces one result. "In some cases," writes Scalia, "originalists will differ among themselves on the correct answer," but this is the "exception, not the rule."[118] This is breaking news to professional historians who have debated, honed, and improved historical methodologies for over a century, yet continue to admit there are a number of questions the evidentiary record cannot answer definitively.

Then there is the issue of historiography. An acceptable historical model written years ago may no longer maintain a historical consensus, or could be substantially altered by new findings.[119] And what about instances where an overwhelming majority of historians disagree with originalist conclusions? These are serious issues. Perhaps Scalia's point is reasonable minds will agree on the historical conclusions that can be reached from the evidentiary record. But this is based upon the false notion that historians and legal scholars are working side-by-side, in agreement, to answer controversial constitutional questions.[120] This is a mirage, especially when so many historians have dissented to the manner history is being employed by the legal community.[121]

It is also necessary to ask, who qualifies as a historian? In a *McDonald v. City of Chicago* concurrence, Scalia defended the Court's turn to history in *District of Columbia v. Heller,* writing, "In the most controversial matters brought before this Court ... *any* historical methodology, under *any* plausible standard of proof, would lead to the same conclusion."[122] He elaborated that the "methodological differences that divide *historians,* and the varying interpretive assumptions they bring to *their work,* are nothing compared to the differences among the American people."[123] Seeing that an overwhelming number of professional historians disagreed with *McDonald* and *Heller*'s methodological approach and conclusions,[124] who qualifies as an historian to Scalia may be downgraded to anyone asserting "a history" with whom he or the respective judge agrees.[125]

One enters a serious dilemma when equating legal scholars, lawyers, originalists or anyone asserting "a history" with professional historians. The legal community often seeks historical meaning through the use of hypothetical word scenarios which they claim prove "public understanding." Historians would mark this approach as a poor combination of social and intellectual history.[126] Certainly how the public understood the Constitution is important for any historical inquiry. However, conducting a highly objective social and intellectual history requires more than parsing text and finding a favorable interpretation.[127] All historical inquiries, including those of social and intellectual history, require historical context. This means the writer must take into account "beliefs, attitudes, philosophies, prejudices, and loyalties that are not of our day."[128] A proper social and intellectual history also must incorporate the most basic methodologies such as comprehensive research, reading and incorporating the seminal accepted works on the subject, separating historical realities from political propaganda, pinpointing what may have intellectually or ideologically influenced the writer, and weighing the credibility of the writer's opinion with others of the same period.[129]

The reality, whether Scalia and other members of the legal community want to admit it or not, is there remains a serious disconnect between universally accepted historical methodologies and the manner in which legal scholars currently employ historical sources. Part of the problem rests with the culture of the legal community. It is what Mark Tushnet has termed the "lawyer as astrophysicist assumption." Once a legal professional reads a "physic book over the weekend," they believe they can "send a rocket to the moon on Monday."[130] In other words, members of the legal community believe as long as they can read the text, their legal education and training is sufficient to "competently master the useful portions of any other discipline."[131]

A primary example of this fallacy is the growth of pro-gun legal scholarship. Beginning in the late 1970s, a number of lawyers, backed by gun advocacy groups like the National Rifle Association, entered the interdisciplinary field of history.[132] They claimed the historical evidence unequivocally proved the founding generation interpreted the Second Amendment as an individual right to possess and use arms, divorced from government sanctioned militias, as a means to check government tyranny through an armed citizenry, provide the means to repel force with force should one be assailed in private or public, and provide for the common defense.[133] The pro-gun scholars did not stop here, even in the wake of dissent from professional historians; dissent which continues into current times.[134] A number of such pro-gun scholars extended their interdisciplinary expertise beyond amateur history. They were now self-proclaimed experts in the fields of philosophy, criminology, sociology, and health. As long as subject included guns, in one form or another, they presented themselves as the omniscient experts.[135] And the findings in each article, irrespective of the interdisciplinary subject(s), were always the same—maintaining, having, and using any type of firearm is a right and their benefits, in public or private, outweigh any societal costs.[136]

There is another name for those who profess to be such jack-of-all-trades: they are the master of none. To become a leading expert in any field takes devoted dedication, extensive training, and a considerable amount of time. The discipline of history is no different. Certainly, one could read the works of prominent early American historians Gordon Wood, Bernard Bailyn, Jack Rakove, Jack P. Greene, and a number of others to obtain a valid understanding of eighteenth-century constitutional history.[137] A rudimentary understanding of the subject does not make one the equivalent of a professional historian. Such expertise requires more than reading a few prominent works. Researching, analyzing, and writing an objective history is a difficult endeavor for even the most seasoned historian. The historian must not only ask the right questions, but know how to answer those questions through extensive research, and reassemble the whole responsibly. Indeed, part of the historian's task is to recreate the past, but the historian should be true to what the historical record provides, not infer or create history that is not there.[138]

Certainly members of the legal community often ask the right questions. They are trained to read the text of the Constitution and recognize major interpretative problems.[139] When these questions are answered, however, words are often taken out of context, extensive research is not adequately conducted, historical assumptions are made, history is explained away to fill the evidentiary gaps, and sometimes dictionaries supplant the ideological, intellectual, and practical origins of constitutional doctrine.[140] Furthermore, subsequent questions are not asked as evidence is compiled.[141] Instead conclusions are reached without there being even the modest link between pieces of historical evidence, and in many cases the wrong follow up questions are asked. These approaches do not meet the basic standards of professional historians and run the serious risk of advancing false notions about the Constitution, which can affect modern perceptions of the historical record.

This is not always the case. In some instances, the employment of subpar historical methodologies, research, and analysis will have a nominal effect on future generations' understanding of the past. Such has been the case in two recent First Amendment decisions—*United States v. Stevens* and *Brown v. Entertainment Merchants Association*—where the Court refused to recognize new categories of unprotected speech absent marking a longstanding historical tradition of treating the speech as unprotected.[142] In *Stevens* the Court struck down, as substantially overbroad, a federal statute that criminalized depictions of animal cruelty. In the process, the Court rejected the government's invitation to hold that depictions of animal cruelty are categorically unprotected by the First Amendment—and the Court stressed that it is disinclined to recognize new categories of unprotected speech.[143] The government proposed a test for recognizing new categories of unprotected speech through categorical balancing of the value of the speech against its societal costs.[144] This prompted the following reaction from Chief Justice Roberts, writing for an 8–1 majority:

> As a free-floating test for First Amendment coverage, that sentence is startling and dangerous. The First Amendment's guarantee of free speech does not extend only to categories of speech that survive an ad hoc balancing of relative social costs and benefits. The First Amendment itself reflects a judgment by the American people that the benefits of its restrictions on the Government outweigh the costs. Our Constitution forecloses any attempt to revise that judgment simply on the basis that some speech is not worth it.[145]

The Chief Justice went on to suggest that speech will be deemed categorically unprotected only if it has so been treated by longstanding historical tradition:

> Our decisions.... cannot be taken as establishing a freewheeling authority to declare new categories of speech outside the scope of the First Amendment. Maybe there are some categories of speech that have been historically unprotected, but have not yet been specifically identified or discussed as such in our case law. But if so, there is no evidence that "depictions of animal cruelty" is among them. We need not foreclose the future recognition of such additional categories to reject the Government's highly manipulable balancing test as a means of identifying them.[146]

In *Brown,* the Court reasserted its reluctance to recognize new categories of unprotected speech, invoking strict scrutiny to strike down a California law that banned the sale or rental of "violent video games" to minors. Writing for a 7–2 majority, Justice Scalia rejected as "unprecedented and mistaken" California's effort "to create a wholly new category of content-based regulation that is permissible only for speech directed at children."[147] States certainly possess "legitimate power to protect children from harm," he wrote, "but that does not include a free-floating power to restrict the ideas to which children may be exposed."[148] Justice Scalia asserted that the holding in *Stevens* "controls this case," because in both cases the government sought to justify categorical restrictions on violent speech by analogizing that speech to obscenity.[149] He stressed that the Court will be unwilling to recognize any new categories of unprotected speech "without persuasive evidence that a novel restriction on content is part of a long (if heretofore unrecognized) *tradition* of proscription."[150]

Thus, in *Stevens* and *Brown,* the Roberts Court relied on tradition to reject the creation of a new Speech Clause doctrine. And in both cases the historical argument was premised on the absence of evidence regulating the categories of speech, not evidence that the categories were constitutionally protected. Certainly, the Court is on point when it infers the framers' placed great value on the pieces and parts of the First Amendment, but the Court failed to address eighteenth-century rights and privileges could be curtailed in the interest of the public good.[151] The public good doctrine stipulated that while the cores of constitutional rights were to be protected, all other interests or categories outside the core could be regulated for the common good.[152] It is a doctrine that makes the Court's "historical tradition" argument in *Stevens* and *Brown* problematic. Both opinions only acknowledge the historical record piecemeal, not in its entirety. It also calls into question whether the judiciary can incorporate the past objectively in order to answer questions of the present without undue bias. Given that such queries are difficult for a professional historian, they are as difficult, if not more so, for a distinguished jurist.

Fortunately, cases such as *Stevens* and *Brown* have had minimal impact on constitutional doctrine and historical understanding. As Michael Stokes Paulsen has put it, cases such as *Stevens* essentially rewrite the First Amendment to read: "The right to freedom of speech and expressive conduct ... shall include ... the right to portray sexual sadism involving the killing of animals."[153] Still, the decisions have not caused an historical backlash—at least not yet. The reason might rest with the stability and public acceptance of modern First Amendment doctrine. The dialogue over its historical scope took place in the first half of the twentieth century, and the resulting jurisprudence reflects a flexible approach allowing for the consideration of modern beliefs. In fact, most scholars would agree that modern First Amendment doctrine is more robust and encompassing than the founding generation could have ever imagined.[154] This shift was the result of changing times more so than the dead hand of the past.

This brings us to another reason why *Stevens* and *Brown* has not caused an historical backlash—neither case delves into the evidentiary record as to minimize or expand the First Amendment's scope. Both opinions adopt a judicial fiat approach to history, i.e., when the Court makes a broad proclamation of the past, which forms a baseline rule for future cases and controversies to be decided.[155] Thus, in a way the Court is not declaring history at all, but merely using it as a guidepost to form a standardized rule. And in the case of the First Amendment, this rule is the legislature must prove a historical tradition of regulation in an area that affects speech and expression for a law to withstand constitutional scrutiny.

The use of historical tradition as a legal guidepost has had its critics. Much like originalism, the use of historical tradition runs the risk of promoting "law office history" in lieu of accepted historical methodologies and total historical context. However, as long as the most basic historical methodologies are followed and a professional historian consensus is adhered to, the Court's use of tradition will ensure history is preserved in the process, with the law retaining its equitable character.[156] As Josiah Quincy wrote, "To Interpret a Law, we must inquire after the Will of the Maker; which may be collected from the words, the Context, the Subject-Matter, the Effects and Consequence, or the Spirit [and] Reason of the Law." Yet, although the meaning and intent are important, and can be derived from any number of historical methods, the entire purpose of legal interpretation and adjudication is to give rise to "EQUITY, or the Correction of wherein the Law (by Reason of its Universality) is deficient."[157]

To state it another way, history does not have to always be a legally binding tool. It is better served as a "learning through experience" tool.[158] This is important because legal professionals are often quick to cling to one quote or authority that they believe proves their interpretation to be the correct one.[159] This is historical reflection through personal identification rather than digesting history in context. In 1875, legal commentator Henry Reed observed this phenomenon in the aftermath of the Reconstruction Amendments, writing:

> Every man has a theory of government under which he lives, and sees it through the medium of his theory. With the government, as seen through this medium, he is either satisfied or dissatisfied. If the former, he is inclined to attribute to its agency a large share of the prosperity and happiness which the people have enjoyed; if the latter, he is equally liberal in charging upon it the adversity and unhappiness they have experienced. In fact, the country appears to these observers to be fortunate or otherwise, and our history and progress respectable or otherwise, accordingly as the government is in conformity or otherwise with their respective theories. With the one, the desire is that the government shall remain as it was created, and the Constitution be interpreted in accordance with recognized canons of legal interpretation; with the other, it is that the Constitution shall be interpreted to agree with his ideas of political expediency, and the government be made to conform to the interpretation.[160]

Today, society's desire for instantaneous answers to legal questions through blogs or opinion editorials has only furthered the divide between ideology and objective constitutional interpretation. It is as if members of the legal community are without the discipline to pause, reflect, and consider what they are reading before they offer their historical opinion (or at least ask a professional historian). As Goebel aptly put it in an observation nearly half a century ago, "There is so much in contemporary life to seduce men from the habits of reading and reflection that should precede the initial agony of putting pen to paper."[161] This criticism is applicable to much, but not all, of the historical scholarship currently published by law reviews.[162] The writing of an objective past is defeated if the primary goal is to understand the past for the sake of the present rather than answer questions of the past for the sake of understanding the past. The first condition of any historical inquiry is "to recognize how much other ages differed from our own."[163] This condition must be kept in mind as one acquires evidence, for the "more we examine the way in which things happen, the more we are driven from the simple to the complex."[164]

Writing in 1931, Herbert Butterfield provided an adequate summary on the role of the historian in this regard:

> [When a historian is engaged upon a piece of research] he comes to his labours conscious of the fact that he is trying to understand the past for the sake of the past, and though it is true that he can never entirely abstract himself from his own age, it is one the less certain that this consciousness of his purpose is a very different one from that of the whig historian, who tells himself that he is studying the past for the sake of the present. Real historical understanding is not achieved by the subordination of the past to the present, but rather by our making the past our present and attempting to see life with the eyes of another century than our own.[165]

Members of the legal community consistently take the opposite approach. History is viewed as subordinate to the present. In other words, the past is not accepted on its own terms and almost never in total context. In its place fragments of historical text are explained away. Lawyers and legal academics either simplify complex issues or seize upon those persons and political parties from the past whose ideas are more analogous to their own.[166] It is a practice that Frank Easterbrook, Chief Justice of the Seventh Circuit Court of Appeals, bluntly describes as "terrible." Easterbrook even admits he does not "pay much attention to purported history in legal briefs because people are always taking things out of context." Instead he relies on the work of "real historians," for they might have "something useful to say even though the lawyers don't."[167]

Internet search engines, while invaluable to contemporary historical research, have only furthered concerns of historical objectivity and understanding. Such tools allow lawyers or commentators to find a few favorable quotes, claim these to be the dominant viewpoint, and denounce the other views as inconsistent with the constitutional meaning or purpose that they believe provides a valid historical thesis from which to advance a predisposed constitutional viewpoint.[168] This is what Butterfield meant by history as a "pathetic fallacy" because it abstracts conclusions apart from what the evidence in its entirety reveals.[169] One must not only place historical quotes, letters, pamphlets, and books in the writer's context, but also in the context of the period, which includes the consideration of intellectual and social influences.

The crux of all this is that substantial history can be difficult. It is a professional discipline that retains its own methodological standards and rules. Yet somehow when history is used for constitutional interpretation the product is diluted as accepted standards are substituted with subpar methods. This should not be the case, especially if jurists are going to rely on history for constitutional adjudication. In a way the proper use of history to adjudicate the law is much like the use of intelligence to execute a military operation. Both scenarios require substantiated and intimately linked evidence to come to a legitimate conclusion; the end goal being minimal errors and the prevention of unintended consequences. In the case of an intelligence officer or analyst, their profession entails collecting as much data as possible, sifting through it, and then being able to provide the chain-of-command an answer based on the most adequate picture in support of a the mission's execution. Should the officer or analyst make assumptions or report poor intelligence, it can affect the success of the mission. Indeed, in some cases poor intelligence can have a nominal effect on mission success. However, more often than not, bad intelligence results in poor execution, which costs money and lives, resulting in political consequences at home and abroad.

Of course not every literate person qualifies as an intelligence officer or analyst. It is a professionally trained skill. One must not only be able to decipher the incoming reports, but also place them within the context of social, political, and military factors. These factors are different dependent upon the region, culture, and country. And in no instance does a commander ask the judge advocate general's office (military lawyers) to reassess the reports and give their inputs. This would be ill-advised to say the least, just as it would be ill-advised for the chain-of-command to ask the intelligence officer to give their analysis on the scope of a multi-lateral treaty, host nation agreement, or the Geneva Convention.

Seeing that it is foolish for legal professionals to assess military intelligence, it begets the question as to why we should give legal professionals deference or equal consideration when assessing historical evidence. Just as the intelligence officer or analyst sifts through the documents of today and the past to provide the most adequate picture possible, the historian does the same with a focus on the past for the sake of understanding the past. In other words, the historian is the intelligence officer or analyst of years past. Yet, unlike the intelligence officer or analyst, the historian must be familiar with languages, societies, and cultures often no longer in existence.[170] It is for this reason that an historian's opinion of the past is more valuable and reliable than a legal professional, who is either unfamiliar with the past or no better than an amateur historian.

Perhaps it can be argued that because a commander's decisions affect immediate life and death situations and those of a jurist adjudicating constitutional questions generally do not, the comparison is unfair. This would be a reasonable criticism. But it overlooks the importance of making impactful decisions based upon the best information and analysis. The rule of thumb applies to any profession if one pauses to consider. And it is the reason there needs to be an agreed upon standard by which the legal community analyzes and jurists apply history. As to what this standard should and should not include will be discussed in subsequent chapters.

The end goal is the retention of historical consciousness when interpreting the Constitution. This requires understanding the Constitution's historical origins and sins before importing the past for use in the present.[171] To be clear, the past must be understood on its own terms. To maintain historical consciousness is not the equivalent of using one's historical imagination. The two are distinct in what the evidentiary record can and cannot provide. The latter—historical imagination—is theoretical, which is dangerous in terms of recreating a historically objective account.[172] It often includes the piecemeal importation of past societal conditions as a means to understand our present.[173] Meanwhile, the former—historical consciousness—is based on total historical context, a substantiated evidentiary foundation, and being true to that which the historical record provides. In other words, historical consciousness requires a generalized awareness of the structure and behavior of society's past as a whole.[174]

2

Historical Consciousness and the Law Considered

The preceding chapter ended with an emphasis on historical consciousness when interpreting the Constitution. In general terms it means knowing the limits of the evidentiary record before applying the dead hand of the past for use in the present. At the same time, it requires understanding the path of the law, which in turn encompasses everything from how the law operates in a particular historical era, to significant jurisprudential shifts, to major societal or cultural developments. It was perhaps Chief Justice Oliver Wendell Holmes who best encapsulated such an approach: "In order to know what [the law] is, we must know what it has been, and what it tends to become." Following the "path of the law" means consulting both "history and existing theories of legislation" to accomplish the "most difficult labor," and then to understand "the combination of the two into new products at every stage."[1] It is what Holmes later referred to as the "oracles of the law." It required having a firm grasp of the "body of reports, of treaties, and of statutes, in this country and in England extending back for six hundred years, and now increasingly annually by hundreds."[2]

Thus, to Holmes, understanding the law meant retaining a thorough grasp of Anglo-American heritage and the development of a codified morality, which is the result of a contextualized process. As Holmes put it, "The law is the witness and external deposit of our moral life. Its history is the history of the moral development of the race."[3] In other words, a historical point in time or certain tradition is not always applicable when interpreting the law. History is merely the starting point, informing us "why a particular law has taken its shape, and more or less if we want to know why" the law exists at all. Holmes elaborated on this point: "The rational study of the law is still to a large extent the study of history. History must be a part of the study, because without it

29

we cannot know the precise scope of rules which it is our business to know. It is a part of the rational study, because it is the first step toward an enlightened skepticism, that is, towards a deliberate reconsideration of the worth of those rules."[4]

Here Holmes' point was not to devalue the past, but rather to give it proper consideration when interpreting present cases and controversies. He remained cognizant of how easily the text and legal principles of the past could be distorted to give "a new and broader scope than it had when it had a meaning."[5] This situation still presents itself today when legal scholars and lawyers assert that historical tradition, original meaning or public understanding should guide judicial decision-making. In this pursuit, text is deciphered with questionable rules of construction, which can lead to results that conflict with historical context and intended legal meaning. The question moving forward and which this chapter hopes to answer is: "Which interpretational approach is just and provides fidelity to the principles embodied by the Constitution?"

In a number of applications and forms, history has always been a contributing factor to interpreting the Constitution. Holmes understood this when he wrote, "Our only interest in the past is for the light it throws upon the present."[6] However, getting to the "bottom of the subject itself" required more than a turn to history. It required following "the existing body of dogma into its highest generalizations by the help of jurisprudence; next, to discover from history how it has come to be what it is; and finally ... to consider the ends which the several rules seek to accomplish, the reasons why those ends are desired, what is given up to gain them, and whether they are worth the price."[7]

Holmes' opinion developed during the late nineteenth century when the "living versus fixed" Constitution debate was coming into the fold. Historian Charles Beard, in particular, observed how it was becoming "widely accepted" for lawyers and laymen to assert the "provisions of the Constitution are clear and fixed—like similar to the multiplication table or natural science."[8] While Beard expressed no doubt that a number of constitutional provisions were intended to be fixed, he maintained reservations concerning the Constitution's "broad and general" clauses such as "due process of law, life, liberty and property, commerce among the states, general welfare, and privileges and immunities." Beard also maintained reservations, given that since 1789 jurists had relied on a myriad of "literary sources, such as the Bible and common law cases, from which aphorisms and information" were "drawn by the judges in elucidating the text and the glosses."[9] In addition, there was the dilemma of multiple meanings. There would always be instances where jurists have to choose between competing interpretations.[10] It was for this reason that Beard felt characterizing the Constitution as "changeless" to be without substance.[11] In Beard's words, the art of judging could never be an exact science, especially when judges must rely upon their "'conscience,' among other things, and matters of conscience are subjective, are matters of personal opinion, and are controlled in expression by inner restraints, not solely by external or objective restraints."[12] It should be noted, however, that Beard did not support a freewheeling judiciary. He cautioned that judges should make the effort to "avoid reading their personal predilections into the Constitution."[13]

English jurist and historian Sir Frederick Pollock was another to witness the push for a fixed Constitution in the early twentieth century. To Pollock, it was not unusual for new generations of lawyers to regard the system they were trained in as "a monster of inhuman perfection." However, Pollock took issue when lawyers asserted the need to cast out the common law approach to constitutional interpretation where precedent and reason dictated the results. In Pollock's mind, to cast out the common law approach was rooted in arrogance. "But the dogmatic assertion that law is the perfection of reason belongs to a later age," wrote Pollock, "an age of antiquarian reverence often falling into superstition and of technical learning often corrupted by pedantry."[14] This is not to say Pollock despised the use of history for legal interpretation. In agreement with Holmes, his friend and correspondent Pollock said that all judgments must look "forward as well as backward." It is a judicial reflection that "not only ends the strife of the parties but lays down the law for similar cases in the future."[15]

Today the living versus fixed Constitution debate is renamed under the subheadings living constitutionalism and originalism. It is a debate that extends to the United States Supreme Court. Antonin Scalia, for one, believes the Constitution has not become "anymore clear or means anything different from what it originally meant." In disagreement, Justice Ruth Bader Ginsburg believes the Constitution can no longer be bound by 1787 or 1791 understanding, especially given that the Constitution has been amended numerous times. But even if 1787 or 1791 is determinative, Ginsburg believes originalists like Scalia are missing the most important point—the framers intended the "Constitution would always be in tune with society that the law is meant to serve."[16] THE C IS MEANT TO SERVE, NOT ENSLAVE US.

The mention of living constitutionalism is enough to raise an eyebrow of any originalist, but to suggest the framers intended the Constitution to be a living document sends them into a tirade. The general reply is originalism offers the lesser of two evils because it ensures jurists are not reading their own personal, economic, moral or political predilections into the Constitution.[17] When it comes to original methods, originalism—interpreting the Constitution in accordance with late eighteenth century rules—the reply is that any living constitutionalism argument is, at best, imbued with abstract meaning. Originalists claim this occurs when interpreters "conclude that possibly abstract language has an abstract meaning without sufficiently considering the alternate possibilities."[18] To be clear, in response to the claim that framers' intended a living Constitution, originalists dismiss it outright.[19]

This begets the question: "What evidence is there proving the Constitution was drafted, ratified, and understood as a fixed document?" A common argument is originalism has always existed and, if anything, the historical evidence suggests the founding generation were originalists. Take for example Antonin Scalia and Bryan Garner's book *Reading Law: The Interpretation of Legal Texts*, in which it is asserted that William Blackstone, "the great 18th-century exponent of English law, was a thoroughgoing originalist."[20] Scalia and Garner provide Blackstone's discussion of an eleventh-century Roman statute forbidding all ecclesiastical persons from purchasing provisions at Rome. The plain text of the statute seemingly extends "to prohibit the buying of grain or other victual." But upon examining the historical record, Blackstone found "the nominations to benefices [ecclesiastical office appointments] were called provisions," meaning that the statute was meant to prohibit bribery, not the purchasing of goods.[21]

Scalia and Garner's claim is interesting, for at no point did Blackstone resort to a methodology that resembles modern day conceptions of intentionalism, textualism or original meaning, yet they somehow identify the late eighteenth-century jurist as being an originalist. And Scalia and Garner are rather forthcoming with this classification: "Blackstone made it very clear that original meaning governed, and the supporters of evolving meaning in legal texts can point to no contemporaneous commentators who differed with him."[22] It is a claim that original method originalists John O. McGinnis and Michael Rappaport echo. "Nothing in the historical record," write McGinnis and Rappaport, "suggests that the original methods including living constitutionalism or other principles permitting interpreters to update the Constitution to reflect changing values."[23] But let us return to Blackstone. At no point did Blackstone limit interpretation to text. He also considered the "effects and consequence" of any particular interpretation. And in the process Blackstone considered the "reason and spirit" of the law because it provided jurists with "the most universal and effectual way of discovering the true meaning of a law." Blackstone was not a proponent of originalism, but of judicial equity. This meant weighing up any number of factors including text, history, custom, and the effects and consequences of any respective interpretation.[24]

Blackstone's approach to law and history was prominent among late eighteenth century American jurists. And what makes it significant today is it undermines the viability of originalist methodologies moving forward. Originalists cannot simply proclaim originalism has always existed because law and history have been intertwined for centuries.[25] The fact remains that originalism does not simply view historical sources as a judicial consideration to weigh among others, but what should bind interpretation. Originalism always gives the past predominance over the present.[26] It does not help matters when legal commentators assume that any historical inquiry is the embodiment of an originalist movement.[27] In the words of David A. Strauss, "To say a view is originalist just because it uses history as a resource—at times and in ways that are determined by non-originalist criteria—is to reveal the manipulability of originalism."[28] To be clear, the popular legitimacy of originalism rests with whether history—in relation to the time when the law or provision was enacted—was essential to the respective court's judgment, or as Strauss has adequately summarized the issue: "To say that the use of history is not 'compelled by fidelity to the constitutional plan' is ... to repudiate the core of originalism."

This is not to say that originalists are not onto something, particularly original methods originalists. They stress the importance of Founding Era interpretive rules. In the beginning, the theory of originalism focused on the intent of the framers before the enterprise was severely discredited by historians.[29] As a result, originalism shifted to original meaning or public understanding; the rationale being that since the Constitution was ratified by "the people," the collective understanding of the Constitution's text must be the means and ends of modern interpretation. Hereto originalism was presented with the constitutional dilemma of accuracy and objectivity, with the Framing Era proving no different.[30] The fact remains that not every interpretation can be deemed reasonable or correct.[31] Moreover, not every person of the late eighteenth century was legally proficient or knowledgeable. However, the theory of original methods originalism is somewhat different. Instead of centering constitutional interpretation from the viewpoint of public intention or meaning, original methods originalism focuses on the Constitution as a late eighteenth-century jurist would have understood it. This viewpoint of constitutional fidelity makes original methods originalism attractive, for it is the first originalist theory to give considerable weight to the judiciary—the branch that gives life, meaning, and authority to the Constitution. In the words of historian Gordon S. Wood: "What ... gave meaning to the Americans' conception of a constitution was not its fundamentality or its creation by the people, but rather its implementation in the ordinary courts of law."[32]

For years originalists ignored the independence of the judiciary, given originalism was a theoretical approach seeking to limit judicial activism.[33] Yet with the advent of original methods originalism it seems originalists are willing to acknowledge the judiciary's discretion to interpret the parameters of the Constitution, albeit according to the late eighteenth-century rules. The question moving forward is what were the eighteenth-century rules of constitutional interpretation? Considering that originalism is a history based theory of interpretation, perhaps a more pressing question is how did late eighteenth-century jurists use and apply historical evidence for constitutional interpretation? To state it another way, what were the late eighteenth-century perceptions of historical consciousness as applied to the law? If late eighteenth-century jurists used and applied the historical record as an outcome determinative tool, then there is an argument to be made that originalism, as currently constituted, is a historically legitimate enterprise. However, if late eighteenth-century jurists merely employed history as a resource and not a command, it raises a series of questions as to how and when that resource was put into effect.[34]

A starting point for answers about the historical role of late eighteenth-century constitutional interpretation is via an examination of the judicial opinions immediately following the ratification of the Constitution, particularly those of the United States Supreme Court. Original methods originalists McGinnis and Rappaport support this approach and conclude there is "strong evidence" to suggest that Framing Era jurisprudential rules were "essentially originalist."[35] In other words, McGinnis and Rappaport agree with the traditional originalist view that the historical evidence supports originalism as a legal theory, whether it be original intent, original meaning or public understanding.[36] But a study conducted by originalist critic William Michael Treanor disputes this. While Treanor is willing to concede that deciphering constitutional text is "one of the relevant factors in constitutional interpretation," he concludes the founding generation "did not have the almost aesthetic sense of the document" to which modern originalists and textualists hold dear. He then supports this conclusion with some notable early Supreme Court opinions preceding *Marbury v. Madison*.

Overall, Treanor believes the historical evidence proves late eighteenth-century jurists adopted an "open-ended interpretive process that consider[ed] many variables and [did] not limit the analysis to text." These variables included "broad principles of governance, policy concerns, and legislative history."[37] To state it another way, Treanor agrees with originalists that history has a role to play in constitutional interpretation. To a degree, he concedes to original methods originalists, like McGinnis and Rappaport, that argue "meaning requires reference to the interpretive rules existing at that time."[38] However,

Treanor distinguishes himself, for he perceives Founding Era interpretive rules as encompassing substantially more than a textualist approach.[39] It was one of many tools employed by eighteenth-century jurists. Thus, in the spirit of late eighteenth-century legal minds like Josiah Quincy and William Blackstone,[40] Treanor understands there is more to legal interpretation than deciphering text to include "drafting history, the spirit of the document, and structual and policy concerns."[41]

Another criticism offered by Treanor is that originalism's appeal rests with its methodological simplicity, not its historical accuracy or superior methods. "One need not be trained as an historian (or know a great deal of history) to recover original meaning," asserts Treanor, for all anyone has to do is access "old dictionaries and grammars" to define the scope of the respective constitutional provision.[42] But what Treanor fails to mention is originalists are not the first to employ these *ad hoc* methodologies. Writing in 1944, historians Julius Goebel, Jr., and T. Raymond Naughton witnessed how lawyers applied the "physic of the dictionary" to "make right" any interpretative inconsistencies. To Goebel and Naughton the approach was nothing short of disturbing. The use of dictionaries cast the "informed and critical reader into a mood of doubting the validity of any conclusions that may be offered on any points of law and practice." Rephrased, the interpreter's judgment is easily "affected by functional considerations," not what the historical record provides.[43]

In response to these critiques, McGinnis and Rappaport assert Treanor's conclusions are both misleading and premature. First, while McGinnis and Rappaport agree the historical evidence does not support a form of "superstrict textualism" or "meanings expressly stated in the text without reference to history, intent, or purpose," they believe the evidence at least supports a flexible textualist approach. What this would embody is taking into account the "meaning of legal terms ... informed by historical understandings incorporated into the text," and any "textual ambiguities are [to be] fairly resolved by resort to constitutional structure, purpose, or intent."[44] Secondly, McGinnis and Rappaport take issue with Treanor concluding Framing Era jurists adhered to "differential levels of scrutiny, depending upon the nature of the case."[45] They claim the founding generation never "enunciated such a principle of differential judicial review," and assert, if anything, the case evidence contradicts Treanor's approach.[46] As a result, McGinnis and Rappaport conclude early case law does not resemble "living constitutionalism" at all, nor does it attempt to "update or infuse the Constitution with values that cannot be found in the text or intent of the enactors."[47]

Despite their disagreement over late eighteenth-century rules of interpretation, Treanor, McGinnis, and Rappaport are in agreement on one essential point—original methods originalism is a valid legal theory. Still, this does little to answer how late eighteenth-century jurists used and applied historical evidence for constitutional interpretation. Neither survey is exhaustive, nor does either provide a detailed framework of eighteenth-century constitutional interpretation. It is a deficiency that McGinnis and Rappaport openly admit, writing their limited review does not provide any "precise interpretive rules."[48] While such intellectual honesty is refreshing, it informs us that most, if not all, of McGinnis and Rappaport's conclusions are premature.[49]

Herein enters an important historical survey by Lorianne Updike Toler, J. Carl Cecere, and Don Willett. It provides insight as to whether the Supreme Court has always applied historical sources when interpreting the Constitution. In line with McGinnis, Rappaport, and other original methods originalists, the study concludes there is evidence of intentionalism. In fact, of the eighty-eight statements made by the Court concerning its interpretative method, fifty-three, or sixty percent, contained intentionalist sounding language. Yet, upon closer examination, the authors found these statements by the Court to be facially misleading.[50] As Toler, Cecere, and Willett detail, the Court's intentionalist statements were more nominal than real, or in their words, the Court was applying "something far more akin to the common law construction and interpretation of statutes, which allowed the use of all historical antecedents in an undifferentiated mass to determine the objectivity obtainable 'intent' of the document."[51] In support of their findings, the authors emphasized the limited extent to which Framing Era sources were actually employed. During the Court's first hundred years, actual citations of Framing Era sources appeared only twenty-one times—less than once every four years.[52]

As a counterpoint, because citations were less frequent in the late eighteenth- and nineteenth-century judicial opinions, originalists may argue little, if any, weight should be given to Toler, Cecere, and Willet's supporting evidence. Historians who have delved into court records can undoubtedly attest as much. It was common for late eighteenth- and nineteenth-century jurists to speak of history in general terms, especially if referencing the intentions or purpose of the framers. This is what historian Alfred H. Kelly referred to the "judicial fiat" and "law office history" approaches to constitutional interpretation. The former—judicial fiat—consists of a broad proclamation of the past that forms a baseline rule. Law office history, by contrast, is the selection of data favorable to the position being advanced without regard to the full historical record and often without context. In either instance, historical understanding assumes more of a subjective rather than objective role.[53]

Yet the use and application of history by late eighteenth-century jurists was more nuanced. History did indeed facilitate placement of the law in context. However, history was more frequently employed as a philosophical and moral tool. Any historian who has perused the prominent and influential legal treatises from the mid- to late eighteenth-century can attest to the number of historical references. Whether it is William Blackstone, Algernon Sidney, David Hume or Jean Louis De Lolme, historical perceptions of the law's development are scattered throughout. Take for instance Blackstone's articulation of the 1328 Statute of Northampton, which stipulated that no person shall "go nor ride armed by Night nor by Day in Fairs, Markets, nor in the Presence of the Justices or other Ministers nor in no Part elsewhere."[54] First, Blackstone referenced the statute to pinpoint its intended scope, which punished by fine and imprisonment those that carry "dangerous or unusual weapons" because it was an act that terrified the "good people of the land." In order to explain the statute's philosophical origins and moral purpose, Blackstone provided an historical justification. He wrote the Statute of Northampton was similar to the "laws of Solon," where "every Athenian was finable who walked about the city in armour."[55] It was an equation Blackstone applied to describe the law's philosophical and moral development in a number of areas. To Blackstone, the law developed through the moral needs of society, which was generally the result of government abuse. It was a perceived theme of English liberty.[56] In Blackstone's words, "But whoever will attentively consider the English history may observe, that the flagrant abuse of any power, by the crown or its ministers, has always been productive of struggle; which either discovers the exercise of that power to be contrary to law, or (if legal) restrains it for the future."[57]

Blackstone's use of history to describe the law's philosophical and moral development was quite common. To the legal minds of the late eighteenth century the law was a science unto itself.[58] Interpreting the law required numerous considerations, including precedent, equity, purposes, consequences, etc. However, in the words of esteemed historian Bernard Bailyn: "The law was no science of what to do next."[59] It is here that history and its methodology proved useful. The law was perceived as a "repository of experience in human dealings embodying the principles of justice, equity, and rights; above all, it was a form of history—ancient, indeed immemorial, history; constitutional and national history; and, as history, it helped explain the movement of events and meaning of the present."[60] And history—at least the founding generation's perception of it—proved crucial in legitimizing the creation of the United States of America. To the supporters of the American Revolution, the ongoing struggle for consensual liberty was perceived as akin to the 1688 Glorious Revolution. For instance, when the Boston Assembly gave instructions regarding the vote for independence, their representatives were reminded that they were on "the verge of a glorious Revolution."[61] In much the same light, Brunswick, Massachusetts, legitimized its support for autonomy due to "their attachment to the system of legal Government established by the glorious Revolution."[62] Also Buckingham County, Virginia, reminded its delegates regarding the vote for independence that it was by the Glorious Revolution, and the choice of the people, that the present royal family was seated on the throne of Great Britain.[63] So it was the Glorious Revolution that came to be revered as the most important historical point in time in support of American independence.[64]

When the revolutionaries referred to the rights of their forefathers, they were undoubtedly including those English forebearers who reaffirmed their constitutional rights with the 1689 Declaration of Rights.[65] South Carolina Judge William Henry Drayton's infamous charge to the grand jury preceding the Declaration of Independence expounds this point.[66] Delivered on April 23, 1776, Drayton judicially declared American independence through the right of self-preservation, but only after listing a long train of English abuses, unanswered petitions, and the colonists being "forced to take up arms in [their] own defence."[67] As historical support, Drayton referred to the Glorious Revolution: "If I turn my thoughts to recollect in history a change of Government upon more cogent reasons, I say I know of no change upon principles so provoking—compelling—justifiable. And in these respects, even the famous Revolution in *England,* in the year 1688, is much inferior. However, we need no better authority than that illustrious precedent."[68]

Drayton went on to detail and compare James II's abuses with those of George III.[69] It led Drayton to conclude, "It is as clear as the sun in meridian that *George* the Third has injured the *Americans* at least as grievously as *James* the Second injured the People of England, but that James did not oppress these in so criminal a manner as *George* has oppressed the *Americans.*"[70] Here Drayton, much like Blackstone, used history as a moral and philosophical guide to contemplate the situation at hand. In particular, he applied history to better demonstrate the legal right of resistance and self-preservation, which dictated a tipping point at which "the people" could cast off an oppressive government and assume a consensual one built upon the people's "happiness."[71]

This view of history—as a repository of experience in human dealings—seemingly developed in late seventeenth century England. And by the mid eighteenth century the writers of the Scottish Enlightenment sought to perfect it.[72] Their views, and notably those of Viscount Henry St. John Bolingbroke and Lord Henry Home Kames, ended up influencing some of the greatest late eighteenth-century American legal minds, which included the likes of Benjamin Franklin, James Otis, Josiah Quincy, James Wilson, John Adams,

Thomas Jefferson and James Madison.[73] Kames, an erstwhile pupil of Adam Smith, wrote of the need to examine the law as a "rational science" suitable for "every person who has an appetite for knowledge." This required having the law's "principles unfolded" and its "connection with manners and politics" surveyed.[74] The key was history. It was a theoretical approach Kames first introduced in his 1758 *Historical-Law Tracts*: "Law in particular becomes then only a rational study, when it is traced historically, from its first rudiments among savages, through successive changes, to its highest improvements in a civilized society. And yet the study is seldom conducted in this manner. Law, like geography, is taught as if it were a collection of facts merely: the memory is employed to the full, rarely the judgment."[75]

Kames' resort to history was not intended to inexplicably bind the present with the dead hand of the past. Instead, he sought to emphasize how the legal profession should not ignore the law's ideological origins or minimize the importance of ancient laws and customs. To Kames it did not make sense to practice the law of the present without acknowledging its historical origins and development.[76] Kames called upon Bolingbroke's *Letters on the Study of History* to make this point. He felt until lawyers applied themselves to make the law a professional science:

> [T]he profession of the law will scarce deserve to be ranked among the learned professions: and whenever it happens, one of the vantage grounds to which men must climb, is metaphysical, and the other, historical knowledge. They must pry into the secret recesses of the human heart, and become well acquainted with the whole moral world, that they may discover the abstract reason of all laws: and they must trace the laws of particular states, especially their own, from the first rough sketches to the more perfect draughts; from the first causes or occasions that produced them, through all the effects, good and bad, that they produced.[77]

Thus, speaking through Bolingbroke, Kames makes a powerful point as to the intersection of law and history. This point being the history of law's progress gives us an adequate philosophical and moral guidepost to deal with the problems of the present. At the same time, Kames foresaw instances where history could be used to unveil legal meaning. As an example, he provided statutory law. "In order to form a solid judgment about any statute, and to discover its *spirit* and *intendment*," wrote Kames, "we ought to be well informed how the law stood at the time, what defect was meant to be supplied, or what improvements made."[78]

Originalists may read Kames as supplying a historical testament to textualism and intentionalism. To do so, however, would be reading Kames out of context and imprinting present attitudes and morals onto the past. This is not history, for the past must be understood through the prism of the period in question, not the present.[79] Kames' illustration of "historical knowledge" proved indispensible to the law as a science.[80] Undoubtedly, determining the intention, meaning, and scope of a statute's text was important in the mid eighteenth century, yet so too was its spirit, including a philosophical understanding of the entire "moral world" through which the statute was born.[81] This was another way of stressing the importance of historical consciousness.[82] And historical consciousness was not acquired by the mere parsing of text, defining it piecemeal, and hypothetical word scenarios. It required historical context or eliciting context to the greatest detail.[83]

It is here that Kames distanced himself from Bolingbroke. In J.G.A. Pocock's words, Bolingbroke was less concerned with studying "how men have lived." Instead he wished to "inculcate the moral and practical lessons of statecraft" by focusing on those "periods likely to contain examples relevant" to the present, which ruled out "the greater part of recorded history."[84] This made Bolingbroke a rather obtuse historian because he detached himself from the past in many ways. Conversely, this detachment allowed him to focus on perfecting the historical process. Unlike some of Bolingbroke's antiquarian brethren, he knew that history did not repeat itself exactly. The past was the past. Thus, in some respects Bolingbroke felt the use of the past for the present was inappropriate.

It was a construction and development that elevated the "law of reason" as a methodological tool.[85] History was used as a means, not an end, in support of rationalizing the law. It provided a framework for explaining the ways in which society translated moral imperatives into positive duties, and provided a record for the defects in the legal system.[86] In Bolingbroke's words: "We ought always keep in mind, that history is philosophy teaching by examples how to conduct ourselves in all the situations of private and public life; that therefore we must apply ourselves to it in a philosophical spirit and manner."[87] Kames delivered similar sentiments in 1754, "Facts and experiments are useless lumber, if we are not to reason about them, nor draw any consequences from them."[88] And in 1799 Kames restated this proposition: "An institute of law ... however perfect originally, cannot long continue so.... The knowledge, therefore, of the progress of law and of its innovation is essential."[89]

The intellectual influence of Scottish Enlightenment writers such as Bolingbroke and Kames had a tremendous impact on American legal education and legal minds. For instance, when James Wilson delivered his lectures on the law, he recommended the writings of Bolingbroke and Kames to his students.[90] Wilson's approach to the law undoubtedly reflected Bolingbroke and Kames' admiration for history. In his introductory lecture, Wilson emphasized the law "should be studied and taught as a historical science."[91] It was a point

Wilson repeated upon teaching the intricacies of the common law. "As has been already mentioned," Wilson wrote, "the most proper way to teach and study the common law is to teach and to study it as a historical science."[92] Wilson even read to his students Bolingbroke's *Letters on the Study of History* verbatim to highlight the role history played in the development of the law.[93] He then placed Bolingbroke and Kames alongside Sir Francis Bacon and informed his students of their importance in the lectures before them:

> Suffer me to recommend most earnestly this outline to the utmost degree of your attention. It comes to you supported with all the countenance and authority of Bacon, Bolingbroke, Ka[mes]—two of them consummate in the practice, as well as in the knowledge of the law—all of them eminent judges of men, of business, and of literature; and all distinguished by the accomplishments of an active, as well as those of a contemplative life. The propriety, the force, and the application of their sentiments will be gradually unfolded, fully explained, and warmly urged to you in the course of my lectures.[94]

Wilson was not the only prominent American legal mind to recommend Bolingbroke and Kames. Writing in 1790 to John Garland Jefferson, Thomas Jefferson emphasized the importance of a well-rounded legal education and recommended works in history, politics, economics, grammar, rhetoric, literature, and style.[95] One of the writers Jefferson recommended was Bolingbroke, whose work "for the sake of style" was deemed "declamatory & elegant."[96] And Bolingbroke's influence extended to Jefferson's intellectual counterpart John Adams. According to historian Zoltan Harastzi, Adams spent much of his life studying Bolingbroke's extensive commentaries to include copying and writing in the margins of his works.[97]

Then there is eminent Boston attorney Josiah Quincy, who cited to and copied from Bolingbroke. Telling is Quincy's reliance on Bolingbroke for the lessons that history can provide for the present: "All men have two ways of improvement, one arising from their own experience, and one from the experience of others: since the first of these ways exposes us to great labour and peril, whilst the second works the same good effect, and is attended by no evil circumstance, everyone ought to take for granted, that *the study of history is the best school* where he can learn how to conduct himself in all the situations of life."[98]

Quincy later elaborated on the use of history as a philosophical and moral guidepost. Relying on Bolingbroke once more, Quincy recalled the principles of the ancient constitution to caution against sacrificing liberty for personal gain: "Our ancestors, in recalling the Constitution to its true principles, guarded with the utmost precaution the subjects Liberty against the open power of the Crown; but they could not be aware that a new monster, called public credit, would be born to besiege that fortress by sap, which they had labored so indefatigably to secure against the attack by storm."[99] Here Quincy invoked history as a moral and practical guide for future governance. This was not an abnormal application of history for use in the present. History was an invaluable tool for highlighting the process of corruption and decay, which many believed would take place if the people ever lost their sense of virtue.[100] As Massachusetts Chief Justice Francis Dana stated in a 1792 charge to the grand jury, "human learning and knowledge" alone is insufficient for "the proper government and well being of any society; for knowledge without virtue will be of but little or no advantage; and unless under the guidance of the right reason, may prove a curse, rather than a blessing to the community."[101]

Kames' influential views on law and history also warrant exploration. Jefferson spent much of his early legal studies copying from the Scottish jurist and philosopher's writings.[102] When Adams joined a private law association in 1765, "for the study of Law and oratory," which was comprised of Jeremiah Gridley, Samuel Fitch, Joseph Dudley and Adams, the group discussed the history of the law from its feudal origins to the present.[103] In the process they read, dissected, and debated Kames' *Historical Law-Tracts*, from which Adams quoted: "The feudal Customs ought to be the Study of every Man, who proposes to reap Instruction from the History of the modern European Nations, because among these Nations, public Transactions not less than private Property, were some Centuries ago, regulated by the Feudal system."[104]

After regurgitating Kames, Adams quoted Jean Jacques Rousseau, who described the feudal system as the "most iniquitous and absurd Form of Government by which human Nature was so shamefully degraded." It was a statement that drew sharp criticism from the association's members. Fitch, for one, defended the feudal system on the grounds it developed the prerequisite societal connections and subordination that is necessary for any government. Dudley followed suit and described the feudal system as the basis that "nations at Peace and in Plenty who live by Commerce and Industry, had adopted such a system," through which Gridley replied it "proves that Rousseau is shallow."[105] Thus, the association agreed with Kames' overlying historical thesis: that the development of liberties and customs could be traced through England's feudal origins and developed over time.

Undoubtedly such familiarity with the law's development proved useful when the founding generation was thrust into the Stamp Act crisis of 1765. In a number of pamphlets prominent writers called upon the ancient constitution or the feudal origins of government, at one time or another, for constitutional support.[106] The use of historical analysis in these instances was not based upon historical fact; it was the substantiation of personal conviction through sources with ostensible gravitas. Take for instance Adams' *Dissertation on the Canon and Feudal Law*. Although he respected the feudal system as a subject of study—particularly to understand the development of the law—Adams thought it to be an unequal and dependent form of government. He even argued the Stamp Act was just one of a series of canon and feudal law attempts to enslave the colonies:

> There seems to be a direct and formal design on foot, to enslave all America. This, however, must be done by degrees. The first step that is intended, seems to be an entire subversion of the whole system of our fathers, by the introduction of canon and feudal law into America. The canon and feudal systems, though greatly mutilated in England, are not yet destroyed. Like the temples and palaces in which the great controversy of them once worshipped and inhabited, they exist in ruins; and much of the domineering spirit in them remains. The designs and labours of a certain society, to introduce the former of them into America, have been well exposed to the public by a writer of great abilities; and the further attempts to the same purpose, that may be made by that society, or by the ministry or parliament, I leave to the conjectures of the thoughtful.[107]

Adams' use of historical narrative for propaganda purposes does not negate the premium late eighteenth-century jurists placed on custom, tradition or the historical development of the law. It does, however, clarify a serious historiographical dilemma. Sometimes the founding generation's understanding of the past was ahistorical, meaning what they may have believed to be historical fact was actually historical fiction.[108] If constitutional interpretation requires us to accept an often illegitimate understanding of the past as legitimate, the resulting jurisprudence can be far from constitutionally objective.

Such a scenario presents a dilemma for objectivity on occasions when jurists import the past for use in the present. H. Jefferson Powell summarizes this quandary, "The [originalist] argument that the founders' wishes must be followed because they wished it so is viciously circular, as well as arguably based on a historical error."[109] It is a criticism that a number of originalists reject on grounds that originalism and history is not one and the same. To originalists, their craft is about eliciting constitutional meaning in line with the founding fathers' wishes, not about getting history right. This generally entails recovering the collective meaning of legal texts at the time the language was adopted by any means necessary. As semantic originalist Lawrence Solum puts it, "[C]ontemporary originalists are not aiming at the same target as some historians, and the methods and assumptions of intellectual history of a certain kind do not provide the appropriate methodology for the recovery of the linguistic meaning of texts." Thus to Solum, historical methodologies can hinder rather than assist the judiciary's ability to discern constitutional meaning. Therefore, it is more prudent to systematically sample and evaluate the "usage" of words "as revealed in a wide variety of sources." The actual "purposes" of words are beside the point, argues Solum, for the only thing that matters is the "patterns of usage at particular times" in a "neutral, systematic, replicable manner."[110]

Solum's distancing of originalism from history is problematic on a number of levels. The most notable is that much of originalism's popularity rests on a perceived legitimacy of and respect for our past.[111] In short, originalism's appeal is linked to the premise that we are following the constitutional path laid by our founding fathers.[112] Originalists cannot employ historical text and sources and simply issue the non-history disclaimer: "Sorry, originalism is not about connecting us with our past, customs, and traditions. Instead it is about breaking down a provision's text, defining those terms in the era written, and reassembling the whole, which will not necessarily reflect the framers' intent or purpose." Originalists are correct to point out that the law is distinct from history in that judicial determinations of intention, meaning, scope and application must be made even where the historical record is unclear. For judges simply to despair and proclaim the relevant text as vague would make the judiciary a useless branch of government.[113] At the same time, the invocation of the past for the present, in any form, and here let us include linguistics, implies that the generation which adopted the language would have collectively agreed with the outcome. This in turn creates a sounding board for lawyers, politicians, and advocacy groups to claim the founding fathers supported "X" or "Y," when in fact historical methodologies reveal the framework as unworkable.[114]

Originalists will, of course, continue to issue the non-history disclaimer as a defense. But when originalists do so, it needs to be clear to everyone involved that any subsequent analysis and conclusions are not the wishes and desires of the founding fathers, but what the contemporary originalist perceives them to be. The fact remains, despite assurances of neutrality, that text can be manipulated easily in any era without eliciting context to the greatest detail.[115] Furthermore, it is not entirely clear why "patterns of usage at particular times" is a more objective and legitimate approach to constitutional understanding than the law in historical context. Considering that one of the primary goals of originalism is fidelity to the Constitution and its text, the burden is on originalists to provide substantiated evidence that late eighteenth-century legal minds agreed with their approach.[116]

However, originalism as it presents itself today is utterly deficient in this respect. When late eighteenth-century jurists engaged in constitutional interpretation, their approach did not rest upon modern conceptions of textualism, intentionalism or linguistics. It was based upon a number of factors, including history, text, and the purposes and consequences of any respective interpretation. Justice Marshall's opinion in *McCulloch v. Maryland* is a prominent example relating to purposes and consequences. Here the Constitution was interpreted holistically by emphasizing the "public good" over textualism.[117] And in terms of history's role in the interpretative process, jurists considered morality, custom, and the development of the law over time, meaning a late eighteenth-century jurist's legal dissection of the Constitution rested on more than the parsing of words. The historical reality is that a number of factors were involved.

Take for instance *Commonwealth v. Dallas* before the Pennsylvania Supreme Court at the turn of the nineteenth century. The case addressed whether the Pennsylvania Assembly could reissue land warrants north and west of the Ohio and Allegheny rivers and Conewango Creek. The question was important because ten years earlier the assembly granted similar land warrants on the condition that the prospective land was settled two years after the warrant's issue. However, a number of the land warrants were not executed according to these conditions, leaving grants open for settlement. Ultimately, the court concluded the new warrants needed to be considered on a case-by-case basis to ensure the terms did not conflict with previous settlements.[118] Of interest is how the court reached its decision. First, the court looked at the text of the statute in question and hoped to identify its "legitimate meaning."[119] However, since the textual query created a number of conflicting hypothetical scenarios, the judges turned to English legal treatises and standard common law principles.[120] When the court applied the statutes to the structure of the Pennsylvania Constitution—as a means to weigh the executive powers of the governor—the judges were again compelled to review English case law and treatises, not textualism, intentionalism or public meaning.[121]

Herein the *Dallas* court incorporated a number of judicial tools to form its decision. In terms of history's role, the court applied the common law approach. It was a consistent theme among turn-of-the-century courts. An example is the Supreme Court case *McIlvaine v. Coxe's Lessee*, which presents how the law of nations and English common law could influence judicial decision making. In *McIlvaine,* the Court upheld a prohibition on aliens taking lands by descent. In determining whether Daniel Coxe was an alien, the Supreme Court first examined whether the New Jersey Constitution superseded the longstanding doctrine of allegiance. While the Court acknowledged the English doctrine of natural allegiance—the perpetual and *unalienable* connection to a nation or society—was extinguished based on the American experience, it upheld the doctrines of perpetual or reciprocal allegiance—an *alienable* connection to a nation or society requiring obedience and loyalty to the rule of law. Considering that the prohibition on aliens owning land was based on the doctrines of permanent and reciprocal allegiance, not natural allegiance, the Court retained no reservation in holding the prohibition to be constitutional.[122]

Even William Patterson's dissent acknowledged the doctrine of allegiance and cited *Blackstone's Commentaries* for the proposition—"The rule of the common law is that all persons may hold lands, except aliens." Patterson disagreed with the majority on the matter that Coxe was a citizen, not an alien.[123] In support of this finding, Patterson examined the history of the American Revolution, including the legal scope of the Declaration of Independence. It was at this juncture Patterson drew support from the broader law of nations and the English common law. Incorporating the treatises of Sir Edward Coke, Emer de Vattel, Henry de Bracton, Matthew Hale, Thomas de Littleton, and others, Patterson stressed: "Let us not, affect to be wiser than the law. Let us not, for idle theories absurd as well as impracticable, depart from those principles which have secured our ancestors the complete enjoyment of their liberty and property."[124] But Patterson did not solely rest his argument on comparative and common law principles. He also put forth a legal reasoning argument:

> But supposing that this doctrine of the common law that the place of birth does conclusively fix the character of a subject, should be considered as not applicable to the case of a revolution by which one part of a nation is severed from the other, becomes independent, and forms a separate government. We must then search ex necessitate for some other principle, as a substitute for the common law principle, and which shall denote who are and who are not members of the new community. Now, the natural, the only practicable substitute is this, that those residing at the time of the revolution in the territory separating itself from the parent country, are subject to the new government, and become members of the new community, on the ground either of tacit consent, evidenced by their abiding in such territory; or on the principle that every individual is bound by the act of the majority. Hence, as birth at the common law denotes the subject, so residence at the time of the revolution will draw with it the same consequence. The great men who conducted the revolution in New-Jersey were at no loss to discover this principle.... Their great object was independence. By [subsequent statutes] they meant to legitimate the revolution by the supreme power of the people. They proclaim their new and republican government. They declare whom they consider as the members composing this new community. They proceed to impose the duties arising out of their new condition, and to enforce the performance of these duties by the sanction of adequate punishment for their violation.... We see an old government dissolved and a new one created. The people at first, and their representatives afterwards, declare by law all men abiding within their territory, subjects of the new government. They pass treason acts, define allegiance, and enforce its duties by the accustomed sanctions of the law. These laws operated on [Coxe]. He was an abider within their territory. They

claim him as a subject, and punish him for refusing to yield obedience. Shall, then, this same government, which with a voice of thunder proclaimed him a subject and punished him as one, or shall an individual under its laws now say to him, you are an alien? Shall he be declared a subject to punish him and an alien to punish him? A subject to take all he has, and an alien to prevent his acquiring any in future? Shall he be made poor by citizenship, and be kept poor for want of it? No, I apprehend not. The government, and all claiming through its laws, are estopped to say he is an alien, and no act of his, as I shall directly shew, would alter his condition.... They had a right to declare the colonists members of the new government on the clear republican principle that the minority must yield to the majority. But they had no intention of going further by illegally taking from them their birth-right—their capacity to inherit lands. These laws also destroy at once the fanciful doctrine of election in case of civil wars.[125]

Of course, *McIlvaine v. Coxe's Lessee* was not the first and only time the Supreme Court incorporated history and custom to assist in its decision making. In *Calder v. Bull,* of the three opinions defining the breadth of the Constitution's prohibition on ex post facto laws, all three refused to read the clause in broad textual terms.[126] Beginning with Associate Justice Samuel Chase, he indeed emphasized the importance of "words" and constitutional "meaning," yet thought it more prudent to approach the clause in context—"The prohibition, 'that no state shall pass any ex post facto law,' necessarily requires some explanation; for, naked and without explanation, it is unintelligible, and means nothing."[127] It is here that Chase compared text with history, contemporaneous state constitutional provisions, and English case law, which led him to conclude "the fact, contemplated by the prohibition, and not to be affected by a subsequent law, was some fact to be done by a Citizen, or Subject."[128] And although the plaintiffs advanced a broad articulation of the principle and as extending to "any law after the fact," Chase rejected the argument given the constraints it would impose on the legislature's ability to enact laws for the good of the whole: "I am under a necessity to give a construction, or explanation of the words, 'ex post facto law,' because they have not any certain meaning attached to them. But I will not go farther than I feel myself bound to do; and if I ever exercise the jurisdiction I will not decide any law to be void, but in a very clear case."[129]

In concurrence, Associate Justice Paterson agreed that it would be in error to read the Ex Post Facto Clause broadly. "The words, ex post facto, when applied to a law," wrote Paterson, "have a technical meaning, and in legal phraseology, refer to crimes, paints and penalties."[130] In support of his reading, Paterson quoted from *Blackstone's Commentaries* and a number of state constitutional provisions; all of which led him to the conclusion that legal meaning and historical context, not popular understanding, were preferred methods of construction.[131] Even Associate Justice James Iredell, who wrote in dissent, ultimately agreed that history in context, particularly comparative history, dispelled a broad reading of the Ex Post Facto Clause:

> [T]he true construction of the prohibition extends to criminal, not to civil, cases. It is only in criminal cases, indeed, in which the danger to be guarded against, is greatly to be apprehended. The history of every country in Europe will furnish flagrant instances of tyranny exercised under the pretext of penal dispensations. Rival factions, in their efforts to crush each other, have superseded all the forms, and suppressed all the sentiments, of justice; while attainders, on the principle of retaliation and proscription, have marked all the vicissitudes of party triumph. The temptation to such abuses of power is unfortunately too alluring for human virtue; and, therefore, the framers of the American Constitutions have wisely denied to the respective Legislatures, Federal as well as State, the possession of the power itself: They shall not pass any ex post facto law; or, in other words, they shall not inflict a punishment for any act, which was innocent at the time it was committed; nor increase the degree of punishment previously denounced for any specific offence.[132]

In summary, cases like *Commonwealth v. Dallas, McIlvaine v. Coxe's Lessee,* and *Calder v. Bull* reveal that text, custom, and history were simply elements of the larger judicial equation of sound legal reasoning. They are not the only late eighteenth- and early nineteenth-century cases where history was incorporated to understand the moral development of the law. *Vanhorne's Lessee v. Dorrance, Chisholm v. Georgia,* and *Respublica v. Oswald* also provide examples.[133] In each case, the historical record was not employed in a manner that resembles a past determinative approach. Certainly, the interpretation of texts—including its intentions, meaning, and understanding at the time of enactment—served as an important judicial guidepost, but so did the consequences of any particular interpretation. It is an interpretational formula that is at odds with how history is most often used and applied by today's legal community. To late eighteenth-century jurists, historical consciousness rested upon the history of the law's development, which in turn would assist in constitutional interpretation. It was a view that Oliver Wendell Holmes unknowingly echoed when he wrote that history informs jurists "why a particular law has taken its shape, and more or less if we want to know why" the law exists at all. Although the "rational study of the law is still to a large extent the study of history," Holmes knew jurists must use and apply the dead hand of the past carefully and in context.[134]

The question moving forward is, how much or what portions of the past can be applied for use in the present? To state it another way, what rules should bind the use of history when interpreting the Constitution? Over the past two decades a number of commentators have taken up this question in hopes of finding a "useable past."[135] Yet the answer as to what constitutes a "usable past" remains elusive. The problem of bias or subjectivity when importing the past for use in the present persists. This dilemma is particularly overriding if one subscribes to originalism in any of its numerous forms, for originalists generally discount a number of interpretational doctrines as incompatible with the Constitution's text, doctrines that were intimately related with late eighteenth-century constitutional interpretation. This issue is taken up in the following chapter, for it is impossible to identify a "usable past" without a better understanding of it.

3

The Complexities of Constitutional Interpretation in the Late Eighteenth Century Considered

The preceding chapter explored how late eighteenth-century legal minds used and applied history for constitutional interpretation. It concluded history was not an outcome determinative tool, but a moral and philosophical guidepost in order to understand the law's development. Should the founding generation's approach hold such sway when it comes to interpreting the Constitution, originalism's approach of intentionalism, textualism, and original meaning must be discarded as incompatible. But the founders' use and application of history is not the only dimension of late eighteenth-century constitutional interpretation at odds with originalism. There are other legal doctrines that many originalists reject on textual grounds. These late eighteenth-century doctrines include a common law approach to constitutional interpretation, the law of reason or giving considerable weight to unwritten constitutional principles, the law of nations, and the public good doctrine in relationship to constitutional rights. Each doctrine embodied facets of living constitutionalism more than fixed constitutionalism. Needless to say, the manner in which late eighteenth-century lawyers argued constitutional cases and late eighteenth-century jurists decided them differs vastly from that of modern day originalism.

Consider for instance the 1787 debt litigation case *Jones v. Walker*, which eventually made its way up to the Supreme Court. John Marshall argued the case and extensively relied upon English case law and statutes.[1] Once the case was on appeal before the Virginia Circuit, Marshall extensively cited the legal treatises of William Blackstone, Emer de Vattel, Hugo Grotius, Jean Jacques Burlamaqui, and Samuel Puffendorf.[2] The case itself involved a bond executed by Daniel Hylton, a Virginia merchant, to the firm of Farell and Jones in 1774. Per the 1777 Virginia Sequestrian Act, enacted in the midst of the Revolutionary War, all debts owed to British citizens could be discharged with depreciated paper currency. Pursuant to the act, Hylton paid a portion of his debt with inflated currency. The creditor responded by suing to collect the outstanding balance, relying on the terms and conditions of the 1783 Treaty of Paris, which guaranteed the removal of all impediments to the collection of pre–Revolutionary debts.[3] In essence, the case rested on whether the 1783 treaty superseded the 1777 Virginia Act, and whether the Constitution dictated the outcome.

Marshall, alongside Patrick Henry and Virginia Attorney General James Innes, argued on behalf of the Virginia debtors.[4] Although Marshall won the case at the district court on state sovereignty grounds, he lost at the Supreme Court. Writing for the Court, Associate Justice Samuel Chase sided with the creditors on Article VI treaty grounds:

> A treaty cannot be the supreme law of the land, that is of all the United States, if any act of a state legislature can stand in its way.... It is the declared will of the people of the United States that every treaty made by the authority of the United States shall be superior to the constitution and laws of any individual state, and their will alone is to decide. If a law of a state, contrary to a treaty, is not void, but voidable only by a repeal or nullification by a state legislature, this certain consequence follows—that the will of a small part of the United States may control or defeat the will of the whole. The people of America have been pleased to declare that all treaties made before the establishment of the national Constitution or laws of any of the states contrary to a treaty shall be disregarded.[5]

It is unlikely that Marshall truly believed in his state sovereignty argument.[6] He was a lawyer representing his client and merely exhausting his arguments. What stands as important, in terms of late eighteenth-century constitutional law, is the manner by which Marshall advocated and its acceptance by the members of the Court. Marshall supported his argument with the common law, English statutes, and the law of nations. The law of nations, in particular, was heavily advanced by all sides. For instance, before the circuit court, Patrick Henry advanced a "Customary Law of Nations" argument.[7] Marshall, in turn, called upon the law of nations to support the seizing enemy property, and even asserted Virginia, as a sovereign state according to international doctrine, had a "Right to legislate over Foreigners," which "goes to rights of all kinds (Lands, other personal property, besides Debts)."[8] And in reply to the likes of Marshall and Henry, lawyer John Wickham argued the "Law of Nations applied to G.B. & America," and thus supported the creditors' rights.[9]

The importance of international law with regard to the case at hand was not overlooked by Chase. Prior to siding with the creditors on Article VI treaty grounds, Chase detailed the pertinent customs and rules, and in doing so acknowledged a deeper understanding of international law and its interrelationship with all nations: "The law of nations may be considered of three kinds—to-wit, general, conventional, or customary. The first is universal, or established by the general consent of mankind, and binds all nations. The second is founded on express consent, and is not universal, and only binds those nations that have assented to it. The third is founded on tacit consent, and is only obligatory on those nations which have adopted it."[10]

Chase's view of the law of nations was quite common in the late eighteenth century. It stipulated there were facets of the law that bound every nation and others that required some form of consent, whether express or tacit.[11] For one, Associate Justice James Wilson, who also wrote an opinion in *Ware v. Hylton,* would have decided for the creditors on international customary grounds: "When the United States declared its independence, it was bound to receive the law of nations in its modern state of purity and refinement."[12] He added:

> By every nation, whatever is its form of government, the confiscation of debts has long been considered disreputable, and we know that not a single confiscation of that kind stained the code of any of the European powers, which were engaged in the war which our revolution produced. Nor did any authority for the confiscation of debts proceed from Congress (that body, which clearly possessed the right of confiscation as an incident of the powers of war and peace), and therefore, in no instance can the act of confiscation be considered as an act of the nation.[13]

The Constitution's text provides us with little, if any, support for the law of nations as an intentional expression of the social compact between the federal government, the states, and the people. Certainly, Articles II and VI confirm the senate's authority to ratify treaties, which supports the recognition of a consensual law of nations.[14] Yet the Constitution makes no reference to international law through either tacit consent or customary practice. The omission leads some originalists to conclude the law of nations has no place in our constitutional jurisprudence except in limited circumstances.[15] It is a view sharply at odds with the historical record,[16] for in the late eighteenth century there remained a vibrant law of nations in a variety of forms, which included its application to constitutional understanding.[17] It is a view found in the writings of a number of prominent jurists and that provides additional evidence why originalism's emphasis on text is incompatible with late eighteenth-century legal understanding.[18]

For example, consider the 1785 case of Charles Julian de Longchamps, who assaulted Francois de Barbe-Marbois, the secretary to the French minister, on the streets of Philadelphia. In response to the incident, the French minister, Chevalier de La Luzerne, demanded the United States deliver and surrender Longchamps to the French authorities. Pennsylvania refused, claiming that its courts, not France, maintained jurisdiction over the matter.[19] The case eventually made its way up to the Pennsylvania Supreme Court. Presiding over the case was Chief Justice Thomas McKean, former delegate and president to the Continental Congress, and signer of both the Declaration of Independence and Articles of Confederation.[20] Of the three questions presented in the case, two involved the law of nations. One was whether Longchamps could be "legally delivered up" to the minister of France. The other concerned whether Longchamps' offenses were in "violation of the Law of Nations being now ascertained and verified, according to the Laws of this Commonwealth."[21] McKean delivered the opinion as follows:

> The first Crime in the Indictment is an Infraction of the Law of Nations; This Law in the full Extent is part of the Law of this State, and is to be collected from the practice of different Nations, and the Authority of Writers.
>
> The Person of a public Minister is sacred and inviolable. Whoever offers any violence to them not only affronts the Sovereign he represents, but also the common Safety and well being of Nations; he is Guilty of a Crime against the whole World.
>
> All the reasons which establish the Independency and inviolability of a Minister apply likewise to secure the immunities of this House. It is to be defended from all Outrage[;] it is under a peculiar protection of the Laws; to invade its Freedom is a Crime against the States, and all other Nations.
>
> The Committee of a Minister or those of his Train partake also of his Inviolability; the independency of a Minister extends to all his household; these are so connected with him, that they enjoy his Privileges and follow his Fate ...
>
> You have then been Guilty of an atrocious violation of the Law of Nations, you have grossly insulted Gentlemen, the peculiar objects of this Law, Gentlemen of admirable Characters, and highly esteemed by the Government of this State in a most wanton and crooked manner. And it is because the Interest as well as the duty of Government to animadvert upon your conduct with a becoming Severity, such a Severity, as may tend to reform yourself, to deter others from the Commission of the like Crime, preserve the honor of the State, and maintain Peace with our great and good Ally and the whole World.[22]

McKean's opinion is interesting because despite the absence of statutory or constitutional support, he found the Pennsylvania Supreme Court retained jurisdiction to enforce the law of nations. Relying on the common law, McKean held there has never been any doubt the "Law of Nations formed a Part of the Law of England, and that a violation of this General Law could be punished by them." As to what constituted a violation of the law of nations, McKean stated the benchmark was the "practice of different Nations, and the Authority of Writers" as well as the written law.[23]

Secretary of Foreign Affairs John Jay concurred with McKean's opinion, writing it was full of "principles" that were "unquestionably true." This included every nation's plenary power over immigration and the intertwining doctrine of allegiance, or, in Jay's words, "every friendly foreigner coming to any Country on Lawful Business, is entitled to the Protection of the Laws of the Country on the one hand, and owes obedience to them during his Residence, on the other." Wherever and whenever a "foreigner breaks the peace or otherwise violates the Laws of the Land," wrote Jay, "he is as amenable to them as any other Person, and that the Sovereign Power of the State has undoubted Right to punish him in the manner and Degree prescribed by the Laws of the State." In terms of the Pennsylvania Supreme Court's holding, Jay agreed with McKean's refusal to extradite Longchamps. Indeed, the legal question was "warranted by the Law of Nations"—a body of law "so deeply and intimately connected with the nature of our Constitutions and Confederation, and so extensive and important in their Consequences, as to require very ample Discussion, much Reflection and serious Consideration." However, it was a "requisition at present [that] cannot possibly be required by the Law of Nations."[24]

Six years after the Longchamps affair, the Constitution was ratified.[25] In terms of foreign affairs powers, the Constitution afforded Congress the authority to "define and punish piracies and felonies committed on the high seas, and offenses against the law of nations,"[26] as well as "regulate commerce with foreign nations."[27] The driving force behind these powers was the need for a more resolute national authority.[28] The framers witnessed how one state's domestic affairs could impact the foreign affairs of the Union.[29] Congress's inability to obtain the consent of three-quarters of the states did not help matters. Just assembling a caucus under the Articles of Confederation was difficult, let alone obtaining the supermajority necessary to enact a bill or ratify a treaty.[30] It was a deficiency admitted by Secretary Jay to Edmund Randolph: "The propriety of [state] Acts [regulating the Law of Nations] appears to me to be questionable, especially as national objects should be regulated by national Laws."[31]

There is nothing in the historical record to suggest the drafters of the Constitution intended to sever the law of nations from American jurisprudence. But more importantly, late eighteenth-century jurists did not interpret the Constitution as discarding the law of nations. The truth of the matter is the law of nations remained an important jurisprudential tool to adjudicate the law. A 1793 charge to the grand jury by then Chief Justice Jay illustrates this point. Jay described the "laws of the United States" as falling under "three heads or descriptions": "1st. All treaties made under the authority of the United States. 2d. The laws of nations. 3d. The constitution and statutes of the United States."[32] Jay defined the "law of nations" as consisting of "those laws by which nations are bound to regulate their conduct towards one another" and "those duties, as well as rights, which spring in relation from nation to nation."[33] In other words, international norms were a wellspring through which jurisprudence could flow. Jay did not accept the law of nations wholesale, however. He understood that the United States was an independent nation capable of enacting laws and signing treaties that defied international norms. In such cases, the United States would be responsible to the court of world and held accountable by other nations for its actions. In Jay's words, "We had become a nation; as such we were responsible to others for the observance of the laws of nations and as our national concerns were to be regulated by national laws, national tribunals became necessary for the interpretation and execution of them both."[34] Jay elaborated on this point—including the interrelationship between the law of nations and the Constitution—as follows:

> You will recollect that the laws of nations make part of the law of this, and of every other civilized nation. They consist in those rules for regulating the conduct of nations towards each other, which resulting from *right reason* receive their *obligation from that principle* and from *general assent and practice.* To this head also belong those rules and laws which become established by agreement between particular nations, and of this kind are treaties, conventions and such like compacts. As in private life a fair and legal contract between two men cannot be altered or annulled by either without the consent of the other, so neither can treaties between nations. States and legislatures may repeal their regulating statutes, but they cannot repeal their bargain—hence it is that treaties fairly made and concluded are perfectly obligatory and ought to be punctually observed.[35]

Jay was not the only person to view the federal government as the gatekeeper of the law of nations and all the sovereign rights, powers, and international duties accompanying it. Months prior to the Constitutional Convention, Madison expressed hope the federal government would be given exclusive power over international affairs. In a letter of April 16, 1787 he wrote to George Washington:

> I would propose next that in addition to the present federal powers, the national Government should be armed with positive and compleat authority in all cases which require uniformity; such as the regulation of trade, including the right of taxing both exports & imports, the fixing the terms and forms of naturalization, &c &c.
> Over and above this positive power, a negative in all cases whatsoever on the

legislative acts of the States, as heretofore exercised by the Kingly prerogative, appears to me to be absolutely necessary, and to be the least possible encroachment on the State jurisdictions. Without this defensive power, every positive power that can be given on paper will be evaded & defeated. The States will continue to invade the national jurisdiction, to violate treaties and the law of nations & to harass each other with rival and spiteful measures dictated by mistaken views of interest.[36]

Madison's view that state laws and policies touching upon foreign affairs should be preempted by federal regulation was also expressed in a pamphlet titled *Vices of the Political System of the United States.* Madison addressed how the Articles of Confederation did not sufficiently curtail the states from violating the Union's international obligations. Not only did he express concern over the states' continued violations of treaty provisions, but also with the potential irregularities that could produce "frequent violations of the law of nations in other respects."[37]

After the ratification of the Constitution by the states, a number of late eighteenth-century legal minds interpreted the Constitution as granting the federal government's inherent authority over the law of nations. Subsequently, its doctrines were perceived as being intertwined with American jurisprudence through the common law. The aforementioned James Iredell issued a charge in 1794 to the grand jury expressing this point of view. In the charge, Iredell stated there are certain duties, by both the individual and the nation, "which can only be ascertained by consulting the law of nations, a law of so much moment to the peace and happiness of mankind if sacredly regarded."[38] Given that the law of nations was based upon the law of nature, Iredell found its principles irrefutable:

> The Law of Nations, by which alone all controversies between nation and nation can be determined, has been cultivated with extraordinary success. Its main principles, as stated by many able writers all civilized nations concur. Those that are really questionable are neither many nor important. Within these few years this law has not only been stated with peculiar accuracy and conciseness, but all its principles have been traced to their source with a *power of reasoning which has commanded universal assent,* and with a spirit of freedom and as enlarged liberality of mind entirely suited to the high improvements the present age has made in all kinds of political reasoning.[39]

Iredell went on to describe the law of nations as part of an Anglo-American tradition: "The Common Law of England, from which our own is derived, fully recognizes the principles of the Law of Nations, and applies them in all cases falling under its jurisdiction, where the nature of the subject requires it."[40] The reference to "jurisdiction" and "nature of the subject" is important because it was commonplace for eighteenth-century jurists to import international legal principles when defining the unknown. In the words of Iredell, seeing that both the common law and law of nations "subsisted in full force ... previous to the Revolution," such legal principles remained in effect until it was "inconsistent with the peculiar circumstances of the country" or "superseded by any special act of legislation."[41]

Two years later, Iredell delivered similar sentiments on the law of nations and its role in American jurisprudence. In particular, he classified the "criminal law of the United States" under three heads or descriptions: (1) offenses against federal statute, (2) offenses against the "universal law of society" outside the territorial limits of the United States, and (3) offenses within the territorial United States, "connected with other nations either by the common tie of the laws of nature, or by any particular treaty or compact."[42] Headings two and three referenced to the law of nations. Although Iredell did not specifically use the term "law of nations" in the headings, the terms "universal law of society" and "laws of nature" were synonymous with the law of nations in the late eighteenth century.[43] Regarding the second description—"offenses against the universal law of society" outside the territorial United States—Iredell wrote that piracy, murder, and other crimes fell under this heading. They were crimes that could be prosecuted even without a statute, for they were "unquestionably a violation of that law of nature by which man is bound to abstain from injuring a fellow creature whenever he meets with him, and more especially from robbing or murdering him." In other words, they were criminal categories that "all civilized nations concur." Considering that every nation maintained the sovereign right to "enforce the law of nature," each nation had the right to decide the "manner [of enforcement] which it conceives most conducive to justice."[44]

The law of nations was applicable even within the territorial United States. According to Iredell, the law of nations generally referred to acts of hostility directed by a citizen of one nation to a citizen of another without the consent or authority of government. Iredell rationalized the importance of this law and its necessary observation by citizens as follows:

> Since ... a whole nation may be answerable, even at the hazard of a war, for any violation of the law of nations which its citizens may commit, and since each citizen is entitled to the full protection of his own government ... it follows that each citizen must be answerable to his own government for a disregard of his duty in this particular, he being indispensably bound to serve his country by every means in his power, and not to injure, much less disgrace it by any.[45]

In 1794, three years after the ratification of the Constitution, Iredell again stated the law of nations applied to the United States because it was part of English common law.[46] Iredell never deviated from this stance in the years that followed. Delivering a charge to the grand jury in 1796, Iredell stated the law of nations was the "result of national reason and propriety." It formed "a part of what is called *the common law*," with or without statutes, "tho' statutes, to give it greater force and efficacy, frequently make express provisions on the subject." Iredell admitted, of course, that Congress could "prescribe different rules" to those dictated by international law and the "citizens of the United States must obey that rule prescribed by the competent authority of their own government," even if inconsistent with the law of nations.[47] However, if Congress was silent on the matter, Iredell felt that American citizens could still be charged in violation of the common law of nations:

> Consequently, when an individual is guilty of a violation of what is usually termed the law of nations in our own territory, he is not chargeable with this in our courts merely as a violation of the law of nations, but as a violation of the law of his own country, of which the law of nations is a part, and of which congress is the sole expositor as to us when it takes that duty upon it. When no act of congress interferes, it is an offence at common law, and in respect to which no particular had passed.[48]

On April 11, 1797, Iredell once again commented on the law of nations in a charge to the grand jury delivered before a Pennsylvania District Court. The purpose of the charge was to highlight the virtues of republican government and to distinguish between the powers afforded the federal and state authorities. To Iredell, the key to a prosperous United States was strict obedience to the laws. Obedience was not only due to legislatively enacted statutes, but also to the "law of nations generally, or any special treaties or conventions in particular, cordially to wish the success of liberty, justice and virtue."[49]

The second Chief Justice of the Supreme Court, Oliver Ellsworth, conveyed a similar understanding of the law of nations in a charge to the grand jury before Chatham County, Georgia. He defined offenses under two heads or descriptions: (1) statutory offenses, and (2) "acts contravening the Law of Nations," or those "acts manifestly subversive of the national government, or of some of its powers specified in the constitution."[50] Given that the scope of the former—statutes—was self-explanatory, Ellsworth only elaborated on the latter:

> Conduct ... clearly destructive of a government or its powers, which the people have ordained to *exist,* must be criminal. It is not necessary to particularize the acts falling within this description because, they are readily perceived; and because also they are ascertained by known and established rules—I mean the maxims and principles of the common law of our land. This law as brought from the country of our ancestors, with here and there an accommodating exception, in nature of local customs, was the law of every part of the Union at the formation of the national compact; and did of course attach upon or apply to it, for the

purposes of exposition and enforcement. It is true, that the parties, acting in their sovereign capacity, might have discontinued that law, with respect to their new relations and the duties hence arising; and have left them to arbitrary decisions. But that they *intend* a discontinuance so contrary to usage in similar cases, and so pregnant with mischief, is certainly not to be *presumed;* and is a supposition, irreconcilable with those frequent reference in the constitution, to the common law, as a living code.[51]

Ellsworth's call to respect both the "written, and the unwritten law," impartially and faithfully, is telling. By the late eighteenth century, the "unwritten law" was another way of referring to immemorial custom, the common law or the law of nations,[52] all of which were intertwined and related as can be seen in the legal works of Matthew Hale, Jean Louis De Lolme, William Blackstone, and Thomas Rutherforth.[53] In the manner of Jay, Madison, and Iredell before him, Ellsworth understood the law of nations to be an extension of the common law; the lynchpin of both being universal reasoning over time.

Such late eighteenth-century legal understanding undeniably refutes the principles of originalism.[54] Whether it is original intent, original meaning, public understanding or original methods originalism, the focus is on the Constitution's text as understood by the generation that adopted it, not *unwritten* doctrines such as the law of nations, universal reasoning or the evolving common law.[55] Moreover, originalists generally reject the notion that the founders practiced any form of living constitutionalism.[56] Yet, as Ellsworth and other late eighteenth-century legal minds inform us, the Constitution was not always explicitly bound by its text. Constitutional doctrine continually grew and evolved based upon custom and reason. Of course, late eighteenth-century American jurists understood the legislature may adopt laws, treaties or policies in contradiction to the existing law of nations or common law.[57] However, in the words of Ellsworth, this was not a matter to be "presumed" by the judiciary.[58] There needed to be evidence dispensing with the "living code" in each and every instance.[59]

The role the law of nations played in late eighteenth-century jurisprudence, particularly its relationship with the common law, is evidence that the law evolved with reason. Given this fact, there is nothing wrong with Ruth Bader Ginsburg querying, "Why shouldn't we look at the wisdom of a judge from abroad with at least as much as we would read a law review article written by a [American] professor?"[60] Yet to the originalist, the invocation of foreign or international law for constitutional interpretation is irreconcilable with the core premise of originalism—text. In other words, the acceptance of foreign law and its sources is perceived as being unfaithful to the Constitution in that it permits jurists to embrace doctrine that fits their personal political and social beliefs.[61]

It is an argument that resonates with originalists and non-originalists alike. It leads to the discussion whether foreign law is incompatible with American beliefs and values. As Antonin Scalia stated in a 2005 discussion with Stephen Breyer, even if one buys into the "evolving Constitution," the jurist should look at the "standards of decency of American society—not the standards of decency of the world, not the standards of decency of other countries that don't have our background, that don't have our culture, that don't have our moral views."[62] Few, if any, will disagree with Scalia that the Constitution embodies American beliefs and values. But the republican beliefs and values codified in the Constitution, particularly the common law method of adjudicating the law, reflect not only the American experience, but also international norms.[63] The law of nations, the common law and law of nature were all built upon universal reasoning as much as local customs, beliefs, and attitudes.[64] To be clear, late eighteenth-century legal minds considered more than just Anglo-American values. The history, jurisprudence, and governments of Western civilization, particularly the Enlightenment, played an important role as well.

A 1774 letter from Lord Mansfield to Lord Drummond expounds this point. When studying the law, Mansfield did not begin his analysis with some form of textualism, intentionalism, or strict constitutionalism. Instead, his starting point was ethics, followed by the "law of nations, which is partly founded on the law of nature, and partly positive." This was the foundation in which the ancient systems of government were studied, especially that of Roman law, Justinian's Institutes, and the feudal law. The feudal law was particularly important, seeing it was "so interwoven with almost every constitution in Europe," and without this foundation it was "impossible to understand Modern History." Only then, after digesting ethics, the law of nations, and the history and development of Western law, did Mansfield suggest the "study of any municipal law, such as the Law of England, Scotland, France, &c. &c."[65]

The importance of ethics, moral philosophy, and reasoning was not solely an English recommendation. Pennsylvania Judge Alexander Addison, for one, emphasized how judges should strengthen their "faculty of reasoning" through mathematics, history, and moral philosophy.[66] This ethical and moral approach to the art of judging included the law of nations. In 1794, the Faculty of Arts at Columbia College—today's Columbia University—instructed this method in a moral philosophy course, which was taught by Professor John Daniel Gross, who had served as a chaplain during the American Revolution. The course began with a study of the laws of nature or the "Principles and Laws resulting from the nature of man, and his natural relations to God, and his fellow creatures." It then progressed on to "ethics" and "natural jurisprudence" within the paradigm of a "well regulated state," including the "universal law of society." And lastly, the course tied in these teachings with the law of nations, which encompassed subjects including war, peace, international trade, treaties, and "national rights of territory and jurisdiction."[67]

A year later Gross published a book on the subject titled *Natural Principles of Rectitude, for the Conduct of Man in All States and Situations in Life.* Much like his course at Columbia College, Gross's book detailed ethics, natural law, and natural jurisprudence in the constraints of a well regulated society and their interrelationship with the law of nations. To Gross, the law of nations not only required nations to respect other nations, but also the actions of individuals against individuals as well states against individuals.[68] Regarding the latter, Gross offered freedom of religion as an illustration. To deny the freedom to worship is "unnatural and more than tyrannical," wrote Gross, especially "if the members thereof are deprived of their indefeasible natural rights of conducting themselves as free and moral agents, responsible in all their actions to their Maker."[69]

Here, the historical record weighs in favor of Ginsburg's view of the Constitution at the time of ratification—since "the birth of the United States as a nation, foreign and international law influenced legal reasoning and judicial decision making."[70] In addition, it supports Ginsburg's overarching judicial philosophy that if our American "experience and decisions may be instructive to systems that have more recently instituted or invigorated judicial review for constitutionality, so too can we learn from others now engaged in measuring ordinary laws and executive actions against fundamental instruments of government and charters securing basic rights."[71] Of course, as Scalia points out, jurists must also keep in mind that our system of government and the Constitution is based upon "We the people" of the United States, not "We the world."[72] And it may seem like the two jurisprudential considerations—the law of nations and our Anglo-American tradition—create a jurisprudential conflict of sorts. But late eighteenth-century jurists did not perceive this to be the case. Instead, when they interpreted the Constitution, the law of nations and our Anglo-American tradition were perceived as operating side-by-side and sometimes in harmony.

Associate Justice James Wilson's writings are instructive here. In a 1793 charge to the grand jury, Wilson stated, "The law of Nations as well as the law of Nature is of obligation indispensible: The law of nations as well as the law of nature is of origin divine." According to Wilson, the "law of nations" could be divided into two categories. The first was founded on "human consent" or "national treaties." The second was "obligatory" or those "universal and unchangeable" principles that cannot be infringed.[73] Wilson elaborated:

> It seems to have been thought, that the laws of nations respects and regulates their conduct only in their intercourse with each other: A very important branch of this law—containing the duties, which a nation owes itself—has a great measure escaped attention. Of a state, as well as an individual, self preservation is a primary duty. To love and deserve an honest fame is another duty of a state as well as of a man. To a state as well as to man, reputation is valuable and an agreeable position. It represses hostility and secures esteem. In transactions without other nations, the dignity of a state should never be permitted to suffer the smallest diminution. Need it be mentioned here, that happiness is the centre, to which states as well as men are universally attracted? To consult its own happiness, therefore is the duty of the nation. When men have formed themselves into a political society, they may reciprocally enter into particular engagements, and contract new obligations in favour of the community or of its members: But they cannot, by their union, discharge themselves from any duties, which they previously owed to those, who form no part of the political association. Under all the obligations due to the universal society of the human race, the citizens of the state still continue. To this universal society it is a duty, that each nation to contribute to the welfare, the perfection and the happiness of others.[74]

In summary, Wilson's argument was the "law of nations" prescribed social compacts that define the duties of both the government and the people. While it was the government's duty to ensure the happiness of the people through its political institutions and the consent of the governed, it was also the duty of the people to obey the law, advance the interests of the state, and be held accountable for their conduct.[75] It was the very principle embodied in the Declaration of Independence, which Wilson himself signed. It proclaimed to the world that "life, liberty, and the pursuit of happiness" were guaranteed on equitable principles through the "consent of the governed."[76]

In addition to dictating the duties of the citizens to the state and the state to citizens, the law of nations embodied a form of customary law. According to Wilson, customary law first developed by "voluntary adoption," second with the "adoption being increased," and then through a lasting "satisfactory experience."[77] It was a body of law that maintained "obligatory force" given its "general utility" to all nations. This did not mean Wilson believed the law of nations, in its entirety, bound each and every country. Like Jay, Iredell, and a number of international law writers before him, Wilson distinguished between the obligatory and consensual law of nations. He admitted the *voluntary* or *positive* portions could "be altered by the municipal legislature of any state, in cases affecting *only* its own citizens."[78] This included the United States where the "law of nations acquires an importance." However, given the Constitution's division of federal-state spheres of government, the law of nations operated in the United States "upon peculiar relations, and upon the relations with peculiar energy."[79] As long as Congress intended to alter or abrogate portions of positive or voluntary international law, those portions would not be binding.

Regardless of the United States' choice to opt out of a particular international rule, doctrine or subject matter, it could not alter or abrogate the continual development of the law of nations.[80] Furthermore, the United States could not opt out of the obligatory law of nations. In Wilson's words, it consisted of "universal, indispensible, and unchangeable" principles which served as an obligation to both nations and their people.[81] Whether the application was to a person or nation, the two objects were linked by the law of reason.[82] As Chief Justice Jay aptly put it, the law of nations consisted of "those rules for regulating the conduct of nations towards each other, which resulting from right reason receive their obligation from that principle and from general assent and practice."[83] Iredell delivered similar sentiments, stating the law of nations can be "traced to their source with a power of reasoning which has commanded universal assent, and with a spirit of freedom and as enlarged liberality of mind entirely suited to the high improvements the present age has made in all kinds of political reasoning."[84]

Such principles and reasoning placed an affirmative duty on government to ensure the happiness of the people through a well-regulated society.[85] As a result "every individual surrendered such a proposition of his private natural rights, as it was inconsistent with the good of the whole."[86] It was the "mass of these surrendered rights" which formed "the whole of that power which we see dispersed in various hands, according to the different modes of government."[87] In the words of Judge David Campbell, the Constitution and the laws resulting from its operation were the "main spring which puts all other wheels of government in motion." Campbell knew that despite the mode or structure of government there would always be individuals "who wish to enjoy the benefits of government, without performing the duties of citizens." This self-centered approach to liberty was the antithesis of the Constitution, for in a "well regulated society, every individual is only at liberty to do what is most conformable to his inclination and his interest, provided it be not inconsistent with the properties, and liberties of others."[88] What Campbell described was the common or public good. It was a doctrine governing late eighteenth-century law that included a presumption of constitutionality. The doctrine was not created by late eighteenth-century American legal minds, but borrowed from earlier commentators such as Algernon Sidney, Francis Hutcheson, Jean Jacques Burlamaqui, Cesare Beccaria, William Blackstone, and others.[89] More importantly, it was in the interest of the public good that the founding generation pushed for a new and more resolute Constitution. Writing in 1785, James Bowdoin touched upon how the Articles of Confederation failed in advancing the public good, and felt there was a need to remind the states of its positive effects:

> [T]hese States in the time of their prosperity, have lost that sense of Honor and Justice, that mutual feeling of Friendship and attachment, and above all, that Public Virtue & Supreme regard to the Interest and safety of *the whole,* which so powerfully actuated them in the Day of Common Danger; and which will be ever essentially necessary, so long as they shall continue to be one great Confederate Commonwealth. It highly concerns *United Sovereign* States only to attend to the ruling Principles of all well regulated Societies; and it concerns them more, because they may be more apt than others to forget, that the Interest of Individuals must be government by that of the whole.[90]

All and all, the public good doctrine dictated that republican constitutions by themselves were "calculated to produce the greatest possible good to the greatest number of people" because the "good, or happiness of the people is acknowledged by all republicans to be the sole end of government."[91] This included laws that affected enumerated rights, for laws adopted by representative governments were presumed constitutional as long as the equitable principle of representation held true.[92] As one anonymous editorial contemporaneous with the adoption of the Constitution stated:

> The proper object of society and civil institution is the advancement of "the greatest happiness of the greatest number." The people as a body, being never interested to injure themselves, and uniformly desirous of the general welfare, have ever made this collective felicity the object of their wishes and pursuit.... "The greatest happiness of the greatest number," being the object and bond of Society, the establishment of truth and justice, ought to be the basis of civil policy and jurisprudence.[93]

A full articulation of this principle can be found in a 1786–87 editorial debate between George Thatcher and the anonymous "Senex" on interpreting constitutional rights. Thatcher, a judge and soon to be member of the First United States Congress, asserted that the rights listed in the 1780 Massachusetts Constitution were not the totality of the people's rights, but a list of constitutional fundamentals that the government could never usurp to protect minority interests.[94] Rights were to be understood through the constraints of the public good, each asserted. Laws that did not abridge a right's intended good or core were presumed constitutional as long as they advanced the "good of the whole,"[95] and complied with the "greatest happiness of the greatest number of people" principle.[96] Thatcher elaborated on this point:

> The right to institute government, and the right to alter and change a bad government, I call the same right: I see no difference between them. The end of this right is the greatest happiness of the greatest number of people, and the means or

object made use of, is government. This right I understand to be a physical power, under the direction of reason, to bring about this happiness. Therefore, when the people have agreed upon a certain set of rules, which they denominate government ... they are binding, on the presumption that they will produce the degree of happiness before mentioned.[97]

Thatcher illustrated this point many times over in his editorial debate with "Senex." Once again, the matter amounted to the underlying principle that rights "prefixed to the constitution" could never be infringed.[98] Meanwhile any activity separate from a right's core were lawful as long as government did not regulate it.[99] Thatcher referred to any activity outside a right's core as "alienable" rights that could be "abridged by the legislature as they may think for the general good."[100] Such laws were presumed constitutional because they will produce the "greatest degree of happiness" for the people as a whole.[101]

Thatcher was just one of many late eighteenth-century jurists to illustrate the importance of the public good in these terms. While modern legal commentators may envision the Constitution as creating a utopian society of individualized liberty, its purpose was to restore societal order at all levels of government and conceptualize a nation based on the consent or happiness of the people.[102] As Judge Israel Smith stated in a 1798 charge before a Cumberland County, New Jersey, grand jury, the "true interest" of the people did not consist of "momentary selfish advantage, but their real and permanent good." Instead of being subject to the whims of "political whoredom," the people needed to have faith in the Constitution and understand "their private and individual interests must give way to that of the public."[103]

A year earlier, Vermont Supreme Court Judge Lot Hall, a Revolutionary War veteran, expressed similar sentiments before a Windham County, South Carolina, grand jury.[104] When "constituting our particular government," stated Hall, "the circumstances of our country, the interest and happiness of the people, the state of society and the manners were taken into consideration; and the establishment made on principles, as nearly as could be, conformable to them all." Such a government, "founded on the interest and happiness of the people," could "derive no pleasure ... but the promotion of their good." Hall was not naïve to assume the Constitution was a perfect instrument, but he knew that "no government, however excellent in its form, can long preserve its liberties, unless it is carried into effect and operation." The only way to effectuate the Constitution's purpose was the enactment and enforcement of laws.[105] As South Carolina Judge Elihu Hall Bay articulated the principle before a Camden grand jury: "Society ... gentlemen, by this noble and venerable institution, has its greatest security, and the laws their firmest support ... that personal safety, and security for the rights and properties of individuals, can only be found and preserved by a due vigorous execution of the laws of their country, by which all who trespass against them, must answer for their offenses."[106]

In 1790 in Exeter, New Hampshire, United States Judge John Sullivan made an analogous statement touching upon American constitutionalism. He felt the "savage and polished Citizen, invariably pursue the same object"—"the pursuit of happiness."[107] Yet the citizen was distinct in that he successfully instituted a government truly based on the consent of the governed:

> The present inhabitants of the United States of America have enjoyed advantages which no other people could ever boast; they, having had in common with others the benefit of reading and considering the various systems of every other country; having been, for a long time, under a government, formerly supposed to approach as near perfection as any that had appeared in the world; and having on trial discovered the defects of many systems invented and practiced upon in America since the late revolution, have at length called forth the united wisdom of America and produced that excellent system.[108]

Here, Sullivan provides us with insight on how jurists understood the Constitution around the time of its ratification, especially with regard to its international character. A former major general in the Continental Army, Sullivan witnessed the development of state constitutions in the midst of the Revolutionary War.[109] In fact, he had written to Meshech Weare on the matter of the New Hampshire Constitution. Sullivan was for instituting as many constitutional checks and balances as to keep the "one Object" or first rule that any republican government should have in view, "namely the Good of the whole." The most important of these checks and balances was "the frequent Choice of the Rulers, by the people," for it reminded government officials that "a new Election would soon Honor them for their good Conduct, or Disgrace them for betraying the Trust reposed in them." Thus, Sullivan was of the opinion that "no Danger can arise" to the social compact where the branches of government are based upon the consent of the people. The rationale being the people "can never suppose ... to have any Thing but the true End of Government (viz their own Good) in View, unless we suppose them Idiots, or self–Murderors."[110]

Taken altogether, this late eighteenth-century judicial commentary reveals jurists did not conceptualize the Constitution in a manner that resembles twenty-first century textualist or originalist paradigms. Rather, the Constitution was viewed as a flexible compact for the establishment of the public good. The Constitution established three branches of government, distinguished the powers divided between the federal, state, and local governments, and proclaimed those essential rights and political qualifications that would ensure liberty was not destroyed. As Scottish Enlightenment writer Viscount Henry St. John Bolingbroke put it, a nation's constitution was an "assemblage of laws, institutions, and customs, derived from certain *fixed principles of reason,* directed to certain fixed objects of *public good,* that compose the general system according to which the community hath agreed."[111]

While it is common today for Americans to romanticize that the founding generation read the Constitution as embodying a presumption of liberty, such an interpretation is at odds with late eighteenth-century judicial understanding.[112] In Judge Richard Peters' words before a Pennsylvania Federal District Court:

> But in a republic there is but one great and leading interest, to wit, that of the whole nation. And in our republic, the majority of our national representatives are judges, legally authorized to declare, under the guards in the constitution, what this general interest is and how it shall be directed. Local interests and particular convenience must yield to this. The parts must make sacrifices to the will and to the ordinances of the whole. These local and temporary sacrifices are fully compensated by the protection and general advantages received from the government, in which everyone partakes, and has as great a weight as it is entitled to. The parts are no more to the whole, than individual in society, who must give up portions both of their personal rights and peculiar advantages to the community of which they are members.[113]

Peters, a Revolutionary War veteran and Washington appointment, understood that "temporary evils" may result from this presumption of constitutionality. However, to accept the opposite was to commit licentiousness or "tear up all government by the roots." Besides, if the "temporary evils" were at odds with desired liberty or were unworkable, the people retained the freedom to "write and speak against them" and the power to "change the representation in the government, by all peaceable and constitutional means."[114]

Pennsylvania Supreme Court Judge Edward Shippen concurred with Peters and other eighteenth-century jurists. He felt the very "essence of a Republican government" was the "will of the *few* must ... submit to the will of the *many*"—not a presumption of liberty. Although sometimes these "numerous blessings of the democratic form" resulted in "inconveniences," it was the form of government adopted by the people, and should the laws be found "oppressive," the people were not left without recourse given the Constitution and the laws could always "be reviewed and reformed."[115]

An additional commentator was Judge Jacob Rush, brother of Benjamin Rush and president of the Third Circuit, who recognized a variety of constitutional theories in circulation during the late eighteenth century.[116] Rush proposed that the Constitution did not retain a "perfect government, perfect laws,

and a perfect administration of justice." To believe otherwise was a theory
solely "in the brains of visionary philosophers" who perceived of the Constitution as distilled to the primary "axiom received amongst" the American people, which "may justly be considered as the basis of all others, namely, that the
majority of the people have a right to govern."[117] Rush elaborated on the government's presumption to carry out the public good:

> Tell [the people] there can be no political freedom, without a sacrifice of some
> portion of those rights which are supposed to be enjoyed in a state of nature; and
> that it is beyond the wit of man, nay, that it is morally impossible, so to arrange
> and combine the powers of society, as to exclude from the virtues that compose
> the character of a good citizen, the duty of obedience *in all cases* where he is
> thrown into *the minority*. Tell them ... that nothing is more opposite to every
> idea of republican government, or more fatally subversive of our democratic sys-
> tems, that an infringement on the great principle, "that a majority of the people
> have a right to govern," without which, it is evident a democracy cannot subsist.[118]

The importance of the public good did not go overlooked by the early
justices of the Supreme Court. In a 1797 charge to the grand jury, Iredell witnessed how private interests are magnified by factious groups, and public interests are "regarded as of comparative insignificance." To Iredell, this was in
conflict with the Constitution's purpose—the "safety of the whole." He elaborated on this point, stating the Constitution ensured "a lesser good is sub-
servient to a greater; and combine, in one general system, every practicable
means of promoting the public welfare consistently with the personal safety,
interest, and happiness of each individual entitled to partake of it."[119] Five years
earlier, in a charge to the grand jury for the District Court of Massachusetts,
Iredell delivered similar remarks, emphasizing how the common good entails
a presumption of constitutionality, given that consensual laws preserve liberty
for all:

> Perhaps in no country in the world have been within so few years exemplified
> such awful and important lessons. We have been taught, not only the value of lib-
> erty, but what it was much more difficult to learn, that liberty itself, in order to
> be truly enjoyed, must submit to *reasonable and considerate restraints.* The
> unbounded liberty of the strongest man is tyranny to the weakest: The unlimited
> sway of a majority is oppression to the minority; Unlicensed indulgence to all the
> passions of men in an impious rejection of the control of reason which Provi-
> dence has given for their government and direction.
> True liberty certainly consists in such restraints, and no greater, on the actions
> of each particular individual as the *common good of the whole requires.* The exact
> medium it may be difficult to find, but we have reason to hope it is most likely to
> be found in that country which can draw forth, by the choice either direct or
> indirect of the people themselves, those characters for the immediate exercise of
> public trusts, in whole abilities and integrity they can place the greatest confi-

dence.... Such have been these governments, as well of the States separately, as of the United States, under which we have the happiness to live.[120]

Chief Justice Jay offered a similar view before the Circuit Courts of New York, Connecticut, Massachusetts, and New Hampshire. The key to "national prosperity" and "inestimable" liberty rested on a "well organized, vigorous government, ruling by wise and equal laws, faithfully executed." Jay added that "civil liberty consists not in a right to every man to do just what he pleases—but it consists in an equal right to all the citizens to have, enjoy, and to do, in peace, security, and without molestation, whatever the equal and constitutional laws of the country *admit* to be consistent with the public good."[121] In a later charge to the grand jury before the Middle Circuit of Virginia, Jay again highlighted the importance of the public good:

> Being a free people, we are governed only by laws, and those of our own making—these laws are rules for regulating the conduct of individuals, and are established according to, and in pursuance of that contract which each citizen has made with the rest, and all with each. He is not a good citizen who violates his contract with society; and when society execute their laws, they do no more than what is necessary to constrain individuals to perform that contract, on the due operation and observance of which the common good and welfare of the community depend; for the object of it is to secure to every man what belongs to him, as a member of the nation; and by increasing the common stock of property, to augment the value of his share in it.[122]

The public good principle even appears in the landmark case *McCulloch v. Maryland,* where the Supreme Court ruled the Second Bank of the United States was a constitutional exercise of congressional power.[123] In writing the opinion, Chief Justice John Marshall placed the public good above what textualist methodologies provided. Despite the words "bank" or "incorporation" being noticeably absent from the Constitution's text, he rejected a reading of the Necessary and Proper Clause that would forfeit Congress's choice of means when exercising either enumerated powers or unlisted "others of inferior importance, merely because they are inferior." Marshall asked, "Can we adopt that construction, (unless the words imperiously require it,) which would impute to the framers of that instrument, when granting these powers of the public good, the intention of impeding their exercise by withholding a choice of means?"[124] Marshall replied in the negative due to the consequences that could result to the public good, i.e., the welfare of the United States: "The baneful influence of this narrow construction on all the operations of the government, and the absolute impracticability of maintaining it without rendering the government incompetent to its great objects, might be illustrated by numerous examples drawn from the constitution, and from our laws."[125]

Marshall and other jurists were not claiming that each and every law advanced the public good. The doctrine merely offered a presumption of constitutionality, and was something that the judiciary was within its right to weigh and consider.[126] Of course a law was clearly invalid if it was adopted through unconstitutional means, enforced via an unconstitutional power or in direct conflict with another constitutional provision.[127] Pennsylvania Chief Justice Thomas McKean neatly condensed the public good in this regard, stating, "It gives the rulers no power but of doing good, and deprives the people of no liberty but of doing evil."[128] This general rule even applied to laws perceived as facially incompatible with constitutional rights. Consider for instance the liberty of the press. It unquestionably protected the right of all persons to seek publication of their opinions. Still, eighteenth-century jurists weighed the utility of each publication through the lens of the public good. In McKean's words, the liberty of the press could only extend to those publications "with an eye solely to the public good," not to those "intended merely to delude and defame," for it is "impossible that any good government should afford protection and impunity" to the latter.[129]

Thus, as to what actions qualified as "good" and "evil" depended upon the structure of the Constitution, the powers of the legislature, and subsequent judicial reasoning and precedent. Associate Justice William Paterson deftly articulated this principle and its application to constitutional limits:

> [Legislatures are] creatures of the constitution—they owe their existence to the constitution—they derive their powers from the constitution—it is their commission; and therefore all their acts must be conformable to it, or else they will be void—The constitution is the work or will of the people themselves, in their original, sovereign, and unlimited capacity. Law is the work or will of the legislature in their derivative and subordinate capacity. The one is the work of the creator, and the other of the creature. The constitution fixes limits to the exercise of legislative authority, and prescribes the orbit, within which it must move. In short ... the constitution is the sun of the political system, around which all legislative, executive, and judicial bodies must revolve.[130]

Paterson acknowledged constitutional rights as one of these limits. Rights were to be given "fundamental" and "sacred" status. As long as they remained in the Constitution, they could "not be worked upon by the temper of the times, nor rise and fall with the tide of events." In other words, constitutional rights reflected "firm and immoveable" principles, "as a mountain amidst the strife of storms, or a rock in the ocean amidst the raging waves."[131] Here, Paterson was not articulating some *ad hoc* presumption of liberty. Instead, he was acknowledging constitutional rights must be respected and it is the judiciary's duty to ensure the legislature does not infringe upon the core of these rights nor negate their utility. As one anonymous 1789 editorial pointed out in the midst of the Constitution's ratification, it was within the purview of the legislature to restrict or limit auxiliary functions of rights because it "prevent[s] the wonton injury and destruction of individuals" and ensures there is a legal "line somewhere, or the peace of society would be destroyed by the very instrument designed to promote it."[132]

When one compares the aforementioned statements of the public or common good to originalist sentiments touching upon the Constitution, it is clear they are not one and the same. Whether it is original intent, meaning or understanding, originalism derives its force by deciphering text in the era it was adopted. Originalists can derive meaning from a number of historical sources; whether it is contemporaneous debates, correspondence, newspaper articles, pamphlets or dictionaries. Late eighteenth-century jurists, however, never quoted or applied such historical sources, nor did they limit and restrict themselves to definitions through the parsing of text, defining its portions, and reassembling the whole to elicit meaning. The purposes and consequences of any respective interpretation, including its relationship to precedent and custom, played a much more vital role. To state it another way, eighteenth-century constitutional interpretation was deeply intertwined with what was often referred to as the "law of reason" or the common law method. Whether it was statutes, constitutional provisions, the law of nations or rights in question, judicial reasoning proved crucial in dictating the outcome; and such reasoning manifested in a variety of forms. When interpreting text, an eighteenth-century jurist could derive multiple meanings. But the spirit, purpose, and application of each meaning had to be weighed in relation to the interpretational consequences.[133] And of course each jurist maintained a unique approach and assigned different variables to text, custom, history, etc.

Here again, the writings of James Wilson are instructive, for they provide us with one late eighteenth-century jurist's approach. To Wilson, the first step in understanding the law was a familiarity with the past. In particular, this applied to the common law. It was a body of law that "should be studied and taught as a historical science."[134] Indeed, while the common law existed in a number of "monuments in writing," wrote Wilson, its true authority rested "on reception, approbation, custom, long and established."[135] It was a view that Wilson no doubt borrowed from Lord Henry Home Kames' treatise *Historical Law-Tracts*. For it was Kames who proposed: "No sort of study contributes more to the knowledge of law, than that which traces it through its different periods and changes."[136] In other words, the common law developed from the virtues of the people, and the most important virtues were "the love of liberty, and the love of law."[137] Consequently, its preservation meant the enactment, enforcement, and improvement of the law to meet the times of the day. Wilson elaborated: "Without liberty, law loses its nature and its name, and becomes oppression. Without law, liberty also loses its nature and its name, and becomes licentiousness. In denominating, therefore, that science, by which the knowledge of both is acquired, it is unnecessary to preserve, in terms, the distinction between them. That science may be named, as it has been named, the science of law."[138]

Here we witness Wilson's view as to how the common law developed based on the "science of law" or the law of reason.[139] Certainly "historical science" gave jurists a better understanding of how the law manifested. However, it was the "science of the law" or reasoning through which the common law flowed. In some instances the common law maintained an "accommodating spirit," in others "its temper [was] decided and firm," yet what endured was that it remained in flux. As Wilson aptly noted, "The means are varied according to the times and circumstances; but the great ends of liberty are kept steadily and constantly in view."[140]

Still, legal reasoning alone was insufficient to garner legitimacy. Interpreting the law also required truths to deduce rationalizations, and the more truths the better the rationale. "We cannot ... begin to reason, till we are furnished, otherwise than by reason, with some truths, on which we can found our arguments," wrote Wilson.[141] This in turn formed the evolving jurisprudence of the state. Its maxims were availed through experience and received additional improvement from every new situation. Wilson viewed this as the manner jurisprudence attained, "in the progress of time, higher and higher degrees of perfection, resulting from the accumulated wisdom of ages."[142] Thus, to Wilson, the rule of law developed based upon the needs of the present. However, in order to maintain legitimacy, the development of the law also required accuracy through reliability. The best way to guarantee this result was through a balance of jurisprudential guideposts or precedent, which prevented errors in legal interpretation, and the more guideposts or precedent on point the better. Wilson proposed, "The more accurately and the more ingeniously men reason, and the farther they pursue their reasonings, from false principles, the more numerous and inveterate will their inconsistencies, nay, their absurdities be."[143]

Here originalists could advance an argument that supports their methodological tenor. This argument being a principled textual approach provides more truths from which to reason, making originalism, in its various forms, more reliable in terms of both accuracy and legitimacy.[144] This argument appears to be facially legitimate. Few historians, if any, will dispute the interpretation of texts played a role in late eighteenth-century constitutional law.[145]

But for such an argument to be truly legitimate requires a showing of textual primacy among late eighteenth-century jurists. To state it another way, we must have evidence that the framers perceived text—and the history of that text—as trumping judicial reasoning.

However, the historical record does not support such a conclusion. Reason was an important variable in deciphering the law. As Josiah Quincy penned in his *Law Commonplace Book,* the laws of England were "grounded, *first* on the Law of Reason," followed by "the Law of GOD" or morality, the "general Customs of the Realm," "Principles that be call'd Maxims," "particular Customs," and lastly statutes. Hence, according to our Anglo-American tradition, a deep understanding of the law's development was a prerequisite before ever examining the text of a statute or constitutional provision. It is interesting how the Anglo origins of American legal thought are often overlooked or cast aside by some modern legal pundits. There is a perception the American Revolution cast off our English origins or, at a minimum, that we should presume the founding generation discarded English law. Yet to proceed down this path would be historically illegitimate. Preceding the Declaration of Independence, the American view was English law applied, just not in its full capacity. The circumstance detailed by Quincy is most interesting. He wrote how different aspects of English law applied to Wales, Scotland, Ireland, and a number of provinces. In some cases, like Wales, English law applied wholesale, and in others, like Ireland, it did not.[146]

Certainly the American perception of English law transformed during the Revolution. In the midst of the Stamp Act crisis, for example, revolutionaries like James Otis stretched the bounds of the law to argue the English common law guaranteed a right to colonial representation.[147] Writing eight years later, in 1772, Samuel Adams similarly called upon on the "eternal law of reason" and the "Common Law of England" to proclaim a right to self-government.[148] And by 1774, the Continental Congress staked out the particulars by which English law applied. Entitled *The Declaration of Rights and Grievances,* Congress wrote the "foundation of English liberty, and of all free government is a right in the people to participate in their legislative council." In addition to this, the Declaration proclaimed the "respective colonies are entitled to the common law of England" and "to the benefit of such of the English statutes, as existed at the time of their colonization; and which they have, by experience, respectively found to be applicable to their several local and other circumstances."[149]

It was a constitutional understanding restated by the delegates of Maryland, Delaware, New Jersey, New York, and Georgia following the Declaration of Independence. Article III of the 1776 Maryland Constitution declared "that the inhabitants of Maryland are entitled to the common law of England ... and to the benefit of such of the English statutes, as existed at the time of their first emigration, and which by experience have been found applicable to their local and other circumstances."[150] Article 25 of the 1776 Delaware Constitution similarly proclaimed: "The common law of *England,* as well as so much of the statute law as have been heretofore adopted in practice in this State, shall remain in force, unless they shall be altered by a future law of the Legislature; such parts only excepted as are repugnant to the rights and privileges contained in this Constitution and Declaration of Rights."[151] Article 22 of 1776 New Jersey Constitution declared: "That the Common Law of England, as well as so much of the Statute Law, as haven heretofore practiced in this Colony, shall still remain in Force, until they shall be altered by a future Law ... such Parts only excepted as are repugnant to the Rights and Privileges contained in this Charter ..."[152] Article 35 of the 1777 New York Constitution declared: "such parts of the common law of England, and of the statute law of England and Great Britain, and the acts of the legislature ... as together did form the law ... on the 19th day of April, in the year [1775] ... shall be and continue to be the law of this State, subject to such alterations and provisions as the legislature of this States shall, from time to time, make concerning the same."[153] Lastly, the 1776 Georgia Constitution did not use the phrase "common law," but did guarantee its protections through the preamble, stating independence was declared by the "people of America ... to assert the rights and privileges they are entitled to by the laws of nature, and reason."[154]

Prior to the drafting of the Declaration of Independence, New Hampshire similarly attributed the Revolution to the denial of common law rights and customs, stating England deprived "us of our natural and constitutional rights and privileges," which was not "agreeable to the laws and customs a long time used here."[155] Meanwhile, other states expressed their approval for the Anglo-American common law through statute. For instance, North Carolina immediately enacted a law declaring "that all such Statutes, and such Parts of the Common Law ... not destructive or, repugnant to, or inconsistent with, the Freedom and Independence of this States ... shall endure, continue, and be in Force."[156] Vermont passed a comparable measure, but made sure to clarify that only the "Common Law, as it is generally practiced and understood in the New-England States" were applicable.[157] Lastly, Virginia passed an ordinance stipulating "that the common law of England, all statutes or acts of parliament made in the aid of the common law prior to the fourth year of the reign of king James the first, and are which of a general nature, not local to that kingdom, together with the several acts of the general assembly of this colony now in force, so far as may consist with the several ordinances, declarations, and resolutions, of the general convention, shall be *the rule of decision,* and shall be considered as *in full force,* until the same shall be altered by the legislative power of this colony."[158]

Clearly, the importance of the common law and its application to American society at large cannot go overlooked when examining late eighteenth-century constitutional understanding.[159] Not only did the common law serve as one of the foundations through which independence was both sought and proclaimed, but it remained a staple of constitutional jurisprudence by the time the Constitution was drafted. Indeed, a reliance on the common law may provide competing interpretations when applied to any respective constitutional question. However, this was why late eighteenth-century jurists weighed the consequences of any prospective interpretation. Moreover, there was general agreement among the founding generation that the common law approach was preferred.[160] As H. Jefferson Powell put it, prominent legal minds gave more consideration to "practice and precedent," as compared to the "historical evidence of the framers' personal intentions."[161]

Powell's conclusion is supported by the jurisprudential tendencies of the Marshall Court. While the justices, including Marshall himself, made a number of intentionalist statements, on closer inspection the evidence reveals a more fluid approach to constitutional interpretation.[162] This is not to say the Marshall Court never cited to or relied upon framing era sources. Of the twelve instances the *Federalist Papers* were cited in the first century of the Supreme Court, the Marshall Court accounted for eight. Yet other than the *Federalist Papers,* the use of framing era sources was few and far between.[163] It is a fact which holds true despite a number of historical sources being made available in print form. The ratification debates of the Massachusetts Convention, Pennsylvania Convention, Virginia Convention, South Carolina Convention, and North Carolina Convention are just a few.[164] Whether originalists wish to acknowledge it or not, there were Founding Fathers who preferred to keep the dead hand of the past out of the political fold.

As an example we know James Madison delayed publication of his convention notes "till the Constitution should be well settled by practice and till a knowledge of the controversial part of the proceedings of its framers could be turned to no improper account."[165] Madison explained, "As a guide in expounding and applying the provisions of the Constitution, the debates and incidental decisions of the Convention can have no authoritative character."[166] Madison was not the only person seeking to subdue political "bias" in the Early Republic.[167] While sitting on the Supreme Court, Chief Justice John Marshall and Associate Justice Bushrod Washington remained cognizant of the impact George Washington's papers could have on the divisive political climate. Bushrod, the venerated Washington's nephew, had been bequeathed the papers through will. Almost immediately after George Washington's death, requests for the papers became common. They were requests Bushrod refused. "Acting with the fairness which shall always mark my conduct," wrote Bushrod to Alexander Hamilton, "I could not upon such a subject refuse to one [political party] what I have granted to the other party, and thus the papers might be used in a way very different from that which I am persuaded was intended by [George Washington] who confided them to my care."[168]

Marshall, a co-custodian of the papers, expressed similar concerns. In a letter to Associate Justice William Paterson, Marshall wrote:

> I form[e]d a resolution shortly after the papers came to my possession, not to use or permit them to be us[e]d, for party purposes. If I open[e]d them to my political friends, I could not refuse like access to those from whom I differ[e]d in opinion. How cou[l]d I, without incurring imputations of unfairness, & subjecting myself to charges which nothing but a resort to the papers could remove. Suppose for instance I should be accus[e]d of publishing partial parts of a correspondence, who cou[l]d I defend myself, & why should I involve myself in difficulties, from which I shou[l]d never be able to extricate myself without opening the papers to both parties? The unmerited abuse of the democratic party I shou[l]d disregard, but were I to use these papers as weapons against them, I should feel myself wrong when they sought aid from them, to refuse their request.[169]

Bushrod and Marshall were more than Supreme Court colleagues. They were longtime friends, classmates, courtroom adversaries, and political allies before ever sitting on the bench together. Bushrod even owed his Supreme Court appointment to Marshall, who had rejected a seat on the bench when first approached, but proceeded to recommend his esteemed friend.[170] In 1802, Bushrod and Marshall were two of the three trustees appointed to create a monument to the memory of George Washington.[171] Two years earlier, Bushrod had recruited Marshall to write a five volume series titled *The Life of George Washington.*[172] It was a project that placed George Washington's papers in their joint possession.

But the importance Bushrod and Marshall placed on shielding the papers from Federalists and Jeffersonian Republicans alike has been overlooked by scholars attempting to understand the use of past for the legal present. Given that Bushrod and Marshall were both sitting on the Supreme Court and known Federalist supporters, this should not be ignored. It would have been easy for either to use the papers for ideological or partisan gain, yet both declined because it would have heightened political hostility, been judicially improper, and may even have sullied George Washington's reputation in the process. In order to place these sentiments in historical context, one must remember Bushrod and Marshall personally witnessed the political turmoil that took place after the elder statesman's retirement. Marshall had even written to George Washington about how it did not matter what bill was presented before Congress, because men "will hold power by any means rather than not hold it; & who would prefer a dissolution of the union to the continuance of an administration not of their own party." In other words, Marshall knew the tumultuous politics of the era would have caused any bill to be "attack'd with equal virulence."[173]

Throughout the Early Republic, George Washington served as the beacon of nationalism. His farewell address was frequently republished and few politicians dared question his wisdom without being subjected to criticism themselves.[174] In short, Washington's past opinions for use in the present was a sought after commodity. So much so that publishers contacted Bushrod about the papers, all to no avail. By 1826, however, Bushrod and Marshall changed their stance. The two friends planned on publishing a three volume set of handpicked letters. The project would prevent the political misuse of the papers as well as preserve Washington's reputation.[175] A year later, Bushrod and Marshall altered their plan by commissioning Jared Spark's to publish a twelve-volume work titled *The Writings of George Washington*. Hereto though, Bushrod and Marshall retained editorial discretion as to which letters were and were not to be published. The contract stipulated that Bushrod and Marshall could withhold "any paper" which they "do not deem suited or proper for publication."[176]

Certainly, the actions of Madison, Marshall, and Bushrod provide us with proof there existed concern over the improper use of historical sources for political purposes, but it does not negate intentionalism as a source for constitutional interpretation. Text, particularly the understanding of text, was undeniably a tool in defining the scope and limits of the Constitution. Yet the interpretation of that text in the late eighteenth-century, including our Anglo-American rights and privileges, was the result of a common law approach, not modern conceptions of textualism. As historians Julius Goebel, Jr., and T. Raymond Naughton have written, "Since the common law was the forest where all manner of constitutional rights had first grown and were duly sheltered, the American, tender of his liberties, was forever coursing in its precincts."[177]

Article III of the Constitution does not expressly command that the judiciary shall follow a common law approach.[178] It is an omission that gives some weight to an intentionalist, textualist or originalist approach. These latter approaches dictate that the interpretation of constitutional text should be limited within the period it was adopted. However, for the vast number of legal historians who have traced the development of the common law, including the ideological evolution of constitutional rights in its process, this is a pathetic fallacy.[179] Late eighteenth-century legal and constitutional interpretation was not formulated at whim. It was carried over from English practice and modified by the American experience.

In contrast, whether it is modern intentionalism, textualism or originalism, the overarching purpose is more to curtail judicial discretion than apply the founding generation's view of the law. To put it another way, intentionalism, textualism, and originalism are essentially rooted in fear and jealousy of the judiciary's power to define the unarticulated content. Such a love-hate affair with judicial discretion predates our Anglo-American constitutional jurisprudence. As Frederick Pollock detailed in his timeless *Columbia Law Review* series on the history of the common law, it is a persistent situation that harks back centuries:

> Suitors in the early age of regular justice [were] highly suspicious of personal favour and caprice and will not hear of giving room for discretion. As they apprehend it, a Court once allowed to relax the customary forms could make of the law itself whatever its members and managers for the time being pleased. The irrational ground goes back to the oldest form of superstition, order than both statecraft and priestcraft, the prehistoric belief in symbolic magic. It is assumed that words have in themselves an operative virtue which is lost if any one word is substituted for any other. He who does not follow the exact words prescribed by the legal ritual does not bring himself within the law.... These two motives, jealously of personal authority and superstitious worship of the letter, are as different as possible in origin and nature, but they are by no means inconsistent. Rather they have been a pair of hands to tie the magistrate fast in bonds woven with the double strand of magic and policy. Between them they have fostered, all the world over, official and professional attachment to form for form's sake, a passion with which we have all made acquaintance at some time, or our greater or less vexation.[180]

Today the applicability of the common law, in terms of constitutional understanding, is less vibrant than it was in the late eighteenth and early nineteenth centuries. Of course, this does not undo the importance that the founding generation placed on the common law, nor does it supersede the time when statutory law was an affirmation of common law principles. Yet, as the United States grew and developed, American society became more reliant on statutory law and the interpretation of texts. Common law principles served less of a purpose. It was a change that soon to be Chief Justice Harlan F. Stone observed: "Judge-made law, which at its best must normally lag somewhat behind experience, was unable to keep pace with the rapid change, and it could find in the law books no adequate pattern into which the new experience could be readily fitted."[181] This change in legal order, however, did not negate continuing the most influential principle of the common law—legal reasoning. Whatever source of law the case or controversy involved, Stone could not contemplate an "adequate reason for our failure to treat a statute much more as we treat a judicial precedent, as both a declaration and source of law, and as a premise for legal reasoning."[182] In other words, the growth of statutory law could never fully extinguish the judiciary's duty of defining the reasonable meaning of the law. It merely began a shift in the structural paradigm. Stone elaborated:

> There is little in the spirit and tradition of the common law to induce us to attempt to reduce the constitutional standard for reasonableness to a detailed formulation of definite propositions. There is neither scope nor historical support for the expansion of constitutional exaction of reasonableness of official action implied in the use of phrases "liberty," "property," "due process," "unreasonable," and the like, into a body of detailed rules attaching definite consequences to definite states of fact.[183]

Stone's view of judicial reasoning is arguably the antithesis of originalism. Stone indeed placed emphasis on the past, but he never perceived the Constitution to be commanding the judiciary to transfix the common law as understood in 1787 or 1791. The "most significant feature of the common law, past and present, and the essential element in its historical growth," wrote Stone, was "the fact that it is preeminently a system built up by gradual accretion of special instances."[184] Stone did not create this view out of thin air. The common law was the basis of legal education leading up to the turn of the twentieth century. However, it was gradually being dispensed with as an approach. In 1898 University of Pennsylvania Law School Dean William Draper Lewis detailed how text books which contained hundreds of cases outlined in their simple legal principles were becoming the new norm. Case studies and critical thinking no longer held the same influence. It was a change Lewis felt to be a "fundamental defect" moving forward, for it hindered the growth of "inductive processes" seeing that "the induction from the reported cases is, after the comprehension of the point in issue, the first step in any serious legal reasoning."[185]

There can be little doubt that defenders of originalism will continue to assert a textual, and albeit *ad hoc* approach to history, confined to the period of ratification, is more principled. This includes limiting the common law to the period of ratification, not as a growing body of law.[186] But this too is a serious dilemma presented by originalism. As Bernadette A. Meyler has detailed, late eighteenth century common law doctrine was "far from a unified field at the time of the Founding, nor was it so conceived, as both the writings of the Founders themselves and contemporary legal commentary demonstrate."[187] "As a consequence," writes Meyler, "a single common law answer to a constitutional question often remains unavailable; instead, several distinct positions may present themselves."[188]

It was a dilemma acknowledged in 1836, when the Massachusetts Assembly and Governor Edward Everett sought codification of the state's common law doctrine. The assembly had approved the appointment of five commissioners to write a report taking "into consideration the practicability and expediency of reducing into a written systematic code, the common law of Massachusetts."[189] The commissioners comprised of Associate Justice Joseph Story, future Massachusetts Supreme Court Judge Theron Metcalf, Harvard Law School professor Simon Greenleaf, Clerk of the Massachusetts House of Representatives Luther S. Cushing, and lawyer Charles E. Forbes. They collectively agreed the task of marshaling the "true nature or character of the common law" would prove difficult:

> [T]he common law consists of positive rules and remedies, of general usages and customs, and of elementary principles, and the developments or applications of them, which cannot now be distinctly traced back to any statutory enactments, but which rest for their authority upon the common recognition, consents and use of the State itself. Some of these rules, usages and principles are of such high antiquity, that the time cannot be assigned, when they had not an existence and use. Others of them are of a comparatively modern growth, having been developed with the gradual progress of society; and others, again, can hardly be said to have had a visible and known existence until our day....
>
> In truth, the common law is not in its nature and character an absolutely fixed, inflexible system, like the statute law, providing only for cases of a determinate form, which fall within the letter of the language, in which a particular doctrine or legal proposition is expressed. It is rather a system of elementary principles and of general juridical truths, which are continually expanding with the progress of society, and adapting themselves to the gradual changes of trade, and commerce, and the mechanic arts, and the exigencies and usages of the country. There are certain fundamental maxims in it, which are never departed from; there are others again, which, though true in a general sense, are at the same time susceptible of modifications and exceptions, to prevent them from doing manifest wrong and injury.[190]

Interestingly enough, the difficulty of the task did not prevent the commissioners from attempting a codification of Massachusetts' common law, albeit carefully.[191] They knew a codification of the entire common law could not be accomplished, especially given that many legal subjects were continually in flux. As a result, the commissioners only agreed to codify those "general principles" from "elementary treatises now extant."[192] Even the identification of such general principles was not an easy task, seeing that portions of the code extended as far back as the English common law, with others no longer reflecting these English principles. Furthermore, there was concern whether the code would be used to constrain judicial authority. It was genuinely feared, following the codification of the state's common law doctrine, that the Massachusetts Assembly would eliminate the remaining "disputable deductions," and in its place proclaim "the positive sanctions of the Legislature ... to be the common law."[193] It was a concern the commissioners dismissed, given the judiciary's implicit authority to decide what the law is:

> [T]he objection has no application to codification, as proposed by the Commissioners; for every thing not governed by the Code is to be left precisely as it now is. Courts of justice are to be at full liberty to apply the existing common law to non-enumerated cases, exactly as they do now. And from the materials thus furnished by judicial decisions, improvements and additions, may, from time to time, be engrafted by the Legislature on the Code itself. It will thus become, what it ought to be, a perpetual index to the known law, gradually refining, enlarging and qualifying its doctrines, and, at the same time, bringing them together in a concise and positive form for public use.[194]

Here, the commissioners' rejection of a transfixed common law and a judiciary constrained by the past derails the claim that originalism has always existed. No one can dispute the Constitution was ratified with supermajority consent and its provisions, to this day, represent the law of the land. However, common law doctrine, which was intertwined with the law of nations, the public good and legal reasoning, was viewed as equally important. Given that the common law was built on custom, tradition, public acceptance, and a long line of precedent, it too was America's birthright.[195] It is important to remember that in every democratic society, including our own, tradition is an essential feature.[196] Therefore, in this sense, originalist claims are somewhat valid. As a people we seek to validate the present through the tradition of the past, and we perceive ourselves to be walking in the footsteps of the founding fathers. But this is impossible. As discussed earlier, the world of today is not that of the late eighteenth century, nor will it ever be. To believe there is some unbroken chain of custom or tradition from the eighteenth century to the present is a Whiggish view of history.[197]

Taken altogether, this presents a legitimacy dilemma when the legal community imports the dead hand of the past for use in the present. We are not one and the same with the founding generation, nor do our modern perceptions of the past necessarily correlate with what the historical record provides. The reality is the legal rationale and reasoning of the past is no longer that of today. Any attempt to fix the Constitution principles of 1787 or 1791 is to undo an essential element of late eighteenth-century constitutionalism—our evolving common law tradition. At the same time, however, for the legal community to completely sever our constitutional past from the present would run counter to the Constitution's purpose, as well as the founding generation's view of history and the law. The use of history and custom to interpret the Constitution was not only commonplace among late eighteenth-century jurists, but it was seen as an important guidepost. The issue moving forward is deciding when a turn to the past is legitimate and when is it not. Moreover, how does the judiciary ensure accuracy in the process by not distorting the historical record or subjectively importing it? It is a problem which has vexed the legal and historical community alike for over a century. The next chapter aims to provide the answers by mapping the historical guidepost approach to constitutional interpretation.

4

Historical Guideposts and Constitutional Interpretation

The role history should play in constitutional interpretation has assumed many forms since the late eighteenth century. To the founding generation, history provided a moral and philosophical guidepost to understanding the law's development. In the mid nineteenth century a shift occurred when a number of jurists began applying history as a tool of judicial restraint.[1] But the use of historical evidence in this fashion presents a number of concerns about legitimacy, objectivity, and accuracy. Such concerns foresee the manipulation of historical record by cherry-picking evidence, the omission of damaging historical facts, and a possible failure to understand sources in historical context. Under the heading "law office history" fall such issues which, to this day, plague constitutional interpretation. And the rise of originalism has only amplified these matters. Instead of considering history in a minority of cases—as nineteenth-century jurists employed it—originalism has brought history into the foray of most constitutional questions and controversies. Thus, it is not uncommon for today's litigants to employ historical evidence when presenting their case before the courts. This in turn creates dueling histories that jurists must weigh, consider, and then with which they must side.

The turn to the dead hand of the past for use in the present is arguably a fruitless endeavor. In 1919, prominent early nineteenth-century historian George Macaulay Trevelyan articulated, "You cannot so completely isolate any historical event from its circumstances as to be able to deduce from it a law of general application."[2] Trevelyan found it problematic when historians, scholars or politicians proclaimed the public at large of an historical era felt and believed a definable conclusion. "The few facts we know [about some persons] may or may not be typical of the rest," wrote Trevelyan. Therefore, the "most important past of its business, history, is not a scientific deduction, but an

83

imaginative guess at the most likely of generalisations."[3] This was not to say history did not serve *any* societal purpose. To Trevelyn, it was quite the contrary. History served any number of important "educational purposes" because it gives society the capability to "reflect on the past."[4] But to "reflect" requires good stewards of history, i.e., diligent, objective, and honest historians. It is the historian's duty not only to educate the public "intelligently in the past," but also to perform it in a manner that "will give the best interpretation" after "having discovered and weighed all the important evidence obtainable."[5] Of course, for historians to accomplish their duties requires they perform some "imaginative or speculative" functions.[6] In other words, Trevelyn understood historians could not answer every question about a particular point in the distant past, and there would be instances where historians paint a canvas with no more than a few shards of historical evidence.

The fact that even professional historians must sometimes guess or make generalizations is reason enough to question whether the use of history for constitutional interpretation is appropriate. But to completely separate history from the law is to undo our Anglo-American tradition and perhaps the Constitution itself.[7] One cannot deny that history, custom, and tradition have always assumed some role in constitutional interpretation. Even when James Madison and other founding fathers took part in drafting the Constitution's text and structure, history played a vital role. In carving out the Constitution's separation of powers framework to include the different checks and balances as well as identifying the essential rights of the people, each maintained a distinct historical pedigree. The role history served in drafting the Constitution was even understood by late eighteenth-century jurists. In a great many subjects, these jurists employed history as a moral and philosophical guidepost: the freedom of the press, the right to trial by jury, crime and punishment, the law of nations, obedience or allegiance to the laws, the rights and duties of citizenship, the parameters of a republican government and the development of the law in general. In these cases, history provided a sense of constitutional legitimacy by explaining the development of the law. At the same time, however, history was not the means of and ends to interpreting the law. It was a consideration to be weighed alongside others. The common law, precedent, judicial reasoning, and the law of nations were equally if not more important in adjudicating constitutional questions and controversies. And of course text—to include its intentions and meaning—served a critical role, but more so in terms of the purposes and consequences of any respective interpretation.

It is within this spirit that the following chapter lays out the historical guidepost approach to constitutional interpretation. In line with our Anglo-American common law tradition, and with respect to the judiciary as an independent branch of government, the historical guidepost approach first relies on precedent to adjudicate constitutional questions and controversies. Relying on precedent first and foremost does not mean applying each and every court expression as dispositive. One must distinguish dictum from holding.[8] In other words, one must weigh whether a respective statement or expression by the judiciary was necessary to the outcome of the case. To borrow from Chief Justice John Marshall in the 1821 case *Cohens v. Virginia:*

> It is a maxim not to be disregarded, that general expressions, in every opinion, are to be taken in connection with the case in which those expressions are used. If they go beyond the case, they may be respected, but ought not to control the judgment in a subsequent suit when the very point is presented for decision. The reason of this maxim is obvious. The question actually before the court is investigated with care, and considered in its full extent. Other principles which may serve to illustrate it, are considered in their relation to the case decided, but their possible bearing on all other cases is seldom completely investigated.[9]

It is only when precedent does not provide a direct answer to the constitutional question or controversy at hand that one should turn to history, custom, and tradition. But the turn to history also requires a respect for historical methodologies. One must maintain a sense of historical consciousness by placing the historical evidence in total context, relying on accepted historical works, knowing the difference between a substantiated historical thesis and an unproven historical theory, differentiating between historical consensus and historical conflict, and recognizing the present is not one and the same with the past. It is only by following these baseline historical methodologies that the use of history in the law can be accurate and therefore legitimate.[10] Undeniably, there will be instances where the past cannot definitively answer the constitutional questions of the present. However, in such cases, it is important one be honest about what the historical record does and does not provide.

Under the historical guidepost approach, one must also distinguish between what the historical record provides at a particular point in time versus custom or tradition. There is a distinction between what history tells about the scope of the Constitution at the time of its 1791 ratification compared with the time of the Fourteenth Amendment's ratification. The same can be said when one compares the Constitution as understood in the mid twentieth-century versus today. This analogy is prevailing since legal understanding changes with time. If one employs the disciplines of history and historiography with due circumspection they can trace these changes in custom, tradition, and understanding in jurisprudence. However, not every legal issue, subject, and controversy has been thoroughly examined by courts. Therefore, there will be cases of first impression and the court will have to weigh the meaning and intent of a constitutional provision against social, political, and cultural tradition. There will also be cases where history may be employed to fill any jurisprudential gaps. Still, whether it is a case of first impression or one merely requiring the assistance of history, the historical guidepost approach does not employ history as a firm outcome–determinative tool. History merely provides moral and philosophical guideposts from which to reason.[11] It cannot be emphasized enough that the past and the present are not one and the same, nor can they ever be. There are a number of social, cultural, political, international and geographic issues to weigh up and consider.[12] More importantly though, when one is faced with a constitutional question or controversy, it is the rare for a modern law, statute, or policy at issue to mirror those found on the books in 1791, 1868 or some other important point in time for understanding the scope of the Constitution.[13]

Lastly, it is worth mentioning the historical guidepost approach is not one and the same with other history-based legal theories such as original intent, new originalism, original methods originalism or framework originalism. In contrast to these latter approaches, the historical guideposts respects basic historical methodologies to ensure accuracy, objectivity, and transparency.[14] History is not a subcontractor or the means to achieve an ideological end.[15] It provides a moral and philosophical guide as an aid to understanding the development of the law. While there is certainly a parallel between original methods originalism and historical guideposts, given both approaches draw inspiration from the late eighteenth-century approach to constitutional interpretation,[16] the historical guidepost approach rejects originalist methodologies outright. Meanwhile original methods originalism embraces originalist methodologies as consistent with framing era thought.[17]

The historical guidepost approach is also different from the new quasi-originalist theory advanced by law professor Jack M. Balkin. Known as framework originalism, on some levels the historical guidepost approach is similar given both theories reject original meaning as a strict outcome–determinative tool. Historical guideposts and framework originalism are also similar given both acknowledge the role the judiciary serves in our constitutional system.[18] But these are the only comparative aspects of constitutional interpretation that historical guideposts and framework originalism have in common. While the historical guidepost approach emphasizes historical consciousness and eliciting context to the greatest detail,[19] framework originalism views the historical record as nothing more than a wellspring from which to pick and choose traditions in line with textual formulations. As Balkin states it, "We must decide in the present which constructions are most faithful to the text; history cannot decide this question for us."[20]

It is rather difficult for proponents of any legal theory, let alone the variants of originalism, to argue their approach is legitimate when the resulting conclusions contradict what a thorough examination of the historical record provides. It is the equivalent of a court deciding a case based upon inaccurate statements of fact. For if a court lays an inaccurate factual foundation, the subsequent legal analysis and case holding will most likely be illegitimate. The historical guidepost approach alleviates this problem by advancing the most accurate history possible. Certainly there will be times when the historical record is either unclear or conflicting, but as long as one is honest about what the historical record does and does not provide, and works through historical conflicts, any subsequent legal analysis will be far more legitimate than cherry-picking historical evidence and discarding historical methodologies wholesale.

Historical Consciousness and Total Historical Context

Before ever applying the past for use in the present, one needs to understand the past according to its own terms. This includes constitutional text. The end goal is not to *infer* or *create* meaning from a sample of historical documents. Such an approach muddles rather than clarifies historical analysis. Instead, the goal is to state results in the form of inner connections traced between ideas or events, and they belong together in an intimate way.[21] It has become far too easy for the legal community to explain away constitutional text or claim that a few historical sources, with virtually little if any connection between them, give meaning or insight into a constitutional doctrine, provision, clause or amendment. Take for example the claims of left-leaning immigration law professors and legal scholars who claim the Declaration of Independence grievance, which stipulates the crown "endeavored to prevent the population of these States; for that purpose obstructing the Laws for migrations hither,"[22] is proof the founding generation believed in a basic right to immigrate.[23] But when the grievance is placed in total historical context one learns it had to do with the crown usurping what was seen as colonial authority, not the recognition of any individualized rights to migrate.[24] It is a point of emphasis that as eighteenth-century American political thought progressed, the idea of virtual representation made less sense, and the colonists sought to establish a government built upon the "consent of the governed" with equitable principles diffused throughout.[25] Furthermore, given the

Declaration's international character and acknowledgment of the law of nations, one would assume late eighteenth-century jurists applied international norms to regulations touching upon immigration law,[26] meaning they agreed with the international premise every nation retains authority over its borders.[27]

The question moving forward is whether this assumption is a historical theory or a historical thesis. What differentiates the two? A historical theory provides a research agenda for other historians to prove or disprove. It is a history in progress so to speak. Meanwhile, a verified historical thesis incorporates substantial and intimately woven evidence that speaks for itself. Initially its findings may not be accepted outright should it not comport with the historical consensus, but this can change with time and subsequent historical exchanges. Of these two options—historical theory or historical thesis—the assumption turns out to be the latter. The right of every nation to legislate over foreigners, to include their entry, exit, and exclusion, was restated by some of America's greatest legal minds. John Marshall, John Jay, William Cushing, James Iredell, Alexander Addison, James Madison, Alexander Hamilton, and Samuel Preston all made statements to this effect. It was a set of powers that were linked with every nation's right of self-preservation.[28] In contrast, there is no historical evidence, at least in context, to suggest that immigration was a right or even rested on notions of prospectivity.[29]

However, for over a century the legal community has advanced a myriad of historical theories touching upon the source of federal immigration power.[30] In recent decades, left-leaning immigration law professors and scholars have claimed the Supreme Court created the plenary power doctrine out of thin air or out of a national sense of peril. And given the Constitution does not expressly grant the federal government immigration powers, they argue federal plenary power over immigration must have some limits and be subject to some form of judicial scrutiny.[31] Originalists advance a similar interpretation on textualist grounds, but do not assert any immigration rights. Instead, they see the textual omission as establishing a complex division of powers between not only executive and legislative branches of federal government, but also among the federal and state governments.[32]

Still, it does not matter whether federal immigration powers are viewed through the prism of legal liberalism or originalism, for in both cases its proponents are explaining away history, not understanding it according to its terms or even attempting to explore the historical record in context. Both ask the right empirical question: "What immigration powers, if any, are afforded the federal and state governments respectively?" Yet neither legal liberalists nor originalists ask any subsequent questions and cannot contemplate going

Historical Thesis v. Historical Theory

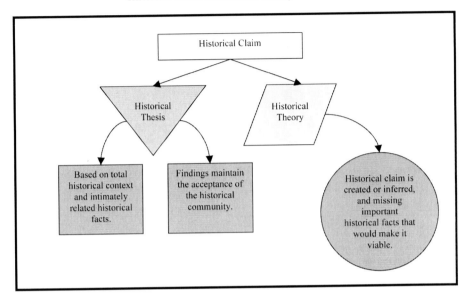

beyond the Constitution's text. It is methodological deficiency that extends to Balkin's framework originalism, which attempts to balance the approaches of both legal liberalism and originalism. Like legal liberalists and originalists, Balkin first turns to the Constitution's text to locate federal immigration powers. While Balkin recognizes the Constitution's Naturalization Clause infers federal power to control immigration, he believes the "obvious" source comes from "Congress's power to regulate commerce with foreign nations and the Indian tribes." What historical support does Balkin produce to support his interpretation? None. Instead, Balkin sidesteps the historical inquiry by explaining away the text. As a result, Balkin audaciously claims the plenary power doctrine was "created" by the Supreme Court and maintains "no basis in the text."[33]

If Balkin is correct that the Supreme Court created the plenary power doctrine, then why did late eighteenth-century jurists stipulate otherwise and link federal power over immigration with the law of nations? Consider for instance James Iredell, who relied on the law of nations to rebut the claim of free migration advocates and defend the constitutionality of the 1798 Alien Act:

> It is believed that it never was suggested in any other country, that *aliens* had a right to go into a foreign country, and stay at their will and pleasure without leave of government. The law of nations undoubtedly is, when an alien goes into

a foreign country, he goes under either an express or implied safe conduct. In most countries of Europe, I believe, an express passport is necessary for strangers. Whence greater liberty is observed, yet it is always understood that the government may order away any alien whose stay is deemed incompatible with the safety of the country.[34]

William Cushing expressed similar sentiments in a charge to the grand jury delivered before the District of Virginia on November 23, 1798. But unlike Iredell, Cushing relied on the broad application of the Constitution's Necessary and Proper Clause and preamble:

> But can any reasonable man suppose, that a government, instituted for the protection of all the States & all the citizens, with full powers to do everything necessary for that important end, has no power to protect itself by laws to prevent crimes which tend directly to its overthrow and destruction? Can it be imagined, that the supreme authority of a government, which is vested with the important powers of war, and of the common defence against public enemies, and of protecting each state against invasions, and is expressly authorised, by the constitution, to make all laws necessary and proper to carry those powers into execution, had no power to remove alien enemies—to remove aliens who belong to, and owe allegiance to a foreign state.[35]

In Balkin's defense, his analysis of federal immigration power was in explanation of the limits and scope of the Commerce Clause.[36] But still, if Balkin continues to make historical claims about constitutional powers, he must pay closer attention to historical methodologies and actually conduct historical research. Of course, Balkin is not the first, nor will he be the last, to explain away history in this fashion. The practice is quite common among members of the legal community. One unproven historical claim is built upon another and so on. Such a domino effect is problematic when the initial point of departure is false, poorly researched or illegitimate. It creates a historically self-perpetuating chain of ill-founded legal scholarship. Such a perversion of the domino effect as is a chain of insecure scholarship may be identified as the "domino defect."

Let us stay on the subject of federal immigration power, for it provides a fitting example of how illegitimate historical claims can result in a domino defect. In the recent Supreme Court case *Arizona v. United States*, at issue were four provisions of Arizona Senate Bill 1070, which aimed to "discourage and deter the unlawful entry and presence of aliens and economic activity by persons unlawfully present in the United States."[37] Only a year earlier the Supreme Court had decided *Chamber of Commerce v. Whiting*, another Arizona immigration test case where the Court upheld a law that revoked the licenses of businesses found guilty of employing unlawful aliens.[38] In *Whiting*,

Arizona won the case by advancing traditional preemption arguments. But in *Arizona v. United States,* a different theory was asserted, known as "attrition through enforcement."[39] The theory stipulated the states retain inherent authority to enforce and strengthen federal immigration law.[40] Surprisingly, the concept of attrition through enforcement developed from the claims of legal liberals and conservatives alike. As a result of the Constitution not granting any express immigration powers, both legal liberals and conservatives carved out theories where the states possessed immigration authority to coincide with federal plenary power. The theory advanced by legal liberals afforded state and local governments the ability to enact sanctuary policies which shielded unlawful aliens from federal detection.[41] Meanwhile, conservatives advanced a theory where the states retained inherent authority to both enforce and strengthen federal immigration law in order to deter unlawful immigration.[42]

In essence, both legal liberals and conservatives built their theories on the historical findings of Gerald A. Neuman, who set out to correct the myth there were no laws regulating immigration until the late nineteenth century.[43] Neuman succeeded in his quest by showing how state immigration regulations developed from 1776 through 1875.[44] But Neuman cautioned that his findings were insufficient to call into question federal plenary power over immigration—a doctrine the Supreme Court did not acknowledge until the late nineteenth-century.[45] It is here that Neuman's history reflects aspects of both an historical theory and historical thesis. While Neuman unequivocally proved the existence of immigration laws from the late eighteenth through to the late nineteenth century, the majority of his legal conclusions were built upon a historical theory. At no point did Neuman delve into the purposes behind the Constitution's ratification, the law of nations as understood in late eighteenth century views, or even the opinions of early American jurists. Instead, Neuman's historical paradigm relied on the unproven theory that it was the institution of slavery which prevented the federal government from passing comprehensive immigration legislation. "The failure to enact uniform immigration policies at the national level resulted from a combination of forces—not just pro-immigration sentiment, but also a desire to keep migration policy within state authority," wrote Neuman. Allegedly, it was only after the ratification of the Thirteenth Amendment and the end of slavery that "national immigration regulation became possible."[46]

To be clear, the only legitimate historical claim made by Neuman was the existence of immigration law before 1875, albeit it at the state level. In the years that followed, members of the legal community stretched Neuman's thesis beyond the bands of historical elasticity when they carved out their respective state immigration theories. This created overlapping domino defects until the subject of state authority over immigration came to a head in *Arizona v. United States*. The majority of the Supreme Court shied away from these false historical claims and applied traditional express and implied preemption doctrine to strike down most of the Arizona Senate Bill 1070. Antonin Scalia, however, built his opinion on the flawed inherent state authority theory, writing that "after the adoption of the Constitution there was *some doubt* about the power of the Federal Government to control immigration, but *no doubt* about the power of the States to do so."[47] Like so many members of the legal community, Scalia made no attempt to explore the historical record, the purposes behind the ratification of the Constitution, or late eighteenth-century perceptions of international law and its relationship to immigration.[48] Instead, Scalia latched onto Neuman's exposition of state immigration regulation from 1776 through 1875.[49] Certainly Scalia would be correct to assert the states passed a number of immigration related measures throughout the late nineteenth-century. But to claim there was "no doubt" of the states' immigration authority is historically unsubstantiated, especially once one refers to the historical record in context.

What this example illustrates is the ease with which history can be misused or explained away. With only one historical fact, Scalia advanced an illegitimate legal theory. Consider this: what if Scalia's dissent was the majority? It would have created an entire strand of jurisprudence and scholarship founded upon a domino defect. Therefore, the legal community, particularly jurists, should proceed cautiously when importing the past for use in the present. This is what makes the consideration of historical context imperative.[50] The first lesson any student majoring in history learns is the importance of context in writing an objective account.[51] Historical context is even more essential in deducing a writer's intentions or written words—what is traditionally referred to as the history of ideas or intellectual history.[52] Historians know words are inert and must be placed in the time of their construction.[53] If the writer's meaning changes it is only due to the "imaginative processes of their human inventors and users" that misinterpreted it, not the original author.[54] Thus, the historian must remain cognizant so as to balance historical texts, images, and theories responsibly, with precision, and connect them to a particular historical world.[55] A historian cannot simply assume meaning with a modern predisposition.[56] The historian must import the language into the proper historical construct, "point out conventions and regularities that indicate what could have could not be spoken in the language, and in what ways the language *qua* paradigm encouraged, obliged, or forbade its users to speak and think."[57]

Perhaps a better way to summarize this placement of text into historical context is to follow Quentin Skinner's three-steps to conducting intellectual history:

1. [We] need to recover an author's intentions in writing in order to understand the meaning of what he writes.
2. In order to recover such intentions, it is ... essential to surround the given text with an appropriate context of assumptions and conventions from which the author's exact intended meaning can then be decoded.
3. This yields the crucial conclusion that a knowledge of these assumptions and conventions must be essential to understanding the meaning of text.[58]

To ignore these rules—i.e., to interpret text loosely—is to commit what historian Herbert Butterfield termed a "pathetic fallacy" because it abstracts conclusions apart from the author's purpose.[59] Yet sadly, this is the interpretative foundation upon which much of today's history based jurisprudence and legal scholarship is built. The dismissal of the most important of all historical methodologies has been accomplished by employing a variety of legal strategies. This includes the turn to originalism which promotes dictionaries and the general usage of words above any contextual, intellectual, social, or ideological framework existing at that time.[60] Not only is originalism's narrowly legalistic approach at odds with historical context, but more importantly, it is in direct conflict with the goal of historical scholarship—to understand the past for the sake of understanding the past.

This last point is crucial, for the historian's primary function is to continuously improve our understanding of the past. This often requires revisiting the evidentiary foundation upon which previous historical writings rest. It also requires engaging in an intellectual discourse with other historians in search of the truth. The law operates slightly differently in order to guarantee some semblance of predictability and reliance. This includes any jurisprudential strands built upon a domino defect, despite the foundation being historically illegitimate. In such cases, the rules of *stare decisis* are the norm, making it difficult to undo any false historical pronouncements. This need not be the case. It is undoubtedly within the purview of the judiciary to correct false history. In fact, one may argue it is the judiciary's duty. In *Moore v. City of East Cleveland,* the Supreme Court seemingly endorsed this view of history and law when it proclaimed the appropriate limits of constitutional rights and governmental power "come not from drawing arbitrary lines, but rather a careful respect for the teachings of history [and], solid recognition of the basic values that underlie our society."[61]

But how is the judiciary, and the legal community in general, supposed to respect the teachings of history when the historical record cannot always supply us with answers we seek? This is why retaining historical consciousness is crucial. To retain historical consciousness is not the same as employing one's historical imagination. The two are distinct in terms of what the evidentiary record can provide. To draw conclusions from one's historical imagination is to build upon speculations and predispositions, not historical facts or findings. Meanwhile, to retain historical consciousness means eliciting context in the greatest detail. To state in another way, members of the legal community should neither read nor infer historical constructs or use their historical imagination. Should members of the legal community feel the need to fill any historical gap(s), they must rely on accepted historical works to do so, not merely a work that supports their predispositions.[62]

Building upon accepted historical works is crucial to ensure historical accuracy. To do otherwise is to proceed down the road of a domino defect, for if the historical foundation is tainted, so too is any subsequent legal analysis. A fitting example of how poor or deficient scholarship can affect historical accuracy is the Supreme Court's landmark Second Amendment decision in *District of Columbia v. Heller.* In *Heller,* the majority was guided by an histor- ical theory dubbed the Standard Model right to arms.[63] Under this model, the Second Amendment provides an individual the right to possess and use arms, divorced from government sanctioned militias, as a means to (1) check government tyranny through an armed citizenry,[64] (2) provide the means to repel force with force should one be assailed in private or public,[65] and (3) provide for the common defense.[66] Indeed, the history supporting an individual right to arms is vast and undeniable. However, the evidence supporting the Standard Model theory is circumstantial at best. In fact a closer consideration of the past four decades of the model's scholarship reveals that it was the repetitive advancement of poor historical paradigms—to include originalist methodologies—that pushed aside accepted historical methodologies, which in turn led to ahistorical conclusions. The errors come in all forms such as *ad hoc* textualism, creating historical myths with circumstantial or no historical evidence, and a minimalist understanding of the ideological and intellectual origins of the right to arms.[67] Still, proponents of originalism and its Second Amendment product, the Standard Model right to arms, foresee little to no problem with distorting history to advance a legal theory. It has become an accepted causality of interpreting the law, but this should not be the case.

For instance, consider Georgetown law professor Randy E. Barnett, who celebrates *Heller* as "the finest example of what is now called 'original public meaning' jurisprudence ever adopted by the Supreme Court."[68] Semantic originalism proponent and legal theorist Lawrence Solum also applauds *Heller* as "the clearest expression of public meaning originalism to be found in a Supreme Court decision."[69] Similarly, co-counsel for the Second Amendment Foundation in *Heller,* Clark M. Neily III, wrote it was "an easy case to get right" and reflects a "spirit of originalism" that should be "justly praised."[70] But despite *Heller* being a victory for originalism, it is undoubtedly a loss in terms of historical accuracy and therefore judicial objectivity. William G. Merkel seemingly foreshadowed this result after *Heller* was adjudicated at the lower District of Columbia Court of Appeals: "From the perspective of constitutional theory, the impending triumph of a historically unsupportable appeal to interpretive fidelity will make a significant victory for results-oriented jurisprudence, and point to the shallowness of originalist claims to neutrality."[71]

To illustrate Merkel's point, as well as the problems associated with *Heller,* originalism, and the Standard Model Second Amendment altogether, it is best to begin from one of the sources. And arguably the most influential Standard Model writer is Joyce Lee Malcolm, for she was the first English historian to assert that Article VII of the 1689 English Declaration of Rights influenced the drafting and protective scope of the Second Amendment. Malcolm's proposed connection between the English and American right to arms has been proven credible. James Madison referenced Article VII in his notes, and a number of early nineteenth-century constitutional commentators viewed the Second Amendment as its lineal descendant.[72] The only significant difference between the two rights was that Article VII was linked to socio-economic status, with the Second Amendment containing no such restriction.[73] Another notable difference between the two rights is how they were understood to operate within their respective governments. England retained one national government, with concurrent power over the militia divided between the crown and Parliament.[74] In the United States, however, it was more complicated. Not only did the Constitution create a division of powers between Congress and the president, but there was also a complex division of federal-state powers, with some of them overlapping.

Beyond linking the Anglo origins of the right to the Second Amendment, Malcolm's thesis fails to meet the historian's burden.[75] The thrust of Malcolm's argument proposes that in the late seventeenth century, arms bearing transformed from a societal duty into a common law right of armed self-defense— in both private and public—and Article VII of the 1689 Declaration of Rights acknowledged this transformation.[76] To date, no historian specializing in late seventeenth-century English history has accepted Malcolm's findings as true. In fact, her writings have been the subject of severe criticism by other historians in the field; criticisms that have yet to be tempered.[77] Malcolm's failure to address these criticisms would be less problematic if other historians or experts had come to Malcolm's defense by supplementing or reinforcing her claims. This has not occurred, however.[78] If anything, the opposite has transpired, with historical antagonism only strengthening over time.[79] Suffice to say, the historical conclusions that Malcolm claims to be substantiated are nothing more than a number of independent historical theories, with little if any connection binding them.[80]

However, Malcolm's work is of significance because it directly influenced Justice Scalia, *Heller*'s architect, who had rebuked any militia reading of the Second Amendment years earlier. Nearly a decade before *Heller* was decided, and citing to Malcolm's work directly, Scalia wrote, "It would ... be strange to find in the midst of a catalog of the rights of individuals a provision securing to the states the right to maintain a designated 'Militia.'" To Scalia, the operative language is all that mattered and it must mean what it says—the people have a right to keep and bear arms, period.[81] What was undoubtedly appealing to Scalia was Malcolm's textual approach. Like Scalia, Malcolm rejected outright any government sanctioned militia limitations on the right to keep and bear arms. First, Malcolm's entire thesis centered on disproving the notion that Article VII of the 1689 English Declaration of Rights was linked to Parliament's right of self-preservation and resistance, and James II's employment of Catholic militia lieutenants.[82] According to Malcolm, any militia reading of Article VII "doesn't qualify as history" because the word "militia" is absent.[83] Instead, Article VII guaranteed a right to personal self-defense because of its "clear language" of an individual right divorced from militia service, and the "accompanying historical record."[84]

The second reason Malcolm rejected any state sanctioned militia reading was her rudimentary understanding of late eighteenth-century militias. From her first publication in 1983, Malcolm made the mistake of equating a well-regulated militia with a mere armed citizenry. She motivates as much by suggesting the Second Amendment's prefatory language is clearly "an amplifying rather than a qualifying clause," and the "twin concepts of a people armed and a people trained to arms were linked, but not inseparably."[85] With this conclusion, Malcolm reveals a rather limited understanding of militia laws. Said laws strictly regulated the arming, arraying, disciplining, mustering, training, and discharging of arms.[86] There is no historical evidence—at least once placed in historical context—to suggest the people maintained an independent right to associate in their own militias without government consent.[87] Nevertheless, Malcolm concluded, "The reference to a 'well regulated' militia was meant to encourage the federal government to keep the militia in good order"—nothing more.[88]

Highlighting these historical errors is important, for they were the means by which Scalia framed *Heller.* To Scalia, the English origins were of particular significance given the Second Amendment's "shall not be infringed" language.[89] It indicated to him that the Second Amendment did not confer the right, but that it was preexisting and understood as one of the fundamental rights of Englishmen.[90] Scalia elaborated:

> This [English] right [to carry weapons in case of confrontation] has long been understood to be the predecessor to our Second Amendment. It was clearly an individual right, having nothing whatever to do with service in a militia. To be sure, it was an individual right not available to the whole population, given that it was restricted to Protestants, and like all written English rights it was held only against the Crown, not Parliament. But it was secured to them as individuals, according to "libertarian political principles," not as members of a fighting force.
>
> By the time of the founding, the right to have arms had become fundamental for English subjects. Blackstone, whose works, we have said, "constituted the preeminent authority on English law for the founding generation," cited the arms provision of the Bill of Rights as one of the fundamental rights of Englishmen. His description of it cannot possibly be thought to tie it to militia or military service. It was, he said, "the natural right of resistance and self-preservation," and "the right of having and using arms for self-preservation and defence."[91]

Considering that the analysis above is based upon inaccurate history and a series of domino defects, it calls into question *Heller*'s legitimacy. This arguably includes the strands of Second Amendment jurisprudence that are reliant upon *Heller*'s historical claims. Lower courts have been forced to wrestle with the variants of Second Amendment history, which in turn has led to a myriad of analyses.[92] As it stands today, a number of courts have solved this dilemma by adopting a historical test that extinguishes the Second Amendment claim should the challenged conduct fall outside the scope of the right circa 1791.[93] It is only when the conduct falls within the protective scope of the Second Amendment that the court applies "some level of 'means-ends' scrutiny to establish whether the regulation passes constitutional muster."[94] However, only a few courts have decided a Second Amendment case or controversy by applying the historical test, leaving open the question as to how history should be employed to decide future Second Amendment issues.[95]

This is not to say *Heller*'s core holding of armed self-defense in the home with a handgun could not have been reached by employing the historical record responsibly. This point will be elaborated on in the discussion below about historical guideposts and tradition. Of note at this stage is that broad and inaccurate historical statements by the judiciary can have dire consequences. Not only can the picking and choosing of history result in illegitimate domino defects, but it can also create entire strands of jurisprudence that are equally questionable.

Historical Guideposts, Custom and Tradition

In the preceding section, the bare bones of the historical guidepost approach were discussed. If faced with a case of first impression, it is acceptable for one to employ history either to determine the scope of a constitutional provision or, at a minimum, to frame the constitutional issue at hand.[96] When doing so, it is important to retain historical consciousness. This means placing history in context, relying on accepted historical works, and not stretching history beyond the bounds of its elasticity. But most cases presented are not of the first impression variety. There are generally a few cases on point to assist us in answering the constitutional question or controversy at hand. It is here that legal custom and tradition can supplement and assist the legal community in providing an answer.

The use of legal custom and tradition becomes particularly useful in cases where the historical record is deficient. In some instances the evidentiary record provides competing interpretations. In others the record is incomplete and provides us with nothing more than a historical theory, not a proven or substantiated historical thesis. Whatever the deficiency, legal custom and tradition helps inform us as to how the law was understood and applied before, during, and after the ratification of a constitutional provision.[97] More importantly, it is by tracing legal custom and tradition that we learn the development of the law. In the words of Oliver Wendell Holmes, "[I]f we want to know why a rule of law has taken a particular shape, and more or less if we want to know why it exists at all, we go to tradition." As with the general rules concerning historical guideposts in ascertaining the scope and meaning of provisions, legal custom and tradition should only be part of a larger "rational study" of the law in that it affords us a "deliberate reconsideration of the worth of [past] rules."[98] This is exactly how late eighteenth-century jurists employed history for constitutional interpretation. They did not simply read the Constitution's text and create a rule of law out of thin air. Late eighteenth-century jurists applied the law as they knew it, considered whether the legal status quo was altered by the Constitution, and then applied common sense legal reasoning. In short, the use of legal custom and tradition was an appropriate tool for the larger purpose of legal reasoning.

The constitutional scope of the First Amendment's Press Clause as understood in the late eighteenth century provides a fitting example. The First

Amendment stipulates that "Congress shall make no law ... abridging the freedom of speech, or of the press."[99] In pure textual terms the prohibition is general—"Congress shall make no law"—yet late eighteenth-century jurists did not view the First Amendment so abruptly.[100] What constituted "free speech" and was suitable for publication in a free press required a turn to the common law and customary practice, which rested on utilitarian principles. This understanding of a free press did not originate in 1776, 1787 or 1791. It developed gradually through a century of Anglo-American intellectual debate, resulting in the doctrine against prior restraint, yet requiring anything published to be the interests of public good. It was believed any publications that did not advance the public good sapped the foundation of free press and were, therefore, outside liberty's umbrella.[101]

This view of a free press was restated by prominent late eighteenth-century jurists before and after the ratification of the Constitution. Pennsylvania Chief Justice Thomas McKean was one such prominent jurist to articulate the customary limits of a free press, and traced the customary doctrine of libel to the Twelve Tables of Rome. The 1776 Pennsylvania Constitution omitted the word "libel" and proclaimed that "the people have a right to freedom of speech, and of writing, and publishing their sentiments; therefore the freedom of the press ought not to be restrained."[102] Despite this, McKean relied on the common law, customary practice, and tradition to limit the constitutional scope of a free press to publications that were "*decent, candid and true* ... for the purpose of reformation and not of defamation, and ... have an eye solely to the public good." Such publications were "not only lawful but laudable." Meanwhile, any publications made to "gratify envy or malice, and contain personal invectives, low scurrility or slanderous charges" were unconstitutional, for they could "answer no good purpose for the community, but on the contrary must destroy the very ends of society." Therefore for McKean, to "censure ... licentiousness" was "to preserve the liberty of the press."[103] In response to the textual assumption that press "ought not to be restrained," McKean applied common sense legal reasoning: "It is equally ridiculous and absurd to supposed, that if one man *speaks* scandalous or defamatory words of another, he may be sued, and ample damages recovered for the injury, but if the same words are put into *writing* or *printed,* no punishment can be inflicted. Such a doctrine may gratify the wishes of envious and malicious cowards and assassins, but must be condemned by all sensible and good men."[104]

Massachusetts Judge Israel Sumner articulated a similar construct of a free press in the constraints of interpreting the 1780 Massachusetts Constitution. Article 16 guaranteed: "The liberty of the press is essential to the security of freedom in a state; it ought not, therefore, to be restrained in this commonwealth." At no point did the article stipulate the liberty of the press could be permissibly restrained, in any form or fashion, yet Sumner rejected a reading that presumed liberty. Instead he applied the custom, tradition, and common sense legal reasoning to conclude:

> This paragraph in our constitution is the boast of every citizen. The security of freedom being the subject matter of this article, there can be no doubt but the citizen has a right to publish his sentiments upon all political, as well as moral and literary subjects; and to point out to the publick such men as he thinks are most suitable to be elected into office; and in many other ways to express his sentiments with freedom, provided he keep within the bounds of the truth; for freedom can never be supported by falsehood. In every instance where falsehood has been propagated of the government or its offices, it has been found to undermine the very principles of freedom, and strikes at the publick peace and happiness. But there is a material difference between the *liberty* and the *licentiousness* of the press; if a man publishes anything to the injury of the publick or individuals, he must answer for it according to the laws of his country. This article, therefore, is appears to me, will not by any means excuse or justify a libelous publication.[105]

Just two years earlier, on February 18, 1789, Massachusetts Chief Justice William Cushing sent a letter concerning the same article. Writing to John Adams, he questioned whether a libel directed against officeholders could be punishable under the clause if "such charges are supportable by the truth of fact."[106] Cushing elaborated:

> But the words of our article understood according to plain English, make no such distinction, and must exclude *subsequent* restraints, as much as *previous restraints*....
>
> The question upon the article is this—What is the liberty of the press, which is essential to the security of freedom? The propagating literature and knowledge by printing or otherwise tends to illuminate men's minds and to establish them in principles of freedom. But it cannot be denied also, that a free scanning of the conduct of the administration and shewing the tendency of it, and where truth will warrant, making it manifest that it is subversive of all law, liberty, and the Constitution; it can't be denied. I think that the liberty tends to the *security of freedom in a State;* even more directly and essentially than the liberty of printing upon literary and speculative subjects in general. Without this liberty of the press could we have supported our liberties against British administration? or could our revolution have taken place? Pretty certainly it could not, at the time it did. Under a sense of impression of this sort, I conceive, this article was adopted. This liberty of publishing truth can never effectually injure a good government, or honest administrators; but it may save a state from the necessity of a revolution, as well as bring one about, when it is necessary....
>
> But this liberty of the press having truth for its basis who can stand before it? Besides it may facilitate a legal prosecution, which might not, otherwise, have been dared to be attempted. When the press is made the vehicle of falsehood and scandal, let the authors be punished with becoming rigour.

But why need any honest man be afraid of truth? The guilty only fear it; and I am inclined to think with Gordon (Vol. 3 No. 20 of Cato's Letters) that truth scarcely adhered to, can never upon the whole prejudice, right religion, equal government or a government founded upon proper balances and checks, or the happiness of society in any respect, but must be favorable to them all.

Suppressing this liberty by penal laws will it not more endanger freedom than do good to government? The weight of government is sufficient to prevent any very dangerous consequences occasioned by *provocations* resulting from charges founded in truth; whether such charges are made in *a legal course or otherwise*. In either case, the *provocation* (which Judge Blackstone says is the sole foundation of the law against libels) being much the same.

But not to trouble you with a multiplying of words; If I am wrong I should be glad to be set right, &c., &c.[107]

Herein Cushing's letter highlights many important aspects of late eighteenth-century constitutional interpretation, particularly as it applies to legal custom and tradition. While acknowledging that the article's text seemingly prohibits restraints altogether, Cushing applied custom and tradition to conclude the liberty of the press could only extend to the truth. Second, Cushing's recollection of the American Revolution highlights a significant historical event that shaped the liberty of the press.[108] But at no point did Cushing give it primacy. Instead the Revolution merely guided Cushing's understanding of its principles, particularly the recognition of utilitarianism to conclude the liberty of the press was an entity that facilitated the voice of the people, which "directly and essentially" contributed to the *"security of freedom in a State."* Cushing even made sure to distinguish between reporting on the "conduct of the administration and shewing the tendency of it" and the "liberty of printing upon literary and speculative subjects in general."[109]

Cushing's view of the liberty of the press circa 1780 is significant, for he would apply the same principles to the First Amendment in the midst of analyzing the 1798 Sedition Act. The act made it a crime to "write, print, utter or publish ... any false, scandalous, and malicious writing or writings against the Government of the United States, or either House of the Congress of the United States, with intent to defame the said government, or either house of said Congress, or the President, or to bring them ... into contempt or disrepute, or to excite against them, or either any of them, the hatred of the good people of the United States."[110] Despite the act's unpopularity and printers "cry[ing] out, that by this law they are abridged the liberty of the press,"[111] Associate Justice Cushing found the law to be within the purview of the First Amendment and a lawful exercise of congressional authority:

[U]nless the liberty of the press comprehends a right to print and propagate scandalous and malicious falsehoods, to the injury of the public; which no man of virtue or modesty will pretend, any more than that liberty of action admits of committing murder, theft, or any other crime.

The law provides a full and sufficient guard to innocents by allowing the party accused, a fair trial by a jury of his country and to acquit himself entirely, only by proving the truth of his own assertions.

That is an important point of the liberty of the press, placed upon the only just and equitable foundations, *safe* to the innocent, and the patriot, by allowing them to publish any truths they please—essential to the preservation of any free government—only forbidding malicious lies and slander, which no man possessed of any principle of virtue or honesty would indulge himself in.[112]

Today it is commonplace for scholars—and even the Supreme Court in the 1964 case *New York Times v. Sullivan*—to proclaim the 1798 Sedition Act was unconstitutional and inviolate of the First Amendment.[113] It is true the Sedition Act led to the rise of Jefferson Republicans, the demise of the Federalist Party, and that the Supreme Court never weighed on its constitutionality before its expiration on March 3, 1801.[114] But to proclaim the Sedition Act unconstitutional in late eighteenth-century terms requires evidence the sitting Supreme Court justices would have struck it down.[115] It is a conclusion that is historically unsupported, for, of the eight justices who filled the five seats during the act's enforcement, the evidence suggests five would have upheld its constitutionality. The five would have included William Cushing (1789–1810), James Iredell (1790–1799), Samuel Chase (1796–1811), Bushrod Washington (1798–1829), and John Marshall (1801–1835). Meanwhile, the remaining three justices, William Paterson (1793–1806), Oliver Ellsworth (1796–1800), and Alfred Moore (1800–1804), may have supported the Sedition Act's constitutionality, but the historical evidence is deficient in this regard.[116]

As already discussed, Cushing supported the constitutionality of the Sedition Act by weighing it against custom and tradition, and applying common sense legal reasoning. Thus, his view needs no further elaboration.[117] In terms of Bushrod Washington and John Marshall, support for the Sedition Act can be found in their correspondence with George Washington and in Marshall's election to Congress in 1798. Not only did both justices concur with Pennsylvania Judge Alexander Addison's pamphlet supporting the Sedition Act's constitutionality as "well calculated," but Marshall refused to denounce the act as unconstitutional when pressed to do so.[118] James Iredell and Samuel Chase also set forth their strong opinions on the subject through charges to the grand jury. To Iredell, the Sedition Act was constitutional because it prevented "mischief" yet preserved the "luster" of the press. In other words, Iredell felt it foolish to contend the publication of falsehoods was "among the indefeasible rights of men, for that would be to make the freedom of liars greater than that of men of truth and integrity":

But, as every human blessing is attended with imperfection, as what produces, by a right use, the greatest good, is productive of the greatest evil in its abuse, so this, one of the greatest blessings ever bestowed by Providence on his creatures, is capable of producing the greatest good or the greatest mischief. A pen, in the hands of an amiable and virtuous man, may enlighten a whole nation, and by observations of real wisdom, grounded on pure morality, may lead it to the path of honor and happiness. The same pen in the hands of a man equally able, but the vices as great as the other's virtues, may, by the arts of sophistry easily attainable, and inflaming the passions of weak minds, delude many into opinions the most dangerous, and conduct them to actions the most criminal.[119]

In reply to the argument that the First Amendment expressly prohibits Congress from making any law touching upon the press, Iredell emphasized the Constitution only guaranteed the "freedom of the press," not its abuse, especially given the "common law principles concerning libel" were applicable:

[Congress is] to make no law respecting an establishment of religion, or prohibiting the free exercise thereof; or abridging the freedom of speech, or of the press. When as to one object they entirely prohibit any act whatever, and as to another object only limit the exercise of the power, they must in reason be supposed to mean different things. I presume, therefore, that Congress may make a law respecting the press, provided the law be such as not to abridge its freedom.[120]

Chase delivered similar sentiments on the Sedition Act to the grand jury during Thomas Cooper's libel trial: "I know of no civilized country, that does not punish similar offenses, and it is peculiarly necessary to the peace and happiness of this country, that such offences should meet with their punishment, as our government is a government founded on the opinions and confidence of the PEOPLE."[121] To Chase, the liberty of the press did not extend to licentiousness because it was something that every virtuous democracy dreaded:

A republican government can only be destroyed by the introduction of luxury and the licentiousness of the press. If you destroy the confidence of the people in their supreme magistrate and the legislature, you effectually sap and undermine the government. The licentiousness of the press is the slow but sure & certain means of destroying confidence of the people, when the confidence, which is the support of the government ceases, the government must fall.[122]

Perhaps what makes Chase's view of the Sedition Act unique was his reliance on international principles. Libels were punished by "all governments" and Chase knew of "no civilized country" that did not punish the offense.[123] It was for this reason that Chase found no First Amendment conflict. More importantly, this view provides us with another example of how late eighteenth-century jurists incorporated history, custom, and tradition to define the law—the law of nations or the universal law of society. As this subject is covered in depth in Chapter 3, it will not be elaborated here. However, it should be noted that late eighteenth-century jurists did not view the law and Constitution in ethno-centric terms as many contemporary conservative legal pundits claim.

As it stands today, the Supreme Court has yet to recognize any distinct or separate constitutional protections to the press as an entity.[124] Instead, the Court's free speech jurisprudence has engulfed the Press Clause.[125] Whether such muddling of First Amendment jurisprudence is consistent with the founding generation's intent has been the subject of debate since the mid twentieth century.[126] The debate centers on whether a free press affords journalists and press entities any distinct First Amendment protections above and beyond or separate from the general people. It is a debate that has been recently brought forward by the justices of the Supreme Court. In the 2012 decision *Citizens United v. Federal Election Commission,* Scalia responded to a particular statement by the dissent in which John Paul Stevens wrote that the text and history of the Constitution suggests at least "one type of corporation, those that are part of the press, might be able to claim special First Amendment status."[127] Scalia replied it would be "strange to interpret the phrase 'the freedom of speech, or of the press' to mean, not everyone's right to speak or publish, but rather everyone's right to speak or the institutional press's right to publish."[128] But in textual terms the First Amendment does not include the words "people" or "publish." It stipulates: "Congress shall make no law respecting an establishment of religion, or prohibiting the free exercise thereof; or abridging the freedom of speech, *or of the press;* or the right of the people peaceably to assemble, and to petition the Government for a redress of grievances."[129] Scalia is indeed correct that press freedoms included every person's right to write and publish their ideas so long as said writings were not libelous.[130] However, Scalia discounts the recognition of any potential press freedoms on the grounds that it is "strange."[131] Just because it is odd or strange to Scalia, and perhaps others unfamiliar with development of press freedoms by the late eighteenth century, this in itself does not push aside what a proper historical inquiry into the Press Clause provides us—distinct press freedoms based upon utilitarianism values.

Therefore the question moving forward is, does this history even matter? Again, the historical guidepost approach operates first and foremost on precedent. If precedent can answer the constitutional case or controversy at hand, then the analysis need not proceed. But what if said precedent is based upon a domino defect or, even worse, on the judiciary's reluctance to provide an answer? If such an argument can be made this scenario presents itself to the Supreme Court's Press Clause jurisprudence. While the Court has indeed addressed the history of the Press Clause on a number of occasions, it has utterly failed to make sense of evidentiary record and apply it to any individual case.[132] Of course, what the future holds for the use of history, custom, and tradition to reinvigorate the Press Clause is unclear. Yet the point remains, the invocation of legal custom and tradition is a valuable tool when interpreting the Constitution. At the same time, however, it is important that custom and tradition are applied in a manner consistent with accepted historical methodologies. One cannot simply proclaim position "X" or "Y" is an accepted custom or tradition. The rules pertaining to historical consciousness must equally apply when invoking custom or tradition for constitutional interpretation. Moreover, one must remain cognizant that traditions and customs can easily change or be extinguished.

As a working example, we return to Supreme Court's decision in *District of Columbia v. Heller.* In the preceding section on historical consciousness and total historical context, the *Heller* Court was criticized for employing the evidentiary record outside the bounds of historical elasticity. That is, the *Heller* Court advanced an unsupported historical theory, therefore making the entire foundation upon which the opinion rests illegitimate. This is not to say, however, the Court's finding that the Constitution guarantees a right armed self-defense in the home with handgun is without historical merit. As historian Frederick Pollock informs us, the right to defend one's home from attack or criminal, what is also known as the castle doctrine, has maintained a "special and privileged" place in English law since the thirteenth century.[133] In support of the exact origins of the castle doctrine, Pollock points to ancient Germanic law,[134] but early English commentators offer a number of origins. In 1643 for example, one anonymous legal commentator associated the castle doctrine with the Magna Carta.[135] Meanwhile, Thomas Digges thought the castle doctrine was linked to every nation's right to self-preservation and resistance, particularly the subject's military duty to repel foreign invasions and secure the national defense.[136]

Whenever and however the castle doctrine developed remains open to historical debate. What is certain is it remained a staple of Anglo-American law through the nineteenth century. Prominent legal commentators William Lambarde, Michael Dalton, Sir Edward Coke, William Hawkins, and William Blackstone all attest to the castle doctrine's privileged status.[137] Thus, if historical custom and tradition is as important as the *Heller* Court suggests, there exists a credible historical guidepost to identify a right to self-defense of one's home. Yet a number of questions about the castle doctrine remain. For one, are handguns a suitable means of exercising this right, or may state or local governments prohibit handguns? Second, assuming handguns are suitable, what police powers, if any, may the government exercise to prevent public injury? Third and lastly, is this right to home bound self-defense with a handgun part of the Second Amendment, Fifth Amendment's substantive due process clause or both?

Before answering these questions it must be emphasized that the historical guidepost approach merely invokes history as a responsible guide, not necessarily as an outcome determinative tool. The fact of the matter is the society of today is not that of our ancestors. More importantly though, the judiciary must function as an independent branch of government, and this requires jurists employ common sense legal reasoning in order to come to a decision, all the while weighing the purposes and consequences of any respective outcome. If we apply this construct to the first question concerning the suitability of handguns, the evidence weighs in favor of finding them constitutionally protected for home bound self-defense. In coming to this conclusion, one must first weigh what the evidentiary record does and does not provide. Consider this example: a number of historians have proven that leading up to the adoption of the Constitution, there were a number of laws prohibiting dangerous weapons in the interest of public safety. This included laws prohibiting certain types of firearms.[138] Moreover, one must recognize not one commentator listed firearms as necessary to exercise the right of self-defense in one's home. These facts indeed call into question recognizing a right to handguns for self-defense in one's home. At the same time, however, one must also acknowledge that since the nineteenth century it has been common for Americans to own, use, and operate handguns for self-defense of one's person, family, and personal property, particularly within the confines of their estate; a number of state constitutional provisions recognize this right, and a number of state court opinions have recognized such a right without significant consequences to ordered liberty.[139] Furthermore, when one considers the accessibility, ownership, and utility of handguns for home bound self-defense over time, it is more than sensible to conclude handguns are a suitable means to defend one's home, and are therefore constitutionally protected.

But to constitutionally recognize the right of self-defense in the home with a handgun does not mean we must extinguish the government's policing powers in the process. As with any right, it must be acknowledged there are acceptable limits in order to preserve the peace, as well as prevent public injury. Hereto history provides us with a responsible guidepost from which to start. From the Norman Conquest, regulations surfaced on the carrying or using of arms as a means to prevent public injury. King Alfred outlined restrictions on the drawing of any weapon "in the king's hall" and the improper carrying of a spear, so as to prevent injury. In 1328, King Edward III implemented restrictions on riding or appearing armed in public places or in the presence of government officials. In 1542, King Henry VIII placed a prohibition on "little short handguns, and little haquebuts," which were a "great peril and continual feare and danger of the kings loving subjects." Meanwhile, in 1787 the Pennsylvania Minority Dissent acknowledged it was lawful to disarm individuals for "crimes committed" or when the legislature determined there may be "real danger of public injury from individuals."[140]

This brief overview reveals that arms regulations to preserve the peace, as well as prevent public injury, are part of our Anglo-American tradition. Whether there is a perfect historical parallel to modern gun control regulations is not the appropriate question for consideration under the historical guidepost approach. For with the advancement of firearm technology, especially the portability, firing rate, and power by which modern firearms operate, it is the rare occurrence that modern gun safety regulations will mirror a historical restriction. Therefore, the preferred question, when applying the history arms regulations, is whether the respective regulation falls within an ideologically or philosophically accepted category that is consistent with governmental police power.[141]

Seeing we have already used history as a guidepost to recognize a right to armed self-defense of one's home with a handgun, while at the same time accepting the government's police power in the process, the question moving forward is, where should this right fall within the text and meaning of the Constitution? Perhaps this question should have been proposed before the historical substantiation. However, the point of this example was to illustrate how legal custom and tradition may be employed as a responsible interpretational guidepost. The answer to question set forth above is secondary to the larger inquiry. To find the answer we must first return to *District of Columbia v. Heller.* At issue in this case was whether a right to armed self-defense of the home with a handgun is the central component of the Second Amendment. The argument presented to the Supreme Court was the right was enshrined by our English forebears in Article VII of the 1689 Declaration of Rights and carried into the Second Amendment. Despite the Second Amendment making no textual reference to the castle doctrine, the home or self-defense, the argument advanced before the Court was the operative language—"the right of the people to keep and bear arms"—could not be limited or purely defined by its prefatory language—"a well regulated militia being necessary to the security of a free State"—meaning the Court should interpret the operative language as providing broad protections for the people at large. History in context, however, dispels this interpretation as stretching the evidentiary record beyond the bounds of historical elasticity. There is no evidence in context to suggest the Second Amendment was a right of confrontation in either public or private, as the *Heller* Court found. Instead, if anything, the spirit and purpose of the Second Amendment was to ensure the existence of a constitutional well-regulated militia as a counterpoise to standing armies, which in turn would guarantee republican liberty.

All and all, given the militia-centric purpose behind the right to keep and bear arms, it is historically problematic to place the right of armed self-defense in the home with a handgun under the umbrella of the Second Amendment. If we are to ensure some semblance of historical accuracy and constitutional legitimacy, it makes more sense to place the right under the umbrella of the Fifth Amendment's substantive due process. The rationale for this being the castle doctrine has retained a privileged status in Anglo-American law for centuries and survives to this day. Even after the crown extended the courts of justice throughout the kingdom in the late thirteenth and early fourteenth century, the castle doctrine remained a critical component of law, particularly as an exception to manslaughter. But if we must place the right to armed defense of the home with a handgun under the umbrella of the Second Amendment, we should do so in a historically responsible manner. The *Heller* Court failed in this pursuit when it proclaimed the right of armed confrontation was the central component of the Second Amendment.[142] Not only does the spirit and militia-centric purpose of the Second Amendment call this finding into question, but it also contradicts the historical evidence which shows carrying dangerous weapons in the public concourse was subject to regulation since the thirteenth century and that the retreat rule dominated late eighteenth-century legal thought.[143] In short, the *Heller* Court was unsuccessful in retaining historical consciousness.

However, there is a more responsible approach to placing the right to armed self-defense of the home under the umbrella of the right to keep and bear arms. This would be to acknowledge the militia purpose of the Second Amendment as the central component, yet find the castle doctrine as an ancillary function of the right. If one of the purposes behind the Second Amendment was to vest the people with a right to defend their life, liberty, and property against enemies, foreign and domestic, through a well-regulated militia—a right that predated the Constitution and was perceived as the birthright of the people—the same principle equally applies to a person's home, for it too is their birthright, predates our Constitution, and has retained a privileged status in Anglo-American law. But it is at this point the analysis must stop and go no further. For one, the issue of contention in the case was whether the Constitution protected a right to armed self-defense in the home with a handgun. Thus, any analysis that goes further than answering this question is unnecessary and arguably dictum. Second and more importantly, as will be seen in Chapter

5, when we apply the historical guidepost approach to the right to keep and bear arms outside the home, the evidentiary record severely calls into question recognizing any other Second Amendment rights divorced from militia service. It provides a case where legal custom and tradition dictates not extending a right.

Historical Guideposts Requires Thinking Historically First, Legally Second

Hopefully as these examples have underlined, whenever one employs history for constitutional interpretation, maintaining historical consciousness and relying on historical context are the keys to ensuring a legitimate foundation upon which to reason legally. Indeed, researching and compiling historical sources and placing them in complete historical context is time consuming, often repetitive, and exhausting. But such sources and their contextualization are the heart of a thorough and objective historical inquiry.[144] Still, even if one performs the historical inquiry properly, history cannot always provide one answer to every constitutional question and controversy. There will be a number of instances where historical consciousness is maintained and context is elicited to the greatest detail, yet multiple conclusions may be reached.[145] Perhaps Max Lerner summed it up best in his 1938 essay *Minority Rule and Constitutional Tradition*: "One may balance the warily expressed desires of the framers against the clear aversion of the people at the time and get nowhere."[146] This unabashed truth has and always will be an associated dilemma with using historical sources to adjudicate the law.[147] Thus, in this respect, even the historical guidepost approach is subject to the same criticism that is generally affiliated with originalism and living constitutionalism—a level of interpretational discretion or subjectivity. But at least the historical guidepost approach is transparent about what the evidentiary record does and does not provide. By maintaining historical consciousness and eliciting context to the greatest detail, one will find it rather difficult to distort the evidentiary record, discard those portions of the historical record that they find disagreeable or latch themselves onto traditions they subconsciously place above others.

Ultimately, when one performs history in law it is essential they first think like and operate as a historian before making any legal conclusions. The historian's burden of proof must be satisfied to ensure accuracy and objectivity, and therefore legitimacy. To do otherwise is to proceed down the path of myth-making. Whether one wants to admit it or not, historical facts can be easily manipulated and distorted. Generally the facts "speak for themselves, and, when properly selected and arranged, provide the basis for a correct interpretation of the past."[148] It has been noted, "A fact is a fact no matter who writes it." At the same time, however, the human mind is susceptible to its own predilections, and people often fall prey to poorly interpreted and narrated facts which propagate myth as historical reality.

Political leanings and affiliations illustrate this point. Whether one leans democrat, republican, liberal or conservative, when history is marshaled and restated, it is done so subjectively to aid a particular point of view. There are a number of examples that historians can draw upon. For continuity, let us return to the immigration theme. In March 2012, I attended an immigration symposium hosted by St. John's University School of Law. At the podium a number of legal academics advocated for either more lenient immigration policies or an end to state immigration laws which criminalized unlawfully present aliens. In terms of putting forth effective and prudent policy objectives the presenters gave many valid points. However, before and after each presenter made their case for immigration reform they called upon false notions of history to deliver their message. In some cases the presenters quoted the infamous words from the Declaration of Independence's preamble—"That all men are created equal; that they are endowed by their Creator with certain unalienable rights; that among these are life, liberty, and the pursuit of happiness"—to claim immigrants, lawful and unlawful alike, are entitled to equal rights alongside United States citizens. In other cases, the presenters selectively recited the words from Emma Lazarus's poem etched at the base of the Statue of Liberty—"Give me your tired, your poor, Your huddled masses yearning to breathe free"—as evidence the United States is a nation of immigrants and we must fulfill this promise.

As the presenters restated these words to substantiate their respective arguments, members of the audience nodded their heads in approval. I thought to myself, how could these legal professionals not know the Declaration of Independence's preamble was about the formation of republican government built upon equitable principles and the actual consent of the government, not the guarantee of equal rights for immigrants? And how could they confuse the actual Statue of Liberty, a gift from the French in the late 1880s, with an American poem that was later inscribed at the base in 1903?" Feeling a duty to correct such false notions of history, I altered my presentation to provide context on these historical matters. I doubt this altered the presiding historical status quo for people will perceive the past as they choose to perceive it.[149] In instances like these, what is being advanced as history is not really history. It is mythistory, or a mixture of history and myth. Paul Horwitz explains this individualized phenomenon as follows: "We *experience* history in one way—

as a set of individualized sensations and emotions which we tie into our own mini-narrative, limited in context, and with no knowledge of the ultimate outcome of the events we are experiencing. We get 'history' in the usual sense of the word when, with knowledge of the outcome of the events we describe, we tie these disparate individual experiences into a coherent, streamlined, narrativized effort to explain what happened."[150]

The public's frequent acceptance of myth in lieu of historical fact is not limited to politically contentious topics such as immigration. It extends to trivial matters such as George Washington's teeth. Ask someone, of what were George Washington's teeth made? Almost without fail the answer they will give is wood. It is uncertain exactly how this answer came to dominate American discourse, but numerous studies by historians and other scholars have all dismissed it as unsupported. The earliest study was a 1948 work entitled *An Introduction to the History of Dentistry.* Written by Bernhard Wolf Weinberger, the two volume work provided the first exhaustive examination of dental history, and found no support for the Washington wooden teeth myth.[151] Later histories reinforced this point, including John Woodforde's *The Strange Story of False Teeth* and Robert Darnton's *George Washington's False Teeth.*[152] The Mount Vernon Ladies Association, which seeks to preserve the history and heritage of Washington, has gone so far as to dedicate a portion of its museum to debunk the wooden teeth myth, even including an informational video from the History Channel.[153] The association also lists the myth on its website as the first "falsehood" worth correcting.[154] There is even a children's book dedicated to the cause. Its purpose being to educate children (and hopefully parents too) that "contrary to popular belief, [Washington] never had a set of wooden teeth."[155]

As of today the wooden teeth myth lives on, and it serves as a contemporaneous example of how difficult it is to remove socially ingrained myths. Just pause to consider that the Washington myth has been academically disproven for over sixty years, yet people still imagine the first president had wooden teeth. And this is a myth that retains no political, philosophical, or ideological affiliation. This last point is significant because when it comes to constitutional interpretation, often an individual or group's understanding is swayed by political, philosophical, or ideological affiliation. Thus, unlike Washington's teeth, constitutional interpretation is generally intertwined with personal identity, and this can hinder the invocation of history for legal interpretation. Frequently, an individual's historical perception of a constitutional provision does not rest on a genuine search for historical truth. Instead, individuals often latch onto evidence for an ideal already maintained. As historian Edward G. Lengel astutely points out, this is because individuals make cognitive choices that "reveal more about us" than they do about what the historical record provides.[156] It is natural for individuals to "define themselves" through their own knowledge and beliefs of history rather than seek historical truth or clarity.

This does not mean, however, the practice of history in law should ever concede to accepting myth as historical fact. We must accept myths will survive no matter how much historical evidence is unearthed or literature is published denouncing them. Few, if any, will disagree that it is every person's right to believe as they wish. However, a person's freedom to believe "X" or "Y" as historical fact does not make it a fact unless it is supported by the employment of proper historical methodologies and gathering substantiating historical evidence in context. Despite historians' best efforts, whether it is individuals, groups, political parties or advocacy groups, they will hold onto the truth as it is perceived through a subjectively filtered lens.

It cannot be stressed enough that the primary role of any historical inquiry must be to explore the past for the sake of understanding the past.[157] This particularly applies to the history of text or what historians refer to as intellectual history. As historian James T. Kloppenberg proposes, "Unless we know what problems individual authors meant to solve, and the conversations in which they took part, we cannot grasp the historical meaning of individual texts."[158] If history in law matters—it is truly essential to constitutional interpretation— it cannot be enough to merely weigh competing historical theories and interpretations, give each mild consideration, and make the desirable choice based upon the needs of today.[159] Historical consciousness requires much more, especially asking the right questions. To borrow from Larry Kramer, it requires "discipline, self-awareness, and a constant process of introspection."[160] In other words, we must continually ask *why*. Why did an author, legislative body or generation choose a particular set of words? Why did they adopt a particular legal idea or constitutional provision? Why did they reject others? We must also continually ask *how*. How did an author, legislative body or generation understand a particular set of words? How did they go about adopting a particular legal idea or constitutional provision? How did they go about rejecting others? The *why* and the *how* are equally, if not more, important than *whether* an author, legislative body or generation wrote, adopted or rejected something because it provides both context and workability.

However, each of these questions cannot be answered without substantiated historical evidence to support it. It is one thing to make claims about an author's, legislative body's or generation's intended meaning. It is another to prove it or meet the historian's burden. Even if one asks all the right questions it does not mean the historical inquiry will be objective, the answers interrogated thoroughly or the facts marshaled honestly. Therefore, history is most susceptible to human error or some slight variant of myth-making. In the words of historian William Wiecek: "Historical facts are inert and in themselves meaningless. They take on meaning only through interpretation. Interpretation in turn is not an automatic process; it begins with the way the historian asks questions, and at all stages is influenced by the historian's own biases (including ideology). History is not made or given by God; it is the product of human minds and therefore liable to error, either of verification or interpretation. There is better and worse history, and certainly false history, but there is no history that is not free of human fallibility."[161]

Wiecek's admission that history maintains a level of subjectivity, no matter how well researched and conducted, is another reason to conclude history in law is no more objective than other interpretational theories. Granted, there will be any number of subjective historical claims. Still, what separates history from the law is the manner in which historians are held professionally accountable for false, sloppy, and mythical claims. Historians not only critique each other in peer-reviewed journals, but they generally answer for those criticisms in subsequent works. It is an intellectual tug-of-war that aids in discovering historical truth. The manner in which historical academia operates is almost akin to how the founding generation perceived a constitutional "free press," the "liberty of the press" or the "freedom of the press." The founders viewed the different newspapers and printings presses as providing a self-correcting pendulum of truth. Whenever the pendulum would swing one way with an argument, the counter viewpoint would swing it to the other side. This allowed the discovery of knowledge which perpetuated and facilitated a balance between truth and falsehood. In other words, a true liberty of the press was continuously self-correcting until the truth was illuminated.[162]

One may argue the legal academia operates in a similar fashion.[163] Certainly, legal professionals participate in open exchanges when interpreting the law and the Constitution. There are distinct accountability and motivational differences, however. In terms of accountability, members of legal academia are not held responsible for historical inaccuracies or blatant subjectivity. If anything, given its adversarial nature, the legal profession encourages such suspension of accountability. Historical inaccuracies are often viewed as nothing more than a failed legal pleading. Even if the author admits to the historical inaccuracies, the author can still assert their legal rationale is sound, in line with precedent or prevents an injustice. There is also the matter of motivational influences for scholarship. With the availability and rapidity of online legal journals and blogs, it is not uncommon for a member of legal academia to present rather timely historical claims in the hope of influencing ongoing litigation. Sometimes these historical claims are rooted in truth. In instances where the historical claims are unsupported or false, the damage may have already taken place in the courts and discourse, creating a domino defect of constitutional jurisprudence and public understanding. Thus, the point to be made about history in law, particularly by legal professionals, is history is employed more as a subcontractor to advance an ideological preference or legal outcome rather than as a means to obtain objective or neutral results.[164]

This is why the historical guidepost approach takes into account the historical consensus of academia when importing the past for use in the present.[165] History—that is what actually took place in the past—is not subject to the whims of a Gallup poll. What constitutes a consensus is not the equivalent of what passes for acceptable history among law professors or the public at large. The manner in which the latter groups view history is more reflective of popular constitutionalism than that which the historical record actually provides. This is not to say legal academia is without historically conscious scholars, lawyers, and jurists. But more often than not this is the exception rather than the rule. To borrow from Sixth Circuit Court of Appeals Judge Jeffrey S. Sutton, we must "distinguish the scholar who has devoted a career to a historical episode from the dilettante or the scholar who has an axe to grind. Just as there is junk science, there is junk history."[166]

One must also take into account historiography when defining what constitutes a historical consensus. Our understanding of the past can easily change dependent upon the period in which it is written, the information collected by the author(s), and the question(s) being asked.[167] The historiography of what has become the Standard Model Second Amendment provides us with a fitting example as to how a historical consensus can be manipulated. Writing in 1982, historian Robert Shalhope published an influential article that seemingly supported the Standard Model interpretation of the right to keep and bear arms.[168] The article was part of a larger exchange with historian Lawrence Delbert Cress over collective versus individual right interpretations. As a result of this exchange historians learned the Second Amendment contained both individual and collective components, yet much was left unanswered.[169] But as more historical information came to light, Shalhope modified his earlier claims and adopted an individual militia-centric interpretation.[170] This modification began in 1985 when Shalhope criticized Standard Model writer Stephen P. Halbrook's book *That Every Man Be Armed* as historically suspect.[171] Then in 2003 Shalhope openly endorsed William G. Merkel and H. Richard Uviller's historical research linking the individual right to keep and bear arms with militia service.[172] Shalhope's final rejection came in 2008 when he signed a historian's amicus brief in *District of Columbia v. Heller* outright dismissing the historical claims of Standard Model writers.[173] However, to this day supporters of the Standard Model claim Shalhope as a historian falling within their camp.[174]

This begets the question: "Why would Standard Model writers claim a historian supports their historical theory when, in fact, it is blatantly false?" Standard Model writers have never given an answer, but seeing that Shalhope openly disavowed the Standard Model as a false prophecy (multiple times), it is fair to assume the mirage is intentional. It masquerades the Standard Model as being academically supported by a consensus, when in fact it is not. And Shalhope is not the only historian whom Standard Model writers claim as falling in their camp. They also point to the work of now deceased Pulitzer Prize winning historian Leonard W. Levy.[175] But Levy never examined, researched or focused any significant efforts on the scope and meaning behind the Second Amendment. Levy merely summed up the historical debate as it stood by the mid–1980s: "Some think [the Second Amendment] upholds a collective right of state militias to bear arms, while others, probably more accurate in so far as original intent is concerned, argue that it protects the right of individuals to keep arms."[176] Here, Levy admitted he was inclined to support an individual right interpretation, but which individual right interpretation? Did Levy view the individual right as intimately linked with militia service or completely divorced from state sanctioned militias as Standard Model writers claim? It is impossible to discern the answer, seeing Levy left just one sentence on the Second Amendment, and he never explored the issue. Still, somehow it is considered acceptable for Standard Model writers to claim Levy as a historian within their camp.

In instances like this, as to what constitutes a historical consensus can easily be manipulated. Just because a prominent historian supported a historical paradigm or interpretation decades ago does not mean they support it today. When new information and findings come to light the historical consensus can change. This is one of the many areas where history and the law diverge. Constitutional analysis and interpretation among legal academics is often broken up into camps based upon theoretical or ideological preference. Historical analysis and interpretation operates a bit differently. Historians indeed apply different methodological approaches to their work dependent upon the disciplinary focus, whether it is social history, intellectual history, etc.[177] Irrespective of their disciplinary focus, there remain methodological standards, particularly the maintenance of historical consciousness and eliciting context in the finest detail. More importantly, historians all share the same pursuit—an objective understanding of the past.[178]

Still, there will be instances when there is no clear historical consensus.

In terms of history in law, this presents conflicting or dueling historical accounts, which can affect the legitimacy of any subsequent legal analysis.[179] In such cases there are three options available. In option one, the constitutional case or controversy should be resolved without resorting to history. Instead, other approaches to constitutional interpretation should be employed such as precedent, weighing the purposes and consequences of each respective interpretation or applying some other neutral principle formula.[180] Option two is to find consensus where there is conflict or to follow the historical path of least resistance. This means relying only on those broader facets of the historical record that are not in dispute. Here history in law can still be employed to frame the issue, but to a lesser degree. Historian and law professor William E. Nelson is an advocate for this approach and frames it as follows: "There will be times ... when two [historical] arguments are genuinely in conflict. On these occasions, a neutral judge must strive to resolve the conflict by searching for a broader principle of consensus that embraces the two competing ones and explains their apparent inconsistencies. Because a judge will not be preferring one conflicting position over another but simply identifying a larger one that identifies both, his neutrality will be preserved."[181]

Ultimately, the underlying premise of Nelson's "find consensus where there is conflict" approach is neutrality. The key to neutrality is transparency about what the record does and does not clearly establish, which provides the perfect segue to the third and final option—choosing conflict when there is conflict. Picking and choosing conflicting historical accounts brings us into the foray of law office history. Since we can select and disregard from historical record at will, this in turn creates a dilemma of objectivity. Further, it must be acknowledged that the manner in which law and history operate is not one in the same. While historians are at liberty (and ethically encouraged) to deliver the proverbial disclaimer "the historical record is unclear," legal professionals, particularly jurists, are often required to provide an answer in one form or another. Thus, as with any manner in which history in law is employed, the historical guidepost approach accepts minor violations of law office history from time to time in order for the law to operate. It is a necessary evil of sorts. However, choosing conflict when there is conflict is not without rules to prevent the abuse of history in law, notably to eliminate the very mythmaking discussed and especially in those instances where one's predilections influence the conflicting choice. Therefore, it is necessary to impose two baseline rules. The first rule is, one must be honest and transparent as to why one made one's respective historical choice. Even when making conflicting choices, one must retain historical consciousness by weighing the purposes and consequences of each choice in historical context. To commit a minor violation of law office history may be dismissible. To create a domino defect could have far reaching consequences. This brings us to the second rule—when "choosing conflict when there is conflict," one cannot build conflict upon conflict. When one conflicting historical account is chosen in preference to another, the enterprise cannot continue. To do so would be in essence mythmaking.

To illustrate "how to" and "how not to" employ choosing conflict when there is conflict, we return to our earlier example of *District of Columbia v. Heller*. In this consideration we will operate under the assumption there is not a historical consensus as to the Second Amendment's militia-centric purpose. Instead, in the foregoing scenario, historians are equally divided as to whether (1) the Second Amendment enshrined an individual right to keep and bear arms in state-sanctioned militia or (2) guaranteed an armed individual right to self-defense in public and private. This places Justice Scalia in a position to choose one of these two conflicting accounts. And according to Scalia, the better choice is to reject any militia-centric reading of the Second Amendment, as the consequence would be the federal government's elimination of the militia:

> If ... the Second Amendment right is no more than the right to keep and use weapons as a member of an organized militia—if, that is, the organized militia is the sole institutional beneficiary of the Second Amendment's guarantee—it does not assure the existence of a "citizens' militia" as a safeguard against tyranny. For Congress retains plenary authority to organize the militia, which must include the authority to say who will belong to the organized force. That is why the first Militia Act's requirement that only whites enroll caused States to amend their militia laws to exclude free blacks. Thus, if [the militia-centric interpretation is] correct, the Second Amendment protects citizens' right to use a gun in an organization from which Congress has plenary authority to exclude them. It guarantees a select militia of the sort the Stuart kings found useful, but not the people's militia that was the concern of the founding generation.[182]

Here, Scalia delivers what seems to be a legitimate historical rationale for choosing the armed individual self-defense interpretation of the Second Amendment. However, under the rules of choosing conflict when there is conflict, Scalia falters at steps one and two. The first problem with Scalia's argument is the lack of historical evidence to suggest the federal government could eliminate state militias under the Constitution's structure. Certainly, a number of Standard Model writers have advanced this theory as historical fact, but they have not unearthed any evidence to prove it.[183] To make any historical claim requires substantiated evidence to support it. Thus, given his inability to maintain historical consciousness, Scalia's rationale easily fails the first rule of choosing conflict when there is conflict. For argument's sake, even if one promotes the Standard Model's militia preemption theory to a conflicting historical account, on a par with accepted historical accounts, Scalia's rationale fails the second rule that eliminates mythmaking. Scalia would have built one conflicting historical account (choosing between the purposes of the Second Amendment) upon another (choosing the conflicting claims of federal-state militia preemption). This is not some minor violation of law office history. It is a prime example of a domino defect.

Historical Guideposts Summarized

This chapter has delved into the complexities of the historical guidepost standard of review. Unlike other history in law applications, the historical guidepost approach applies history in a responsible manner. It seeks to employ the historical record thoroughly, accurately, and objectively. This in turn provides a more legitimate foundation from which to reason. History is not the means and ends of constitutional interpretation. It is merely a philosophical and moral guide towards understanding the laws' development in historical context. History in context provides an invaluable tool from which to reason. During this process, however, it is important to retain historical consciousness and not to infer or create history that is not there. This is what essentially separates historical guideposts from originalism, which perceives historical sources as merely a subcontractor to determine legal meaning.

Perhaps what is most intriguing about originalism is its proponents' claim that originalist methodologies are the best means in an imperfect world. Originalism is argued to be better suited than history in context, given the dangers originalist methodologies impose upon history are perceived as nominal compared to the dangers historical methodologies can impose on constitutional interpretation. The rationale for such a claim is historians misunderstand the task facing originalists and are thus ill-equipped to interpret the Constitution.[184] If originalists are correct in making this point, it may logically be inferred the legal community is better equipped to handle everything from science in law to medicine in law. But why would anyone seek the opinion of the legal community to answer questions about science or medicine? Why not rely primarily on scientists and medical doctors? Chapter 1's example of military intelligence illustrates this point succinctly. Just as it makes little sense for a military commander to seek the opinion of the unit's Judge Advocate General (JAG) to assess intelligence and executing the mission plan, it is equally nonsensical to give primacy to legal professionals when answering questions about history. Just because the legal community can read and digest the English language does not make it the most reliable source from which to draw historical conclusions. Perhaps originalists will someday find some legitimate reason originalism and originalist methodologies are preferable to history and historical methodologies. But as it stands today the excuse for performing law office history is that it is better than history office law. Thus they propose, conclusions—even historical ones—derived from within the legal world will suffice better than historical conclusions for the legal realm.

In the remaining chapters the historical guidepost approach will be weighed and considered alongside others. In preparation, here follows a three step summary to the historical guidepost approach. Step one is determining whether or not to apply the historical guidepost approach. We must first ask whether this is a case of first impression. If the answer is yes, the historical guidepost approach may be employed. If the answer is no, then a subsequent series of questions should be asked. For one, it must be determined whether precedent answers the question in full. If the answer is no, then historical guideposts may be employed to frame or guide interpretation. However, if the answer is yes, then the use of history in law is unnecessary unless following the rules of *stare decisis* are unworkable.

Step two requires determining how to employ the historical guidepost approach as a historian. There will be instances where the common law, the law of nations, custom or tradition is applicable; the historical record cannot provide an answer; the historical record provides more than one answer; and

Step One Flowchart—The Basics of the Historical Guidepost Approach

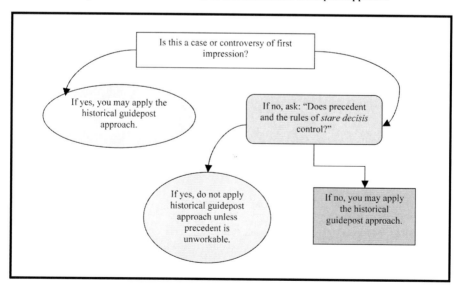

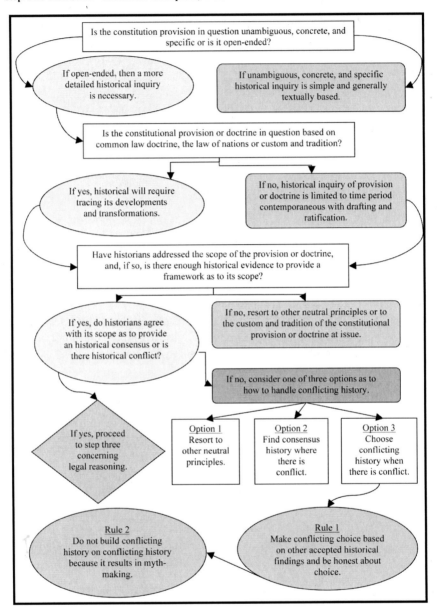

Is the constitution provision in question unambiguous, concrete, and specific or is it open-ended?

If open-ended, then a more detailed historical inquiry is necessary.

If unambiguous, concrete, and specific historical inquiry is simple and generally textually based.

Is the constitutional provision or doctrine in question based on common law doctrine, the law of nations or custom and tradition?

If yes, historical will require tracing its developments and transformations.

If no, historical inquiry of provision or doctrine is limited to time period contemporaneous with drafting and ratification.

Have historians addressed the scope of the provision or doctrine, and, if so, is there enough historical evidence to provide a framework as to its scope?

If yes, do historians agree with its scope as to provide an historical consensus or is there historical conflict?

If no, resort to other neutral principles or to the custom and tradition of the constitutional provision or doctrine at issue.

If no, consider one of three options as to how to handle conflicting history.

If yes, proceed to step three concerning legal reasoning.

Option 1
Resort to other neutral principles.

Option 2
Find consensus history where there is conflict.

Option 3
Choose conflicting history when there is conflict.

Rule 2
Do not build conflicting history on conflicting history because it results in myth-making.

Rule 1
Make conflicting choice based on other accepted historical findings and be honest about choice.

there is no historical consensus or conflicting historical accounts, and so forth. Throughout step two the key is to retain one's sense of historical consciousness by employing historical methodologies. At this step, one must place constitutional text, philosophy, events, and so forth in complete historical context. Furthermore, one must rely on accepted historical works, know the difference between a substantiated historical thesis and an unproven historical theory, and be able to differentiate between historical consensus and historical conflict. In short, step two requires applying the historical method, not the legal method. This in turn provides a thorough, accurate, and objective historical foundation from which to reason at step three.

We have summarized how to assess which occasions warrant the historical guidepost approach and how to apply it in historical terms. The matter remaining is how to employ the historical guidepost approach responsibly. Again, it is worth emphasizing this approach merely provides a framework from which to reason. History is not the gravitas of all constitutional interpretation, nor should it be. Since the Constitution's ratification, American jurists have weighed and considered a number of factors when interpreting its provisions, and there is no reason why this should not hold true today. To do otherwise is to strip the judiciary of its independence. However, when invoking history to interpret the Constitution, there are two basic guidelines which prevent its abuse. First, it must be remembered the past and the present are not the same, nor can they ever be. There will be instances where reason dictates that relying on the past hinders rather than assists settling a modern case or controversy. There will also be instances where the modern statute, regulation or policy at issue does not mirror its historical predecessors. Here, one will have to consider the larger philosophical and ideological purpose of the law to determine its constitutionality.

The second guideline calls one to take cognizance of what the historical record does and does not provide and to only reason from what is known. The goal is to not infer or create history. This phenomenon generally results in mythmaking and may also be referred to as invoking one's "historical imagination." This was observed in the example of *Arizona v. United States,* where Justice Scalia reasoned a historical record of state immigration regulation suggests the Constitution vested the states with some powers concerning immigration.[185] But an unpacked historical record unequivocally calls this claim into question. Not only was one of the purposes behind the Constitution to prevent the states from interfering with international and national interests, but every late eighteenth-century jurist to address the subject of immigration authority vested such powers with the federal government. To summarize, in order to employ the historical guidepost approach responsibly, as with step two, the key to step three is retaining one's sense of historical consciousness when following the path of the law. To paraphrase Oliver Wendell Holmes once more, this is undoubtedly the "most difficult labor," for it requires understanding and weighing the past with the present at every stage.[186]

5

Historical Guideposts, the Second Amendment and Firearms Outside the Home

In the preceding chapter the historical guidepost approach to constitutional interpretation was described in detail and then simplified into three steps. In this chapter those steps will be applied to a constitutional issue that is currently making its way through the courts—the Second Amendment and carrying firearms outside the home. In *District of Columbia v. Heller* and *McDonald v. City of Chicago*, the Supreme Court held the Second Amendment was not a right limited to service in a well-regulated militia, but an individual right of the people to keep and bear arms for self-defense—particularly armed self-defense the home with a handgun—that applied to both the federal and state governments.[1] In the wake of these landmark decisions, a number of lawsuits were brought challenging federal and state laws governing the carrying of firearms in public.[2] Some of the lawsuits challenged laws that banned the carrying of firearms within the public concourse.[3] Some challenged state or local laws that prohibited the carrying of firearms in only certain public places such as churches and campuses.[4] Meanwhile others challenged state laws that allowed for the public carrying of firearms, but only if the applicant could show a proper cause or necessity to do so.[5]

But before applying the historical guidepost approach to the Second Amendment and carrying firearms outside the home, it is worth summarizing how originalists have traditionally handled the subject. To the originalist the foremost guide is text. In *Heller* this interpretational approach won the day when the Supreme Court held the Second Amendment's prefatory language—"A well regulated militia being necessary to the security of a free State"—does not limit or constrain its operative language—"the right of the people to keep and bear arms, shall not be infringed." To be clear, according to the tenets of originalism, the Second Amendment protects the right to "keep arms" and the right to "bear arms." The right to "keep arms" embodies a right to retain, have in custody or have weapons, and right to "bear arms" is understood as a right to carry.[6] When originalists apply this textual approach to firearms outside the home, the natural conclusion is *Heller*'s right to armed self-defense with a handgun must extend beyond one's home. As Owen McGovern has framed it: "[If] the Second Amendment guarantees an individual right to bear arms in defense of both an individual and the state, this must imply the ability to carry those arms outside of one's home. It is difficult to imagine how one could exercise the right to bear arms in defense of the state from the confines of one's living room."[7]

A similar legal argument is advanced by National Rifle Association lawyer and Standard Model scholar Stephen P. Halbrook. But Halbrook distinguishes himself from McGovern, given his originalist approach centers around the absence of the word "home" and the inclusion of the word "militia" in the Second Amendment, as well as the text and structure of the Bill of Rights as a whole:

> [The Second Amendment] guarantees not only the right to "keep" arms, such as in one's house, but also to "bear arms," which simply means to carry arms without reference to a specific place. The explicit reference to the militia indicates that the right is not home-bound, nor is the right to bear arms limited to militia activity. When a provision of the Bill of Rights relates to a house, is says so plainly—the Third Amendment requires the consent of the owner for a soldier to "be quartered in any house." First and Second Amendment rights are not limited to one's house or other premises—the people have the right to "the freedom of speech, [and] of the press," "peaceably assemble, and to petition the government for redress of grievances," and to "keep and bear arms." Nothing in the text guaranteeing these rights limits them to the home.[8]

Then there is UCLA law professor Eugene Volokh, who relies on the originalist understanding of "bear arms" to reach the conclusion "self-defense has to take place wherever the person happens to be" and nearly any "prohibition on having arms for self-defense in a particular place ... is a substantial burden on the right to bear arms for self-defense."[9] Like Halbrook, Volokh also draws upon history to support his take on the Second Amendment. In Volokh's words, by the late eighteenth century, only "public carrying 'accompanied with such circumstances as are apt to terrify the people' was ... seen as prohibited; 'wearing common weapons' in 'the common fashion' was legal."[10] It is a frequent claim among supporters of the Standard Model Second Amendment. This perception is linked to the historical theory that arms regulations leading up to the late eighteenth century were few and far between, never impeded on an individual's ability to defend themselves in private or public, and those regulations that did exist were merely an antecedent of slavery.[11] Allegedly, it was not until the nineteenth century that regulations touching upon the public carrying of arms developed and the right to keep and bear arms came under attack.[12] Therefore, under the originalist and Standard Model constructs of the Second Amendment, most modern day arms regulations should be viewed as presumptively unconstitutional given they go beyond the framers' view of armed self-defense.[13] George Mason law professor Nelson Lund sums up this view succinctly: "The logic of Justice Scalia's theory that the Second Amendment codified a preexisting right would render virtually all modern gun control regulations unconstitutional because few regulations existed in 1791 (leaving everyone with the right to do anything that was not forbidden) and there is no historical record individating what kinds of regulations were not then adopted would have been considered permissible."[14]

Originalist arguments pertaining to the Second Amendment are not limited to when the Constitution was ratified. They extend to the period surrounding the adoption of the Reconstruction Amendments, particularly the Fourteenth Amendment's Privileges or Immunities Clause, where history reveals members of Reconstruction Congress sought to apply the Bill of Rights to the states.[15] Thus, to many originalists, the Reconstruction period offers a second founding moment from which to derive constitutional meaning.[16] And in terms of the Second Amendment, the conclusion generally reached is the right to keep and bear arms was understood as an individual right protecting against both private and public violence.[17] It is a claim some strengthen by relying on a number of mid to late nineteenth-century state court opinions that distinguished between the "open carrying" and "concealed carrying" of weapons.[18]

Taken altogether, originalism's focus on text leads to the conclusion that the Second Amendment protects an armed right to self-defense beyond the home. Although originalists may vary in opinion as to what types of weapons are suitable to exercise this right and where it may be limited in the interests of public safety, they generally agree that limiting the right to the confines of the home is unfaithful to the Second Amendment's text. But is limiting the right to the home (at least the self-defense with a firearm) unfaithful to history, especially once the evidentiary record is unpacked and historical methodologies are employed? It is here that the historical guidepost approach will be applied step by step. The first question to be asked is whether this is a case of first impression. To state it more succinctly, the question is whether there is any precedent dictating the Second Amendment does or does not extend beyond the home. Those advocating for robust Second Amendment rights claim *Heller* and *McDonald* answer this question in the affirmative. It is a conclusion reached much in the same way originalists interpret the Second Amendment's text. However, the constitutional issue in both *Heller* and *McDonald* was whether armed self-defense in the home, with a handgun, was protected by the Second Amendment, not the extent of any rights outside the home. Thus, one may also claim the issue of the Second Amendment outside the home is a case of first impression.[19]

Fortunately, there are two considerations that put an end to this stalemate and weigh in favor of continuing the historical guidepost approach. The first is *Heller*'s conflicting dictum on the scope of the right outside the home.[20] At one point the *Heller* Court seemingly endorsed an armed right to self-defense outside the home: "[T]he right [to arms] secured in 1689 as a result of the Stuarts' abuses was by the time of the founding understood to be an individual right protecting against both public and private violence."[21] But later the Court backed off from this pronouncement: "From [William] Blackstone through the 19th-century cases, commentators and courts routinely explained that the right was not a right to keep and carry any weapon whatsoever in any manner whatsoever and for whatever purpose."[22] When one takes the two statements together it leaves much unanswered. For instance, if the Second Amendment protects against both "public and private violence," yet does not extend to "any weapon" in "any manner," what is the scope of the right beyond the home? Also does judicial balancing or history determine the answer?

This brings us to the second consideration that weighs in favor of employing the historical guidepost approach—*Heller*'s endorsement of history.[23] Justice Scalia's majority opinion was clear to point out the Court's historical analysis was not "exhaustive," and that it would "expound upon the historical justifications" in future cases or controversies.[24] It was a view that Scalia restated in *McDonald* in a concurring opinion, "Historical analysis can be difficult ... [b]ut the question to be decided is not whether the historically focused method is a *perfect means* of restraining aristocratic judicial Constitution-writing; but whether it is the *best means available* in an imperfect world."[25]

Now that we have established employing the historical guidepost is proper, we can move to step two and examine whether the Second Amendment protects a right to firearms outside the home through the lens of history. This first requires a resort to the Second Amendment's text, which is at best ambiguous. As discussed earlier, the originalist argument is that "bear arms" implies a right to carry arms and must logically be understood as extending the doctrine of armed self-defense beyond the home. Although this reading is plausible, it raises more questions than it answers and certainly tells us nothing about its limitations.[26] Therefore a deeper historical inquiry is preferred. But before conducting any historical inquiry we must ask the right questions. This

The Second Amendment Outside the Home and Historical Guideposts—Step One

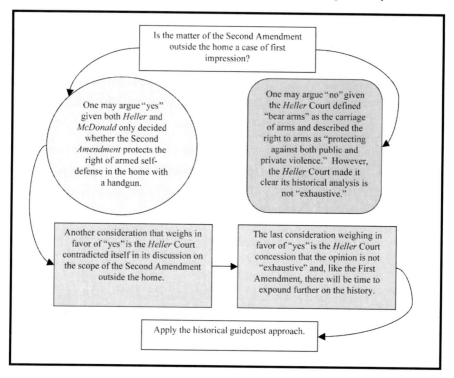

Is the matter of the Second Amendment outside the home a case of first impression?

One may argue "yes" given both *Heller* and *McDonald* only decided whether the Second *Amendment* protects the right of armed self-defense in the home with a handgun.

One may argue "no" given the *Heller* Court defined "bear arms" as the carriage of arms and described the right to arms as "protecting against both public and private violence." However, the *Heller* Court made it clear its historical analysis is not "exhaustive."

Another consideration that weighs in favor of "yes" is the *Heller* Court contradicted itself in its discussion on the scope of the Second Amendment outside the home.

The last consideration weighing in favor of "yes" is the *Heller* Court concession that the opinion is not "exhaustive" and, like the First Amendment, there will be time to expound further on the history.

Apply the historical guidepost approach.

contextually frames the issue and sets forth a research agenda from which to begin. In terms of the Second Amendment outside the home, a number of empirical questions are presented. For instance, seeing that the *Heller* Court held the framers' Second Amendment embodied a right to self-defense, in both public and private, it is worth looking into the late eighteenth-century perception of armed self-defense for some answers. We must ask, what were the rules pertaining to self-defense in the late eighteenth century? Did people maintain a right to carry any and all weapons? In what places, if any, could this right be curtailed? Furthermore, seeing that the *Heller* Court admitted its historical analysis was not "exhaustive," it is worth looking into the history of arms regulation to test the viability of any armed self-defense rights outside the home. Thus, we must ask questions like, when did the public regulation of arms begin in Anglo-American law? How did this body of law develop or change leading up to the late eighteenth century? What were its tenets? Which areas of regulation were deemed acceptable by the late eighteenth century? Also, which areas of regulation, if any, were deemed unacceptable by the late eighteenth century?

Lastly, if custom and tradition matter in determining the scope of the Second Amendment outside the home, we must also ask questions touching upon self-defense and arms regulation after the ratification of the Constitution. This would mean tracing the concept of armed self-defense and the history of arms regulation from the Early Republic through today. This is what historians refer to as a historiographical inquiry. However, before seeking the answers to any of these questions, it is important to again stress the retention of historical consciousness. It cannot be emphasized enough that the historical guidepost approach seeks to establish a legitimate historical foundation from which to legally reason. This is accomplished by placing text, events, doctrines, and so forth in their proper context. Retaining historical consciousness also requires incorporating accepted historical works on the topic, knowing the difference between a substantiated historical thesis and an unproven historical theory, and being able to differentiate between historical consensus and historical conflict.

Now that we have reestablished what historical consciousness embodies, we may proceed to answer our historical questions. In terms of the first inquiry—what were the rules pertaining to self-defense in the late eighteenth century—there are a number of places one may look, but late eighteenth-century legal treatises, statutes, and court records provide the best evidence.[27] And upon sifting through the evidence one immediately learns how the common law treated private and public self-defense differently. On the one hand, private or home bound self-defense retained a privileged status with what was referred to as the castle doctrine.[28] The doctrine stipulated (and continues today) that any person who is in fear of their life may employ deadly force within the confines of the home. In the late eighteenth century, however, the castle doctrine was not viewed as an absolute right to employ deadly force wherever on one's property. The common law required the act of self-defense take place in the person's "mansion or dwelling house" or those buildings that are its "parcel," not to "distant barn[s], warehouse[s], or the like."[29]

Public self-defense, on the other hand, was much more complicated and dependent upon the facts of the case.[30] Despite the *Heller* Court classifying the Second Amendment as a right to "carry weapons in case of confrontation," the justices seemingly omitted an important historical fact.[31] In the late eighteenth century the common law required a person retreat to the wall before the doctrine of self-defense excused the employment of deadly force.[32] As James Davis articulated the principle in his 1774 treatise *The Office and Authority of a Justice of the Peace,* "Self-Defence is excusable only upon inevitable Necessity: The Party assaulted must giv[e] Back as far as he can, without endangering his own Life, and the mortal Wound must not be given till after such Retreat, otherwise it is Manslaughter."[33] John Haywood articulated the principle in similar terms, stipulating: "[T]he law requires that the person who kills another in his own defence, should have retreated as far as be conveniently or safely can to avoid the violence of the assault, before he turns upon his assailant."[34] But unlike Davis, Haywood added self-defense was not a "preventive" right: "This right of natural defence does not imply a right of attacking, for instead of attacking one another for injuries past or impending, man need only have recourse to the proper tribunals of justice. They cannot therefore legally exercise this right of preventive defence."[35] Certainly, if a person was faced with an imminent threat, and could not retreat without endangering their own life, deadly force was authorized. However, this was the exception, not the general rule.

Now that we have outlined the contours of self-defense by the late eighteenth century, it is worth exploring what role, if any, the preparatory wearing of firearms served in this process. To state it another way, we must ask what areas of public firearms regulation were permissible by the late eighteenth century. The historical record reveals a number of laws regulating the use, carrying, and operation of firearms to include laws punishing the discharging of weapons in public, preventing the unlawful assembling and training of militia arms without the consent of government, and prohibiting armed bodies of people without the consent of government.[36] Taken altogether, what these laws reveal is it was within the purview of the government to prevent public injury, particularly any injuries which may result from the improper use of firearms in the public concourse.[37] Still, one may argue these laws do not directly address whether late eighteenth-century society could prohibit or license the individual carrying of firearms in the public concourse for preparatory self-defense. Was the carrying of firearms in the public concourse perceived as an individual right as originalists and Second Amendment advocates claim, or was it based on the consent of government? And if the preparatory carrying of firearms was perceived as a right, were there restrictions as to the type of weapons that could be carried?

The answer to these questions can be found by exploring the origins, purpose, and enforcement of the Statute of Northampton. Initially signed into law in 1328, the Statute of Northampton stipulated that no person—except government officials and those under the license of government—shall "go nor ride armed by Night nor by Day in Fairs, Markets, nor in the Presence of the Justices or other Ministers nor in no Part elsewhere." Violation of the statute was a misdemeanor resulting in forfeiture of arms and up to thirty days imprisonment.[38] The statute was of such importance that its tenets survived for over five hundred years with the states of Massachusetts, North Carolina, and Virginia adopting it after the ratification of the Constitution. In Massachusetts, for instance, the law reaffirmed the justice of the peace's common law power to stay and arrest "all affrayers, rioters, disturbers, or breakers of the peace, and such as shall ride or go armed offensively, to the fear or terror of the good citizens of this Commonwealth."[39] North Carolina began its law by listing the common exceptions to the rule—government officials in performance of their duty and the hue and cry—then stipulated that no one shall bring "force in an affray of peace, *nor* to go nor ride armed by day nor by night, in fairs, markets, nor in the presence of the King's Justices, or other ministers, nor in no part elsewhere."[40] Meanwhile, the Virginia law differed slightly. Like North Carolina, Virginia began its restatement with the exceptions to the rule. But Virginia incorporated different operative language by stipulating that no one should bring "force and arms" to government officials, "nor go nor ride armed by night nor by day, in fairs or markets, or in other places, in terror of the Country."[41]

Given the survival and existence of the Statute of Northampton in American law following the ratification of the Constitution, one would logically presume the founding generation did not perceive the carrying of firearms for self-defense as a constitutional right. This presumption is amplified by the fact late eighteenth-century law dictated a duty to retreat or the need to prevent needless death. But those that subscribe to the Standard Model view of the Second Amendment proclaim the Statute of Northampton should only be read as applying to the "carrying arms in ways that caused public terror." In making this claim, however, Standard Model writers have never provided a working historical example or any substantiated evidence that supports it. It is a characterization that leads Standard Model writers to conclude by the late eighteenth century there were no laws regulating "peaceful carrying [of firearms] for self-defense or otherwise."[42] But as will be detailed below, such claims contradict the historical evidence.[43] To begin, it must be noted that prohibitions on going armed in the public concourse actually preceded the Statute of Northampton and developed out of the common law in the mid thirteenth century.[44] In the years that immediately followed, a number of royal proclamations were issued to enforce this rule of law.[45] In 1320, one proclamation was issued in the town of Oxford following armed assaults on the university's clerks, scholars, and masters. The chancellor requested the "King's peace" be enforced and the "bearing of arms should be completely forbidden, by the laity as well as clerks, and that the chancellor, in default of the mayor, may punish them on all occasions which are necessary."[46] The king's council replied and instructed the mayor to "forbid any layman *except town officials* to wear arms in the town."[47] On April 28, 1326, another proclamation was issued by Edward II "prohibiting any one going armed without his licence, except the keepers of his peace, sheriffs and other ministers, willing that any one doing the contrary should be taken by the sheriff or bailiffs or the keeps of his peace and delivered to the nearest gaols."[48]

Edward II would end up fleeing in the midst of social and political turmoil.[49] But two years later, Parliament codified these proclamations as part of the Statute of Northampton.[50] The statute was crucial in extending the king's courts of justice and provided the basis of English legal reform for centuries to come.[51] It purged corruption within local government, unified the kingdom under a body of law, and ensured the public peace was kept.[52] In terms of the statute's enforcement, it was enforced to prevent crime, murder, and breaches of the peace. Then in 1396 the statute was amended by Richard II to guarantee its provisions would not apply to government officers. The amendment also clarified the misdemeanor punishment by stipulating a forfeiture of arms or a fine and possible imprisonment.[53] After Richard II's death the statute was reissued in one form or another by subsequent monarchs to include Henry IV, Henry VI, Elizabeth I, and James I.

Elizabeth I's reign is of particular significance given the statute's prohibition was extended to modern weaponry, particularly guns, firearms, pistols and the like.[54] It was an amendment that legal commentators took notice of from the late sixteenth century through the eighteenth century. For instance, William Lambarde, arguably the most prominent lawyer of the Elizabethan period, described the Statute of Northampton in the following terms:

> [I]f any person whatsoever (except the Queenes servants and ministers in her presence, or in executing her precepts, or other offices, or such as shall assist them and except it be upon Hue and Crie made to keep the peace, and that in places where acts against the Peace do happen) shall be so bold, as to go, or ride armed, by night, or by day, in Faires, Markets, or any other places: then any Constable, or any other of the saide Officers, may take such Armour from him, for the Queenes use, & may also commit him to the Gaole. And therefore, it shall be good in this behalf, for the Officers to stay and arrest all such persons as they shall find to carry Dags or Pistols, or to be apparelled with privie coates, or doublets: as by the proclamation [of Queen Elizabeth I].[55]

Lambarde's understanding of the Statute of Northampton proved influential. He was cited, reprinted or paraphrased by a number of prominent commentators to include Abraham Fraunce, Michael Dalton, Edward Coke, William Hawkins and others. In the case of Michael Dalton's *The Countrey Justice,* it was the first restatement to distinguish between non-dangerous weapons and dangerous weapons. In terms of non-dangerous weapons the person would have had to employ it "offensively." At the same time, "offensively" spoke to the general carriage of dangerous weapons, meaning when it came to dangerous weapons like guns, pistols, and firearms in the public concourse, the prohibition was general and at the discretion of the justice of the peace or constable to enforce.[56] As Dalton put it, the peace may be enforced to "all such as shall go or ryde armed (offensively) in Fayres, Markets, or elsewhere; or shall weare or carry any Dagges or Pistolls charged: it seemeth any Constable seeing this, may arrest them and may carrie them before the Justice of the Peace. And the Justice may binde them to the peace, yeah though those persons were so armed or weaponed for their defence; for they might have had the peace against the other persons: and besides, it striketh a feare and terror into the Kings subjects."[57]

What Dalton and Lambarde's restatements make abundantly clear is that the act of carrying dangerous weapons was sufficient to amount an affray, "strike a feare"[58] or "striketh a feare."[59] Although Dalton and Lambarde would go on to influence a number of subsequent restatements, citations to their work are noticeably absent from Sir Edward Coke's *The Third Part of the Institutes of the Laws of England* discussion "against going or riding armed." Coke merely restated the Statute of Northampton's text.[60] He did not employ the word "offensively," nor did he list firearms as being prohibited in the public concourse. Instead Coke differentiated between "force and armed," bringing "force in affray of the people," and the act of going and riding armed.[61] But there is nothing to suggest that Coke maintained a different view from Lambarde and Dalton given Coke correctly distinguished between the misdemeanor Statute of Northampton and the felony 25 Edw. 3, stat. 5, c. 2 § 13,[62] which maintained a *mens rea* element and was to be "adjudged ... according to the laws of the realme of old time used, and according, as the case requires."[63] Moreover, Coke understood and applied the general exceptions to the rule— government officials, military duty, and the hue and cry.[64] He even proceeded to list the castle doctrine as an exception twice, but emphasized that preparatory self-defense with dangerous weapons did not qualify: "But he cannot assemble force, though he be extreamly threatened, to goe with him to Church, or market, or any other place, but that is prohibited by this Act."[65]

The English commentators that followed each restated the Statute of Northampton in different terms, but each cited or paraphrased Lambarde, Dalton, and Coke's treatises. For instance, Richard Crompton paraphrased the Statute of Northampton: "Any (except the Kings Officers and their companie doing their service) riding or going armed, or bring force in affray of the people, are to be imprisoned, and lose their armour."[66] William Sheppard and Joseph Keble included the prohibition on firearms, but omitted the word *offensively*.[67] George Meriton and Robert Gardiner included the word *offensively* and referenced the prohibition on firearms.[68] Meanwhile, John Layer omitted any reference to firearms, yet included word *offensively*.[69] But even in Layer's case it is important to note that he listed the legal exceptions—government officials, military muster, and the assembling of the hue and cry.[70]

By the turn of the eighteenth century some commentators began substituting *offensive weapons* in lieu of *offensively*. The phrase, as understood in the eighteenth century, encompassed dangerous weapons such as guns, pistols, firearms, hangers, cutlasses, and bludgeons.[71] For instance, in the 1707 treatise *A Compleat Guide for Justices of Peace,* John Bond wrote the Statute of Northampton stands for the legal proposition that "persons with offensive Weapons in Fairs, Markets or elsewhere in Affray of the King's People, may be arrested by the Sheriff, or other the King's Officers[.]"[72] Bond made sure to clarify that the prohibition applied to persons "that carry Guns charged."[73] William Forbes also streamlined the legal principle: "By the *English* law, a Justice of Peace ... may cause [to] Arrest Persons with offensive Weapons in Fairs, Markets, or elsewhere in Affray, and seize their Armour."[74]

What makes these restatements so important is they would go on to influence writers like Hawkins, Blackstone, and American commentators.[75] For instance, James Davis's *The Office and Authority of a Justice of the Peace* cited Dalton and read: "Justices of the Peace ... may apprehend any Person who shall go or ride armed with unusual and offensive Weapons, in an Affray, or among any great Concourse of the People."[76] John Haywood borrowed from *Blackstone's Commentaries,* writing that "riding or going armed with dangerous or unusual weapons, is a crime against the public peace, by terrifying the good people of the land, and is prohibited by statute upon the pain of forfeiture of the arms."[77] Meanwhile, James Wilson, in his lectures on the law, copied directly from Hawkins' *Pleas of the Crown,* "In some cases, there may be affray, where there is no actual violence; as where a man arms himself with dangerous and unusual weapons, in such a manner, as will naturally diffuse a terror among the people."[78]

Thus, once we take the evidentiary record in its entirety and place it in historical context, we can deduce three historical conclusions. First, prohibitions on going armed in the public concourse were deeply embedded in Anglo-American law for over five hundred years. Second, such prohibitions applied to dangerous weapons to include firearms. A 1686 New Jersey statute, entitled *An Act Against Wearing Swords, &c.,* is one of many evidentiary sources that proves this point. The statute prohibited "Persons [from] wearing Swords, Daggers, Pistols, Dirks, Stilladoes, Skeines, or any other unusual and unlawful Weapons" in public because it induced "great Fear and Quarrels" among the inhabitants.[79] Third, both the Statute of Northampton and the common law dictated a person would be inviolate of the law if they were carrying said weapon(s) without the license of government. In contrast to these findings, and despite the breadth of the historical evidence in support, those who subscribe to the Standard Model insist on a different reading of the Statute of Northampton and the common law touching upon the public carriage of firearms. For instance, David B. Kopel and Clayton Cramer claim the statute requires "arms carrying with the *specific intent* of terrorizing the public."[80] David T. Hardy similarly deduces the statute stands for the punishment of dangerous conduct, not the act itself. He believes the "key to the offense was not so much the nature of the arm, as the *specific intent* to cause terror."[81]

On their face, the competing claims of Standard Model writers may lead some to conclude there is not a historical consensus as to scope of permissible armed carriage by the late eighteenth century.[82] But not one Standard Model writer has ever delved into the historical record to support their conclusions. Still, if one believes they are faced with legitimate conflicting history under the historical guidepost approach, there are three options available. One may either relinquish history as an interpretational and guiding tool, find historical "consensus where there is conflict" or "choose conflicting history where there is conflict." Should the first option be chosen, the historical inquiry is extinguished. However, if the second or third option is chosen, one must conduct an even deeper historical inquiry, and this is where retaining historical consciousness produces dividends. When faced with competing or conflicting historical claims it is necessary to familiarize oneself with historiography. In other words, it is important to go to the source material from which the competing claims are derived. It is only at this level one can learn how the respective interpretations developed.

In the case of the Standard Model interpretation, the evidence ultimately leads to one source—the historical works of Joyce Lee Malcolm.[83] A consistent theme among Malcolm's writings is that England maintained an armed society that was virtually unaffected by the Statutes of the Realm. According to Malcolm: "It is apparent that the regulations in effect before 1640 did not interfere with the basic duty of the English people to keep arms for the defence of themselves, their neighbors or the realm."[84] Allegedly, it was not until the Restoration that arms regulations took hold to include the enforcement of the Statute of Northampton. Writing in 1980, for example, Malcolm dismissed virtually every weapons statute on the books, and as a result characterized the statute as prohibiting the "brandish[ing of] a firearm so as to terrify others."[85] Over a decade later Malcolm again cast aside the statute as nothing more than a law "against riding armed in disturbance of the peace" that was no longer enforced.[86] And upon publishing her book in 1994, Malcolm continued to claim the statute "had never been enforced" and only applied in circumstances that may "terrorize" the public.[87]

It is here one must contrast Malcolm's claims with the preceding historical findings in this chapter. And upon doing so what becomes clear is Malcolm's conclusion that the Statute of Northampton was never enforced directly contradicts the historical evidence. Not only was the statute enforced by numerous monarchs from the fourteenth century through the seventeenth century, but it was restated by every prominent legal commentator leading up to the turn of the nineteenth century. However, this is just the beginning of the historical problems associated with Malcolm's work on the Statute of Northampton. Another deficiency presents itself upon reviewing Malcolm's account of a 1686 case where Sir John Knight was acquitted of violating the Statute of Northampton. According to Malcolm, James II prosecuted Knight under the statute as part of a larger plan to disarm political dissidents. Malcolm alleges the King's Bench rejected interpreting the statute in line with its text because it would "disarm law-abiding citizens."[88] First, it must be noted that a close examination of Malcolm's evidence provides no support for the claim that James II intended to use the Statute of Northampton as a vehicle to disarm all of England. There is not one document, letter, pamphlet or secondary account that supports it. It is a finding Malcolm seems to have created out of thin air. At best Malcolm's finding on this point is nothing more than a unsubstantiated historical theory, not a proven historical thesis. But what's worse is the *English Reports* and the history of Sir John Knight's case cannot remotely be read to support Malcolm's analysis concerning the court's interpretation. The King's Bench held the intent of the Statute of Northampton was "to punish people who go armed to terrify the King's subjects," affirming the act of "going armed" was a "great offence at the *common law,* as if the King were not able or willing to protect his subjects; and therefore this Act is but an affirmance of that law."[89] This legal definition takes nothing away from the prosecutorial scope of the statute. If anything it supports the proposition of the legal commentators stated earlier—going armed with dangerous weapons in the public concourse, without the license of the government, terrified the people.

More importantly, the King's Bench stipulated the narrow holding that it could not inflict any other punishment than what the statute directed. In this case, Sir John Knight was cloaked with governmental authority because he committed the act in accordance with the mayor and aldermen of Bristol.[90] Thus, under the terms of the Statute of Northampton, Knight qualified as one of the "King's Officers and Ministers in doing their Office," and would have been exempted from punishment.[91] This explains why the jury acquitted Knight, and nothing further could be done according to the statute.[92] At the trial itself, the political nature of Knight's prosecution was well known. Despite facilitating and taking part in the seizure of the priest, the mayor and aldermen of Bristol were acquitted of all charges, yet the attorney general still prosecuted Knight.[93] In an attempt to separate Knight from the other government officials, the attorney general sought prosecution under the Statute of Northampton by attempting to prove that Knight was disaffected to government, and could not be exempt by law. As evidence of his legal theory, the attorney general offered that Knight had refused a "Commission to be a Captain in the time of Monmouth's Rebellion" and was outside the protective scope of governmental immunity.[94] Knight countered with "very good proofe" that he acted as one of the crown's officials, and only refused the commission because of the distances involved.[95] If anything, Knight felt his refusal of the king's commission had done more of a service in that he offered prudent advice to the crown's ministers.[96]

The indictment even accused Knight of being a *"very disloyall and Seditious and ill affected man* [that] had caused Musketts or Armes to be carried before him in the Streets, and into the Churck to publick service to the terror of his Majesties Leige people."[97] Knight admitted that he was armed upon going to the church, but refused to concede that he was disaffected.[98] In explaining the turn of events, Knight also informed the King's Bench of an assault and identifiable threat to his person.[99] Days earlier, two Irishmen had been waiting outside Knight's home to assault his person. After waiting to no avail, the Irishmen approached a woman for Knight's whereabouts, and brutally beat her for failing to reveal the location.[100] In addition to this incident, there was another involving Mack Don, who Knight claimed to have assaulted his person, although no charges were ever brought against Don.[101] It was for these reasons that Knight confessed to the court that he always "rode with a Sword and a Gun," and had a number of armed attendants,[102] which had been an exception under the common law.[103]

But Knight never rested his innocence or legal defense on preparatory self-defense or the common law exception. It was not the act Knight was being charged with, nor were any of the "attendants" charged in violation of the statute. Instead, Knight defended the case in terms of "active Loyalty" to the crown and even cited Richard II's statute exempting governmental officials from punishment.[104] It is a historical point of emphasis that when Knight was armed to apprehend the priest he was under the license of the king's service. It is for this reason the King's Bench doubted the conduct "came within the equity and true meaning of the Statute of Northampton about goeing armed[.]"[105] The chief justice even scolded the attorney general for indicting Knight. The chief justice stated, "[I]f there be any blinde side of the Kings business[s] you will al[ways] lay your finger upon it, and shew it to the Defendants[.]"[106]

Here again, we see an example as to why employing accepted historical methodologies to elicit total historical context matters. There will often be instances where what seems to be viable historical conclusion is nothing more an unsupported theory. Therefore, when faced with conflicting historical accounts we must unpack, examine, and weigh the competing claims. But this is not the only lesson to be learned from this example. It also illustrates the ease by which an entire body of legal scholarship can be susceptible to a domino defect. For over thirty years Standard Model writers have cited and relied on Malcolm's mischaracterization of the Statute of Northampton, all without ever researching the subject in full. This in turn has propped up the myth there were no laws regulating the carry of arms for self-defense.[107] It is a costly mistake that even the most recent Second Amendment casebook made when discussing the Statute of Northampton:

> The 1328 Statute of Northampton imposed a very broad restriction on arms-carrying, although there appears to be little evidence of it actually been much enforced....
>
> Over three centuries later, a charge under the statute was brought against a notable political opponent of the despotic King James II. The opponent had gone to church armed, and was acquitted by the jury.... The Chief Justice explained that the statute only applies to persons "who go armed to terrify the King's subjects." While the statute "is almost in desuetudinem," it would apply "when the crime shall appear malo animo" (with evil intent). The Chief Justice noted "a general connivance to gentlemen to ride armed for their security." The limiting construction of the case was treated as the authoritive rule thereafter.[108]

Other than pointing out that the Statute of Northampton was enacted in 1328 and Sir John Knight was, in fact, prosecuted, the casebook's statement is completely inaccurate. This particularly applies to the authors' final sentence proclaiming the "limiting construction of the case was treated as the authoritive rule thereafter."[109] As support for this proposition the authors cite William Blackstone's *Commentaries on the Laws of England.* However, at no point did Blackstone mention, reference, quote or cite Sir John Knight's case, nor did he limit the statute's construction, as the authors would have us believe. What Blackstone wrote was: "The offence of *riding* or *going armed,* with dangerous or unusual weapons, is a crime against the public peace, by terrifying the good people of the land, and is particularly prohibited by the statute of Northampton."[110] Blackstone then illustrated the Statute of Northampton's scope with a historical parallel. It was viewed as similar to the "laws of Solon" where "every

Athenian was finable who walked about the city in armour."[111] Here we find that Blackstone did not deviate at all from the Statute of Northampton's purpose—a prohibition on carrying dangerous weapons in the public concourse without the license of government, for in such instances an individual's security was vested with society and the laws governing it.[112] This point is only strengthened upon examination of Blackstone's other sections. For instance, when discussing the hue and cry—the doctrine applicable to pursuing criminals—Blackstone wrote that any person raising it "must acquaint the constable of the vill[age] with all the circumstances which he knows of the felony, and the person of the felon" before the pursuit could be approved.[113] The castle doctrine was the only exception to this rule.[114]

William Hawkins' *Pleas of the Crown* also contradicts how the Second Amendment casebook summarizes the Statute of Northampton in law and history, thus further disproving the notion of a "limiting construction" being the "authoritive rule thereafter." Writing in 1716, Hawkins stated that "any Justice of the Peace, or other person ... impowered to execute" the Statute of Northampton may "seize the Arms" of "any Person in Arms contrary" to its provisions.[115] This included the seizure of arms for preparatory self-defense in the public concourse. As Hawkins aptly put it, "[A] Man cannot excuse the wearing such Armour in Publick, by alledging that such a one threatened him, and that he wears is for the Safety of his Person from his Assault."[116] There were three exceptions to the general prohibition. The first was home bound self-defense. The rationale being "because a Man's House is ... his Castle," there shall be no penalty for a person "assembling his Neighbours and Friends in his own House, against those who threaten to do him any violence therein."[117] The second exception applied to persons carrying arms with the license of government. There was no legal presumption to "terrify the People" if a "Person of Quality," i.e., person licensed for public carriage, wore "common Weapons" approved by law.[118] And the last exception was the assembling of arms for the hue and cry, *posse comitatus* or militia. In the words of Hawkins, there is no violation of the Statute of Northampton when a person "arms himself to suppress or resist such Disturbers of the Peace or Quiet of the Realm."[119] This exception was not a free license to enforce the peace at an individual's leisure. Instead, the assembling of the hue and cry, *posse comitatus* or militia was solely at the discretion of government. Yet somehow supporters of the Standard Model Second Amendment arrive at the opposition conclusion. They read the licensing exception as the general rule, which would swallow Hawkins' other sections as superfluous and erase the intent and enforcement of the statute for four centuries.[120] Furthermore, in order for the Standard Model interpretation to even be plausible, historians would

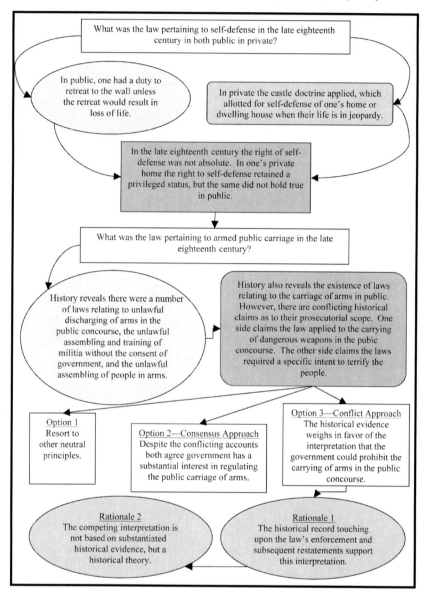

have to exclude legal commentators like Joseph Keble and Michael Dalton. But this is not history in context. It is law office history and mythmaking at its finest.

In summary, if one proceeds down the historical guidepost approach upon reaching the conflicting views concerning the Statute of Northampton, there are two interpretational options available. If one chooses the second option—choosing consensus where there is conflict—it is safe to conclude the historical record shows the public carriage of arms, to include firearms, was a subject of government regulation by the late eighteenth century. And if we proceed to the third option—choosing conflict where there is conflict—the historical inquiry concludes it is within the purview of government to ban the carrying of dangerous weapons in the public concourse. Of course, if one proceeds to the third option, this does not necessarily lead to the conclusion that the Statute of Northampton was enforced everywhere and anywhere.[121] In the late eighteenth century, the majority of Americans lived outside city centers, towns, and other populated enclaves.[122] Certainly when traveling on unprotected highways or through the unsettled frontier it would have been common for late eighteenth century Americans to arm themselves (whether this was perceived as a constitutional right is another matter). But even taking these historical observations into consideration, it does not negate the fact that it is was within the government's police power to regulate the public carriage of arms to prevent public injury. This was the entire purpose behind the Statute of Northampton and other late eighteenth-century laws touching upon dangerous weapons. None of which were called into questioned as a violation of the Second Amendment or a right to bear arms.

It was not until the nineteenth century, when a number of states began enacting concealed carry laws, to guarantee the public safety, that legal challenges were brought.[123] It is at this juncture that the historiography of the right to bear arms takes an interesting turn. While a number of state courts upheld the laws as a constitutional exercise of governmental power, other courts found them to be inviolate of the respective state's bear arms provision. What further complicates matters is that the courts employed different interpretational approaches. In the 1822 decision *Bliss v. Commonwealth,* for example, the Kentucky Supreme Court assumed a libertarian approach to strike down the state's concealed carry law:

> The right existed at the adoption of the constitution; it had then no limits short of the moral power of the citizens to exercise it, and it in fact consisted in nothing else but in the liberty of the citizens to bear arms. Diminish that liberty, therefore, and you necessarily restrain the right; and such is the diminution and restraint, which the act in question most indisputably imports, by prohibiting the citizens wearing weapons in a manner which was lawful to wear them when the constitution was adopted. In truth, the right of the citizens to bear arms, has been as directly assailed by the provisions of the act, as though they were forbid carrying guns on their shoulders, swords in scabbards, or when in conflict with an enemy, were not allowed the use of bayonets; and if the act be consistent with the constitution, it cannot be incompatible with that instrument for the legislature, by successive enactments, to entirely cut off the exercise of the right of the

citizens to bear arms. For, in principle, there is no difference between a law prohibiting the wearing concealed arms, and a law forbidding the wearing such as are
exposed; and if the former be unconstitutional, the latter must be so likewise.[124]

Twenty years later, in *State v. Buzzard,* the Arkansas Supreme Court
upheld a concealed carry provision and noted the above mentioned Kentucky
Supreme Court's interpretation was "specious" given it would negate the "fundamental principles upon which the government is based." The Arkansas
Supreme Court elaborated on this point: "The dangers to be apprehended
from the existence and exercise of such [a] right, not only to social order,
domestic tranquility and the upright and independence administration of the
government, but also to the established institutions of the country, appears so
obvious as to induce the belief that they are present to every intelligent mind,
and to render their statement here unnecessary."[125]

Weighing the interests of the government in preserving the peace, preventing injury, and guaranteeing the public safety against a right to armed
self-defense was the prevailing approach assumed by Southern courts.[126] It is
here that the Standard Model Second Amendment narrative finds support in
tradition and becomes persuasive. In the words of Standard Model scholar
Michael P. O'Shea: "It should be uncontroversial that when historical claims
are made about the existence or nonexistence of a particular tradition in American legal history, the decisions and opinions of American Courts are important evidence of that tradition."[127] In other words, it is because a number of
nineteenth-century courts acknowledged a right to armed self-defense outside
the home with dangerous weapons that O'Shea believes it is a right worth recognizing in line with traditional American values. But to only weigh the values
and tradition of Southern courts runs the risk of subjective and illegitimate
history, for the Northern courts viewed the public carriage of dangerous
weapons much differently. The respected jurist Peter Oxenbridge Thacher
aptly articulated the Northern view in a charge to the grand jury, stating:

> In our own Commonwealth [of Massachusetts], no person may go armed with a
> dirk, dagger, sword, pistol, or other offensive and dangerous weapon, without
> reasonable cause to apprehend an assault or violence to his person, family, or
> property. Where the practice of wearing secret arms prevails, it indicates either
> that the laws are bad; or that they are not executed with vigor; or, at least, it
> proves want of confidence in their protection. It often leads to the sudden com-
> mission of acts of atrocious injury; and induces the individual to rely for defence
> on himself, rather than on society. But how vain and impotent is the power of a
> single arm, however skilled in the science of defence, to protect its possessor from
> the many evil persons who infest society. The possession of a concealed dagger is
> apt to produce an elation of mind, which raises itself about the dictates both of
> prudence and law. The possessor, stimulated by a sensitive notion of honor, and

constituting himself the sole judge of his rights, may suddenly commit a deed; for which a life of penitence will hardly, even in his own estimation, atone. When you survey the society to which you belong, and consider the various wants of its members;—their numbers, their variety of occupation and character,—their conflicting interests and wants ... what is it, permit me to ask, preserves the common peace and safety? I know of no answer, but THE LAW:—it is the law, which makes every man to know his own place, compelling him to move in it, and giving him his due.[128]

Here we see how the government's interest in preserving the peace and preventing injury trumped any individual liberty to carry dangerous weapons in the public concourse. It was a view emulated by a number of states in the nineteenth century. Maine, Delaware, Wisconsin, Pennsylvania, Oregon, and Minnesota all placed the burden on the person carrying arms to show a reasonable fear of "assault or other injury or other violence" in order to escape prosecution.[129] Thus, much like the Statute of Northampton, these laws prohibited the carrying of dangerous weapons in the public concourse.[130] However, the nineteenth-century provisions were unique in that they expressly acknowledged a defense of "reasonable" fear from assault. Certainly, a person could not claim this defense as an everyday preparatory measure, but it does show the variations of public carriage that developed in the United States by the time the Fourteenth Amendment was ratified.

This fact is crucial because there are a number of constitutional theorists that assert it is the understanding of the Second Amendment at the time of the Fourteenth Amendment's ratification that matters most, not the late eighteenth-century understanding. But when the Fourteenth Amendment was ratified there was hardly a consensus as to the constitutional scope of armed public carriage.[131] Some courts, like the North Carolina Supreme Court in *State v. Huntly,* applied the history of the Statute of Northampton to uphold broad restrictions on the carrying of dangerous weapons in the public concourse.[132] Others, like the Georgia Supreme Court in *Nunn v. State,* upheld a prohibition on the carrying of concealed weapons on the grounds the law permitted open carry.[133] A lack of consensus among the courts was even noted by some of the more prominent nineteenth-century legal commentators. Later editions of James Kent's *Commentaries on American Law,* for example, stated, "There has been a great difference of opinion on the question" of concealed weapons laws. At the same time, however, given "the practice of carrying concealed weapons has been often so atrociously abused," the treatise concluded "it would be very desirable, on principles of public policy, that the respective legislatures should have the competent power to secure the public peace, and guard against person violence by such a precautionary provision."[134] Meanwhile, other legal commentators, to include the likes of William Oldnall Russell and Francis Wharton, opined that laws regulating the carriage of arms were supported by the English common law.[135]

The overall point to be made is simple. At the time of the Fourteenth Amendment's ratification there was an abundance of views relating to the right to bear arms outside the home. And when one applies these conflicting views within the constraints of the historical guidepost approach, it serves as an example where history does not always provide the answers we seek. Of course, there is always the first option when faced with conflicting history, which would be to extinguish the historical inquiry altogether and resort to other modes of constitutional interpretation. The second option—choosing consensus where there is conflict—essentially leads us down the same path because the consensus view provides three undisputed historical facts. First, much like in the late eighteenth century, there were a number of laws punishing the discharging of weapons in public, preventing the unlawful assembling and training of militia arms without the consent of government, and prohibiting armed bodies of people without the consent of government.[136] What these laws reveal is, it was within the purview of government to prevent public injury, particularly any injuries which may result from the improper use of firearms in the public concourse.[137] Second, we know at the time the Fourteenth Amendment was ratified there were a number of state prohibitions on the individual carriage of arms in the public concourse. Third and lastly, it can be stated with certainty that state courts not only varied as to whether such prohibitions were constitutional, but they also varied in their interpretational approach. Some resorted to textualism, some balanced individual liberty against public safety, some considered the history of regulation, and so forth. Thus, taken altogether, the second option does not truly provide us with any limiting guideposts from which to reason, meaning it is likely we will have to resort to some other form of neutral interpretation.

This brings us to the third and last option when faced with conflicting history—choosing conflict where there is conflict. Here again, given the variety of interpretations in the nineteenth century and the complex historiography, to proceed down this path would lead us to building conflict upon conflict. This places us in the realm of law office history and mythmaking. Certainly there is an argument to be made that one can proceed to "choose conflict where there is conflict" by limiting our choices to the Southern and Northern views of the right to carry arms. To do so, however, would lead us down the path of subjective and illegitimate history more so than an objective and legitimate history.

Up to this point we have seen how applying the historical guidepost approach to different eras can lead to different results. The constitutional

The Second Amendment Outside the Home in the Reconstruction Era—Step Two

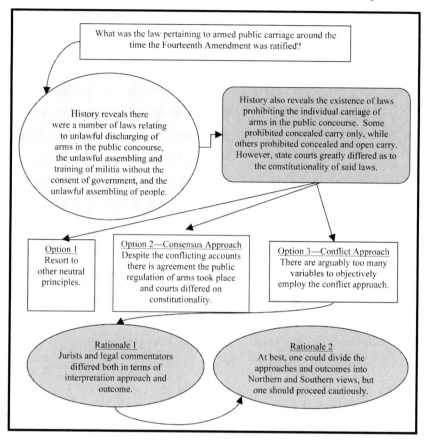

scope of carrying dangerous weapons in the public concourse, to include firearms, at the time of the Constitution's ratification is a clearer guidepost than at the time the Fourteenth Amendment was ratified. The historiography only gets more complicated as we approach modern times. Today it is common for jurisdictions to permit concealed carry, but in the late nineteenth century it was perceived as cowardly and immoral.[138] Today the majority of states maintain "shall issue" laws, which grant to persons qualified a license to carry firearms so long as they meet a set of statutory requirements. However, just a few decades ago, a majority of states subscribed to "may issue" laws, which only granted licenses to carry firearms if the person showed a necessity to do so.[139] Today a majority of jurisdictions do not require a person to retreat to the wall, but during the late eighteenth century this was the majority view. And let us not forget the political and social impact of the Supreme Court's decisions in *District of Columbia v. Heller* and *McDonald v. City of Chicago.* A historian would be hard pressed to find examples of any late eighteenth-century or nineteenth-century politician using the right to bear arms in political campaigns. Today, however, one's stance on Second Amendment rights is a politically sensitive topic, begetting the question: "What role if any should these societal changes play into interpreting the Second Amendment outside the home?"[140]

It depends upon the reasoning employed or how much weight the respective interpreter wants to give to history, tradition, custom, purposes, consequences, and so forth. The historical guidepost approach merely ensures a legitimate historical foundation from which to legally reason. It is not intended to give primacy to one interpretational approach over the other. Thus, for example, let us say a jurist finds the period of the Constitution's ratification as dispositive in determining the scope of the Second Amendment outside the home. Upon applying the historical guidepost approach, the jurist has the option of selecting a number of legitimate historical narratives, dependent upon whether the jurist follows the path of consensus or conflict history. A similar scenario presents itself if a jurist prefers the period of the Fourteenth Amendment's ratification. But what if the jurist places greater emphasis on custom and tradition when examining the scope of the Second Amendment outside the home? In such a case, the jurist will examine the history of multiple eras and apply the historical guidepost approach at each point in time. Still, the jurist must be honest about changes in custom and tradition in the process. For instance, when discussing the rules pertaining to self-defense in public, the jurist must acknowledge how jurisdictions began to shift away from the retreat rule in the late nineteenth century. The same holds true should the jurist explore the history of concealed carry regulations. Arguably the first such prohibition appeared in a 1350 English statute under the reign of Edward III.[141] By the late nineteenth century, such prohibitions were common in the United States.[142] However, as of today, most jurisdictions allow for the concealed carry of firearms dependent upon the respective state's licensing scheme.[143]

All and all, the purpose of step three is to ensure an honestly marshaled evidentiary record is applied responsibly. The goal is to not infer or create history. It must be kept in the back of our minds that past and the present are not one and the same, nor can they ever be. Thus, when using the past for the present, it is essential to be cognizant of differences in culture, technology, societal problems, and so forth. This is arguably the toughest labor because it is easy to fall trap to one's own predilections. Let us take for example a commonplace argument by Second Amendment originalists, who proclaim any firearm, magazine or ammunition limitations are unconstitutional because they impede the ability of the people to defend themselves.[144] As historical support, Second Amendment originalists point to the fact that the founding generation did not impose identical restrictions.[145] This is a valid legal argument if one subscribes to the constitutional theory that society cannot be regulated any further than it was by the generation ratifying the constitutional provision in question. But if one accepts this argument as valid, it must also be accepted that most modern day government regulations are legislative overreach because they go beyond the limits of past regulation. This in turn would negate the bedrock principle of any constitutional republic—legislating in the interest of the public good, which evolves dependent upon the ills and problems of society.[146]

Here we see an important consequence of applying past for use in the present. But it is not the only consequence of such a strict originalist approach. Such a narrow construction would mean discarding a number of other historical considerations on social cost. For instance, in the late eighteenth century the repeating rifle or pistol had not been invented yet, meaning the founding generation was never faced with the societal problem of today's mass shootings. And what about taking into account the value the founding generation placed on life with the duty to retreat before employing lethal self-defense?[147] Lastly, what about a consideration of late eighteenth-century laws that prohibited the discharging of firearms to prevent public injury? One such law was passed in 1768 by the Boston Town Council because its "inhabitants have been lately surprised and endangered by the firing of Muskets charged with Shot or Ball on the Neck, Common, and other Parts of the Town."[148] Two decades later, the town of Newburyport, Massachusetts, followed suit and passed an ordinance outlawing the discharging of firearms, excepting the lawful purpose of organized militia musters controlled by State officers:

> That no person (excepting the militia, when under arms, on muster-days, and by the command of their officer) shall fire off any sort of gun, pistol ... or other thing charged or composed in whole, or in part of gun-powder, in array of the streets, lanes or public ways in this town, nor so near as to affright any horse, or in any sort tend to affright, annoy or injury any person whatever—nor shall any person discharge at a mark or otherwise any gun, charged with ball, at any time or front of any place within this town, nor in any direction but such only as from time to time *shall be approved of and licensed by the town, or by the select-men thereof.*[149]

What can be logically deduced in terms of eighteenth-century social costs from these discharging laws? The answer is the prevention of negligent discharges by single-shot firearms was deemed suitable in the interests of the public good, and during an era where maintaining a loaded and properly charged firearm could be compromised by the surrounding conditions. More importantly, it comes at a point in history where the standard rifleman could discharge, on average, no more than two to three rounds per minute depending upon the skill of the shooter.[150] Thus, given the technology available to the founding generation, we can calculate the eighteenth-century social cost associated with firearms at a ratio of two or three potential deaths per minute.[151]

Now in terms of modern firearms, a standard handgun can fire anywhere between six (standard .357 magnum revolver) to over a dozen bullets (standard magazine loaded handgun), and can be easily loaded in seconds. Thus, a social cost estimate ranges the modern handgun between the ratio of twelve and twenty-four potential deaths per minute, with a trained marksman capable of killing up to forty-eight people per minute.[152] These are low estimates. They operate on the assumption the person is firing well aimed shots and reloading at a normal speed. The estimates do not take into account factors such as extended magazine clips, the carrying of multiple firearms or the rapid firing capabilities of assault weapons. If one applies any of these factors, the death per minute ratio would be the social cost equivalent of a rather large eighteenth-century riot, which was unquestionably prohibited by law in the interests of public safety.[153] Not even eighteenth-century cannons could successfully achieve a social cost ratio that high.

The purpose of providing this historical parallel is not to limit the types of arms that may be acquired in accordance with the Second Amendment. This is an entirely separate constitutional issue in itself, and it is well-settled in our constitutional jurisprudence that rights must evolve with accepted technologies. Instead, the point is that the social costs associated with firearms has risen exponentially since the late eighteenth century, and this does not even include substantial demographic changes by comparing eighteenth- and twenty-first-century census or population data. It also does not take into account the lethality of modern ammunition and the extended distances projectiles can now travel. If the past matters, if it truly matters, in weighing the constitutionality of modern gun regulations, historical consciousness dictates a number of considerations. It is not enough to simply proclaim the founding generation did not have equivalent legal restrictions. For if one retains historical consciousness, as applied to the scope of the Second Amendment outside the home, the logical conclusion is if the founding generation believed it legally sufficient to prevent firearm injuries with a two or three death per minute ratio, it is difficult to question the constitutionally of laws that prevent firearm injuries measuring at a twelve, twenty-four, or as high as forty-eight potential deaths per minute.[154]

The same may be said of modern laws regulating the carrying of dangerous weapons period. Whether the state or local law at question is shall issue, may issue, requires professional certification or training to carry a firearm in the public concourse, and so forth, it is not enough to proclaim the founding generation did not maintain similar restrictions. Given the regulation of arms carriage dates back to the Norman Conquest, and were unquestioned until challenges to concealed carry prohibitions took place in nineteenth-century America, history weighs in favor of presuming the regulation is constitutional. This is not to say that each and every modern law regulating weapons in the public concourse is a constitutional exercise of government power. It just means historical consciousness requires us to take into account a number of factors and reason accordingly.

6

Historical Guideposts, the Fourteenth Amendment and Citizenship by Birth

One of the most controversial issues in American constitutional law is that of citizenship by birth. The Fourteenth Amendment prescribes the constitutional rule: "All persons born or naturalized in the United States, and subject to the jurisdiction thereof, are citizens of the United States and of the State wherein they reside."[1] These twenty-eight words have fueled numerous constitutional questions as to its protective scope. Is every person born in the territorial United States a citizen of the United States? May a person's immigration status impact whether they are "subject to the jurisdiction thereof"? Also, does the Fourteenth Amendment allow Congress any flexibility to legislate who is "subject to the jurisdiction" of the United States?

Much like the discussion over the Second Amendment outside the home, the answers to these questions differ depending on who is asked. If one asks left-leaning academics, the answer is virtually all persons born in the United States must be citizens within the meaning and intent of the Fourteenth Amendment, excluding the children of Indians, diplomatic officials, and foreign military. Take for instance Gerald L. Neuman, who concludes that the "status of the alien parents is irrelevant" when applying the Citizenship Clause of the Fourteenth Amendment to persons born in the United States.[2] Thus, according to Newman, the Citizenship Clause guarantees citizenship to all children born of "permanent residents, lawful nonimmigrants, or unlawfully present" immigrants.[3] And anyone that asserts otherwise, such as limiting birthright citizenship to "children of citizens and permanent residents," Neuman believes is a revisionist historian.[4] Saby Ghoshray arrives at a similar conclusion: "Codified within the Citizenship Clause in Section 1 of the Fourteenth Amendment is the universal guarantee of birthright citizenship for persons born within the geographical boundary of the United States."[5] According to Ghoshray it was not until recent years that a "nativist" or limiting interpretation of the Citizenship Clause developed, which must be cast as "erroneous on constitutional, historical, and moral grounds."[6]

What Neuman describes as "revisionist" and Ghoshray as "nativistic" is dubbed the consensualist model. The model became influential in the late twentieth century, and subscribes to the view that unlawful immigrants are not "subject to the jurisdiction" of the United States within the original meaning and spirit of the Fourteenth Amendment, and therefore their children cannot be granted citizenship.[7] A similar scholarly approach adopts the view that the children of unlawful immigrants are citizens of the United States with the caveat that Congress may exclude them through the plenary power doctrine.[8] While this scholarly contingent agrees that the children of unlawful immigrants are not within the intended spirit of the Fourteenth Amendment, it recognizes that the United States Code must be amended in order to exclude unlawful immigrants from citizenship.[9]

Although the consensualist model is derived from textualism and originalist methodologies, not all originalists agree with its interpretation.[10] Take for instance Michael D. Ramsey, who argues the "Constitution's text plainly grants birthright citizenship to the children of illegal aliens born in the United States." In coming to this conclusion, Ramsey relies almost exclusively on the original meaning of the word "jurisdiction." "[I]f we look at the way the relevant language was used in the nineteenth century, when the Amendment was adopted," stated Ramsey in a panel discussion at the University of San Diego, "it becomes clear that 'jurisdiction' referred not just to the power of the court, but to the power of nations."[11] Matthew Ing also employs an originalist approach and concludes the original public meaning of "jurisdiction" proves the consensualist interpretation is incorrect on "originalist grounds."[12] Where Ing distinguishes himself from Ramsey is his reliance on original expected applications originalism (coming to the outcomes the framers expected), step by step, to dismiss the consensualist model.[13]

Then there are more historically based scholars such as Garrett Epps and Mark Shawhan who argue history in context cannot conceivably support the consensualist model. Epps is rather forthright in this claim, classifying the consensualist model as a "right wing myth," and writing the "history of the Amendment's framing lends *no support* to the idea that native-born American children should be divided into citizen and non-citizen classes depending on the immigration status of their parents."[14] Providing one of the most detailed legislative histories on the Citizenship Clause to date, Epps contends that the constitutional text is straightforward. He interprets the phrase "subject to the jurisdiction thereof" as applying to the moment of birth, and in no way can be limited by the immigration status of the parents.[15] In other words, Epps believes the legal question of birthright citizenship rests on whether the child is subject to American law at birth, which would make almost every child born on United States territory "subject to the jurisdiction thereof."

Shawhan concurs with Epps' bottom line conclusion, yet distinguishes himself by asserting the legislative history of the 1866 Civil Rights Act is equally if not more important when deciphering the Citizenship Clause.[16] The act stipulated "that all persons born in the United States and not subject to any foreign power, excluding Indians not taxed, are hereby declared to be cit-izens of the United States."[17] When one compares the text of the Citizenship Clause and the 1866 Civil Rights Act, the difference is telling. Still, Shawhan rationalizes the two must be interconnected because "Congress added the Clause to constitutionalize the citizenship guarantee of the Civil Rights Act, and because the Clause's substance drew heavily from the Act."[18]

Herein, one may deduce there is a consensus as to the scope of the Citi-zenship Clause, and any limited or conditional reading of the Citizenship Clause fails in both historical context and legal application. To do so, however, would be to rush to judgment, for there is growing parallel body of scholarship questioning the validity of such historical judgments. First, it is asserted such a broad interpretation of the Citizenship Clause would be to prescribe a con-stitutional redundancy. Given the Fourteenth Amendment already requires birth in the territorial United States as a condition, it is argued that it is super-fluous to interpret "subject to the jurisdiction thereof" as being merely "subject to the laws."[19] Thus, critics of the broad interpretation view "subject to the jurisdiction thereof" as meaning something more, such as an affirmation of national consent or "complete jurisdiction."[20] Second, commentators in sup-port of a broad interpretation of the Fourteenth Amendment omit the impor-tance nineteenth-century nationality law placed on domicile and residence when defining political rights to include citizenship, especially its link with the legal tenets of allegiance and personal subjection.[21] Lastly, commentators who support broad interpretation overlook the role international law served in determining "jurisdiction" and hence citizenship by birth. International perceptions of jurisdiction and allegiance were highly influential at the time the Fourteenth Amendment was ratified, and, if history truly matters, this must have some bearing as to how we interpret the Citizenship Clause today.[22]

Taken altogether, the conflicting historical and legal accounts present a serious objectivity concern. One can easily fall victim to their own predilec-tions by picking and choosing the historical narrative in line with their philo-sophical, ideological, and political viewpoint. It is in instances like this that retaining historical consciousness is crucial, for it ensures the past is not abused for use in the present. What this requires is looking at the motivations of each writer, breaking down the methodologies employed, weighing the competing historical claims, and discarding those that prove to be unsubstantiated. In other words, one must familiarize themselves with the historiography of the Citizenship Clause. The point to be made here is what may seem like an acceptable historical model written years ago may no longer maintain historical acceptance or could be substantially altered by new findings.[23]

In a recent article, historian Robert E. Mensel nicely summed up this objectivity dilemma and offered prudent advice if we must use history as a guidepost for interpreting the Citizenship Clause today:

> Today's debate over the extent to which citizenship by birthright was intended to be limited by the language of the Civil Rights Act and Fourteenth Amendment has descended into a contest of competing certainties.... Each side claims the unambiguous support of what it claims to be a clear historical record.... The historical record of the Congressional debates, and the historical context preceding those debates, are rife with contradiction and uncertainty. The conclusions that can be drawn from the relevant history must be recognized as based not on the certainty of the record, but on a process of assessing and balancing the contradictions therein. The best we can do is to weigh the competing bodies of evidence and assess their relative weight.[24]

But before delving into the evidentiary record, we must consider step one of the historical guidepost approach and explore whether the constitutional scope of the Citizenship Clause is a case of first impression. In this instance, the answer is "no," given the Supreme Court explored the scope of the Citizenship Clause in a number of late nineteenth-century cases. This does not mean, however, that history, custom, and tradition are useless moving forward. It merely triggers the inquiry: "What does this late nineteenth-century precedent answer in terms of the Citizenship Clause's constitutional scope?" Those questions that precedent cannot answer, the historical guidepost approach may be employed to frame or guide constitutional interpretation moving forward.

The first Supreme Court decision to address the Citizenship Clause did so in dictum. Within just five years of the Fourteenth Amendment's ratification, in the 1873 *Slaughterhouse Cases*, the Supreme Court stated:

> [The Citizenship Clause] declares that persons may be citizens of the United States without regard to their citizenship of a particular State, and it overturns the *Dred Scott* decision by making all persons born within the United States and subject to its jurisdiction citizens of the United States. That its main purpose was to establish the citizenship of the negro can admit of no doubt. The phrase, "subject to its jurisdiction" was intended to exclude from its operation children of

ministers, consuls, and citizens or subjects of foreign States born within the United States.[25]

Here, the Court's analysis is seemingly in line with those commentators that denounce any consensual, limited, or restricted interpretation of the Citizenship Clause. However, it is unclear what the Court meant by "subjects of foreign States." Did the Court intend to acquiesce to *jus sanguinis* citizenship or citizenship based upon the nationality of the father? Did the Court interpret the Citizenship Clause in conjunction with the text of the 1866 Civil Rights Act—"subject to no foreign power"—or was the Court implicitly affirming the conditions precedent for birthright citizenship to vest? The answers to these questions are unclear.[26]

Eleven years later, in *Elks v. Wilkins,* the Court again addressed the scope of the Citizenship Clause. This time the issue before the Court was one of national citizenship. In particular, the question was whether a person born of Indian parents was "subject to the jurisdiction thereof." The Court read Section 1 of the Fourteenth Amendment in conjunction with Section 2 to hold John Elk—a child born of Indian parents—did not fall within the legal scope of the Citizenship Clause and therefore could not claim voting protections under the Fifteenth Amendment.[27] In terms of all non–Indian persons born in the territorial United States, the Court stated in dicta:

> The evident meaning of ["subject to the jurisdiction thereof"] is, not merely subject in some respect or degree to the jurisdiction of the United States, but completely subject to their political jurisdiction, and owing them direct and immediate allegiance. And the words relate to the time of birth in the one case, as they do to the time of naturalization in the other. Persons not thus subject to the jurisdiction of the United States at the time of birth cannot become so afterwards, except by being naturalized, either individually, as by proceedings under the naturalization acts, or collectively, as by the force of a treaty by which foreign territory is acquired.[28]

Here again, the Court left much wanting in terms of scope of the Citizenship Clause. What did the Court mean by "completely subject" to the political jurisdiction of the United States? At what point did "direct" or "immediate allegiance" vest? If the Court meant birth in itself vested allegiance, the rest of the paragraph would be superfluous. And if one examines Justice Harlan's dissent, we find citizenship by birth to be dependent upon factors such as the parents being "subject to taxation and other public burdens" in accordance with the text of the 1866 Civil Rights Act.[29] According to Harlan, the same would have held true for the Fourteenth Amendment, for "the former [1866 Civil Rights Act] urged the adoption of the latter."[30]

Despite the Supreme Court's decisions in the *Slaughterhouse Cases* and

Elks v. Wilkins, the issue of whether persons born of alien parents in the territorial United States were in fact citizens remained unsettled as a jurisprudential matter. Following the ratification of the Fourteenth Amendment, there were a number of views with the debate centering on the coexisting 1866 Civil Rights Act and Citizenship Clause.[31] The two legal provisions were perceived as operating in conjunction. The rationale was the Citizenship Clause did not override the 1866 Civil Rights Act, given that Section 5 of the Fourteenth Amendment allotted Congress the "power to enforce, by appropriate legislation the provisions of this article."[32] Thus, to late nineteenth-century commentators, decoding who and who was not a citizen by birth meant determining not only whether a person born in the territorial United States "subject to the jurisdiction thereof," but also "not subject to any foreign power."[33]

Before the Supreme Court would hear *Wong Kim Ark* and seemingly answer this jurisprudential question, Marshall B. Woodworth analyzed the case in light of the district court opinion.[34] Woodworth put forth a number of important legal considerations. First, the district court opinion conflicted with the dictum in the *Slaughterhouse Cases*. Second, international law generally adhered to two doctrines of citizenship—*jus soli* and *jus sanguinis*.[35] Third, there was very little substantive case law directly addressing whether the Citizenship Clause applied to the child of two alien parents residing in the territorial United States.[36] Like other late nineteenth-century commentators, Woodworth perceived the constitutional question to rest on the relationship between the 1866 Civil Rights Act and the Citizenship Clause: "These two expressions [of the law] are, to all intents and purposes, the same in meaning, for it may well be said that one who is subject to the jurisdiction of the United States is not subject to any foreign power. Taking the phrase as it is contained in the constitutional provision, and the question presents itself, what is intended to be the application of the word 'jurisdiction?' Does it mean to be subject to the 'laws' of the United States, or has it another and a more extended meaning?"[37]

Woodworth answered these questions by asserting the Citizenship Clause required three conditions for citizenship by birth to vest. The person had to (1) be within the territorial United States, (2) be "under the protection of [its] laws," and (3) had "the *consequent obligation to obey them, when obedience can be rendered.*" It was only after meeting all three conditions that the person was "subject by their birth ... within the terms of the amendment."[38] Thus to Woodworth, "subject to the jurisdiction thereof" did not mean mere presence in the territorial jurisdiction. It required something more in line with the rules pertaining to allegiance, domicile, and personal subjection. Woodworth, of course, admitted every nation "may affix conditions or regulate the acquisition of citizenship, in accordance with what it may deem most conducive to its policy, stability, and prosperity,"[39] with the United States electing citizenship on *jus soli* principles. At the same time, however, Woodworth acknowledged that the subject of citizenship was "co-extensive with the right of a nation to *admit* or *exclude* aliens and to prescribe terms of their *admission* or *exclusion.*"[40] The right to admit or exclude aliens according to any condition was a long-standing international norm and unquestioned by jurists from the late eighteenth to the turn of the twentieth century.[41] Embedded within this sovereign right was the doctrine of allegiance, which stipulated an alien could not gain the full protection of the host nation without fully submitting to it.[42] This explains why discussions on citizenship were always intertwined with references to allegiance, residence, domicile, and personal subjection. As Woodworth aptly put it, in the late nineteenth century the doctrines were "co-extensive" with each other, and no one could expect to be afforded political rights or benefits on any footing other than legal admission and acceptance into the community.[43]

It is through this contextual and historical lens one must read the Supreme Court's 1898 decision in *Wong Kim Ark.* The case concerned the birth in the territorial United States of Wong Kim Ark, whose parents were both of Chinese descent and residents of California.[44] Of particular importance was how the Court emphasized that its previous cases touching upon the Citizenship Clause did not present these facts, and even made sure to note said facts were crucial to the decision at numerous points.[45] The Court then stated that residence, domicile, and allegiance were all requisites that citizenship by birth rested upon:

> The foregoing considerations and authorities irresistibly lead us to these conclusions: the Fourteenth Amendment affirms the ancient and fundamental rule of citizenship by birth within the territory, *in the allegiance and under the protection of the country,* including all children here born of *resident aliens,* with the exceptions or qualifications (as old as the rule itself) of children of foreign sovereigns or their ministers, or born on foreign public ships, or of enemies within and during a hostile occupation of part of our territory, and with the single additional exception of children of members of the Indian tribes owing direct allegiance to their several tribes. The Amendment, in clear words and in manifest intent, includes the children born, within the territory of the United States, of all other persons, of whatever race or color, *domiciled within the United States.* Every citizen or subject of another country, *while domiciled here, is within the allegiance and the protection, and consequently subject to the jurisdiction,* of the United States. His allegiance to the United States is direct and immediate, and, although but local and temporary, continuing only so long as he remains within our territory.[46]

In summary, what the *Wong Kim Ark* Court held was a person born of alien parents, domiciled within the territorial United States, was a citizen thereof—nothing more, nothing less. This limited holding is confirmed by legal commentary immediately following the Court's decision. Take for instance an 1898 case note published by the *Yale Law Journal.* The author wrote *Wong Kim Ark* stood for the proposition that the "alien must be permanently domiciled" in the United States for citizenship by birth to vest, unlike "Great Britain [where] birth during mere temporary sojourn is sufficient to render the child a British subject."[47] A 1905 article in *The American Lawyer* read *Wong Kim Ark* at a similar light. Written by John W. Judd, the article stressed the importance of domicile and residence: "Under this holding [the immigrant parents of the person born] should be permanently domiciled here."[48] Then there was an article Marshall Woodworth had written about the case in detail before the *Wong Kim Ark* decision. Woodworth stressed the necessity of allegiance for birthright citizenship to vest: "The Fourteenth Amendment affirms the ancient and fundamental rule of citizenship by birth within the territory, in the allegiance and under the protection of the country, including all children here born of resident aliens."[49]

Wong Kim Ark remains the last time the Supreme Court addressed the scope of the Citizenship Clause. At no point did the Court fully address the legal parameters and limits of domicile, residence or allegiance. The Court merely stipulated Wong Kim Ark's parents met the requirements. This leaves open a number of legal considerations such as what is the citizenship of a child born to immigrant parents that are only temporarily present or traveling in the United States? Is the Fourteenth Amendment's Citizenship Clause triggered in such cases? Does the answer change if one of the parents is a United States citizen? It is common today for left-leaning legal commentators to read the *Wong Kim Ark* decision as affirmatively answering such questions. They claim the decision supports the proposition that all persons born in the territorial United States—excluding the children of Indians, diplomatic officials, and foreign military personnel—are United States citizens.[50] However, this reading is idealistic at best, given a number of late nineteenth- and early twentieth-century commentators did not interpret the Court's holding in such broad terms.[51]

Therefore, given there remain unanswered questions as to the scope of the Citizenship Clause, it is prudent to proceed with the historical guidepost approach. It is here, proceeding to step two, that the retention of historical consciousness is paramount, for the historiography of the Citizenship Clause is wrought with errors, misconceptions, and unsubstantiated claims. It is important to keep in mind that most of the scholarship to explore the Citi-

The Fourteenth Amendment's Citizenship Clause and Historical Guideposts—Step One

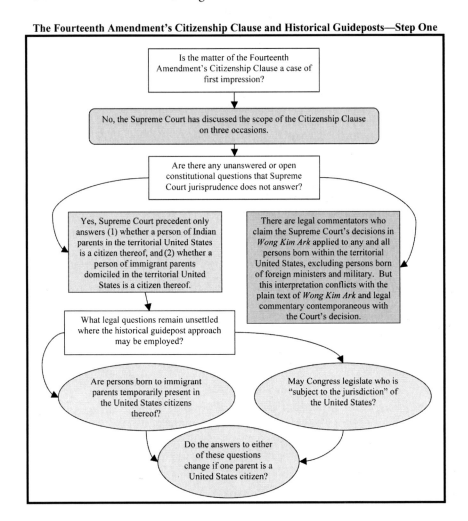

zenship Clause has been driven by the politics of unlawful immigration.[52] To be clear, scholars writing on the meaning of the Citizenship Clause often commit the error of exploring the past for the sake of the understanding the present, not exploring the past for the sake of understanding the past.[53] They seek late nineteenth-century answers to twenty-first century questions such as: what is the citizenship of a child born to unlawful immigrants?[54] Does the Fourteenth Amendment's Citizenship Clause apply to the children of unlawful immigrants? Does the answer change if one of the parents is a United States citizen?

Certainly the applicability of the Citizenship Clause to the children of unlawful immigrants provides a set of unanswered questions for today's legal academy, but to center the historical inquiry around these questions muddles rather than clarifies analysis. Examples can be found in the different interpretational approaches to the Citizenship Clause. In the case of those scholars subscribing to the consensualist model, they ahistorically equate the legal status of Indians, in the nineteenth century, as being compatible with the unlawful immigrants of today, all without providing a proper legal correlation.[55] A similar error is made by scholars supporting a broad interpretation when they equate the status of late nineteenth-century Chinese immigrants and gypsies with today's unlawful immigrants.[56] And then there is an objectivity issue in the writings of scholars who omit or mischaracterize the importance of domicile and residence in defining political rights, especially its interconnection with the legal tenets of allegiance, personal subjection, and international law from the mid to late nineteenth century.

Whether it is scholarship endorsing the consensualist model or a broad interpretation of the Citizenship Clause, the problem is its authors are not seeking the answer to historical questions, but twenty-first-century legal questions. Certainly the different accounts offer interpretations that are historically plausible. However, the methodologies employed raise more questions than provide answers. More importantly, in the constraints of the historical guidepost approach, it leaves us without a historical consensus as to the constitutional scope of the Citizenship Clause. And when faced with conflicting history there are three options available. One may either relinquish history as an interpretational and guiding tool, find historical "consensus where there is conflict" or "choose conflicting history where there is conflict."

Should the first option be chosen, the historical inquiry is extinguished. However, if the second or third option is chosen, one must conduct a deeper historical inquiry. To begin, one must ask the right questions. It contextually frames the issue and sets forth a research agenda from which to begin. And perhaps the most pressing question is the purpose for including the Citizenship Clause in the Fourteenth Amendment. Then there are more specific questions, such as, what were the rules pertaining to citizenship by birth at the time the Fourteenth Amendment was ratified? Did the drafters of the Fourteenth Amendment perceive the Citizenship Clause as providing a fixed constitutional rule, or could citizenship by birth be tailored through legislation or treaty? How were claims of citizenship by birth adjudicated following the ratification of the Constitution? How did prominent legal commentators interpret the Citizenship Clause? Lastly, given the Supreme Court in *Wong Kim Ark* stressed the importance of legal domicile and allegiance in coming to its decision, how did these legal tenets operate by the late nineteenth century?

In terms of the first question—what was the purpose for including the Citizenship Clause in the Fourteenth Amendment—there are a number of places one may find the answer, but scholars are in agreement that the impetus for including Citizenship Clause was to overturn the Supreme Court's decision in *Dred Scott v. Sanford,* and therefore prevent the Southern states from enacting discriminatory legislation under the rationale that free blacks were not citizens. Initially, the 1866 Civil Rights Act was enacted to remedy this concern, but members of Congress questioned whether a constitutional amendment would be necessary to effectively overturn *Dred Scott.*[57] As a result, the Citizenship Clause was put forward, with its text clarifying that United States citizenship was not only superior to state citizenship, but by obtaining of the former the latter was guaranteed: "All persons born or naturalized in the United States, and subject to the jurisdiction thereof, are citizens of the United States and the State wherein they reside."[58] This purpose behind the Citizenship Clause was commonly understood following the ratification of the Fourteenth Amendment. As late nineteenth-century legal scholar Samuel T. Spear wrote in an 1877:

> The Fourteenth Amendment, so far from introducing an absolutely new theory into the Constitution with respect to citizenship, simply extended an old theory to persons not previously embraced within its provisions, giving additional protection to certain citizen rights, and in this way enlarging the applications of the theory. The primary purpose of the amendment was to bring the emancipated negroes of this country within the category of citizenship in both of its forms [state and federal], and thus place them on a equal footing with the white race about whose citizenship there was no dispute.[59]

When placed in this context, the purpose for including the Citizenship Clause into Section 1 of the Fourteenth Amendment is not even remotely controversial. It is history that easily falls into the category of "choosing consensus where there is conflict." What is controversial, however, is what the drafters meant by the phrase "subject to the jurisdiction thereof," and how the Citizenship Clause was to operate within the confines of the Fourteenth Amendment as a whole. Beginning with the meaning of "subject to the jurisdiction thereof," scholars are deeply divided as to whether the phrase was synonymous with "subject to the laws" or meant something more. If "subject to the jurisdiction thereof" simply meant "subject to the laws," all that is required for citizenship by birth to vest is the parents fall within the legal jurisdiction of the United States.[60] Scholars endorsing this interpretation draw from the congressional debates of the 1866 Civil Rights Act, the Fourteenth Amendment, and textualist based arguments. To them, the evidentiary record is clear. The Citizenship Clause enshrined the common law doctrine touching upon citizenship by birth to all persons, with only the children of Indians, diplomatic officials, and foreign military exempted.

Critics of this interpretation do not dispute the Citizenship Clause as being inapplicable to the children of Indians, diplomatic officials, and foreign military. Thus, here again we have a historical finding that falls into the category of "choosing consensus where there is conflict." But it is last point of agreement between the conflicting historical accounts. A point of contention remains over nineteenth-century conceptions of allegiance, particularly its interrelationship with citizenship by birth. For when critics of an all encompassing Citizenship Clause bring up notions of allegiance, one of three rebuttals is given.[61] The first is one of textual omission. It is claimed if the drafters of the Fourteenth Amendment intended the doctrine of allegiance to be implicit within "subject to the jurisdiction thereof," they would have expressly included the word "allegiance."[62] It is a hypocritical argument given the text of the Fourteenth Amendment does not state "subject to the laws," yet it is claimed this is what the drafters meant by the phrase "subject to the jurisdiction thereof."

This brings us to the second rebuttal, which asserts any allegiance qualification is legally satisfied so long as the parents and child are "directly subject" to the "sovereign power" of the United States.[63] In other words, any allegiance conditions precedent are perceived as akin to being "subject to the laws."[64] But such an argument operates on the assumption that the word "allegiance" was synonymous with legal jurisdiction in the nineteenth century—an assumption the evidentiary record does not conceivably support. This argument also overlooks the complexities of allegiance doctrine, particularly its variants to include natural allegiance, perpetual allegiance, temporary allegiance, and local allegiance.

This brings us to the third and last rebuttal. It is claimed the debates over the Citizenship Clause make it clear that allegiance was not the central point of contention in deciphering citizenship. Instead, invoking the doctrine of allegiance was a consideration for defining citizenship by birth that the framers rejected. Therefore, while it is acknowledged that members of Congress discussed the doctrine of allegiance, it is argued that we must place such discussions aside because the phrase "subject to the jurisdiction thereof" settled the dispute. As Saby Goshray puts it, "[T]here appeared to be legitimate concerns over the impact of allegiance, which the framers seem to have successfully overcome via the jurisdiction requirement of the Citizenship Clause."[65]

What is perplexing about all three rebuttals is they claim to be historically supported, yet not one comports with the legal tenets of allegiance as applied to citizenship by birth in the nineteenth century or the legislative history of the 1866 Civil Rights Act and the Citizenship Clause. Beginning with the legal tenets of allegiance as applied to citizenship by birth, the 1844 case of *Lynch v. Clarke* is arguably the most important American case on point to the address the subject.[66] The case concerned whether Julia Lynch, who was born in New York of "alien parents, during their temporary sojourn," was a citizen.[67] In conclusion, Judge Lewis H. Sandford held that by the current "law of the United States, every person born within the *dominions and allegiance* of the United States, whatever were the situation of his parents, is a natural born citizen."[68] And by "allegiance" Sandford meant that "general allegiance" owed to the "confederated sovereignty of the United States" by aliens within its territorial limits.[69] Here, Sandford was likely referring to temporary and local allegiance, which is a full submission to the authority of the nation as the tacit condition of protection.[70]

At no point, however, did Sandford claim or infer citizenship by birth vested automatically upon territorial presence or that it was an unalterable constitutional right. In fact, Sandford expressly acknowledged the federal government's authority to prescribe rules affecting citizenship by birth:

> In reference to another class of the future inhabitants of the country [following the ratification of the Constitution]—those who were born here of alien parents—it is claimed that the common law continued in force, which will be a subject for inquiry presently. Whether it did or did not, *their condition was to be ascertained by a national law.* In reference to aliens, *legislation would be necessary; and the power to legislate, was conferred upon Congress.* From what has been stated, it follows that such power was intended to be, and necessarily must be exclusive. And being exclusive, it cannot, as we have seen, be controlled by the *unwritten or common law* of one of the states, any more than it can be altered by the statute law of such state. And whether or not the Constitution enabled Congress to declare that the children born here of alien parents who never manifested an intention to become citizens, are aliens or are citizens—*it is clear that the decision of that question must be by some general rule of law,* applicable to affecting our whole nation. It must be determined by what may be called the *national law,* as contra-distinguished from the local law of the several states. It is purely a matter of national jurisprudence, and not of state municipal law.[71]

In summary, *Lynch* does not stand for the sole proposition that mere birth in the United States constitutionally vests citizenship as some modern legal scholars have proclaimed.[72] Sandford noted how the parties were in agreement that Congress had not yet legislated on the subject. In such cases the common law applied until Congress regulated the subject. "[I]n the absence of constitutional or congressional provision on the subject [of citizenship by birth], it must be regulated by the principles of the common law, if they are pertinent and applicable," wrote Sandford.[73] In the case of *jus soli* citizenship, the common law required the parents to be in accord with the doctrine of allegiance by maintaining "general allegiance" to the United States.[74] And the court found Julia Lynch's parents to fall within the terms of "general allegiance" likely because they were domiciled in the United States at the time of her birth.

This form of allegiance required by aliens that are domiciled in a country—often referred to as temporary or local allegiance—required more than being physically present and "subject to the laws." In England, it often required the announcing of one's presence and taking an oath. The same held true in the United States. As Noah Webster aptly put it, local allegiance imposes "an obligation upon every member of a state or body politic, the moment he steps within its jurisdiction, to submit peaceably to such positiv[e] injunctions of that state's, as hav[e] been judged necessary for its welfare."[75] Webster noted that the purpose of the doctrine of allegiance was the need for *moral law, which has for its object the good of society.*"[76] In other words, allegiance was perceived as a legal determination that could be regulated dependent upon the needs and political self-preservation of the nation.

This understanding of allegiance was often restated during the congressional debates over the 1866 Civil Rights Act and the Citizenship Clause. These debates took place at a time when the United States was immersed in the international politics of dual allegiance.[77] This included issues pertaining to the status of foreigners born on United States soil.[78] For instance, in the midst of the Civil War, the French government stipulated ten rules of citizenship as a means to exempt its citizens from United States military service. The list included French citizens who were temporarily resident in the United States, and also "minor sons, even those born in [the United States], of French parents who are naturalized Americans, if they were born before their naturalization of their father."[79] Secretary of State William H. Seward responded that the United States would not "sanction all the positions assumed" by the French government.[80] Instead, Seward thought it best to handle any citizenship issues within the tenets of international and constitutional law "as the cases actually arise."[81] It was a policy the Department of State continued throughout the late nineteenth century in which a number of adjudications were based on international conceptions of citizenship by birth. However, before we get to that historical point in time, it is important to capture the congressional debates on the subject.

Beginning with the 1866 Civil Rights Act, it stipulated "that all persons born in the United States and not subject to any foreign power, excluding Indians not taxed, are hereby declared to be citizens of the United States."[82] Herein, the textualist would argue the act makes no reference to the doctrine of allegiance, and therefore should have no bearing in our interpretation of citizenship by birth. But what this line of argument overlooks is the doctrine of allegiance was implicit in citizenship law. This is confirmed by the 1866 Civil Rights Act's sponsor, Illinois Senator Lyman Trumbull, who made a number of statements to this effect. For instance, in an exchange with Pennsylvania Senator Edgar Cowan, Trumbull openly declared the children of German and Asiatic parents born in the United States would qualify as citizens of the United States.[83] During this declaration Trumbull did not stipulate any conditions for United States citizenship to vest.[84] However, Trumbull later clarified the rule of law when he stated the doctrine of allegiance was implicit within citizenship law, for the next day Trumbull qualified his position in the following terms: "My own opinion is that all these persons born in the United States and under its authority, *owing allegiance* to the United States, are citizens without any act of Congress. They are native-born citizens. That is my judgment about it; but there is a difference in opinion upon that subject."[85]

This statement alone is evidence enough that Trumbull viewed citizenship by birth to be intertwined with the doctrine of allegiance and being a member of the political community. As an example of persons who did not qualify, Trumbull declared Indians must be excluded, given they "do not recognize nor are they made subject to the laws of the United States."[86] Here, Trumbull's use of the phrase "subject to the laws" cannot be equated with mere legal jurisdiction—that is civil and criminal jurisdiction—given Indian parents could be held legally accountable for actions committed outside their tribal jurisdiction, yet any children born outside the same tribal jurisdiction were not "subject to the jurisdiction thereof." Thus, Trumbull understood the phrase "subject to the laws" as embodying something more, such as political jurisdiction. This finding is supported by a later statement where Trumbull discussed the legal status of Indians: "They make and administer their own laws; they are not counted in our population; [and] they are not represented in our Government."[87]

Still, from Trumbull's statements on the subject of citizenship by birth, it is unclear whether not falling under the "authority" and "allegiance of the United States" was satisfied upon meeting *all* the stated conditions or *any* of them. One may assert that Trumbull was only referencing the political status of Indians, and such status could not conceivably extend to any other classes of people.[88] But this view is called into question upon reading Trumbull's statements of February 1, 1866:

> The Senator [John B. Henderson] from Missouri and myself desire to arrive at the same point precisely, and that is to make citizens of everybody born in the United States who owe allegiance to the United States. We cannot make a citizen of a child of a foreign minister who is temporarily residing here. There is a diffi-

culty in framing the amendment so as to make citizens of all the people born in the United States and who owe allegiance to it. I thought that might be the best form in which to put the amendment at one time, "That all persons born in the United States and owing allegiance thereto are declared to be citizens"; but upon investigation it was found that a sort of allegiance was due to the country from persons temporarily resident in it whom we would have no right to make citizens, and that that form would not answer.[89]

What this statement informs us is the 1866 Civil Rights Act was not intended to make citizens of all persons born in the legal jurisdiction of the United States. There was the perception that certain conditions were necessary before citizenship by birth would vest. In terms of nineteenth-century international law this meant persons born of parents temporarily present in the United States would not satisfy the requisite allegiance. A statement by Iowa Representative James F. Wilson on the 1866 Civil Rights Act shares this view and that preceding conditions may be imposed on birthright citizenship:

> It is in vain we look into the Constitution of the United States for a definition of the term "citizen." It speaks of citizens, but in no express terms defines what it means by it. *We must depend on the general law relating to subjects and citizens recognized by all nations for a definition,* and that must lead us to the conclusion that every person born in the United States is a natural-born citizen of such States, except it may be that children born on our soil to *temporary sojourners* or representatives of foreign governments, are native-born citizens of the United States.[90]

Indeed, during the 1866 Civil Rights Act debates, congressional members often spoke of birthright citizenship in broad terms. This included Trumbull.[91] But this does not mean citizenship by birth was an absolute command with no conditions precedent or that it could not be tailored by international law, treaty or legislative act. It is a historical point of emphasis that the act's citizenship provision was merely declaratory of the law as the Reconstruction Congress understood it.[92] As Trumbull stated to the Illinois Assembly on the matter: "It was the generally received opinion that after the adoption of the Constitutional Amendment abolishing Slavery, all native born persons were citizens. If not citizens, what were they? ... The [Civil Rights Act's] words declaring 'all persons born in the United States, and not subject to any foreign Power, to be citizens' were only declaratory of what the law already was."[93]

It is worth restating that at least one scholar—Garrett Epps—believes the legislative history of the 1866 Civil Rights Act should have no bearing as to how the Fourteenth Amendment's Citizenship Clause is interpreted or understood. Epps finds it problematic to compare the language of the two provisions, given the Citizenship Clause maintains "different wording; it emerged from a different political situation; it was adopted under different procedures and had different authors, and it was approved by different voting bodies."[94] It is for these reasons that Epps concludes the Citizenship Clause's "meaning must stand on its own."[95] There is no disputing with Epps that the two provisions maintain different language. But the two provisions were understood as encompassing the same body of law.[96] It is a fact supported by the debates concerning the Fourteenth Amendment's Citizenship Clause.

When the Fourteenth Amendment was first proposed by Michigan Senator Jacob M. Howard to the Senate, it did not have a provision touching upon citizenship by birth. Section 1 only declared: "No State shall make or enforce any law which shall abridge the privileges or immunities of the citizens of the United States; nor shall any State deprive any person of life, liberty, or property without due process of law; nor deny any person within its jurisdiction the equal protection of the laws."[97] On May 23, 1866, Ohio Senator Benjamin F. Wade sought to amend Section 1 by removing the word "citizen" and substituting language that barred states from abridging "the privileges or immunities of persons born in the United States or naturalized by the laws thereof."[98] Wade knew the courts, including the Supreme Court in *Dred Scott v. Sanford*, disagreed on the definition of citizen. Thus, Wade sought to mirror Section 1 to reflect the legal proposition afforded by the 1866 Civil Rights Bill, for he "always believed that every person, of whatever race or color, who was born within the United States, was a citizen of the United States."[99]

In response to Wade's view of citizenship by birth, Maine Senator William P. Fessenden queried: "Suppose a person is born here of parents from abroad temporarily resident in this country."[100] Wade replied that he only knew of "one instance, in the case of the children of foreign ministers who reside 'near' the United States" that this would be the case.[101] He elaborated that is was by a "fiction of law" that such persons were not "residing here," and not citizens of the United States.[102] There is no disputing that Wade's definition of citizenship by birth is distinct from the debates concerning the 1866 Civil Rights Act, particularly as it applied to persons temporarily resident or who were outside the allegiance of the United States. Wade's reason for such an all encompassing interpretation was it comported with the legal maxim *de minimis lex non curat*, or the law does not concern itself with trifles. He thought it "better to put this question beyond all doubt and all cavil by a very simple process" with the language he proposed.[103]

It was at this juncture that Senator Howard, the sponsor of the 1866 Civil Rights Act, intervened and added the following language to precede Section 1: "All persons born in the United States and subject to the jurisdiction thereof are citizens of the United States wherein they reside."[104] Howard described the purpose of the amendment in the following terms:

> This amendment which I have offered is simply declaratory of what I regard as the law of the land already, that every person born within the limits of the United States, and subject to their jurisdiction, is by virtue of natural law and national law a citizen of the United States. This will not, of course, include persons born in the United States who are foreigners, aliens, who belong to the families of ambassadors or foreign ministers accredited to the Government of the United States, but will include every other class of persons. It settles the great question of citizenship and removes all doubt as to what persons are or are not citizens of the United States. This has long been a great desideratum in the jurisprudence and legislation of this country.[105]

Standing on its own, one can interpret Howard's speech in one of two ways. The first interpretation runs parallel to Senator Wade's interpretation, and would affirm that only the children of foreign ministers and ambassadors were excluded from citizenship by birth. In contrast, a second interpretation gives weight to Howard's mention of "natural law and national law," and must conclude that international norms and national legislation could impact which "foreigners" or "aliens" were "subject to the jurisdiction thereof." Given the previous statements by members of Congress when debating the 1866 Civil Rights Act, the second interpretation seems more likely. In the words of historian Robert E. Mensel, "It ... appears that [Howard] wished to link the meaning of the proposed [Wade] amendment with the meaning of the Civil Rights Act.... The Act was to be clarified by the Amendment."[106] It is a view that finds support in the remaining debates concerning the Citizenship Clause.

The primary objection to Howard's amendment was it did not sufficiently clarify the status of Indian children. Senators Edgar Cowan of Pennsylvania, James R. Doolittle of Wisconsin, and William Fessenden of Maine each expressed concern as to whether Indian children would be excluded.[107] It is here that Senator Trumbull chimed in to confirm that "subject to the jurisdiction thereof" would be synonymous with the purpose of the 1866 Civil Rights Act:

> The provision is, that "all persons born in the United States, and subject to the jurisdiction thereof, are citizens." That means "subject to the complete jurisdiction thereof." Now, does [Senator Doolittle] pretend to say that the Navajoe Indians are subject to the complete jurisdiction of the United States? What do we mean by "subject to the jurisdiction" of the United States? Not owing allegiance to anybody else. That is what it means. Can you sue a Navajoe Indian in court? Are they in any sense subject to the complete jurisdiction of the United States. By no means. We make treaties with them, and therefore they are not subject to our jurisdiction.[108]

Thus, in line with Trumbull's statements on the 1866 Civil Rights Act, we find citizenship by birth was a bit more complicated than mere birth in the territorial United States and falling within its legal jurisdiction. The doctrine of allegiance and being a member of the political community were also factors in defining who was "subject to the jurisdiction thereof" or what Trumbull referred to as the "complete jurisdiction." Conversely, Garrett Epps and scholars in support of a broad interpretation of the Citizenship Clause interpret Trumbull's reference to "complete jurisdiction" narrowly, and focus intently on the reference to suing Navajoes in a court of law. From this sentence it is deduced "complete jurisdiction" must equate to legal jurisdiction.[109] It is an interpretation that conflicts with the evidentiary record as a whole, given Trumbull later stipulated allegiance and personal subjection were important conditions in addition to being within the legal jurisdiction of the United States.[110]

It was at this juncture that Maryland Senator Reverdy Johnson stood up in support of an amendment "excluding Indians not taxed." However, before Johnson elaborated on the importance of such an amendment, he defined the law touching upon citizenship by birth as follows:

> Now, all this amendment provides is, that all persons born in the United States and not subject to some foreign Power ... shall be considered as citizens of the United States. That would seem to be not only a wise but a necessary provision.... I know of no better way to give rise to citizenship than the fact of birth within the territory of the United States, born of parents who at the time were subject to the authority of the United States.[111]

This statement further supports the view that the Citizenship Clause and the 1866 Civil Rights Act embodied the same body of law. Indeed, citizenship by birth was often restated in very general terms, but its tenets rested on factors such as the doctrine of allegiance, personal subjection to the jurisdiction, and being a member of the political community. Following Johnson's statement, Trumbull even assuaged any concerns over the Citizenship Clause, stating, "We propose to make citizens of those brought under our jurisdiction in that way."[112] When was an individual "brought" under the United States jurisdiction? Using the political situation of Indians as an example, Trumbull stated it required "owing allegiance solely to the United States."[113] Hence, the Citizenship Clause's language "subject to the jurisdiction thereof" was never intended to remove the 1866 Civil Rights Act's understanding of citizenship by birth. Instead, the language "subject to the jurisdiction thereof" was intended to quell any concerns on the issue state versus federal citizenship.[114] This point was clarified when Senator Doolittle questioned the difference in language. Howard replied the change was "to put this question of citizenship

... beyond the legislative power of such gentlemen [from the states that] would pull the whole system up by its roots and destroy it, and expose the freedmen again to the oppressions of their old masters."[115] To be clear, "subject to jurisdiction thereof" sought to affirm once and for all that United States citizenship was superior to state citizenship.[116]

The question moving forward is under what circumstances was a person not "subject to the jurisdiction thereof." Here again, it is worth delving into the congressional debates, but it is nearly impossible to find a dispositive answer.[117] Take for instance, a statement by Illinois Representative Jehu Baker, who thought the Citizenship Clause to be "plainly just" and without objection.[118] It ensured those who were "subject to taxation, to military service, both State and national, *ought,* upon every principle of manly justice, to receive in turn from society that protection which is involved in the *status* of citizenship."[119] Cleary, Baker did not perceive citizenship by birth to vest as a result of territorial presence and being subject to the legal jurisdiction. There were a number of considerations to be weighed, yet it is unclear exactly what precisely those considerations are and how they should be weighed. What remains certain, however, is exploring nineteenth-century contours of jurisdiction provides an invaluable key, as is evidenced in a speech by Oregon Senator George H. Williams:

> In one sense, all persons born within the geographical limits of the United States are subject to the jurisdiction of the United States, but they are not subject to the jurisdiction to the United States in every sense. Take the child of an ambassador. In one sense, that child born in the United States is subject to the jurisdiction of the United States, because if that child commits the crime of murder, or commits any other crime against the laws of the country, to a certain extent he is subject to the jurisdiction of the United States, but not in every respect; and so with these Indians. All persons living within a judicial district may be said, in one sense, to be subject to the jurisdiction of the court in that district, but they are not in every sense subject to the jurisdiction of the court until they are brought, by proper process, within the reach of the power of the court. I understand the words here "subject to the jurisdiction of the United States," to mean fully and completely subject to the jurisdiction of the United States. If there was any doubt as to the meaning of the words, I think that doubt is entirely removed and explained by the words in the subsequent section [on apportionment].[120]

Williams' reference to Section 2 provides a clue to the historical riddle as to what was meant by members of Congress that referred to "complete" or "political" jurisdiction. If the parents were eligible to be counted for federal apportionment, their children born in United States territory were "subject to the jurisdiction" and a citizen thereof. It is an interpretation that finds support in the congressional debates over apportionment. The question repeatedly asked and answered, in terms of apportionment, was whether non-citizens, women, and minors should be counted. Despite numerous attempts to limit apportionment to voters or male citizens twenty-one years and older, the basis of apportionment was decidedly affirmed to be total population.[121] But total population did not include every person present in the United States at the time. The drafters of the Fourteenth Amendment understood that apportionment would not extend to those temporarily present or who were not deemed part of the political community.[122] Thus, in constitutional terms, Section 1 and Section 2 are intimately linked.[123] During the debates of both sections, references to domicile, allegiance, and being a contributing member of the political community were frequent. They were factors that could be legislated in terms of defining who is within the jurisdiction of the United States.[124] Judge Timothy Farrar's *Manual of the Constitution of the United States* coincides with this understanding. Discussing the Fourteenth Amendment, Farrar wrote:

> Who are the *"persons in each State"* to be counted? Citizens, inhabitants, residents—temporary or permanent, strangers, aliens, Indians, &c.? "Indians not taxed" are not altogether excluded; although before it was by some considered doubtful whether they were excluded only from the first class. This total exclusion is compatible with the preceding section, only on the ground that the Constitution has made them aliens, and so not "subject to the jurisdiction" of the United States, otherwise than aliens by temporary residence; for otherwise they are, by that section and by birthright, actual "citizens of the United States, and of the States wherein they reside." ... "The whole number of persons in each State" cannot mean everybody on the soil at a particular time, nor exclude everybody who may happen not to be on it at the same time, and of course should be authoritatively construed by the law-making power.[125]

Farrar never expressly defined who constituted as "persons" in terms of the Fourteenth Amendment, but in a previous section he wrote "persons" included "citizens or aliens, natural-born or legally admitted, or otherwise constituted as such," and expressly included that portion of those *"bound to service."*[126] Farrar's definition runs parallel with many who advocated for the adoption of the Fourteenth Amendment. There had to be a legal line somewhere that Congress may "enforce, by appropriate legislation, the provisions of this article."[127] Massachusetts Senator Charles Sumner, a member of the Reconstruction Congress and strong advocate for the Thirteenth, Fourteenth, and Fifteenth Amendments, supported this view, writing the Fourteenth Amendment's "definition of Citizenship" could be enforced by "appropriate legislation."[128] Then there is a letter from Senator Trumbull to President Andrew Johnson which stipulated the 1866 Civil Rights Act only made citizens of "'all persons' born of parents *domiciled* in the United States, except untaxed Indians."[129] To be domiciled is not the same as being within the United

States' legal jurisdiction. It requires the requisite of allegiance, a full submission to the laws, and an intention to permanently reside.[130]

As it stands today, scholars that advance a broad interpretation of citizenship by birth have yet to answer for the historical evidence that supports interpreting the Citizenship Clause through the other provisions of the Fourteenth Amendment—that is Sections 1 and 2 are linked, and Section 5 permits some form of legislation to define who is "subject to the jurisdiction thereof." There is, however, a competing holistic interpretation which would require interpreting "subject to the jurisdiction thereof" only in conjunction with the other Section 1 clauses.[131] In the words of Saby Ghoshray: "While the Citizenship Clause announces a declaration of rights, the other three clauses, the Privileges or Immunities Clause, the Equal Protection Clause, and the Due Process Clause, act as the foundational pillars upon which the Citizenship Clause can exist for eternity. Here, these foundational pillars are to act as a bulwark against any attempt to abrogate the natural rights of citizens that the framers conceived of under the doctrine of *jus soli*."[132]

In support of this legal theory, its supporters attempt to draw from the evidentiary record.[133] Ghoshray, in particular, highlights the "timeless arguments of John Bingham" concerning the Fourteenth Amendment, yet omits Bingham's personal views touching upon citizenship by birth.[134] What arguably makes Bingham's understanding of great significance was his personal involvement in drafting the Fourteenth Amendment. It has even been asserted by some that Bingham's interpretation should be the one most relied upon when interpreting the Fourteenth Amendment.[135] However, Bingham did not perceive citizenship by birth in broad and unlimited terms. Take for instance a speech delivered by Bingham seven years prior to the debates of the 1866 Civil Rights Act and the Citizenship Clause, where the issue of citizenship by birth arose over the admission of the Oregon Territory into the Union. Discussing the contents of the 1857 Oregon Constitution, Bingham defined United States citizenship in the following terms:

> Who are the citizens of the United States? Sir, they are those, and those only, who *owe allegiance* to the Government of the United States, not the base [perpetual] allegiance imposed upon the Saxon by the Conqueror, which required him to mediate in solitude and darkness at the sound of the curfew; but the *allegiance* which requires the citizen not only to obey, but to support and defend, if need be with his life, the Constitution of his country. All free persons born and *domiciled* within the jurisdiction of the United States, are citizens of the United States from birth.[136]

Here, much like the debates over the 1866 Civil Rights Act and the Citizenship Clause, Bingham placed citizenship by birth in the constraints of

domicile, allegiance, and being a member of the political community. As
applied to the doctrine of allegiance, it is unlikely that Bingham was referencing natural allegiance or that which is possessed by citizens at birth, for he
stated citizenship by birth applied to all free persons that are "domiciled."
Thus, it is likely Bingham was referring to allegiance in terms of temporary or
local allegiance, which requires full obedience and submission to the laws of
the nation as the condition of protection. It is an interpretation that finds support after reading the rest of Bingham's speech. He confirmed numerous times
that birthright citizenship extended to those "free inhabitants, born and *domiciled* within the United States."[137] In these latter instances, Bingham did not
reference the doctrine of allegiance, but that this does not displace the doctrine
was universally understood. In fact, in a speech three years later Bingham confirmed his acceptance of the doctrine when debating emancipation within the
District of Columbia:

> I undertake to say, by the decision of your Federal tribunals, that women—that
> all the women of this Republic born upon the soil—are citizens of the United
> States.... The Constitution leaves no room for doubt upon this subject. The
> words "natural-born citizen of the United States" occur in it.... Who are the *nat-
> ural-born citizens* but those born in the Republic? Those born within the Repub-
> lic, whether black or white, are citizens by birth—natural born citizens ... all
> other persons born within the Republic, of parents *owing allegiance* to no other
> sovereignty, are natural born citizens. Gentlemen can find no exception to this
> statement touching natural-born citizens except what is said in the Constitution
> in relation to Indians. The reason why that exception was made in the Constitu-
> tion is apparent to everybody. The several Indian tribes were recognized at the
> organization of this Government as independent sovereignties. They were treated
> with as such; and they have been dealt with by the Government ever since as sep-
> arate sovereignties. Therefore, they were excluded from the general rule.[138]

Taken altogether, Bingham's statements only further undermine those
scholars who claim the framers of the Fourteenth Amendment intended for
citizenship by birth to apply to all persons in the territorial United States,
except for the children of Indians, diplomatic officials, and foreign military
personnel. Certainly, on its face, such an interpretation of the Citizenship
Clause offers a viable historical theory. But once the evidentiary record is
unpacked and placed into historical context, the complexities of citizenship
by birth in the nineteenth century cannot be so easily cast aside or rewritten.
To borrow once more from historian Robert E. Mensel on this subject: "Nineteenth century citizenship and subjecthood cannot be understood without a
grasp of the concept of allegiance. Allegiance was the link between subject
and sovereign that created the obligations of each to the other."[139]

Therefore, if we apply the aforementioned historical evidence to the third option of employing conflicting history under the historical guidepost approach—choosing conflict where there is conflict—it must be concluded the Citizenship Clause was not an absolute guarantee of citizenship by birth with no exceptions. The language "subject to the jurisdiction thereof" was viewed as a phrase of limitation that may take into consideration such factors as allegiance, domicile, and being a member of the political community. While detractors will continue to claim no one interpreted the Citizenship Clause in such terms, they are intently ignoring the rich historical evidence following the ratification of the Fourteenth Amendment. Take for example Margaret Stock, who has claimed the State Department "never interpreted" the Citizenship Clause in a manner that would deny citizenship to persons born in the territorial United States.[140] Stock comes to this conclusion without ever researching the claim. It is a common "law office history" mistake where an author declares history "X" or "Y" to be true, when in fact it is not.[141]

Throughout the nineteenth century the United States maintained lenient rules regarding immigration and naturalization. This public policy, however, did not negate the right of every sovereign nation to deny persons entry. It was a right the United States rarely enforced, but it was invoked from time to time. In the mid-nineteenth century, for example, the historical record shows United States' visas were denied to persons "whose loyalty to the Union ... has not the most complete and satisfactory evidence."[142] Affording citizenship to persons born in the United States was also fairly lenient. But here too there were instances where citizenship was denied to persons born in the United States on the grounds the parents were not domiciled or in the allegiance of the United States, even after the ratification of the Fourteenth Amendment. In order to clarify the rule of law on this point and prevent any international incidents, in 1874 the Department of State and Foreign Affairs Committee submitted a bill to define what constituted domicile and residence in order to acquire United States citizenship by birth, both abroad and in the territorial United States.[143]

The bill came at the recommendation of President Ulysses S. Grant, and its purpose was to "mark out and define when and how expatriation can be accomplished."[144] Grant acknowledged that the Fourteenth Amendment, once and for all, extinguished the "feudal doctrine of perpetual allegiance," yet pleaded to Congress that there remained international disagreement as to when foreign citizenship attached or United States citizenship was lost.[145] Thus, there remained disagreement as to when temporary allegiance attached or there was sufficient personal subjection for birthright citizenship to vest.

Multiple times, in 1873, members of president's cabinet defined the constitutional scope of the Fourteenth Amendment in this regard. The first occurred in response to an application for a United States passport. Secretary of State Hamilton Fish wrote that citizenship attaches "by reason of birth within the jurisdiction of the United States, or by reason of naturalization therein."[146] Both cases required a "personal subjection to their jurisdiction" in order for citizenship to vest, and "make the constitutional right complete."[147] Fish later confirmed this interpretation in a letter to President Grant, writing, "The fourteenth amendment of the Constitution makes personal subjection to the jurisdiction of the United States an element of citizenship."[148] Fish concurred with the drafters that the "child born of alien parents in the United States is held to be a citizen thereof," but this was understood to only vest on the tacit condition of "personal subjection."[149]

In 1873, former Oregon Senator George H. Williams, who voted both in favor of the 1866 Civil Rights Act and Fourteenth Amendment, came to a similar understanding as United States attorney general.[150] The word "jurisdiction," Williams wrote to President Grant, "must be understood to mean absolute or complete jurisdiction, such as the United States had over its citizens before the adoption of this amendment."[151] He recognized that aliens were "subject to the United States only to a limited extent."[152] Hence, "in the absence of treaties and legislation by Congress" on the subject, the rules of allegiance and personal subjection were "to be drawn from writers upon international and public law, who do not always agree, and therefore it will be difficult for Government to act upon any such rules without a chance of controversy."[153]

It is for these reasons that the Foreign Relations Committee sought to adopt uniform standards for vesting citizenship by birth.[154] The bill was authored by Massachusetts Representative Ebenezer R. Hoar, a former Massachusetts state judge and United States attorney general who had failed in his nomination to the Supreme Court.[155] The bill defined the terms "domicile" and "reside" as "implying a fixed residence at a particular place, with direct or presumptive proof of an intent to remain indefinitely."[156] The definition applied to both United States citizens living abroad and immigrants in the territorial United States. In terms of the latter, the following rule was prescribed:

> [A] child born within the United States of parents who are not citizens, and who do not reside within the United States, and who are not subject to the jurisdiction of the United States, shall not be regarded as a citizen thereof, unless such child shall reside in the United States, or unless his or her father, or in case of death of the father his or her mother, shall be naturalized during the minority of such child, or such child shall within six months after becoming of age file in the Department of State, in such form and with such proof as shall be prescribed by the Secretary of State, a written declaration of election to become such citizens, or shall become naturalized under general laws.[157]

What makes this provision of such importance is that it conditioned citizenship on the tenets of allegiance and domicile. In particular the provision disqualified from citizenship the children of immigrant parents temporarily present. Indeed, the bill provided numerous exceptions to this general rule, but these exceptions were only intended to reciprocate the rules that the United States applied to its own citizens abroad.[158] Those that opposed the bill mainly took issue with the distinctions made between native and naturalized citizens, and there were virtually no claims the bill violated the Citizenship Clause.[159] In fact, the *Boston Daily Globe* endorsed the bill as "properly" excepting "a child born within the United States of parents who are neither residents, nor have been naturalized during its minority."[160] Meanwhile, other newspaper accounts merely summarized the debate proceedings and provided no commentary as to its constitutionality under the Fourteenth Amendment.[161] Throughout the debates, only one person questioned congressional authority in this regard. On the third day, New York Representative Robert S. Hale prepared a long speech attacking the bill on numerous grounds. Hale's primary objection was that of other opponents; the bill treated citizens born abroad differently than those born in the United States.[162] Hale's second objection was the bill conflicted with the duties of government in terms of international norms.[163] He then objected on the grounds of the Fourteenth Amendment: "The general rule is that every person born within a sovereignty is by birth a subject of that sovereignty.... This rule has no respect to the circumstances under which the person may have been born, or the status of the parents at the time of his birth; whether the father of the child born here is permanently domiciled within our borders, or is here for temporary and commercial purposes, or is a mere visitor or a casual traveler within our boundaries. If the child is born within the United States, by that birth he is a citizen of the United States."[164]

Those scholars who support a broad interpretation of the Fourteenth Amendment may claim this is why the bill was never put to vote. However, this conclusion does not find support in the legislative record. No one else on the House floor objected to Hoar's bill on this ground. The bill was debated for four days, and opponents emphasized their disfavor on the grounds of distinction between naturalized and born citizens, not unequivocal birthright citizenship. In defense of the bill, Hoar stated it determined "who shall be regarded as citizens, in order that there may not be any question" further on the subject.[165] To quell the fears of those who thought the bill took United States citizenship away from citizens abroad, Hoar stated: "We are not undertaking to take any man's citizenship away; but the United States have certain duties in regard to their citizens abroad. That provision of the Constitution does not take away the right of a citizen of the United States to become naturalized in a foreign country; it does not relate to it. Its object was to provide who should be citizens of the United States within its jurisdiction. [The Fourteenth Amendment's] object, in short, was to reverse the *Dred Scott* decision. That was the great purpose of it."[166]

Hoar's understanding of "jurisdiction" was based on notions of national sovereignty concerning foreign affairs, immigration, and citizenship, not mere legal jurisdiction. To prevent foreign embarrassments, the bill's supporters, including the president's cabinet, hoped to finally settle the terms of residency for purposes of citizenship, both at home and abroad. Even after the bill was withdrawn for revisions, the main objection to the bill remained the same in that it deprived American citizens of jurisdiction after two years of residing abroad. Pennsylvania Congressman Leonard Myers, an opponent of the bill, was happy to see the bill withdrawn, yet attested to its legitimate purpose: "The very able replies of the Cabinet, with the documents appended ... for the most valuable collection upon expatriation, naturalization, *domicile,* and *citizenship* we have.... I say, therefore, that no question ever came more legitimately before a committee, and none better deserves to occupy the attention, challenging nevertheless, as it should, the closest scrutiny."[167]

Myers also agreed with Secretary of State Hamilton Fish that "personal subjection"[168] was an element of the Fourteenth Amendment: "Jurisdiction is but another word for sovereignty."[169] This sovereignty required the United States to protect its citizens abroad absent an avowal or act removing their allegiance, but it also required allegiance or personal subjection with the intent of domicile from those within its territorial jurisdiction. Unfortunately, the lack of any legislation defining residency or domicile proved problematic for the Department of State in adjudicating United States citizenship claims moving forward. Ebenezer Hoar's bill sought to remedy the different outcomes affected by treaties, international law, and the doctrine of allegiance, but proved to be too burdensome on United States citizens domiciled abroad. Thus, absent congressional guidance, the Department of State continued its practice of adjudicating United States citizenship claims on a case by case basis.

One such case was that of Ludwig Hausding, who was born of persons "temporarily in the United States," yet never dwelled nor applied for citizenship in the United States.[170] Given these facts, Secretary of State Frederick Theodore Frelinghuysen knew Ludwig could only assert citizenship on the ground of birth in the United States. However, Frelinghuysen found the legal claim to be "untenable, for by Section 1992, Revised Statutes, it is made a condition of citizenship by birth that the person be not subject to any foreign power."[171] Frelinghuysen elaborated: "Sections 1992 and 1993 of the Revised

Statutes clearly show the extent of existing legislation: that the fact of birth, under circumstances implying *alien subjection,* establishes of itself no right of citizenship; and that the citizenship of a person so born is to be acquired in some legitimate manner through the operation of statute."[172]

Frelinghuysen's mention of "alien subjection" is important because it denotes that Hausding's parents had not personally subjected themselves to the jurisdiction of the United States as to qualify for his citizenship. Hausding's case was not the only one to rest on qualifications of personal subjection, residence, or allegiance. In 1885, former Democrat Kentucky representative and current United States ambassador Boyd Winchester wrote to Secretary of State Thomas F. Bayard on the matter of Richard Greisser, who desired papers to establish American citizenship.[173] The facts stipulated that in 1869 Greisser was born of two non-citizen parents in Delaware, Ohio, but was removed to Switzerland within a year. Neither Greisser nor his family ever returned to the United States, yet he sought "citizenship on the ground of being born in the United States."[174] However, Winchester did not view the Fourteenth Amendment as unequivocally granting citizenship to everyone born in the United States. Instead, Winchester found the "precedents and instructions" to be "so unsatisfactory and conflicting" that he "declined to do anything until specially instructed from the Department."[175] On the one hand, he read State Department precedent as granting a "right of election of citizenship on arriving at maturity" to persons born in the United States.[176] On the other, Winchester found authorities vesting citizenship according to the nationality of the father.[177] If he had to choose an interpretation, however, Winchester found it to be "intimated, if not expressly held, that there should be a personal subjection to the jurisdiction of the United States to complete and maintain [a person's] character of or claim of citizenship."[178]

Bayard replied to Winchester that "on general principles of international law I do not consider ... Richard Greisser ... a citizen of the United States."[179] Bayard had "no doubt" that Greisser was born in the United States, but the facts presented made him "subject to a foreign power" and "not subject to the jurisdiction of the United States."[180] Again, the Department of State's reliance on international law in this instance was deemed necessary given the absence of congressional legislation. The statutes did not prescribe any right of election, thus Bayard felt he must follow international precedent and grant citizenship if Greisser had remained in the country. At the same time, however, Bayard acknowledged that any rules concerning citizenship by birth could be superseded by legislation when he acknowledged the 1866 Civil Rights Act as a constitutional exercise as to whom is "subject to the jurisdiction thereof."[181]

A year later, Bayard again referred to the international rules respecting

election to adjudicate the citizenship of Friedrich de Bourry, who had been
born in New York on December 4, 1862, of Austrian parents temporarily resident:

> It is not claimed that his father was ever naturalized, or made the requisite decla-
> ration of his intention to become a citizen of the United States, or in any way sig-
> nified his intention formally to abjure his Austrian allegiance. Nor is it pretended
> that ... the present memorialist arrived at full age, he took any steps to make or
> record his election of citizenship in the United States.... Under these circum-
> stances it is not necessary for me to consider the question whether Friedrich de
> Bourry was, at the time of his birth, a citizen of the United States under the natu-
> ralization statutes and the fourteenth amendment of the Constitution of the
> United States.[182]

The right of election to citizenship was never part of our Anglo-American
tradition. It developed as an international norm in the mid to late nineteenth
century, and in terms of statutory law, the United States maintained no rules
pertaining to the subject. Indeed, Ebenezer Hoar's 1874 bill sought to codify
a right to election to certain classes. However, the bill's defeat left the secretary
of state to adjudicate United States citizenship on a case by case basis according
to international precedent.

Take for instance a query from the Belgium government as to whether
all persons born "upon the soil" were citizens of the United States.[183] Bayard
replied that both the 1866 Civil Rights Act and Fourteenth Amendment controlled but found the issue was a bit more complicated than mere birth in the
United States: "[Q]uestions arising thereunder must be considered upon the
facts presented in actual cases in which a ruling becomes necessary, giving due
heed to the general principle that the right of election of citizenship commonly
pertains to the individual himself on becoming *sui juris*," or upon their consent
and being competent.[184] ONE WHO HAS FULL RIGHTS

Once again, Bayard relied on the international rules respecting election
to determine United States citizenship. He also acknowledged that any "subsequent" statutes in time would control future determinations, implying that
"subject to the jurisdiction thereof" gave Congress flexibility in defining which
alien classes qualified.[185]

When William F. Wharton assumed the position of secretary of state, he
too implied Congress was not foreclosed from legislating which alien classes
were "subject to the jurisdiction thereof." In 1891, Wharton wrote to F.D.
Grant that "[t]here has not been a little diversity of opinion as to the scope
to be given to the words 'not subject to any foreign power'" in the 1866 Civil
Rights Act.[186] Wharton conveyed confidence that a "diplomatic officer" fell
within the exception, for "the 'children of ambassadors' form an exception to

the rules as to persons being born in the allegiance of a sovereign who are born on this soil."[187] Wharton's reference to allegiance once again confirms how legal commentators perceived the doctrine to be implicit with the Citizenship Clause. Citizenship by birth required something more than being subject to the laws.

It is in this context one should read the Supreme Court's references to allegiance and domicile in *Wong Kim Ark*. In the late nineteenth century, the two legal premises of allegiance and domicile were viewed as operating in conjunction. By establishing lawful domicile, with the intent to remain, the requisite allegiance for citizenship by birth attached to the parents in accordance with international law.[188] However, if domicile was not established, the person did not possess the necessary allegiance to be within the complete jurisdiction of the United States. This understanding of domicile and allegiance was the dominant view in the late nineteenth century and often restated by commentators. In 1880 for instance, Samuel T. Spear wrote on the importance of residence and the Fourteenth Amendment. First, Spear addressed Section 2 and its definition of "persons" for purposes of apportionment. Spear agreed with Timothy Farrar that "*persons* are meant *resident persons,* inhabitants within the boundaries of a state."[189] To state it another way, apportionment did not apply to persons merely present in the United States. They needed to be residents or accepted members of the polity. Not surprisingly, Spear applied the same rule of law to the subject of citizenship by birth. In Spear's words, the "political significance which attaches to the place of birth grows out of the fact that is usually accompanied with *subjection to the jurisdiction* and taken to indicate the jurisdiction to which the person is subject."[190] It all boiled down to domicile: "'Domicile is residence as a final abode. To constitute it, there must be: 1, residence, actual or inchoate; 2, the non-existence of any intention to make domicile elsewhere.' ... The *animus manendi* [or intention of remaining to acquire domicile] is the chief point ... and distinguishes a legal residence, or one that involves citizenship, from a temporary or transient occupancy which carries with it no change of citizenship."[191]

Lawyer, intellectual, and former United States ambassador William L. Scruggs offered a similar take on domicile, allegiance, and citizenship by birth. To Scruggs, the Citizenship Clause reversed the "Jefferson order of allegiance" from state to federal sovereignty, and codified the English common law touching upon citizenship by birth, but on the caveat that "personal subjection to our jurisdiction" remained an "element of citizenship."[192] In other words, Scruggs interpreted the Citizenship Clause as neither embodying a pure "test by place of birth, nor that by the nationality of the parent, without important qualifications."[193] It was the lack of congressional guidance as to who was and was not "subject to the jurisdiction" of the United States that vexed Scruggs and his fellow diplomats: "How or under what circumstances a citizen may be deemed to have changed his allegiance, and to have obliterated all obligations resulting from his previous allegiance, has been among the vexed questions connected with our administration of foreign affairs."[194]

If one follows the congressional debates of the 1866 Civil Right Act and Citizenship Clause, the answer is the establishment of lawful domicile or when persons become part of the political jurisdiction as to qualify for representation. But even this answer proved unsatisfactory throughout the late nineteenth century, for the Department of State was forced to resort to international principles to define who had, in fact, established the requisite domicile for citizenship by to vest.

Irving Berdine Richman was another late nineteenth century intellectual who interpreted the Citizenship Clause as an affirmation of common law principles that ultimately rested on establishing domicile. The author of numerous histories, Richman may have provided the first historical analysis on the Citizenship Clause, often quoting members of the Thirty-Ninth Congress at length.[195] While recognizing the different opinions among the courts and scholars, Richman believed the "great weight of opinion" supported the notion that "citizenship of the United States was not created but simply declared by the Fourteenth Amendment."[196] This meant that aspects of both the English common law and international law applied.[197] Therefore, the children of "visiting" or "non-resident" foreigners could be constitutionally excluded from citizenship: "'[C]itizenship' and 'state membership' being convertible terms, the citizenship of a parent may truthfully be said to attach immediately at birth to a child born out of the jurisdiction of the parent's state; for by a temporary absence from his state an individual manifestly does not lose his membership therein."[198]

Perhaps the most forthright intellectual to take up the constitutional scope of the Citizenship Clause was the United States Chief Justice of the Samoa Islands Henry C. Ide. He posed the question: "[D]oes not the very fact of birth in our country render one 'subject to the jurisdiction thereof' and 'not subject to any foreign power?'"[199] Ide recognized the constitutional tradition of *jus soli* over *jus sanguinis* citizenship, yet also understood the importance of domicile as a means to define the former according to the tenets of allegiance:

> When does the new principle of place of birth begin to extinguish the nationality? When does it complete that destruction and itself assume full sway and clothe the descendant with the new citizenship? It is no answer to say that the child is born with the stamp of his father's nationality upon him. He is likewise

born with the stamp of his father's actual domicile and intention never to renew or recognize his former allegiance and to adhere to the new one. Which is the more indelible and controlling? Ultimately the latter controls in all cases. According to our national theories, as expounded in our foreign relations and as suited to our conditions, the new stamp is controlling from the first birth in the new country, not from the second or later generations.

But the question of domicile is important in this connection [of *jus soli* citizenship]. *One born of parents temporarily in our country is not born with the stamp of domicile and intention to reside here. Those are two elements of jurisdiction wanting.*[200]

The question that lingered is what constituted as domicile. Again, according to statements by members of Congress who debated the 1866 Civil Rights Act, the Citizenship Clause, and the failed 1874 expatriation bill, the matter could be legislated on. It is an understanding that Ide agreed with on the grounds of United States sovereignty and international law. "[W]here an alien is actually domiciled in our country, fixed for life as an inhabitant," wrote Ide, "his original nationality is so far weakened that our institutions ought not to consent that its inanimate shadow shall rest upon his offspring and deprive them of the inherent rights which are theirs by birth."[201]

This brings us to the last prominent intellectual to interpret the Citizenship Clause in terms of allegiance, domicile, and personal subjection, Boyd Winchester. In 1885, as a United States ambassador, Winchester acknowledged the competing interpretations of "subject to the jurisdiction," and concluded it must require some form of "personal subjection."[202] Twelve years later and removed from political service, Winchester maintained the Citizenship Clause did not grant citizenship to everyone within the territorial and legal jurisdiction of the United States: "The United States claim all persons born within their territory as native born citizens, whatever may have been the nationality of their parents. There are, however, exceptions to this rule, resulting from the requirement of *personal subjection* to the "jurisdiction thereof"—(of the United States). This excludes Indians, the children of foreign diplomatic representatives born within the limits of the United States, and the *children of persons passing through or temporarily residing in this country.*"[203]

Winchester supported the exclusion of temporary resident immigrants and sojourners on the grounds of domicile and allegiance. "Family domicile is the factor of prime importance," wrote Winchester, when determining *jus soli* citizenship, and is the "great defect" of *jus sanguinis* citizenship.[204] He admitted there were differing internationalist theories as to when domicile attached,[205] but acknowledged the doctrine of allegiance still applied in order for the full protection of the nation to vest, including any rights to citizenship: "Citizenship is an attribute of national sovereignty and not merely of individual or local existence. It is a sacred right, full of grave consequences, granted with solemn formalities, and its existence should always be *well defined* and *indisputable.*"[206]

Modern scholars who support a broad, all encompassing view of the Citizenship Clause may argue this commentary preceded the Supreme Court's decision in *Wong Kim Ark* and is therefore historically insignificant. Modern scholars may also claim that since *Wong Kim Ark*, the subject of citizenship by birth was generally understood as applying to all persons born in the territorial and legal jurisdiction of the United States. Rachel E. Rosenbloom recently advanced this line of argument in an article exploring how, in the twentieth century, any restrictive interpretations of the Citizenship Clause were intimately tied in with exclusionist immigration politics.[207] "*Wong Kim Ark* may have settled the doctrinal questions regarding the scope of the Citizenship Clause," writes Rosenbloom, "but it did not quell the political fervor surrounding the issue."[208]

Rosenbloom is indeed correct to note that, throughout much of the twentieth century, immigration exclusionists sought to tailor the Citizenship Clause to meet their political goals, but she and others would be wrong to assume *Wong Kim Ark* settled all matters pertaining to persons born within the United States. A number of commentators read *Wong Kim Ark* as affording citizenship by birth to the children of immigrants domiciled in the United States. However, the decision did not answer whether the children of immigrants temporarily resident fell under the scope of the Citizenship Clause. The same can be said for any immigrants excluded or denied entry into the United States. Were their children intended to be under the umbrella of the Citizenship Clause?

It is a historical point of emphasis that before and after *Wong Kim Ark,* the Department of State was facing problems associated with dual allegiance and citizenship.[209] Thus in terms of United States constitutional jurisprudence, much remained unsettled as to whether citizenship by birth applied to the children of immigrants temporarily resident or sojourning in the United States. What the evidentiary record does convey is the law of nations distinguished between the status of immigrants temporarily present and permanently domiciled. Moreover, it was unquestionably within the sovereign right of each nation to define the terms of allegiance, settlement, and citizenship.[210] As John Hopkins University political science professor W.W. Willoughby observed in 1907:

> In the interest of peace, and for mutual convenience and self-interest, certain more or less definite rights and responsibilities have been recognized to belong and attach to every independent political power. Chief and fundamental among

these international principles thus developed is that according to which it is held that some one governing power is held to have general control over each portion of the earth's territory, and, reciprocally, is held ultimately responsible for what occurs there.

The government which claims the right of jurisdiction is presumed to have the power to exercise it effectively, and in no case is it permitted by other power to plead a *non possumus* either because of lack of physical force, or because of peculiarity of constitutional structure. In the international world, nations are not concerned with the legal legitimacy, but with the actual ability of a government to fulfill its international obligations.[211]

Here, Willoughby provides insight as to how jurisdiction and allegiances overlapped by the turn of the twentieth century. Just as the United States could claim the citizenship of persons born of its own citizens overseas, foreign nations could also claim the citizenship of persons born of their citizens. But this created a number of international disputes in terms of obligations and duties, both by the nations involved and its citizens. During this period, the law of nations dictated that persons born of immigrants temporarily resident or sojourning did not satisfy the requisite allegiance for citizenship by birth to attach.[212] This is not to say, however, that a nation could not exercise its sovereignty and make such persons citizens at birth. But the opposite proposition held true as well, meaning any nation, to include the United States, could have excluded certain classes of immigrants from falling with its jurisdiction, whether it be through legislation or treaty. This in turn diminished any number of international disputes from dual military obligations to dual taxation. What it all boiled down to was sovereignty and the willingness of the respective nation or nations to exercise it.

Today we are far removed from the political world of the late nineteenth and early twentieth centuries. Thus, it is easy for modern commentators to read the Citizenship Clause and "subject to the jurisdiction thereof" as mere legal or territorial jurisdiction. To do so, however, is to read one's own predilections into the past, rather than understanding the past according to its terms. It must be remembered that the Fourteenth Amendment was ratified at a time where it was not only important to secure the citizenship of Freedman from state encroachment, but also to prevent foreign conflicts and embarrassments.[213] If one relies on modern notions of textualism and originalism, these contextual aspects of history are easily overlooked. For commentators who rely on textualism and originalism, the language of the Citizenship Clause is plain and clear—"subject to the jurisdiction" means "subject to the legal jurisdiction." In terms late nineteenth-century legal vocabulary, it is indisputable that the word "jurisdiction" was often understood as being subject to the legal jurisdiction or the civil and criminal jurisdiction. However, the word "juris-

The Citizenship Clause and Historical Guideposts—Step Two

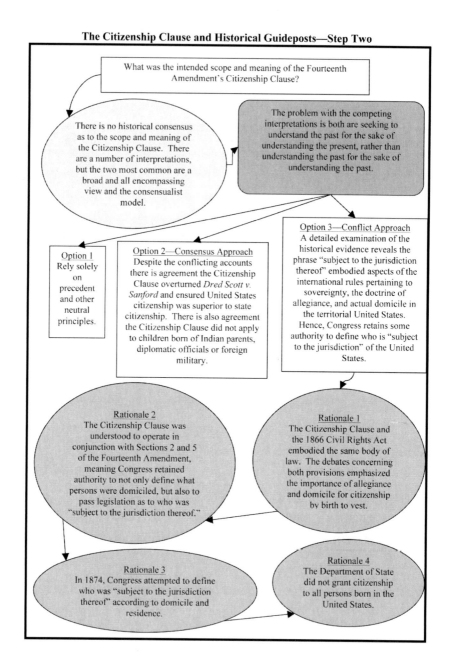

diction" also denoted the larger premise of national sovereignty, meaning the United States, like other nations, retained its sovereign right to determine what foreigners may domicile within its territory and retained the necessary allegiance to be "subject to the jurisdiction thereof." And there is no indication, from either the debates of the 1866 Civil Rights Act or the Citizenship Clause, the drafters and ratifiers of the Fourteenth Amendment intended to relinquish United States sovereignty. If anything, the evidentiary record suggests the opposite.

Therefore, if one proceeds down the historical guidepost approach, upon reaching the conflicting views concerning the Citizenship Clause, there are two interpretational options available. If one chooses the second option—choosing consensus where there is conflict—it is safe to conclude the historical record conveys the Citizenship Clause was ratified to overturn *Dred Scott v. Sanford* and ensure United States citizenship was superior to any notions of state citizenship. There is also agreement among scholars that the Citizenship Clause did not apply to children born of Indian parents, diplomatic officials or foreign military. But if we proceed to the third option—choosing conflict where there is conflict—the historical inquiry concludes the phrase "subject to the jurisdiction thereof" cannot conceivably be interpreted as being synonymous with mere legal jurisdiction. It embodied something more consistent with the international rules pertaining to sovereignty, the doctrine of allegiance, and actual domicile in the territorial United States. What this means is Congress retains some latitude to define who is in fact "subject to the jurisdiction" of the United States. Of course, if one proceeds to the third option, this does not overturn the Supreme Court's decisions in *Elk v. Wilkins* and *Wong Kim Ark*. The historical guidepost approach simply provides a historical foundation from which to determine those unanswered constitutional questions identified at the beginning of this chapter, such as, what is the citizenship of a child born to immigrant parents that are only temporarily present or traveling in the United States? Is the Fourteenth Amendment's Citizenship Clause triggered in such cases? Does the answer change if one of the parents is a United States citizen? And how do the answers to these questions apply to today's present dilemma of unlawful immigration?

Again, it is worth noting the historical guidepost approach does not seek to use history as an outcome-determinative tool. It merely lays an accurate and legitimate historical foundation from which to legally reason. For instance, let's say we take the path of choosing consensus where there is conflict, and at issue is a federal statute that expressly denies citizenship to children born of immigrant parents not domiciled, to include the children of unlawfully present immigrants because they have not personally subjected themselves to the jurisdiction of the United States. Even applying the broader historical foundation surrounding the Citizenship Clause, one still has to weigh and consider the differences between the past and the present, tradition, and the purposes and consequences of any respective interpretation. In terms of tradition, the language of the Citizenship Clause and corresponding federal statute have mirrored one another since 1940.[214] During this period, no one born in the territorial United States, excluding the children of Indians, diplomatic officers, and foreign military, has been denied citizenship at birth. This tradition certainly weighs in favor of striking down any statute denying citizenship. But one must also consider the purposes and consequences of this choice. On the one hand, to strike down the federal statute would mean undermining or stripping the United States of its sovereignty, which may have jurisprudential consequences for other statutes that distinguish between immigrant classes. On the other hand, to uphold the statute would arguably lead to unforeseen burdens such as statelessness.

Even if we take the path of "choosing conflict where there is conflict," one cannot neglect considerations like tradition or the purposes and consequences of any respective interpretation. Undoubtedly in the case of choosing conflict where there is conflict, the historical foundation from which to reason is more instructive. In the late nineteenth century, domicile, allegiance, and personal subjection were all understood as requirements for citizenship by birth to vest. Given the hypothetical statute only denies United States citizenship to the children of parents that do not meet these late nineteenth-century requirements, the statute seemingly passes constitutional muster. At the same time, however, it must be acknowledged the United States has never denied citizenship by birth in such broad terms. Thus, here again we are faced with considering the purposes and consequences of upholding or striking down the statute. No matter the legal question pertaining to the scope of the Fourteenth Amendment and citizenship by birth, historical consciousness requires more than honestly marshaling the past. It also includes applying the past to the present responsibly, which requires the interpreter to take into account a number of factors and reason accordingly.[215]

Epilogue

This book explored the subject of history in law in great detail. In doing so a number of lessons were learned, particularly the difficulty in producing a thorough, well-researched, and objective historical foundation from which to legally reason. Another lesson is that performing the role of historian is not an easy task. While advocates of originalism and other historically based approaches to interpreting the Constitution will continue to argue history is history no matter who writes it, there is a distinction between claiming proposition "X" or "Y" is true through *ad hoc* methodologies and proving it through accepted historical methodologies. This was illustrated in a number of examples such as federal-state immigration powers, the freedom of the press, the carrying of firearms outside the home for individual self-defense, and citizenship by birth, just to name a few. There are indeed others, but the point to be made is that any interpretational approach's legitimacy rests on its ability to produce accurate results. This includes originalism. Still, originalists will argue originalism brings us closer to the framers' Constitution than any other interpretational approach available, and it is an approach that does not require the assistance of professional historians. It is argued, if anything, legal professionals are better suited for the task, given their training in the interpretation of legal texts. In the words of Georgetown law professor and originalist Randy E. Barnett:

> [L]awyers are experts in identifying the meaning of language in legal context; historians are not and, to their credit, don't even try (unless they are submitting amicus briefs to the Supreme Court). In addition to describing past events, historians are particularly interested in explaining why what happened in the past happened, why people did what they did; as a result, they are very concerned with identifying motives, or other causal influences. Historians have no particular interest in the meaning of authoritative legal texts, unless they are legal historians who are very often also lawyers. The fact that a legal text is old sometimes makes the identification of meaning more difficult, but far

from impossible in most cases. For one thing, the meaning of language hasn't changed that much....

If it was genuinely not possible to identify the meaning of language at a previous point in time, then old contracts could not be enforced according to their meaning at the time of their formation (which is what the law of contracts requires), old statutes would be a mystery and impossible to follow or enforce, and classic Supreme Court opinions would be impossible to understand. The only language that is claimed to be inscrutable mystery to lawyers (but not historians) is the foundational law provided by the U.S. Constitution. How are we lawyers able to follow the 200 [plus] year-old-opinions in *Marbury, Gibbons* and *McCulloch,* but not the Constitution itself, written a mere 30–40 years earlier? Has anyone seriously suggested that lawyers need to consult historians to tell them the communicative content of these precedents?

The reason for claiming that the Constitution alone among legal texts is inaccessible to lawyers is not that its original communicative content is unclear, but that *some* of its original meaning is all too clear and some people don't like it, so it must be gotten rid of somehow. The Progressives were very candid about this, referring to the "Horse-and-Buggy" Constitution. They knew what it meant, but it got in their way. So, for better or worse, the written opinions of long dead New Deal and Warren Court Justices have replaced important parts of the written text of the Constitution. You don't need to be a historian to know there's a difference in meaning between the two sources of law, but it helps to be a lawyer.[1]

Barnett's preference for legal professionals over historians when interpreting the Constitution is commonplace among originalists.[2] However, it remains unclear why it is acceptable for the legal community to make claims about history, yet it is unacceptable for historians to make claims about the law, at a particular point in time that they are experts in, by employing historical methodologies. According to Barnett, we should accept this double standard because the Constitution's language has not changed that much in two hundred years and legal professionals are better trained to interpret legal texts. This is certainly news to intellectual historians who specialize in the interpretation of texts, to include their philosophical origins, meaning, and influence in the public discourse, politics, and law. More importantly though, as has been discussed and illustrated throughout this book, the employment of historical methodologies provides a much higher standard than what is being offered by originalists. The former requires substantiated evidence and eliciting context to the greatest detail, while the latter is rooted in what the writer can make the text mean.

But even if Barnett is correct and the meaning of the Constitution's text has not changed that much, the overarching body of law existing at a particular time, to include the culture and society with which it operates, has changed substantially. One cannot merely extract those legal principles and lessons one likes and discard the others. This is what makes history in law such a contentious topic among historians, for originalists want to carry forward those portions of the past they agree with and are more analogous to their own beliefs. Even Barnett is not immune from this criticism. Take for instance, Barnett's "presumption of liberty" when weighing the constitutionality of legislative acts.[3] Barnett opines: "[I]f the purpose of recognizing property rights is to permit people to put their personal and local knowledge into action in pursuit of happiness, peace, and prosperity, then they should be able to use their rightfully owned resources in any manner they wish. Only in this way will they be able to put their knowledge into action; and no third party will usually know better than they how to do this. At a minimum, this suggests that freedom of action is to be presumed rightful and that any constraints on this freedom require justification."[4]

As a matter of modern individual political virtue there are no problems with Barnett's presumption. However, as a matter of eighteenth-century constitutionalism and political thought, the presumption is void of historical context, for Barnett's thesis is almost solely reliant on a modern libertarian perception of Locke's writings. Take for instance this passage from Barnett's work entitled *Restoring the Lost Constitution*:

> Locke ... claimed whatever liberty or powers are given up when one enters society are given up ... only with an intention in everyone the better to preserve himself and his Liberty and Property.... "The power of the Society, of *Legislative* constituted by them, can never be suppos'd to extend farther than the common good." Locke distinguished the two powers that were given up, either entirely (the executive power) or to be regulated by law (the power of self-preservation), from a third species of natural rights that he does not claim a person surrenders upon entering civil society or upon forming government. The third species is "the liberty he has of innocent Delights." We might also call this the right to the *pursuit of happiness*. Provided that such pursuits do not unjustly interfere with the rights of others, the civil authority has no role in the prohibition or even the regulation of "innocent Delights."[5]

Indeed, Locke was highly influential among members of the founding generation, but historians have long understood that Locke's writings do not provide the sole or primary answer in tracing the legal origins and meaning of the "pursuit of happiness."[6] Locke was just one of infinite sources read by the founding generation and often too much weight is placed on Locke's work as the instrument of American constitutionalism. This does not mean that Locke's understanding of *happiness* is without some merit. As historian Darrin M. McMahon informs us, happiness in both the Lockean liberal and classical republican form "most likely coexisted in [Jefferson's] mind and even overlapped."[7] In terms of eighteenth-century American constitutionalism, Lockean liberalism is reflected in constitutional rights or what McMahon refers to as barriers "against the governments, institutions, and individuals that invariably [seek] to impede our natural due."[8] Meanwhile, the classical republican view of happiness, this being a society based upon the consent of the governed, is reflected in the democratic structure of American constitutionalism. It is a model that links civic virtue and the advancement of the public good to the happiness of society.

Where Barnett's historical analysis falters is it misapplies Lockean liberalism, and also mischaracterizes what constituted the "common good" or "public good" in late eighteenth-century constitutionalism. Barnett claims that the common or public good embodied a legal presumption of liberty. Thus, "like the Constitution itself," Barnett writes that the presumption of liberty is "a means to the end of achieving justice—which itself is a means to facilitating the pursuit of happiness by each person living in society with others."[9] But once the evidentiary record is unpacked and the text is placed in the constraints of historical context, Barnett's interpretation cannot survive.[10] If anything, Barnett's take on history falls into the category of historical revisionism, for he views the ancient constitution with the impairment of modern influences.[11] It is a dilemma that resurfaces in other areas of history explored by Barnett such as the Second Amendment, given his strict adherence to the original meaning originalism.[12] Then there is Barnett's take on the Necessary and Proper Clause. Not only does Barnett overlook the influential writings of Alexander Addison, but he also omits James Iredell's broad view of the Necessary and Proper Clause while sitting on the Supreme Court bench.[13]

The point here is not to single out Barnett. He is just one of many originalists who proclaim originalist methodologies are superior to historical methodologies. Instead the point is to further illustrate how absurd it is for originalists to proclaim that legal professionals are better qualified to recover the Constitution's intentions, meaning, and purpose through textualist and originalist methodologies than historians are able to through historical methodologies. It is the equivalent of proclaiming product "X" is better than product "Y" without ever having used product "Y." The fact of the matter is most legal professionals, including originalists, have never been trained as historians. Therefore, when non-historically trained legal professionals, like Barnett, opine on the abilities of historians, they do so from an outsider's perspective. Personally, having been trained in both legal and historical methodologies, I can attest that the two professions are educated differently. The manner in which today's legal professionals are trained is based on notions of textualism and what the respective interpreter can make the text mean. It is about convincing others that proposition "X" is right and counter proposition "Y" is wrong. This is arguably why originalism remains so attractive to members of the legal profession. Its methodologies are familiar. The only caveat is that originalists are interpreting texts that are often centuries old. And one does not have to be familiar with history or historical methodologies to be an originalist. One just has to be proficient in interpreting texts.[14]

Although originalism has become a gravitational force to members of the legal professional, it has yet to garner acceptance among historians, and for good reason—it often leads to ahistorical results. Certainly there are instances where originalist findings run parallel with what the historical record provides. However, as this book illustrated many times over, originalism's focus on text is frequently at odds with the historical evidence. And seeing that history is the very core of originalism, whether its proponents want to admit it or not, it is absolutely mindboggling how originalists can proclaim constitutional accuracy and legitimacy when the results defy history in context.[15] This is not to say historical methodologies are not without their own deficiencies when it comes to interpreting the Constitution, but historical methodologies require a much heavier burden of proof and provide a stronger foundation from which to reason.

As to what role history should play when interpreting the Constitution is a separate matter. It is a debate that has been increasingly ongoing since the turn of the twentieth century. Those who subscribe to fixed constitutionalism, in one form or another, draw heavily from the dead hand of the past. Meanwhile, those who subscribe to living constitutionalism, in whatever form, place emphasis on precedent, and the purposes and consequences of a particular interpretation. This book contends both sides are right and wrong. The use of history in law is a time honored tradition, whether it is a historical event, tradition or custom. Each has been drawn upon, at one time or another, to provide a moral and philosophical guide to the law's development. But as this book argues, the dead hand of the past should be used sparingly as an outcome determinative tool. The fact remains that the society of today is not that of our ancestors. Moreover, except in a few cases, since the ratification of the Constitution, history has been used sparingly as an outcome-determinative tool. The purposes and consequences of any respective interpretation, including its relationship to precedent and custom, have played a much more vital role. Thus, much like history, this too must be given due consideration when interpreting the Constitution.

Notes

Chapter 1

1. For the social development of the American colonies in the eighteenth century, see Jack P. Greene, *Pursuits of Happiness: The Social Development of Early Modern British Colonies and the Formation of American Culture* 66–68, 90–91, 125–27, 144–45, 187–88 (Chapel Hill: University of North Carolina Press, 1988).

2. For a classic study, see Bernard Bailyn, *Education in the Forming of American Society* (New York: W.W. Norton, 1972).

3. St. George Tucker, *View of the Constitution of the United States with Selected Writings* 44 (Clyde N. Wilson fwd., Indianapolis, IN: Liberty Fund, 1999).

4. For a history, see Daniel G. Lang, *Foreign Policy in the Early Republic: The Law of Nations and the Balance of Power* 67–163 (Baton Rouge: Louisiana State University Press, 1985).

5. The intended purpose of the Constitution's militia powers and the Second Amendment was to safeguard a well-regulated militia functioning in support of nation's interests. For a detailed history of the constitutional significance of a well-regulated militia in American thought, see Don Higginbothom, "The Federalized Militia Debate: A Neglected Aspect of Second Amendment Scholarship," 55 *William & Mary Quarterly* 39, 42–43 (1998); Patrick J. Charles, "The Constitutional Significance of a 'Well-Regulated' Militia Asserted and Proven with Commentary on the Future of Second Amendment Jurisprudence," 3 *Northeastern Law Journal* 1 (2011). For a detailed English history of the antistanding army ideology, see Lois G. Schwoerer, *No Standing Armies! The Anti-Army Ideology in Seventeenth Century England* (Baltimore: Johns Hopkins University Press, 1974).

6. This view of the Early Republic was often conveyed in charges to the grand jury. However, it was President George Washington's 1796 farewell address that had the largest influence. It was republished during times of national crisis and often used as persuasive political authority. *See, e.g.*, Francois Furstenberg, *In the Name of the Father: Washington's Legacy, Slavery, and the Making of a Nation* 1–12,

21–22, 34–45, 52–59, 74–78, 93–99, 156–60 (New York: Penguin Press, 2006).

7. Julius Goebel, Jr., "Constitutional History and Constitutional Law," 38 *Columbia Law Review* 555, 557 (1938).

8. Ibid. at 562.

9. Ibid.

10. Antonin Scalia and Bryan A. Garner, *Reading Law: The Interpretation of Legal Texts* 89 (St. Paul, MN: West, 2012) ("The conclusive argument in favor of originalism is a simple one: It is the *only objective standard* of interpretation even competing for acceptance") (emphasis added).

11. *See, e.g.*, Robert H. Bork, *The Tempting of America: The Political Seduction of the Law* 143–60 (New York: Free Press, 1997).

12. *See, e.g.*, Antonin Scalia, "Originalism: The Lesser Evil," 57 *University of Cincinnati Law Review* 849 (1989).

13. Randy Barnett, "The Original Meaning of the Commerce Clause," 68 *University of Chicago Law Review* 100, 105 (2001); Vasan Kesavan and Michael Stokes Paulsen, "The Interpretive Force of the Constitution's Secret Drafting History," 68 *Georgetown Law Journal* 1113, 1144–45 (2003).

14. For the beginnings of semantic originalism, see Ronald Dworkin, "Comment," in *A Matter of Interpretation: Federal Courts and the Law* 115, 119 (Princeton, NJ: Princeton University Press, 1997).

15. John O. McGinnis and Michael Rappaport, "Original Methods Originalism: A New Theory of Interpretation and the Case Against Construction," 103 *Northwestern University Law Review* 751, 753 (2009).

16. Ibid. at 786–801.

17. *See* Robert W. Gordon, "The Arrival of Critical Historicism," 49 *Stanford Law Review* 1023 (1997); Robert W. Gordon, "Historicism in Legal Scholarship," 90 *Yale Law Journal* 1017 (1981); Roger S. Ruffin, "The Constitution and the Dilemma of Historicism," 6 *San Diego Law Review* 171 (1969).

18. For a discussion, see William E. Nelson, "History and Neutrality in Constitutional Adjudication," 72 *Virginia Law Review* 1237 (1986).

19. For some discussions, see John Hart Ely, "Constitutional Interpretivism: Its Allure and Impossibility," 53 *Indiana Law Journal* 399 (1977); Mark V. Tushnet, "Following the Rules Laid Down: A Critique of Interpretivism and Neutral Principles," 96 *Harvard Law Review* 781 (1983); Raoul Berger, "Mark Tushnet's Critique of Interpretivism," 51 *George Washington Law Review* 532 (1983); Martin H. Redish, "Interpretivism and the Judicial Role in a Constitutional Democracy," 19 *Harvard Journal of Law and Public Policy* 525 (1996).

20. For some discussions, see Alfred H. Kelly, "Clio and the Court: An Illicit Love Affair," 1965 *Supreme Court Review* 119 (1965); Paul Murphy, "Time to Reclaim: The Current Challenge of American Constitutional History," 69 *The American Historical Review* 64 (1963).

21. For some discussions, see John Philip Reid, "Legal History," 1966 *Annual Survey of American Law* 669 (1966); William M. Wiecek, "Clio as Hostage: The United States Supreme Court and the Uses of History," 24 *California Western Law Review* 227 (1987).

22. For a historian's view on the use of history for constitutional interpretation before the rise of originalism, see G. Edward White, "The Arrival of History in Constitutional Scholarship," 88 *Virginia Law Review* 485 (2002). For an early critique of originalism from a historian's perspective, see Wiecek, "Clio as Hostage" at 266–68.

23. Cass Sunstein has referred to this as "hard originalism." *See* Cass Sunstein, "Five Theses on Originalism," 19 *Harvard Journal of Law and Public Policy* 311, 312 (1996).

24. Paul W. Kahn, *Legitimacy and History: Self-Government in American Constitutional Theory* 59 (New Haven, CT: Yale University Press, 1992).

25. Ibid.

26. For some critiques of originalism on this point, see Paul Finkelman, "The Constitution and the Intentions of the Framers: The Limits of Historical Analysis," 50 *University of Pittsburgh Law Review* 349 (1989); Saul Cornell, "The Original Meaning of Original Understanding: A Neo-Blackstonian Critique," 67 *Maryland Law Review* 150 (2007); Tara Smith, "Originalism's Misplaced Fidelity: 'Original' Meaning is Not Objective," 26 *Constitutional Commentary* 1 (2009).

27. *See, e.g.*, Saul Cornell, "Originalism on Trial: The Use and Abuse of History in *District of Columbia v. Heller*," 69 *Ohio State Law Journal* 625, 626–31 (2008). *See also* Larry Kramer, Two (More) Problems with Originalism," 31 *Harvard Journal of Law and Public Policy* 907 (2008); Caleb Nelson, "Originalism and Interpretive Conventions," 70 *University of Chicago Law Review* 519 (2003).

28. Saul Cornell, "The People's Constitution vs. The Lawyer's Constitution: Popular Constitutionalism and the Original Debate Over Originalism," 23 *Yale Journal of Law and Humanities* 295, 295–304 (2011). *See also* Gordon Wood, "Rhetoric and Reality in the American Revolution," 23 *William and Mary Quarterly* 3 (1966) (discussing the histo-

rian's dilemma in separating political propaganda, changing arguments, and political realities).

29. *See* J.G.A. Pocock, *Virtue, Commerce, and History: Essays on Political Thought and History, Chiefly in the Eighteenth Century* 10 (Cambridge, NY: Cambridge University Press 1985); J.G.A. Pocock, Gordon Schochet, and Lois G. Schwoerer, "The History of British Political Thought: A Field and its Futures," *British Political Thought in History, Literature and Theory, 1500–1800*, at 10, 11 (David Armitage ed., Cambridge, NY: Cambridge University Press, 2006); Quentin Skinner, "Hermeneutics and the Role of History," 7 *New Literary History* 214, 216 (1975).

30. Mark Tushnet argues originalist writings should be treated separately from other works that invoke history for support. It is what Tushnet refers to as "history-in-law" because in originalism, "history functions ... as a decoration rather than authority." *See* Mark Tushnet, "Interdisciplinary Legal Scholarship: The Case of History-in-Law," 71 *Chicago-Kent Law Review* 909, 914 (1996).

31. *McDonald v. City of Chicago*, 130 S. Ct. 3020, 3057–58 (2010) (Scalia, J., concurring).

32. Ibid.

33. For some recent discussions, see Frank H. Easterbrook, "Textualism and the Dead Hand," 66 *George Washington Law Review* 1119 (1998); William Michael Treanor, "Taking Text Too Seriously: Modern Textualism, Original Meaning, and the Case of Amar's Bill of Rights," 106 *Michigan Law Review* 487 (2007); Thomas B. Colby, "The Sacrifice of the New Originalism," 99 *Georgetown Law Journal* 713 (2011).

34. Wiecek, "Clio as Hostage" at 268.

35. Robert W. Gordon, "The Struggle Over the Past," 44 *Cleveland State Law Review* 123, 133 (1996).

36. For a recent critique of New Originalism, see generally Cornell, "The People's Constitution vs. The Lawyer's Constitution" at 295–337. *See also* Laura Kalman, *The Strange Career of Legal Liberalism* 193 (New Haven, CT: Yale University Press, 1996) (stating as of 1996 there has still not been an open discussion on the "gap between historians' and lawyers' history"); Gordon, "Historicism in Legal Scholarship" at 1055 (arguing for an open dialogue between legal theory and legal history); Morton J. Horwitz, "History and Theory," 96 *Yale Law Journal* 1825, 1835 (1987) (arguing for an awareness about "legal historiography and the ways in which controversies over political and legal theory influence legal historical inquiry").

37. *See* Michael Rappaport, "History Office Law," *The Originalism Blog* (December 27, 2010) (discussing how "history office law" is a larger problem than "law office history").

38. David Thomas Konig, "*Heller*, Guns, and History: The Judicial Invention of Tradition," 3 *Northeastern Law Journal* 175, 177–78 (2011).

39. Murphy, "Time to Reclaim" at 77–78.

40. This formula is often referred to as the Cambridge School of Intellectual History founded by

J.G.A. Pocock and Quentin Skinner. *See* Quentin Skinner, 2 *The Foundations of Modern Political Thought* (Cambridge, NY: Cambridge University Press, 1978); J.G.A. Pocock, *Politics, Language and Time* (Chicago: University of Chicago Press, 1971).

41. David A. Strauss, "Can Originalism Be Saved?" 92 *Boston University Law Review* 1161, 1170 (2012).

42. Wiecek, "Clio as Hostage" at 267.

43. The most notable example is that of Michael A. Bellesiles, who was found to have violated basic norms of historical scholarship in his 2000 book *Arming America. See* Stanley N. Katz, Hanna H. Gray, and Laurel Thatcher, *Report of the Investigative Committee in the Matter of Professor Michael Bellesiles* (July 10, 2002); Michael A. Bellesiles, *Arming America: The Origins of a National Gun Culture* (New York: Alfred A. Knopf, 2000).

44. Kelly, "Clio and the Court" at 155; Buckner F. Melton, Jr., "Clio at the Bar: A Guide to Historical Method for Legists and Jurists," 83 *Minnesota Law Review* 377, 377–88 (1998).

45. Herbert Butterfield, *The Whig Interpretation of History* 16 (London: G. Bell and Sons, 1931). *See also* J.G.A. Pocock, "The Origins of Study of the Past: A Comparative Approach," 4 *Comparative Studies in Society and History* 209, 211–14 (1962) (discussing the importance of a historian's "social awareness" of the past before one can ever relate history to the present).

46. Robert H. Jackson, "Full Faith and Credit: The Lawyer's Clause of the Constitution," 45 *Columbia Law Review* 1, 6 (1945).

47. Murphy, "Time to Reclaim" at 72–77.

48. Ibid. at 77.

49. Ibid. at 78.

50. Ibid. at 79.

51. Kelley, "Clio and the Court" at 155.

52. Ibid. at 123.

53. Ibid. at 156.

54. Ibid. at 157.

55. Ibid.

56. Ibid. at 158.

57. Julius Goebel, Jr., and T. Raymond Naughton, *Law Enforcement in Colonial New York: A Study in Criminal Procedure (1664–1776)*, at xxxiii (Montclair, NJ: Patterson Smith, 1944).

58. Ibid. at xxxiii–xxxiv.

59. Alfred L. Brophy, "Introducing Applied Legal History," 31 *Law and History Review* 233, 233–34 (2013).

60. *See* David B. Kopel and Clayton E. Cramer, "Credentials are No Substitute for Accuracy: Nathan Kozuskanich, Stephen Halbrook, and the Role of the Historian," 19 *Widener Law Journal* 343, 378 (2010).

61. Wiecek, "Clio as Hostage" at 266–67.

62. Butterfield, *The Whig Interpretation of History* at 62–63.

63. For a discussion on the importance of total historical context, see Quentin Skinner, "The Limits of Historical Explanations," 41 *Philosophy* 199 (1966).

64. Julius Goebel, Jr., "Ex Parte Clio," 54 *Columbia Law Review* 450, 451 (1954).

65. Ibid. at 467.

66. *See, e.g.*, David A. Strauss, "Common Law Constitutional Interpretation," 63 *University of Chicago Law Review* 877, 885–86 (1996) (explaining the "dead hand" problem).

67. Tushnet, "Interdisciplinary Legal Scholarship" at 917–26.

68. Wiecek, "Clio as Hostage" at 227–28.

69. Konig, "*Heller*, Guns, and History" at 177–78.

70. *See, e.g.*, Allison Orr Larsen, "Confronting Supreme Court Fact Finding," 98 *Virginia Law Review* 1255 (2012). *See also Ogden v. Saunders*, 25 U.S. 213, 332 (1827) ("Much too has been said concerning the principles of construction which ought to be applied to the Constitution of the United States. On this subject also, the Court has taken such frequent occasion to declare its opinion as to make it unnecessary, at least, to enter again into an elaborate discussion of it. To say that the intention of the instrument must prevail; that this intention must be collected from its words; *that its words are to be understood in that sense in which they are generally used by those for whom the instrument was intended*; that its provisions are neither to be restricted into insignificance nor extended to objects not comprehended in them, nor contemplated by its framers is to repeat what has been already said more at large and is all that can be necessary.") (emphasis added)

71. One could easily be enticed into assuming Jack M. Balkin was the first to attempt a model considering both, a doctrine Balkin refers to as "framework originalism." *See* Jack M. Balkin, *Living Originalism* 21–34 (Cambridge, MA: Harvard University Press, 2011). However, Balkin's rules for "framework originalism" are nothing new. They may have been influenced, borrowed or copied from other commentators, most notably historian William M. Wiecek, who offered a similar construct twenty-three years earlier. *See* Wiecek, "Clio as Hostage" at 231–33.

72. *See* Lorianne Updike Toler, Joseph Carl Cecere, and Don R. Willett, "Pre-'Originalism,'" 36 *Harvard Journal of Law and Public Policy* 277 (2012) (finding that the first hundred years of Supreme Court precedent does not support "anything like the modern idea of Originalist philosophy").

73. *McCulloch v. Maryland*, 17 U.S. 316 (1819).

74. Finkelman, "The Constitution and the Intentions of the Framers" at 368; Kelly, "Clio and the Court" at 123–25.

75. *McCulloch*, 17 U.S. at 415.

76. Ibid.

77. *United States v. Fisher*, 6 U.S. 358 (1805).

78. Ibid. at 396.

79. *McCulloch*, 17 U.S. at 415.

80. 4 *The Debates in the Several State Conventions on the Adoption of the Federal Constitution* 166–67 (Jonathan Elliot ed., Philadelphia: J.B. Lippincott 2d ed., 1907).

81. In recent years, debate over the scope of the Necessary and Proper Clause has reached new

heights. But none of the scholars, supporting either a narrow or broad reading, has cited to or referred to Iredell's charge to the grand jury, despite the charge being available in two prominent source books. *See* Francis Wharton, *State Trials of the United States During the Administrations of Washington and Adams with References, Historical and Professional, and Preliminary Notes on the Politics of the Times* 458 (Philadelphia: Carey and Hart, 1849); Griffith J. McRee, 2 *Life and Correspondence of James Iredell: One of the Associate Justices of the Supreme Court* 550 (New York: D. Appleton, 1858). This author ran across the charge reading late eighteenth-century newspapers.

82. James Iredell, "Charge Delivered to the Grand Jury for the District Court of Pennsylvania," Part II, April 11, 1799, reprinted in *The Independent Chronicle and the Universal Advertiser* (Boston, MA), May 30, 1799, at 1, col. 3.

83. Ibid.; James Iredell, "Charge Delivered to the Grand Jury for the District Court of Pennsylvania," Part III, April 11, 1799, reprinted in *The Independent Chronicle and the Universal Advertiser* (Boston, MA), June 3, 1799, at 1, col. 1.

84. *See* Kurt T. Lash and Alicia Harrison, "Minority Report: John Marshall and the Defense of the Alien and Sedition Acts," 68 *Ohio State Law Journal* 435, 485–509 (2007).

85. *See* Patrick J. Charles, "Originalism, John Marshall, and the Necessary and Proper Clause: Resurrecting the Jurisprudence of Alexander Addison," 58 *Cleveland State Law Review* 529 (2010).

86. Alexander Addison, *Liberty of Speech and the Press: A Charge to the Grand Juries of the County Courts of the Fifth Circuit of the State of Pennsylvania* (Albany: Loring Andrews, 1798).

87. 4 *The Papers of John Marshall* 3–4 (Charles T. Cullen ed., Chapel Hill: University of North Carolina Press, 1984).

88. Charles, "Originalism, John Marshall, and the Necessary and Proper Clause" at 565–70.

89. Ibid. at 563–65.

90. 6 *The Papers of John Marshall* 278 (Charles F. Hobson ed., Chapel Hill: University of North Carolina Press, 1990).

91. Charles, "Originalism, John Marshall, and the Necessary and Proper Clause" at 563–65.

92. The first Supreme Court case to take a detailed historical approach was *Dred Scott v. Sandford*, 60 U.S. 393 (1857), which was extremely controversial in its conclusions. *See* Mark A. Graber, *Dred Scott and the Problem of Constitutional Evil* (Cambridge, NY: Cambridge University Press, 2006); Daniel A. Farber, "A Fatal Loss of Balance: *Dred Scott* Revisited," 39 *Pepperdine Law Review* 13 (2011). *See also* John Philip Reid, "The Touch of History: The Historical Method of a Common Law Judge," 27 *The American Journal of Legal History* 157 (1964) (discussing the development of a historical method by Judge Charles Doe in the mid-nineteenth century).

93. *City Gazette and Commercial Advertiser* (Charleston, SC), Apr. 15, 1821, at 2 (col. 1). It

should be noted that the following letter was published well after Addison's death. The letter was reprinted to commemorate his wisdom.

94. A fitting example is that of American jurist and framer James Wilson. Wilson frequently used history to explain the development of the law, but not bind it. He admitted "the most proper way to teach and to study the common law is to teach and study it as a historical science." James Wilson, "Of the Common Law," Chapter XII, in 2 *The Collected Works of James Wilson* 749, 769 (Kermit L. Hall and Mark David Hall eds., Indianapolis, IN: Liberty Fund, 2007). At the same time, however, Wilson viewed the common law as an evolving body of law that does not necessarily bind the present. Because the common law's "authority rests on reception, approbation, custom, long and established," wrote Wilson, the "same principles, which establish it [must also] change, enlarge, improve, and repeal it." Ibid. at 773.

95. *See, e.g.,* Calder v. Bull, 3 U.S. 386 (1798).

96. 2 *Portrait of a Patriot: The Major Political and Legal Papers of Josiah Quincy Junior: The Law Commonplace Book* 215 (Daniel R. Coquillette and Neil Longley York eds., Boston: Colonial Society of Massachusetts, 2007).

97. Associate Justice Antonin Scalia is a strong proponent for the use of dictionaries to ascertain meaning:

> The external sources you're talking about [to define the law]—a dictionary, the cases that define a term of art, and so on—just go to the ordinary meaning of the words in their context.... I don't mind using legislative history just to show that a word could mean a certain thing. We are trying to ascertain how a reasonable person uses language, and the way legislators use language is some evidence of that, though *perhaps not as persuasive evidence as a dictionary.* That is using legislative history as (mildly) informative rather than authoritative: "the word can mean this because the people sometimes use it that way, as the legislative debates shows," rather than "the word must mean this because that is what the drafters said it meant."

Antonin Scalia and John F. Manning, "A Dialogue on Statutory and Constitutional Interpretation," 80 *George Washington Law Review* 1610, 1616 (2012) (emphasis added).

98. 2 *Portrait of a Patriot* at 217.

99. Goebel, "Constitutional History and Constitutional Law" at 562. Indeed, historical assumptions are likely to arise at the beginning of most historical inquiries. However, these assumptions should not affect the end analysis "if we are conscious that they are assumptions," for it would be "the most fallacious thing in the world ... to organize our historical knowledge upon an assumption without realizing what we are doing, and then make inferences from that organization and claim that these are the voice of history." Butterfield, *The Whig Interpretation of History* at 23–24.

100. Antonin Scalia, "Common-Law Courts in a Civil Law System: The Role of the United States

Federal Courts in Interpreting the Constitution and Laws," in *A Matter of Interpretation* 3, 45; Scalia and Manning, "A Dialogue on Statutory and Constitutional Interpretation" at 1615–19.

101. *See, e.g.*, Stephen E. Sachs, "Constitutional Backdrops," 80 *George Washington Law Review* 1813 (2012). A fitting example is Article VII of the 1689 English Declaration of Rights. Although Article VII makes no mention of a militia, the history of its adoption proves it was adopted to give Parliament concurrent authority over the militia; an issue of serious debate from the mid to late seventeenth century. *See* Patrick J. Charles, "'Arms for Their Defence?' An Historical, Legal, and Textual Analysis of the English Right to Have Arms and Whether the Second Amendment Should Be Incorporated in *McDonald v. City of Chicago*," 57 *Cleveland State Law Review* 351 (2009); Patrick J. Charles, "The Right of Self-Preservation and Resistance: A True Legal and Historical Understanding of the Anglo-American Right to Arms," 2010 *Cardozo Law Review de novo* 18 (2010).

102. *See, e.g.*, Alfred H. Kelly and Winfred A. Harbison, *The American Constitution: An Account of the Development of the American Constitution and of American Constitutionalism from its Origins in England, Europe, and the Colonies to Our Time* 1–3, 7–156 (5th ed., New York: W.W. Norton, 1976).

103. For a larger discussion of these issues, see Jack Rakove, *Original Meanings: Politics and Ideas in the Making of the Constitution* 9–22 (New York: Alfred A. Knopf, 1996). For the importance of interpreting the Constitution through both custom and significant events, particularly the American Revolution, see Jack P. Greene, *The Constitutional Origins of the American Revolution* (Cambridge, NY: Cambridge University Press, 2011).

104. The first Supreme Court Justice to accurately make this connection was Potter Stewart. *See* Potter Stewart, "Or of the Press," 26 *Hastings Law Journal* 631 (1975). Today, however, Supreme Court jurisprudence does not embrace distinct press protections. *See Nebraska Press Ass'n v. Stuart*, 427 U.S. 539, 559 (1976); *New York Times Co. v. Sullivan*, 376 U.S. 254, 256 (1964); *Gitlow v. New York*, 268 U.S. 652, 664 (1925); *Abrams v. United States*, 250 U.S. 616, 618–19 (1919). And in some scholarly circles the Press Clause is viewed as nothing more than a right to print technology. *See, e.g.*, Eugene Volokh, "'The Freedom ... of the Press,' From 1791 to 1868 to Now: Freedom for the Press as an Industry or the Press as a Technology," 160 *University of Pennsylvania Law Review* 459 (2011).

105. Such a disagreement presented itself in the midst of the American Revolution when loyalist printers were denounced as inviolate of the "liberty of the press," shut down, and destroyed. For a discussion, see Patrick J. Charles and Kevin Francis O'Neill, "Saving the Press Clause from Ruin: The Customary Origins of a 'Free Press' as Interface to the Present and Future" 2012 *Utah Law Review* 1691, 1728–43 (2012).

106. For a discussion of the emergence of the First Amendment and its intellectual development through the 1798 Sedition Law debates, see Leonard W. Levy, *Emergence of a Free Press* 221–81 (New York: Oxford University Press, 1985).

107. Scalia, "Common-Law Courts in a Civil Law System" at 45.

108. Ibid. at 45–46.

109. Richard A. Posner, "Past Dependency, Pragmatism, and Critique of History in Adjudication and Legal Scholarship," 67 *University of Chicago Law Review* 573, 573 (2000).

110. Ibid. at 591, 596.

111. Ibid. at 595.

112. Stephen Breyer, *Making Our Democracy Work: A Judge's View* 77 (New York: Alfred A. Knopf, 2010).

113. Ibid. at 76.

114. Ibid. at 76–77.

115. *See, e.g.*, Amanda L. Tyler, Frank H. Easterbrook et al., "A Dialogue with Federal Judges on the Role of History in Interpretation," 80 *George Washington Law Review* 1889, 1896, 1908–9 (2012) (comments of Jeffrey S. Sutton). For more on Sutton's view on the use of history and the law, see Jeffrey S. Sutton, "The Role of History in Judging Disputes About the Meaning of the Constitution," 41 *Texas Tech Law Review* 1173 (2009).

116. J. Harvie Wilkinson, Cosmic Constitutional Theory: Why Americans Are Losing Their Inalienable Right to Self-Governance 50 (New York: Oxford University Press, 2012).

117. Michael Rappaport, "Posner on Scalia and Garner's Reading Law III: Are Judges Up to the Job of History?" *The Originalism Blog* (September 10, 2012). *See also* Michael Rappaport, "Historians, Originalists, and Pauline Maier," *Liberty Law Blog* (August 17, 2013).

118. Scalia and Garner, *Reading Law* at 401.

119. Paul L. Murphy made this critique in 1963 and it remains a problem today as legal professionals pick and choose historical works they are aligned with ideologically. *See* Murphy, "Time to Reclaim" at 77.

120. Scalia and Garner, *Reading Law* at 401.

121. This is what happened after the Supreme Court's most originalist opinion in *District of Columbia v. Heller. See* Paul Finkelman, "It Really Was About a Well-Regulated Militia," 59 *Syracuse Law Review* 267 (2008); Saul Cornell, "*Heller*, New Originalism, and Law Office History: 'Meet the New Boss, Same as the Old Boss,'" 56 *UCLA Law Review* 1095 (2009); David Thomas Konig, "Why the Second Amendment Has a Preamble: Original Public Meaning and the Political Culture of Written Constitutions in Revolutionary America," 56 *UCLA Law Review* 1295 (2009); William G. Merkel, "*Heller* as Hubris, and How *McDonald v. City of Chicago* May Well Change the Constitutional World as We Know It," 50 *Santa Clara Law Review* 1221 (2010); William G. Merkel, "*District of Columbia v. Heller* and Antonin Scalia's Perverse Sense of Originalism," 13 *Lewis and Clark Law Review* 349 (2009); Nathan Kozuskanich, "Originalism, His-

tory, and the Second Amendment: What Did Bearing Arms Really Mean to the Founders?" 10 *Pennsylvania Journal of Constitutional Law* 413 (2008).

122. *McDonald v. City of Chicago*, 130 S. Ct. 3020, 3057–58 (Scalia, J., concurring) (2010).

123. Ibid. (emphasis added).

124. *See, e.g.*, Brief for English/Early American Historians as Amici Curiae Supporting Respondents, *McDonald*, 130 S. Ct. 3020 (2010) (No. 08–1521) (supported by twenty-one scholars and historians).

125. This is a legitimate critique of originalism—it lacks objectivity. However, as long as judges rely on professional historical analysis, some of this is alleviated. *See* Tyler, Easterbrook, et al., "A Dialogue with Federal Judges on the Role of History in Interpretation" at 1890, 1896–97.

126. *See* Cornell, "The People's Constitution vs. The Lawyer's Constitution" at 297–304; Barry Friedman, "Discipline and Method: The Making of 'The Will of the People,'" 2010 *Michigan State Law Review* 877, 891 (2010) (agreeing with historians that legal works need to adhere to reasonable historical "standards regarding how they search, what claims they make, on what evidence, and to what end").

127. *See* Quentin Skinner, "Motives, Intentions an Interpretation of Texts," 3 *New Literary History* 393, 407–8 (1972) (stating the importance of interpreting historical text is focusing on the "writer's mental world" and any factors linked to the text's creation); Quentin Skinner, "Meaning and Understanding the History of Ideas," 8 *History and Theory* 3, 6–7 (1969) (discussing how a focus on text often brings to "bear some of one's own expectations about what he must have been saying" and converting "scattered and quite incidental remarks" into doctrine).

128. Melton, "Clio at the Bar" at 378.

129. Ibid. at 389–96, 451.

130. Mark Tushnet, "Constitutional Scholarship: What Next?" 5 *Constitutional Commentary* 28, 31 (1988).

131. Neil M. Richards, "Clio and the Court: A Reassessment of the Supreme Court's Uses of History," 13 *Journal of Law and Politics* 809, 890 (1997).

132. For a history, see Carl T. Bogus, "The History and Politics of Second Amendment Scholarship: A Primer," 76 *Chicago-Kent Law Review* 3 (2000).

133. *See, e.g.*, David I. Caplan, "Restoring the Balance: The Second Amendment Revisited," 5 *Fordham Urban Law Journal* 31 (1976). *See also* Don B. Kates, "A Modern Historiography of the Second Amendment," 56 *UCLA Law Review* 1211 (2009) (discussing the growth and findings of the Second Amendment from a pro-gun viewpoint).

134. See Saul Cornell, *A Well-Regulated Militia and the Origins of Gun Control in America* (New York: Oxford University Press, 2006); H. Richard Uviller and William G. Merkel, *The Militia and the Right to Arms, or, How the Second Amendment Fell Silent* (Durham: Duke University Press, 2003); The

Second Amendment in Law and History: Historians and Constitutional Scholars on the Right to Bear Arms (Carl T. Bogus ed., New York: New Press, 2000).

135. Although there are a number of examples to include (such as authors Stephen P. Halbrook, David B. Kopel, and Joyce Lee Malcolm), the most prominent is attorney Don B. Kates. In 1983, Kates wrote one of the most influential pro-gun history articles on the Second Amendment. *See* Don B. Kates, "Handgun Prohibition and the Original Meaning of the Second Amendment," 82 *Michigan Law Review* 204 (1983). Almost a decade later, Kates wrote a philosophy centered article endorsing a right to bear arms against both public and private balance. *See* Don B. Kates, "The Second Amendment and the Ideology of Self-Protection," 9 *Constitutional Commentary* 87 (1992). Then there is criminology and sociology centered articles endorsing the same bottom line. *See* Don B. Kates, "The Value of Civilian Handgun Possession as a Deterrent to Crime or a Defense Against Crime," 18 *American Journal of Criminal Law* 113 (1991); Don B. Kates and Gary Mauser, "Would Banning Firearms Reduce Murder and Suicide: A Review of International and Some Domestic Evidence," 30 *Harvard Journal of Law and Public Policy* 649 (2007); Don B. Kates and Clayton E. Cramer, "Second Amendment Limitations and Criminological Considerations," 60 *Hastings Law Journal* 1339 (2009). Lastly, there is even a public health article. *See* Don B. Kates, Henry E. Schaffer, John K. Lattimer, and George B. Murray, "Guns and Public Health: Epidemic of Violence or Pandemic of Propaganda," 62 *Tennessee Law Review* 513 (1995). The pro-gun conclusion is not surprising seeing that Kates' and other pro-gun scholars' research is largely being funded by groups like the National Rifle Association. *See, e.g.*, NRA Civil Rights Defense Fund, "Supported Research," available at http://www.nradefensefund.org/supported-research.aspx (showing $264,000 in research grants for a four month period to Standard Model writers that include David T. Hardy, Don B. Kates, David B. Kopel, and Kenneth Klukowski). Yet, at the same time, pro-gun scholars accused their literary opponents as being influenced by anti-gun funding. *See, e.g.*, George A. Mocsary, "Monopoly of Violence," *Claremont Review of Books* 46 (2010). ("To date, the best research on the Second Amendment has been done by legal scholars. Historians have largely been funded by organizations that favor gun control, with predicable results.")

136. For a general summary of the rise of pro-gun scholarship, see Adam Winkler, *Gun Fight: The Battle over the Right to Bear Arms in America* (New York: W.W. Norton, 2011).

137. Kalman, *The Strange Career of Legal Liberalism* at 143–63.

138. Butterfield, *The Whig Interpretation of History* at 100–2.

139. Scalia and Garner, *Reading Law* at 309–402.

140. Butterfield, *The Whig Interpretation of His-*

tory at 105 (discussing that the "sin" in historical composition is not "bias," but when the writer seeks "to abstract events from their context and set them up in implied comparison with the present day, and then to pretend that by this 'the facts' are being allowed to 'speak for themselves'").

141. Ibid. at 7 ("the more we are discussing and not merely enquiring, the more we are making inferences instead of researches, then the more whig our history becomes if we have not severely repressed our original error" being honest and self-critical).

142. United States v. Stevens, 130 S. Ct. 1577 (2010); *Brown v. Entertainment Merchants Association*, 131 S. Ct. 2729 (2011).

143. *Stevens*, 130 S. Ct. at 1586.

144. Ibid. at 1585.

145. Ibid.

146. Ibid. at 1586.

147. *Brown*, 131 S. Ct. at 2735.

148. Ibid. at 2735–36.

149. Ibid. at 2734.

150. Ibid. (emphasis added).

151. For some examples by eighteenth-century legal minds, see Scribble Scrabble, *The Cumberland Gazette* (Portland, ME), December 8, 1786, at 1 (editorial by Judge George Thatcher under pen name Scribble Scrabble); Alexander Addison, *Charges to the Grand Juries of the Counties of the Fifth Circuit in the State of Pennsylvania* 93, 157–58 (1800); William Blackstone, 1 *Commentaries on the Laws of England* 135, 139 (1765); Jean Louis De Lolme, *The Constitution of England; Or, An Account of the English Government* 199 (David Lieberman ed., Indianapolis, IN: Liberty Fund, 2007).

152. See Patrick J. Charles, "Restoring 'Life, Liberty, and the Pursuit of Happiness' in Our Constitutional Jurisprudence," 20 *William and Mary Bill of Rights Journal* 457, 502–17 (2011).

153. Michael Stokes Paulsen, "Our Perfect, Perfect Constitution," 27 *Constitutional Commentary* 531, 538–39 (2011).

154. Modern First Amendment jurisprudence is based on a libertarian view rather than as it existed in the late eighteenth century. This libertarian version was ahistorically advanced by Zechariah Chafee, Jr. See Zechariah Chafee, Jr., "Freedom of Speech in War Time," 32 *Harvard Law Review* 932 (1919); Zechariah Chafee, Jr., *Free Speech in the United States* (Cambridge, MA: Harvard University Press, 1941). Chafee's theory was sufficiently defeated by Leonard W. Levy, and later by David M. Rabban. See Leonard W. Levy, *Legacy of Suppression: Freedom of Speech and Press in Early American History* (Cambridge, MA: Harvard University Press, 1960); David M. Rabban, "The First Amendment in its Forgotten Years," 90 *Yale Law Journal* 514 (1981).

155. See Kelly, "Clio and the Court" at 122; John Philip Reid, "Law and History," 27 *Loyola Los Angeles Law Review* 193, 219 (1993); Barry Friedman and Scott B. Smith, "The Sedimentary Constitution," 147 *University of Pennsylvania Law Review* 1, 23–24 (1998).

156. A number of historians have advocated for a similar approach in order to balance objective history with the rule of law. See Nelson, "History and Neutrality in Constitutional Adjudication" at 1277–94 (arguing for the use of history on neutral principles by accepting consensus history and discarding conflict history); Wiecek, "Clio as Hostage" at 233–34 (arguing history can frame the question, but cannot always answer it); Finkelman, "The Constitution and the Intentions of the Framers" at 398 (arguing the past can illuminate the problems of the past, but cannot always answer how we should rule ourselves today).

157. 2 *Portrait of a Patriot* at 87.

158. See, e.g., Calvin Woodard, "History, Legal History, and Legal Education," 53 *Virginia Law Review* 89, 105–6 (1967).

159. Alan Harding, *A Social History of English Law* 8 (Peter Smith, 1966).

160. Henry Reed, "American Constitution in 1787 and 1866," 2 *The International Review* 604, 619 (1875).

161. Julius Goebel, Jr., "Learning and Style in the Law—An Historian's Lament," 61 *Columbia Law Review* 1393, 1400 (1961).

162. See Robert J. Spitzer, "Historical Approach: Why History Matters: Saul Cornell's Second Amendment and the Consequences of Law Reviews," 1 *Albany Government Law Review* 312 (2008); Robert J. Spitzer, *Saving the Constitution from Lawyers: How Legal Training and Law Reviews Distort Constitutional Meaning* (Cambridge, NY: Cambridge University Press, 2008).

163. Butterfield, *The Whig Interpretation of History* at 36.

164. Ibid. at 21.

165. Ibid. at 16. See also Pocock, "The Origins of Study of the Past" at 211–14 (discussing the importance of an historian's "social awareness" of the past before one can ever relate history to the present).

166. For a more in depth discussion on these problems, see Larry D. Kramer, "When Lawyers Do History," 72 *George Washington Law Review* 387 (2003); Laura Kalman, "Border Patrol: Reflections on the Turn to History in Legal Scholarship," 66 *Fordham Law Review* 87 (1997); Martin S. Flaherty, "History 'Lite' in Modern American Constitutionalism," 95 *Columbia Law Review* 523 (1995).

167. Tyler, Easterbrook, et al., "A Dialogue with Federal Judges on the Role of History in Interpretation" at 1890.

168. See, e.g., Nathan Kozuskanich, "Originalism in a Digital Age: An Inquiry into the Right to Bear Arms," 29 *Journal of the Early Republic* 585 (2009).

169. Butterfield, *The Whig Interpretation of History* at 30.

170. As Mark Tushnet writes: "[T]he historian demonstrates that the past is a foreign country where people managed to think that things we find inconsistent were entirely compatible, indeed sometimes entailed by each other. The historian shows how complicated yesterday's ideas and institutions were.

The simple fact that people in the past used words we use today does not mean that those words meant to them what they mean to us." Tushnet, "Interdisciplinary Legal Scholarship" at 916.

171. *See* J.G.A. Pocock, "British History: A Plea for a New Subject," 47 *The Journal of Modern History* 601, 614–15 (1975).

172. In an oral argument before the 7th Circuit Court of Appeals, Judge Richard Posner asked the defendant to use their "historical imagination" in terms of carrying firearms in the eighteenth century. Thus, instead of objectively examining the legal history of public arms regulation, he wanted defendant's counsel to reflect on an imaginative past. Posner would go on to write the opinion for the case, relying upon his "historical imagination" rather than any history of regulation to extend the Second Amendment outside the home:

> And one doesn't have to be a historian to realize that a right to keep and bear arms for personal self-defense in the eighteenth century could not rationally have been limited to the home. Suppose one lived in what was then the Wild West, the Ohio Valley for example..., where there were hostile Indians. One would need from time to time to leave one's home to obtain supplies from the nearest trading post, and en route one would be as much (probably more) at risk if unarmed as one would be in one's home unarmed.

See "Oral Argument Audio," *Moore v. Madigan*, No. 12–1269 (7th Cir. June 8, 2012), available at http://www.ca7.uscourts.gov/fdocs/docs.fwx?caseno=12–1269&submit=showdkt&yr=12&num=1269; *Moore v. Madigan*, 2012 U.S. App. LEXIS 25264 (7th Cir., 2012).

173. Butterfield, *The Whig Interpretation of History* at 16, 105.

174. J.G.A. Pocock, *Political Thought and History: Essays on Theory and Method* 189 (Cambridge, NY: Cambridge University Press, 2009).

Chapter 2

1. Oliver Wendell Holmes, *The Common Law* 5 (1881).

2. Oliver Wendell Holmes, "The Path of the Law," reprinted in 52 *Boston University Law Review* 212, 212 (1972).

3. Ibid. at 213.

4. Ibid. at 221.

5. Ibid. at 224.

6. Ibid. at 225.

7. Ibid. at 226.

8. Charles A. Beard, "The Act of Constitutional Interpretation," 1 *National Law Guild Quarterly* 9, 12 (1937).

9. Ibid. at 13–14.

10. *Compare* Randy E. Barnett, *Restoring the Lost Constitution: The Presumption of Liberty* 126 (Princeton, NJ: Princeton University Press, 2004) (stating one should choose the meaning that advances constitutional legitimacy) *with* Jack M.

Balkin, "Framework Originalism and the Living Constitution," 103 *Northwestern Law Review* 549, 609 (2009) (stating multiple factors should decide the choice such as "text, structure, history, precedent, prudence, and national ethos"). *See also* Rakove, *Original Meanings* at 8–11 (discussing the historian's dilemma of determining original meaning or understanding).

11. *See, e.g., Home Building and Loan Ass'n v. Blaisdell*, 290 U.S. 398, 451 (1934). *See also South Carolina v. United States*, 199 U.S. 437, 448 (1905); *Hawke v. Smith*, 253 U.S. 221, 227 (1920).

12. Beard, "The Act of Constitutional Interpretation," at 16.

13. Ibid.

14. Frederick Pollock, "The Genius of the Common Law I: Our Lady and Her Knights," 12 *Columbia Law Review* 189, 189–90 (1912).

15. Frederick Pollock, "The Expansion of the Common Law I: The Foundations of Justice," 3 *Columbia Law Review* 505, 522 (1903).

16. Steve Eder, "Justice Ginsburg on Opera and the Constitution," *The Wall Street Journal*, August 3, 2012.

17. *See, e.g.*, Michael W. McConnell, Laurence H. Tribe, and Paul D. Gewirtz, *The Senate, the Courts, and the Constitution* 12 (Washington, D.C.: Center for National Policy, 1986).

18. John O. McGinnis and Michael Rappaport, "The Abstract Meaning Fallacy," 2012 *Illinois Law Review* 737, 739 (2011).

19. For a discussion on the conflict between a living constitution and originalism, see Robert Post and Reva Siegel, "Originalism as a Political Practice: The Right's Living Constitution," 75 *Fordham Law Review* 545, 568–74 (2006). For a discussion that proposes originalism is consistent with the living constitution, see Jack Balkin, "Original Meaning and Constitutional Redemption," 24 *Constitutional Commentary* 427, 456–57–491, 493–6, 504–11 (2007). For dissent against Balkin's claim, see Andrew Koppelman, "Why Jack Balkin is Disgusting," 27 *Constitutional Commentary* 177 (2010).

20. Scalia and Garner, *Reading Law* at 79.

21. Blackstone, 1 Commentaries on the Laws of England at 60.

22. Scalia and Garner, *Reading Law* at 404.

23. McGinnis and Rappaport, "Original Methods Originalism" at 802.

24. Blackstone, 1 *Commentaries on the Laws of England* at 60–62.

25. For arguably the most detailed study on the continually changing use of historical sources for constitutional understanding, see J.G.A. Pocock, *The Ancient Constitution and the Feudal Law: A Study of English Historical Thought in the Seventeenth Century—A Reissue with a Retrospect* (Cambridge, NY: Cambridge University Press, 1987). *See also* J.G.A. Pocock, "The Origins of Study of the Past: A Comparative Approach," 4 *Comparative Studies in Society and History* 209 (1962). Originalism, as a crystallized legal theory, did not come into form until an influential essay in 1980. *See* Paul Brest,

"The Misconceived Quest for the Original Understanding," 60 *Boston University Law Review* 204 (1980).

26. *See, e.g.*, H. Jefferson Powell, "Rules for Originalists," 73 *Virginia Law Review* 659, 662–63 (1987).

27. *See, e.g.*, Jeffrey Rosen, "If Scalia Had His Way," *New York Times* (January 8, 2011). *See also* Jamal Greene, Nathaniel Persily and Stephen Ansolabehere, "Profiling Originalism," 111 *Columbia Law Review* 356 (2011) (discussing the rise and influence of originalism).

28. Strauss, "Can Originalism Be Saved?" at 1170.

29. *See, e.g.*, H. Jefferson Powell, "The Original Understanding of Original Intent," 98 *Harvard Law Review* 885 (1988). For a historian's conditional acceptance of original intent, see Leonard W. Levy, *Original Intent and the Framers' Constitution* (New York: Macmillan, 1988).

30. *See* Rakove, *Original Meanings* at 3–22. *See also* Kramer, "Two (More) Problems with Originalism," at 907–16; Nelson, "Originalism and Interpretive Conventions," at 519–98.

31. *See* Gordon S. Wood, "Rhetoric and Reality in the American Revolution," 23 *William and Mary Quarterly* 3 (1966).

32. Gordon S. Wood, *The Creation of the American Republic 1776–1787*, 291 (2d ed., Chapel Hill: University of North Carolina Press, 1998).

33. *See* Jonathan O'Neill, *Originalism in American Law and Politics: A Constitutional History* 94–132 (Baltimore: Johns Hopkins University Press, 2005); Keith E. Whittington, "The New Originalism," 2 *Georgetown Journal of Law and Public Policy* 599, 599–603 (2004). For early originalist attacks on the Warren Court, see Bork, *The Tempting of America* at 69–95, 130–2; Edwin Meese III, "Interpreting the Constitution," in *Interpreting the Constitution* (Jack N. Rakove ed., Boston: Northeastern University Press, 1990); Richard S. Kay, "Adherence to the Original Intentions in Constitutional Adjudication: Three Objections and Responses," 82 *Northwestern University Law Review* 226 (1988); Raoul Berger, *Government by Judiciary: The Transformation of the Fourteenth Amendment* 283–99, 363–72 (Cambridge, MA: Harvard University Press, 1977).

34. Strauss, "Can Originalism Be Saved?" at 1170.

35. McGinnis and Rappaport, "Original Methods Originalism" at 752.

36. Ibid.

37. William Michael Treanor, "Against Textualism," 103 *Northwestern University Law Review* 983, 985 (2009).

38. McGinnis and Rappaport, "Original Methods Originalism" at 753.

39. Treanor, "Against Textualism" at 986.

40. *See* 2 *Portrait of a Patriot* at 87; 1 William Blackstone, *Commentaries on the Law of England* 61 (Oxford: Clarendon Press, 1765).

41. Treanor, "Against Textualism" at 986.

42. Ibid. at 984.

43. Goebel and Naughton, *Law Enforcement in Colonial New York* at xxxiii.

44. McGinnis and Rappaport, "Original Methods Originalism" at 794.

45. Ibid.

46. Ibid. at 795–801.

47. Ibid. at 802.

48. Ibid. at 752, 795.

49. The point here is that McGinnis and Rappaport's thesis is not fully developed. It is a historical theory, not a historical thesis, and McGinnis and Rappaport's bottom line conclusions are no better than those found in Charles Beard's infamous *Economic Interpretation of the Constitution*. Writing in 1913, Beard asserted the framers were economically motivated to adopt the Constitution, and in doing so, cherry-picked historical evidence to support it. It was a deficiency Beard admitted, and later negated the thesis as viable. *See, e.g.*, O.G. Libby, "Review: An Economic Interpretation of the Constitution of the United States," 1 *The Mississippi Valley Historical Review* 113, 114 (1914) ("Beard has undoubtedly very much weakened his case by attempting to combine in one presentation the functions of investigation and judge, especially since his basis for judgment is so obviously limited.... As a whole the work is principally at fault in its lack of perspective; the period of constitution making is too narrowly limited.").

50. Toler, Cecere, and Willett, "Pre-'Originalism'" at 301.

51. Ibid. at 314. The authors believe their findings are in line with H. Jefferson Powell's powerful dissent against originalism as a valid legal theory. *See generally* Powell, "The Original Understanding of Original Intent" at 885–948.

52. Toler, Cecere, and Willett, "Pre-'Originalism'" at 304–6. It was not until the Warren Court that framing era sources were employed more frequently and resembled anything close to modern day originalism. *See* Frank B. Cross, "Originalism: The Forgotten Years," 28 *Constitutional Commentary* 37 (2012).

53. Kelly, "Clio and the Court" at 122–23. Today virtually any court opinion's legitimacy and accuracy requires supporting evidence through detailed citations. *See* Matthew J. Festa, "Dueling Federalists: Supreme Court Decisions with Multiple Opinions Citing *The Federalist*," 31 *Seattle Law Review* 75 (2007) (discussing how citing to *The Federalist* gives constitutional opinions historical legitimacy); Robert J. Hume, "Two Studies of the U.S. Supreme Court: The Use of Rhetorical Sources by the U.S. Supreme Court," 40 *Law and Society Review* 817 (2006) (discussing how the justices can use content and sources strategically to enhance the legitimacy of decisions). Yet prior to the turn of the twentieth century it was common for legal treatises, law reviews, and legal opinions to rely on precedent only, i.e., the common law method of adjudicating cases and controversies. Furthermore, in the late eighteenth century citations were often noticeably absent. *See, e.g.*, C. Paul Rogers III, "Scots Law in Post-

Revolutionary and Nineteenth-Century America: The Neglected Jurisprudence," 8 *Law and History Review* 205, 209 (1990) (acknowledging the influence of the Scottish Enlightenment on late eighteenth-century American jurisprudence, yet noting citations as noticeably absent). This fact may lead some to conclude that framing era legal minds were textualists first and foremost, seeking to build a distinct body of law based upon the public meaning of the Constitution's text. *Compare* Akhil Amar, *America's Constitution: A Biography* (New York: Random House, 2005) *with* H. Jefferson Powell, "Grand Visions in an Age of Conflict," 115 *Yale Law Journal* 2067 (2006). Such a conclusion, however, would be dangerously misleading, for late eighteenth-century legal doctrine was far more complex and encompassed portions of Anglo-American common law, English case law, and the law of nations. *See, e.g.*, Kramer, "Originalism and Pragmatism" at 907–16 (discussing how there were multiple approaches to constitutional interpretation in the late eighteenth century).

54. 2 Edw. 3, c. 3 (1328) (Eng.).

55. William Blackstone, 4 *Commentaries on the Laws of England* 148–49 (Oxford: Clarendon Press, 1769).

56. *See, e.g.*, Blackstone, 3 *Commentaries on the Laws of England* at 133–35 (discussing the history of the writ of habeas corpus).

57. Ibid. at 135.

58. *See, e.g.*, Wilson, 1 *Collected Works of James Wilson* at 501–48 (describing law as a science).

59. Bernard Bailyn, *The Ideological Origins of the American Revolution: Enlarged Edition* 31 (Cambridge, MA: Harvard University Press, 1992).

60. Ibid.

61. 6 *American Archives: Documents of the American Revolution*, 1774–1776, at 279 (Fourth Series, Peter Force ed., Washington, D.C.: n.p., 1833–46).

62. Ibid. at 556.

63. Ibid. at 604.

64. *See, e.g.*, J.G.A. Pocock, *Three British Revolutions: 1641, 1688, 1776* (Princeton, NJ: Princeton University Press, 1980).

65. Patrick J. Charles, *Irreconcilable Grievances: The Events that Shaped the Declaration of Independence* 55–64 (Bowie, MD: Heritage Books, 2008).

66. For some histories of William Henry Drayton, see William M. Dabney and Marion Dargan, *William Henry Drayton and the American Revolution* (Albuquerque: University of New Mexico Press, 1962); J. Russell Snapp, "William Henry Drayton: The Making of a Conservative Revolutionary," 57 *The Journal of Southern History* 637 (1991); Keith Drawczynski, *William Henry Drayton: South Carolina Revolutionary Patriot* (Baton Rouge: Louisiana State University Press, 2001).

67. "Judge Drayton's Address to the Grand Jury at Charlestown, South Carolina," in 5 *American Archives: Documents of the American Revolution, 1774–1776*, at 1025, 1028 (Fourth Series, Peter Force ed., Washington, D.C.: n.p., 1833–46). For an intellectual history of the right of self-preservation and

resistance, see Charles, "The Right of Self-Preservation and Resistance" at 18–60. For more on the history of the right of resistance and self-preservation, see Skinner, 2 *The Foundations of Modern Political Thought* at 302–48; J.C.D. Clark, *The Language of Liberty 1660–1832: Political Discourse and Social Dynamics in the Anglo-American World* 249–89 (Cambridge, NY: Cambridge University Press, 1994).

68. "Judge Drayton's Address to the Grand Jury at Charlestown, South Carolina," in 5 *American Archives: Documents of the American Revolution, 1774–1776*, at 1028.

69. Ibid. at 1028–30.

70. Ibid. at 1031.

71. *See, e.g.*, Charles, "Restoring 'Life, Liberty, and the Pursuit of Happiness' in Our Constitutional Jurisprudence" at 482, 488.

72. *See* David Lieberman, "The Legal Needs of a Commercial Society: The Jurisprudence of Lord Kames," in *Wealth and Virtue: The Shaping of Political Economy in the Scottish Enlightenment* 203–34 (Istvan Hont and Michael Ignatieff eds., Cambridge, NY: Cambridge University Press, 1983); Donald Winch, *Adam Smith's Politics: An Essay in Historiographic Revision* 46–69 (Cambridge, NY: Cambridge University Press, 1978); Duncan Forbes, *Hume's Philosophical Politics* 3–90 (Cambridge, NY: Cambridge University Press, 1975).

73. *See* Dalphy I. Fagerstrom, "Scottish Opinion and the American Revolution," 11 *The William and Mary Quarterly* 252 (1954); Ronald Hamowy, "Jefferson's Declaration of Independence," 36 *The William and Mary Quarterly* 503 (1979); Douglas L. Wilson, "Thomas Jefferson's Early Notebooks," 42 *The William and Mary Quarterly* 433 (1985); Daniel Walker Howe, "Why the Scottish Enlightenment Was Useful to the Framers of the American Constitution," 31 *Comparative Studies in Society and History* 572 (1989); Robert A. Ferguson, *The American Enlightenment, 1750–1820* (Cambridge, NY: Cambridge University Press, 1994); Samuel Fleischacker, "Adam Smith's Reception Among the American Founders, 1776–1790," 59 *The William and Mary Quarterly* 897 (2002); William Ewald, "James Wilson and the Scottish Enlightenment," 12 *University of Pennsylvania Journal of Constitutional Law* 1053 (2010); James E. Pfander and Daniel D. Birk, "Article III and the Scottish Judiciary," 124 *Harvard Law Review* 1613 (2011). *See also* Rogers III, "Scots Law in Post-Revolutionary and Nineteenth-Century America" at 205–35.

74. Henry Home Kames, *Elucidations Respecting the Common and Statute Law of Scotland* xiii (Edinburgh: Adam Neill, 1777).

75. Henry Home Kames, 1 *Historical Law-Tracts* i–ii (Edinburgh: Bell & Bradfute, 1758).

76. Lieberman, "The Legal Needs of a Commercial Society" at 206.

77. Kames, 1 *Historical Law-Tracts* at xi–xii (quoting Henry St. John Bolingbroke, *Letters on the Study of History* 150–51 (London: W. Richardson and S. Clark, 1752).

78. Kames, 1 *Historical Law-Tracts* at ix (emphasis added).

79. *See* Butterfield, *The Whig Interpretation of History* at 16. *See also* Gordon S. Wood, *The Purpose of the Past: Reflections on the Use of History* (New York: Penguin Press, 2008) ("It is natural for us to want to discover the sources, the origins, of our present circumstances. But the present should not be the criterion for what we find in the past. Our perceptions and explanations of the past should not be directly shaped by the issues and problems of our own time."); Pocock, "The Origins of Study of the Past: A Comparative Approach" at 211–14 (1962) (discussing the importance of an historian's "social awareness" of the past before one can ever relate history to the present).

80. Kames, 1 *Historical Law-Tracts* at ix.

81. Ibid. at xi.

82. Kames most likely borrowed from Bolingbroke concerning the importance of a law's "spirit," which was also an implicit reference to the common law. *See* Kunal M. Parker, *Common Law, History, and Democracy in America, 1790–1900* at 46–50 (Cambridge, NY: Cambridge University Press, 2011). For a discussion of historical consciousness, see Pocock, "British History" at 614–15.

83. Skinner, "The Limits of Historical Explanations" at 214.

84. Pocock, *The Ancient Constitution and the Feudal Law* at 246. For the politics behind Bolingbroke's history, see Quentin Skinner, "The Principles and Practice of Opposition: The Case of Bolingbroke versus Walpole," in *Historical Perspectives: Studies in English Thought and Society in Honor of J.H. Plumb* 93–128 (Neil McKendrick ed., London: Europa Publications, 1974).

85. Pocock, *The Ancient Constitution and the Feudal Law* at 246–47.

86. Lieberman, "The Legal Needs of a Commercial Society" at 209.

87. Bolingbroke, *Letters on the Study of History* at 48.

88. Henry Home Kames, "Of the Laws of Motion," in 1 *Essays and Observations: Physical and Literary* 2–3 (Edinburgh: G. Hamilton and J. Balfour, 1754).

89. Henry Home Kames, *Select Decisions of the Court of Sessions, from the Year 1752 to the Year 1768* at iii (2d ed., Edinburgh: Bell & Bradfute, 1799).

90. Wilson, 1 *Collected Works of James Wilson* at 457–58, 583.

91. Ibid. at 432.

92. Wilson, 2 *Collected Works of James Wilson* at 769.

93. Wilson, 1 *Collected Works of James Wilson* at 457–58.

94. Ibid. at 458.

95. Morris L. Cohen, "Thomas Jefferson Recommends a Course of Law Study," in *The History of Legal Education in the United States: Commentaries and Primary Sources* 169, 171 (Steve Sheppard ed., Pasadena, CA: Salem Press, 1999).

96. Letter of Thomas Jefferson to John Garland Jefferson, June 11, 1790, in 5 *The Writings of Thomas Jefferson* 181 (New York: Putnam's, 1895). For more on Bolingbroke and Kames' influence on Jefferson's perception of history, see Hannah Spahn, *Thomas Jefferson, Time, and History* 107–14 (Charlottesville: University of Virginia Press, 2011).

97. *See* Zoltan Haraszti, *John Adams and the Prophets of Progress* (Harvard University Press, 1952); 1 *The Diary and Autobiography of John Adams: Diary 1755–1770*, at 11–12, 35–36, 38, 40, 73, 176, 200, 210, 253 (L.H. Butterfield ed., Cambridge, MA: Harvard University Press, 1961).

98. 1 *Portrait of a Patriot* at 149.

99. Ibid. at 157.

100. Ibid. at 157–58. *See also* Forrest McDonald, "A Founding Father's Library," in 1 *Literature of Liberty: A Review of Contemporary Legal Thought* (Leonard P. Liggio ed., Menlo Park, CA: Cato Institute, 1978).

101. Francis Dana, "Charge to the Grand Jury Delivered to the Court of Common Pleas of Portland, Massachusetts," June 4, 1792, reprinted in *The Eastern Herald* (Portland, Mass.), June 4, 1792, at 2, col. 3.

102. Wilson, "Thomas Jefferson's Early Notebooks" at 449–50.

103. 1 *The Diary and Autobiography of John Adams* at 251–55.

104. Ibid. at 254.

105. Ibid.

106. Bailyn, *Ideological Origins of the American Revolution* at 80–81.

107. John Adams, "A Dissertation on the Canon and Feudal Law," in 3 *The Works of John Adams, Second President of the United States* 447, 464 (Charles Francis Adams ed., Boston: Little, Brown, 1851).

108. The majority of the founding generation prescribed to the Whig version of history. They "assumed an ancient constitution, which, through immemorial common law, guaranteed the rights of Englishmen in perpetuity." Robert A. Ferguson, *Law and Letters in American Culture* 14 (Cambridge, MA: Harvard University Press, 1984). *See also* Gordon, "The Struggle Over the Past" at 126. ("The Revolutionaries shared with other Englishmen a dynamic view of political history, according to which those ancient liberties had been gradually recovered over centuries of struggle and finally confirmed in the constitutional settlement of the Glorious Revolution of 1689. Americans believed that the English Crown and Parliament were reversing the course of history and once again conspiring against traditional liberty in their treatment of the colonies.").

109. Powell, "Rules for Originalists" at 662.

110. Robert W. Bennett and Lawrence Solum, *Constitutional Originalism: A Debate* 58 (Ithaca, NY: Cornell University Press, 2011). For another argument detailing that originalism and history are not one and the same, see Tushnet, "Interdisciplinary Legal Scholarship" at 914.

111. This was particularly true of original intent originalism. *See* Berger, *Government By Judiciary* at 314–15 ("To thrust aside the dead hand of the

Framers is to thrust aside the Constitution. The argument that new meanings may be given to words employed by the Framers aborts their design; it reduces the Constitution to an empty shell into which each shifting judicial majority pours its own preferences."); Raoul Berger, "Original Intent and Boris Bittker," 66 *Indiana Law Journal* 723, 755 (1991) (arguing the "great merit of originalism" is that it is a "simple concept"). *See also* Jamal Greene, "Selling Originalism," 97 *Georgetown Law Journal* 647, 662 (2009) (noting that originalism's "simplicity is also one of its chief selling points, and therefore, one of its greatest strengths").

112. It is what Justice Scalia had drawn from to support his turn to originalism. *See* "Scalia Defends Originalism as Best Methodology for Judging Law," University of Virginia Law School News & Events, April 20, 2010, available at https://www.law.virginia.edu/html/news/2010_spr/scalia.htm. *See also* Eric Posner, "Why Originalism is So Popular," *The New Republic*, January 15, 2011; Reva B. Siegal, "Dead or Alive: Originalism as Popular Constitutionalism in *Heller*," 122 *Harvard Law Review* 191 (2008); Tara Smith, "Why Originalism Won't Die: Common Mistakes in Competing Theories of Judicial Interpretation," 2 *Duke Journal of Constitutional Law and Public Policy* 159 (2007).

113. This is not to say that it has not happened. A notable example is Chief Justice Burger's failure to define the "press" in the First Amendment. *See First National Bank of Boston v. Bellotti*, 435 U.S. 765, 801–2 (1978) (Burger, C.J., concurring).

114. The Standard Model Second Amendment is a notable example in this regard. *See* Patrick J. Charles, "The Second Amendment in Historiographical Crisis: Why the Supreme Court Must Reexamine the Embarrassing 'Standard Model' Moving Forward, 39 *Fordham Urban Law Journal* 1727 (2012). For a counter argument, which asserts that a Standard Model should be followed as the eighteenth-century concept of the right is unacceptable, see Nicholas J. Johnson, "Rights Versus Duties, History Department Lawyering, and the Incoherence of Justice Stevens *Heller* Dissent," 39 *Fordham Urban Law Journal* 1503 (2012).

115. *See* Cornell, "*Heller*, New Originalism, and Law Office History" at 1098–1106. *See also* Thomas W. Merrill, "Originalism, Stare Decisis and the Promotion of Judicial Restraint," 22 *Constitutional Commentary* 271, 277–78 (2005) (stating originalism is no better than arguing from precedent in that both can be manipulated by lawyers).

116. *See* Whittington, "The New Originalism" at 609 ("The primary virtue of new originalism is one of constitutional fidelity, not of judicial restraint or democratic majoritarianism."); John O. McGinnis and Michael Rappaport, "Original Interpretive Principles as the Core of Originalism," 24 *Constitutional Commentary* 371, 374–75 (2007) (defending original methods originalism on the grounds fidelity to founders' constitution). *See also* Jamal Greene, "On the Origins of Originalism," 88 *Texas Law Review* 1, 8–9 (2009) (stating "fidelity to the Constitution" is

one purpose of originalism, but it also seeks to prevent "organic alterations" to constitutional text "through social change and judicial innovation").

117. *McCulloch v. Maryland*, 17 U.S. 316, 408, 417–18 (1819).

118. *Dallas v. Commonwealth*, 4 U.S. 237 (1802).

119. Ibid. at 240.

120. Ibid. at 242.

121. Ibid. at 244.

122. *McIlvaine v. Coxe's Lessee*, 6 U.S. 280, 280–92 (1804). The preamble of the 1776 New Jersey Constitution acknowledged the doctrine of reciprocal allegiance and the breaking of allegiance ties with Great Britain, but makes no mention of alienage. *See* N.J. Const. of 1776, preamble ("Whereas all the constitutional authority ever possessed by the kings of Great Britain over these colonies, or their other dominions, was, by compact, derived from the people, and held of them, for the common interest of the whole society; *allegiance and protection are, in the nature of things, reciprocal ties*, each equally depending upon the other, and liable to be dissolved by the others being refused or withdrawn. And whereas George the Third, king of Great Britain, has refused protection to the good people of these colonies; and, by assenting to sundry acts of the British parliament, attempted to subject them to the absolute dominion of that body; and has also made war upon them, in the most cruel and unnatural manner, for no other cause, than asserting their just rights—all civil authority under him is necessarily at an end, and a dissolution of government in each colony has consequently taken place.") (emphasis added).

123. *McIlvaine*, 6 U.S. at 292–98 (Patterson, J., dissenting).

124. Ibid. at 311–12 (Patterson, J., dissenting).

125. Ibid. at 312–15 (Patterson, J., dissenting).

126. In *Calder v. Bull*, the legal approach taken by all three justices undercuts originalism. *See* Alison L. LaCroix, "Temporal Imperialism," 158 *University of Pennsylvania Law Review* 1329, 1337–43 (2010) (discussing the complex judicial layers of *Calder v. Bull*); Treanor, "Against Textualism" at 1003; Thomas B. McAffee, "The Constitution Based on the Consent of the Governed—Or, Should We Have an Unwritten Constitution," 80 *Oregon Law Review*, 1245, 1256–62 (2001) (discussing the "unwritten" constitution dilemma); Michael C. Dorf, "Integrating Normative and Descriptive Constitutional Theory: The Case of Original Meaning," 85 *Georgetown Law Journal* 1765, 1774–75 (1997); Maeva Marcus, "The Effect (or Non-Effect) of Founders on the Supreme Court Bench," 80 *George Washington Law Review* 1794, 1804–5 (2012) (discussing how *Calder v. Bull* shows "how unsettled constitutional meaning was in 1787"). But a number of originalists do not see *Calder v. Bull* as defying originalism. *See* McGinnis and Rappaport, "Original Methods Originalism" at 757 n. 18; Randy E. Barnett, "The People or the State? *Chisholm v. Georgia* and Popular Sovereignty," 93 *Virginia Law Review* 1729, 1752 (2007); Bork, *The Tempting of America* at 19–20, 25.

127. *Calder v. Bull*, 3 U.S. 386, 390 (1798).
128. Ibid. at 392.
129. Ibid. at 395.
130. Ibid. at 395 (Paterson, J., concurring).
131. Such an approach was common in the late eighteenth century and it was certainly within the purview of the judiciary to define the Constitution's text with standard legal reasoning. *See* Powell, "The Original Understanding of Original Intent" at 895–96, 910–11.
132. *Calder v. Bull*, 3 U.S. 386, 390, 399–400 (1798) (Iredell, J., dissenting).
133. *Respublica v. Oswald*, 1 U.S. 319, 325 (1788) (weighing the English history of libels to understand the scope of the Pennsylvania Constitution's Press Clause); *Vanhorne's Lessee v. Dorrance*, 2 U.S. 304, 305–12 (1795) (weighing the history of Parliamentary powers to the constructs of the Pennsylvania Constitution); *Chisholm v. Georgia*, 2 U.S. 419, 470–71 (weighing the history of the American Revolution and Declaration of Independence to understanding the scope of the Constitution); ibid. at 437–44 (Iredell, J., dissenting) (analyzing the history of the English crown to suits by citizens). *See also* Powell, "The Original Understanding of Original Intent" at 922–93 (discussing the rules of construction employed in *Chisholm*).
134. Holmes, "The Path of the Law" at 221.
135. *See* Jeffrey S. Sutton, "The Role of History in Judging Disputes About the Meaning of the Constitution," 41 *Texas Tech Law Review* 1173 (2009); Matthew J. Festa, "Applying a Usable Past: The Use of History in Law," 38 *Seton Hall Law Review* 479 (2008); Cass R. Sunstein, "The Idea of a Useable Past," 95 *Columbia Law Review* 601 (1995).

Chapter 3

1. R. Kent Newmyer, *John Marshall and the Heroic Age of the Supreme Court* 98 (Baton Rouge: Louisiana State University Press, 2001).
2. James Iredell, *Middle Circuit, 1793, Virginia* (1793) (Library of Congress Rare Books Division, Washington, D.C.).
3. *Ware v. Hylton*, 3 U.S. 199, 199–207 (1796). For the text of the 1783 Treaty of Paris, see Roger L. Kemp, *Documents of American Democracy: A Collection of Essential Works* 143 (Jefferson, NC: McFarland, 2010).
4. Although Patrick Henry lost the case, Iredell detailed in a letter how persuasive the prominent Virginia lawyer had been in court:

P[atrick] Henry has been speaking these two days, & tho' he spoke 4 hours each day I was not in the least tired. He is certainly the first orator I ever heard—speaks with the most ease, the least embarrassment, the greatest variety, and with an illustration of imagery altogether original but perfectly correct. His manner too in respect to his adversaries is very gentlemanly, and I am told it always is, and that notwithstanding he is the Idol of every popular Assembly he never was known to say anything per-

sonally offensive but in his own defense and then he is always sure to make his adversaries repent their attack. He is a much more solid character and better Reasoner than I expected to find him, and I have every reason to believe from accounts received of him here by many gentlemen that he is a man of real benevolence and integrity. You may imagine as to his oratory I am quite impartial for in the course of many points he has argued he has not satisfied me in the slightest degree as to anything but the Payments into the Treasury about which I still hesitate. I am astonished to find that the Defendant's Lawyers here, who are certainly very able Men [which includes John Marshall] think the defence as to the breach of the Treaty by G.B. seriously tenable. But I was much more so to find that Mr. Johnson and Mr. Griffin were doubtful about it, and I believe for this reason principally directed a second argument. On this point neither Mr. [Chief Justice John] Jay or myself had a shadow of a doubt for one moment. Perhaps we may differ eventually about the payments into the Treasury but I am not sure. The indication of my opinion at present is in support of them. The court will certainly not be over till next week but what time in the week I can't conjecture. I will not fail to acquaint you of our determination.

James Iredell to Mr. Johnston (May 29, 1793) (on file with the Library of Congress Manuscripts Division, Washington, D.C.).
5. *Ware v. Hylton*, 3 U.S. 199, 236–37 (1796).
6. Newmyer, *John Marshall and the Heroic Age* at 100–101.
7. Iredell, *Middle Circuit* at 2.
8. Ibid. at 6, 10.
9. Ibid. at 50.
10. *Ware v. Hylton*, 3 U.S. 199, 227 (1796).
11. *See, e.g.*, 1 Wilson, *Collected Works of James Wilson* at 501–48.
12. *Ware v. Hylton*, 3 U.S. 199, 281 (1796) (Wilson, J., concurring).
13. Ibid.
14. U.S. Const. Art. II, § 2; U.S. Const. Art. VI, § 2.
15. *See* John O. McGinnis, "Contemporary Foreign and International Law in Constitutional Construction," 69 *Albany Law Review* 801 (2006); John O. McGinnis and Ilya Somin, "Should International Law Be Part of Our Law?" 59 *Stanford Law Review* 1175 (2007); Michael D. Ramsey, "*Missouri v. Holland* and Historical Textualism," 73 *Missouri Law Review* 969 (2008).
16. This may also hold true if one is a flexible textualist. *See* Edwin D. Dickinson, "The Law of Nations as Part of the National Law of the United States," 101 *Pennsylvania Law Review* 26, 34–46 (1952).
17. For my previous writings on this subject, see Patrick J. Charles, "The Plenary Power Doctrine and the Constitutionality of Ideological Exclusion: An Historical Perspective," 15 *Texas Review of Law and Politics* 61 (2010); Patrick J. Charles, "Decoding the Fourteenth Amendment's Citizenship Clause: Un-

lawful Immigrants, Allegiance, Personal Subjection, and the Law," 51 *Washburn Law Journal* 211 (2012); Patrick J. Charles, "Recentering Foreign Affairs Preemption in *Arizona v. United States*: Federal Plenary Power, the Spheres of Government, and the Constitutionality of S.B. 1070," 60 *Cleveland State Law Review* 133 (2012).

18. For some scholarship asserting a larger "law of nations" role consistent with originalism, see Francisco Forrest Martin, "Our Constitution as Federal Treaty: A New Theory of United States Constitutional Construction Based on an Originalist Understanding for Addressing a New World," 31 *Hastings Constitutional Law Quarterly* 269 (2004); Johan D. Van Der Vyver, "Prosecuting Offenses Against the Law of Nations in the United States," 20 *Emory International Law Review* 473 (2006); Gerald L. Neuman, "International Law as a Resource in Constitutional Interpretation," 30 *Harvard Journal of Law and Public Policy* 177 (2006); Daniel A. Farber, "The Supreme Court, the Law of Nations, and Citations of Foreign Law: The Lessons of History," 95 *California Law Review* 1335 (2007); Anthony J. Bellia, Jr., and Bradford R. Clark, "The Federal Common Law of Nations," 109 *Columbia Law Review* 1 (2009).

19. *See* Alfred Rosenthal, "The Marbois-Longchamps Affair," 63 *The Pennsylvania Magazine of History and Biography* 294 (July 1939); G.S. Rowe and Alexander W. Knott, "Power, Justice, and Foreign Relations in the Confederation Period: The Marbois-Longchamps Affair, 1784–1786," 104 *The Pennsylvania Magazine of History and Biography* 275 (July 1980); Peter P. Hill, *French Perceptions of the Early Republic, 1783–1793*, at 16–17 (Philadelphia: American Philosophical Society, 1988).

20. For more on Thomas McKean, see John M. Coleman, "Thomas McKean and the Origin of an Independent Judiciary," 34 *Pennsylvania History* 111 (April 1967); G.S. Rowe, "A Valuable Acquisition in Congress: Thomas McKean, Delegate from Delaware to the Continental Congress, 1774–1783," 38 *Pennsylvania History* 225 (July 1971); G.S. Rowe, "Thomas McKean and the Coming of the Revolution," 96 *The Pennsylvania Magazine of History and Biography* 3 (1972).

21. Court Opinion *Commonwealth of Pennsylvania v. Charles Julian de Longchamps* (McKean, J.), Supplement in John Jay to Congress, February 16, 1785, in *John Jay Papers Digital Collection* (Columbia University Library) (originals at National Archives and Records Administration, Washington, D.C.).

22. Ibid.

23. Ibid.

24. John Jay to Congress, February 16, 1785, in *John Jay Papers Digital Collection* (Columbia University Library) (originals at National Archives and Records Administration, Washington, D.C.). Left-leaning immigration law professors have falsely proclaimed the Supreme Court's plenary power over immigration was created out of thin air. *See* L. Henkin, "The Constitution and United States Sovereignty:

A Century of Chinese Exclusion and its Progeny," 100 *Harvard Law Review* 853 (1987); Hiroshi Motomura, "Immigration Law After a Century of Plenary Power: Phantom Constitutional Norms and Statutory Interpretation," 100 *Yale Law Journal* 545 (1990). There are commentators who declare the Supreme Court created the doctrine out of sense of national peril. *See* Matthew J. Lindsay, "Immigration, Sovereignty, and the Constitution of Foreignness," 45 *Connecticut Law Review* 743 (2013); Matthew J. Lindsay, "Immigration as Invasion: Sovereignty, Security, and the Origins of the Federal Immigration Power," 45 *Harvard Civil Rights–Civil Liberties Law Review* 1 (2010). However, the history of the Constitution and law of nations weighs heavily in favor of the plenary power doctrine. It is a legal doctrine that can be traced as far back as the fifteenth century. *See generally* Charles, "The Plenary Power Doctrine and the Constitutionality of Ideological Exclusions" at 61–126.

25. The deficiencies with the Articles of Confederation and its differences with the Constitution are significant in understanding the scope of the Constitution, for Federalists often compared the two documents to achieve ratification. *See* Rakove, *Original Meanings* at 11.

26. U.S. Const. Art. I, § 8, paragraph 10.

27. U.S. Const. Art. I, § 8, paragraph 3.

28. Charles, "The Plenary Power Doctrine and the Constitutionality of Ideological Exclusion" at 93–107. A number of James Bowdoin's letters convey how the Articles of Confederation were insufficient to deter Great Britain from taking advantage of the individual states. *See* James Bowdoin to Nicholas Van Dyke, July 10, 1786, in *The Papers of Nicholas Van Dyke* (Library of Congress, Washington, D.C.) ("It is a misfortune to the Union, that no proper Regulations of Trade have been yet adopted by the States, to counteract those of Great Britain, which are manifestly calculated to render the States in every respect insignificant, though at the same time they operate to their own advantage."); James Bowdoin to Nicholas Van Dyke, July 22, 1785, in *The Papers of Nicholas Van Dyke* ("It is much to be desired that Congress may be vested with a well guarded power to regulate the Trade of the United States.... In the meantime it is to be relied on, that the mutual Friendship ... of the several States towards each other"). *See also* James Iredell, *Answers to Mr. Mason's Objections to the New Constitution Recommended by the Late Convention at Philadelphia* 7 (Newbern, NC: Hodge and Wills, 1788) (stating offenses against the law of nations "immediately" affect "the security, the honour or the interest of the United States at large, and of course must come within the sphere of the Legislative authority which is entrusted with their protection.").

29. *See, e.g.*, John Jay to Nicholas Van Dyke, January 29, 1785, in *The Papers of Nicholas Van Dyke* ("It will be unnecessary to remark to your Excellency the influence of our domestic Affairs on our foreign; their intimate connection with each other and how necessary it is that they who are concerned in con-

ducting the latter should be accurately informed of the State of the former."). *See also* Tucker, *View of the Constitution of the United States* at 190–92.

30. *See* Congress Circular to Nicholas Van Dyke, July 2, 1783, in *The Papers of Nicholas Van Dyke* ("Congress for sometime past generally consisted of less than" the nine States necessary to pass any legislation, whereas the "public ... has suffered and continues to suffer great delay and embarrassment"); Congress Attendance 7–19 February 1784, in *The Papers of Nicholas Van Dyke* (showing attendance reached delegates as low as five states and no higher than seven states); Congress Circular to Nicholas Van Dyke, November 11, 1784, in *The Papers of Nicholas Van Dyke* (delegates from Georgia, South Carolina, Virginia, and New Jersey expressing disappointment in attendance, an "important matter which nearly concerns the welfare & happiness of the Union").

31. John Jay to Edmund Randolph, September 24, 1788, in *John Jay Papers Digital Collection* (Columbia University Library) (original available at Columbia University, Butler Library, Rare Books Division).

32. John Jay, "A Charge to the Grand Jury," reprinted in *The City Gazette and Daily Advertiser* (Charleston, SC), August 14, 1793, at 2, col. 1.

33. Ibid.

34. John Jay, *The Charge of Chief Justice Jay to the Grand Juries of the Eastern Circuit* 7 (1790).

35. Ibid. at 11–12 (emphasis added).

36. James Madison to George Washington, April 16, 1787, reprinted in *The Debates in the Federal Convention of 1787 Which Framed the Constitution of the United States* 592–94 (Oxford University Press, 1920).

37. James Madison, "Vices of Political System of the United States," reprinted in *Selected Writings of James Madison* 35, 36 (Indianapolis, IN: Hackett, 2006). For more on Madison's concerns about state power and the need to distribute federal-state spheres, see Charles F. Hobson, "The Negative on State Laws: James Madison, the Constitution, and the Crisis of Republican Government," 36 *The William and Mary Quarterly* 215 (1979). For more on the law of nations and its impact on drafting the Constitution, see Andrew Lenner, "A Tale of Two Constitutions: Nationalism in the Federalist Era," 40 *The American Journal of Legal History* 72 (1996); Andrew Lenner, "Separate Spheres: Republican Constitutionalism in the Federalist Era," 41 *The American Journal of Legal History* 250 (1997).

38. James Iredell, "Charge Delivered to the Grand Jury for the District of South Carolina," May 12, 1794, reprinted in *Gazette of the United States and Daily Evening Advertiser* (Philadelphia, PA), June 12, 1794, at 2, col. 1.

39. Ibid. at col. 2 (emphasis added).

40. Ibid. at 3, col. 1.

41. Ibid.

42. James Iredell, "Charge Delivered to the Grand Jury for the Circuit Court of Pennsylvania," April 12, 1796, reprinted in *Federal Gazette and Bal-*

timore Daily Advertiser (Baltimore, MD), April 21, 1796, at 2, col. 2.

43. For some examples see, 2 *Portrait of a Patriot* at 181; Blackstone, 1 *Commentaries on the Laws of England* at 43 (showing the interrelation between the law of nature, municipal law, and the law of nations); 4 Blackstone, 4 *Commentaries on the Laws of England* at 66–67 (same); Emer De Vattel, *The Law of Nations* 68–72 (Knud Haakonssen ed., Indianapolis, IN: Liberty Fund 2008) (discussing how the "*law of nations* is originally no other than the *law of nature applied* to nations"); James Wilson, "Charge to the Grand Jury of the Circuit Court of Pennsylvania," July 22, 1793, reprinted in *The North-Carolina Journal* (Halifax, NC), August 21, 1793, pg. at 1, col. 2 ("The Law of Nature when applied to states or political societies receives a new name—that of the Law of Nations.... The law of *Nations* as well as the law of *Nature* is of *obligation indispensible*: the law of nations as well as the law of nature is of *origin divine*.").

44. James Iredell, "Charge Delivered to the Grand Jury for the Circuit Court of Pennsylvania," April 12, 1796, reprinted in *Federal Gazette and Baltimore Daily Advertiser* (Baltimore, MD), April 21, 1796, at 2, col. 3.

45. James Iredell, "Charge Delivered to the Grand Jury for the Circuit Court of Pennsylvania," April 12, 1796, reprinted in *Federal Gazette and Baltimore Daily Advertiser* (Baltimore, MD), April 22, 1796, at 2, col. 2.

46. James Iredell, "Charge Delivered to the Grand Jury for the District of South Carolina," May 12, 1794, reprinted in *Gazette of the United States and Daily Evening Advertiser* (Philadelphia, PA), June 14, 1794, at 3, col. 1.

47. James Iredell, "Charge Delivered to the Grand Jury for the Circuit Court of Pennsylvania," April 12, 1796, reprinted in *Federal Gazette and Baltimore Daily Advertiser* (Baltimore, MD), April 22, 1796, at 2, col. 2.

48. Ibid.

49. James Iredell, "Charge Delivered to the Grand Jury for the District Court of Pennsylvania," April 11, 1797, reprinted in *American Mercury* (Hartford, CT), May 1, 1797, at 2, col. 3.

50. Oliver Ellsworth, "Charge Delivered to the Grand Jury for the District Court of Chatham County," reprinted in *Columbian Museum and Savannah Advertiser* (Savannah, GA), May 14, 1799, at 3, col. 3.

51. Ibid.

52. Of course, references to the "unwritten law" predate the eighteenth century. For some examples, see John Cowell, *The Institutes of the Lawes of England Digested Into the Method of the Civill or Imperiall Institutions* 5 (London: Tho. Roycroft, 1651) ("The unwritten Law consists of ancient customes of the Realme which are observed for Law and to the observation of which our Kings at their coronations were obliged, by Oath; notwithstanding any of these customes may be altered or nulled by Statute."); Thomas Hobbes, "A Dialogue Between a Phylosopher and a Student, of the Common-Laws

of England," in *The Art of Rhetoric, With a Discourse of the Laws of England* 1, 3 (London: William Crooke, 1681) (describing the common law as "being unwritten, and consisting in nothing else but right Reason").

53. Matthew Hale, *The History and Analysis of the Common Law of England* 1 (Stafford: J. Nutt, 1713) (referring to the common law as the "unwritten law"); De Lolme, *The Constitution of England* at 84 ("The *Unwritten Law* is thus called, not because it is only transmitted by tradition from generation to generation; but because it is not founded on any known act of the Legislature. It receives its force from immemorial custom, and, for the most part, derives its origin from Acts of Parliament enacted in the times which immediately followed the Conquest."); Blackstone, 1 *Commentaries on the Laws of England* at 63 ("The *lex non scripta*, or unwritten law, includes not only *general customs*, or the common law properly so called; but also the *particular customs* of certain parts of the kingdom; and likewise those *particular laws*, that are by custom observed only in certain courts and jurisdictions."); William Blackstone, *An Analysis of the Laws of England* 16–17 (Oxford: Clarendon Press, 1756) (describing the "unwritten law" as synonymous with the common law, which included "general customs," "particular customs," and "particular laws"); Thomas Rutherforth, 1 *Institutes of Natural Law: Being the Substance of a Course of Lectures on Grotius De Jure Belli et Pacis* 284, 287–88, 452 (3d ed., Philadelphia: William Young, 1799).

54. Thomas Jefferson also embraced the law of nations as binding every nation. *See* Charles M. Wiltse, "Thomas Jefferson on the Law of Nations," 29 *American Journal of International Law* 66 (1935); Louis Martin Sears, "Jefferson and the Law of Nations," 13 *American Political Science Review* 379 (1919).

55. For some discussions, see Peter J. Smith, "Sources of Federalism: An Empirical Analysis of the Court's Quest for Original Meaning," 52 *UCLA Law Review* 217 (2004); Balkin, "Original Meaning and Constitutional Redemption" at 520–22; Greene, "On the Origins of Originalism" at 8–18.

56. *See, e.g.*, McGinnis and Rappaport, "Original Methods Originalism" at 802 ("Nothing in the historical record we have seen ... suggests that the original methods included living constitutionalism or other principles permitting interpreters to update the Constitution to reflect changing values.").

57. *See, e.g.*, James Iredell, "Charge Delivered to the Grand Jury for the District of South Carolina," May 12, 1794, reprinted in *Gazette of the United States and Daily Evening Advertiser* (Philadelphia, PA), June 14, 1794, at 3, col. 1 (discussing how acts of legislation can supersede the law of nations and common law).

58. Oliver Ellsworth, "Charge Delivered to the Grand Jury for the District Court of Chatham County," reprinted in *Columbian Museum and Savannah Advertiser* (Savannah, GA), May 14, 1799, at 3, col. 3.

59. Ibid.

60. Adam Liptak, "Ginsburg Shares Views on Influence of Foreign Law on Her Court, and Vice Versa," *New York Times*, April 11, 2009.

61. *See, e.g.*, Greene, "On the Origins of Originalism" at 11, 56.

62. Antonin Scalia and Stephen Breyer, "Relevance of Foreign Legal Materials in U.S. Constitutional Cases: A Conversation Between U.S. Supreme Court Justices," 3 *International Journal of Constitutional Law* 519, 526 (2005).

63. *See, e.g.*, Frederick Pollock, "The Continuity of the Common Law," 11 *Harvard Law Review* 423 (1899) (discussing the international nature and growth of the common law on both sides of the Atlantic). For evidence the interrelationship between the law of nations and constitutions, see Vattel, *Law of Nations* at 91–96; *see also* J. Whitla Stinson, "The Common Law and the Law of Nations," 9 *California Law Review* 470 (1920). For a survey of foreign law in American constitutional interpretation, see Paul Finkelman, "Foreign Law and American Constitutional Interpretation: A Long and Verable Tradition," 63 *New York University Annual Survey of American Law* 29 (2007).

64. This is reflected in a number of early nineteenth-century American writings on the law of nations. For some examples, see James Mackintosh, "A Discourse on the Study of the Law of Nature and Nations," 1 *Journal of Jurisprudence* 344 (1821); "Definition and History of the Law of Nations," 28 *American Jurist and Legal Magazine* 1 (1842); "Definition and History of the Law of Nations," 28 *American Jurist and Legal Magazine* 249 (1843).

65. "Course of Study in Law, Recommended by Lord Mansfield, to Mr. Drummond, 1774," in *The New York Magazine, or Literary Repository* 235 (April 1793).

66. Alexander Addison, Open Letter, in *City Gazette and Commercial Advertiser* (Charleston, SC), Apr. 15, 1821, at 2, col. 1.

67. "The Present State of Columbia College, in New York," in *The New York Magazine, or Literary Repository* 291–92 (May 1794).

68. John Daniel Gross, Natural Principles of Rectitude, for the Conduct of Main in All States and Situations in Life 401–6 (1795).

69. Ibid. at 411. The infringement of other rights was viewed as inviolate of the law of nations. *See, e.g.*, Thomas Smith to Joseph Shippen, April 13, 1774, in 1 *American Archives: Documents of the American Revolution, 1774–1776*, at 273 (Fourth Series, Peter Force ed., Washington, D.C., 1833–46) (stating a trial by one's peers was part of "natural justice" or the "law of nations").

70. Ruth Bader Ginsburg, "A Decent Respect to the Opinions of [Human]kind": The Value of Comparative Perspective in Constitutional Adjudication, International Academy of Comparative Law, American University (July 30, 2010).

71. Ibid.

72. Scalia and Breyer, "Relevance of Foreign Legal Materials in U.S. Constitutional Cases" at 526.

73. James Wilson, "Charge Delivered to the

Grand Jury for the District Court of Pennsylvania," July 22, 1793, reprinted in *The North-Carolina Journal* (Halifax, NC), August 21, 1793, at 1, col. 2.

74. Ibid.

75. *See* Wilson, 1 *Collected Works of James Wilson* at 502–7, 532–34. See also Gross, *Natural Principles of Rectitude, for the Conduct of Main in All States and Situations in Life* at 347–64, 382–86 (New York: T. and J. Swords, 1795).

76. *See, e.g.,* Charles, "Restoring 'Life, Liberty, and the Pursuit of Happiness' in Our Constitutional Jurisprudence" at 477–523. The Declaration was not the first or only instance where the founding generation relied on the law of nature and nations as support for republican liberty. *See, e.g., The Votes and Proceedings of the Freeholders and Other Inhabitants of the Town of Boston* 3 (Boston: Edes and Gill, 1772) (*"Just and true Liberty, equal and impartial Liberty"* in matters spiritual and temporal constitute "a Thing that all Men are clearly entitled to, by the external and immutable Laws of God and Nature, as well as by the Law of Nations, and all well grounded municipal Laws, which must have their Foundation in the former."); Benjamin Franklin to M. Dumas, December 19, 1775, in 4 *American Archives: Documents of the American Revolution, 1774–1776,* at 352 (Fourth Series, Peter Force ed., Washington, D.C.: n.p., 1833–46) (acknowledging receipt of Vattel and promising to frequently consult the law of nations); "Candidus, on Independence," in 5 *American Archives: Documents of the American Revolution, 1774–1776,* at 88 (Fourth Series, Peter Force ed., Washington, D.C.: n.p., 1833–1846) (asserting the posting of a standing army "without our consent, or a single farthing taken from us in the like manner" was a violation of the law of nations).

77. Wilson, 1 *Collected Works of James Wilson* at 494–95.

78. Ibid. at 333.

79. Ibid. at 527.

80. Ibid. at 333, 528–29. It is likely that Wilson, Jay, and Iredell took this principle from Jean Jacques Burlamaqui's popular treatise. *See* Jean Jacques Burlamaqui, 1 *The Principles of Natural and Political Law* 199 (2d ed., London: J. Nourse, 1763) ("All that can be said on this subject is, that when customs of an innocent nature are introduced among nations; each of them is reasonably supposed to submit to those customs, so long as they have not made any declaration to the contrary. This is all the force or effect that can be given to received customs; but a very different effect from that of a law properly called.").

81. Wilson, 1 *Collected Works of James Wilson* at 529.

82. Ibid. at 498, 531.

83. Jay, *The Charge of Chief Justice Jay to the Grand Juries of the Eastern Circuit* at 11.

84. James Iredell, "Charge Delivered to the Grand Jury for the District of South Carolina," May 12, 1794, reprinted in *Gazette of the United States and Daily Evening Advertiser* (Philadelphia, PA), June 12, 1794, at 2, col. 2.

85. Wilson, 1 *Collected Works of James Wilson* at 503–5, 537. *See also* Charles, "Restoring 'Life, Liberty, and the Pursuit of Happiness' in Our Constitutional Jurisprudence" at 502–17.

86. Alexander Widcocks, "Charge to the Grand Jury for the City of Philadelphia," September 17, 1794, reprinted in *The Oracle of the Day* (Portsmouth, NH), October 7, 1794, at 1 col. 3.

87. Ibid.

88. David Campbell, "Charge to the Grand Jury Delivered in the Ohio Territory," August 1791, reprinted in *The Freeman's Journal; Or, the North-American Intelligencer* (Philadelphia, PA), November 9, 1791, at 3 cols. 2–3.

89. *See generally* Cesare Beccaria, *An Essay on Crimes and Punishment* (London: J. Almon, 1764); Francis Hutcheson, *An Inquiry Into the Original of Our Ideas of Beauty and Virtue* (London: J. Darby, 1726). *See also* 1 Blackstone, *Commentaries* at 135; Burlamaqui, *The Principles of Natural and Political Law* at 89. ("In states where the people have some share in the government, every individual interests himself in the public good, because each, according to his equality or merit, partakes of the general success, or feels the loss sustained by the state.") Hutcheson and Beccaria were particularly influential in late eighteenth-century thought. See Charles Maurice Wiltse, *The Jeffersonian Tradition in American Democracy* 70–71 (Chapel Hill: University of North Carolina Press, 1935); Henry Steele Commager, "The American Enlightenment and the Ancient World: A Study in Paradox," 83 *Proceedings of the Massachusetts Historical Society* 3 (1971); Donald S. Lutz, "The Relative Influence of European Writers on Late Eighteenth-Century American Political Thought," 78 *The American Political Science Review* 189 (1984); Daniel Walker Howe, "Why the Scottish Enlightenment Was Useful to the Framers of the American Constitution," 31 *Comparative Studies in Society and History* 572 (1989); Mark David Hall, "James Wilson's Law Lectures," 128 *The Pennsylvania Magazine of History and Biography* 65, 68 (2004).

90. James Bowdoin to Nicholas Van Dyke, July 22, 1785, in *The Papers of Nicholas Van Dyke.*

91. "To the Hon. Eldridge Gerry, Esq.," in *The Massachusetts Centinel* (Boston, MA), November 14, 1787, at 2, col. 3.

92. *See* Ray Raphael, *Constitutional Myths: What We Get Wrong and How to Get it Right* 68–72 (New York: New Press, 2013).

93. "The Citizens of America," in *The Freeman's Journal; Or, the North-American Intelligencer* (Philadelphia, PA), July 16, 1788, at 1, col. 1.

94. *See* Patrick J. Charles, "Scribble Scrabble, the Second Amendment, and Historical Guideposts: A Short Reply to Lawrence Rosenthal and Joyce Lee Malcolm," 105 *Northwestern Law Review* 1821, 1827–29 (2011).

95. George Thatcher, "Scribble Scrabble," in *The Cumberland Gazette* (Portland, ME), December 8, 1786, at 1, col. 3.

96. George Thatcher, "Scribble Scrabble," in *The*

Cumberland Gazette (Portland, ME), January 26, 1787, at 1, col. 2.

97. George Thatcher, "Scribble Scrabble," in *The Cumberland Gazette* (Portland, ME), March 23, 1787, at 4, col. 1.

98. George Thatcher "Scribble Scrabble," in *The Cumberland Gazette* (Portland, ME), December 8, 1786, at 1, col. 3.

99. George Thatcher, "Scribble Scrabble," in *The Cumberland Gazette* (Portland, ME), January 26, 1787, at 1, col. 3. ("Whatever right the people had to use arms in a state of nature, they retain at the present time, notwithstanding the 17th article of the Bill of Rights.")

100. George Thatcher, "Scribble Scrabble," in *The Cumberland Gazette* (Portland, ME), December 8, 1786, at 1, col. 3. *See also* ibid. at 1, cols. 1–2. ("'All power resides originally in the people' and in the very few instances, if any, is the declaration of rights immediately restrictive of the rights and powers of the people: But it rather vests powers in the legislature to controul, modify and direct the alienable rights of the people, from time to time, as the legislature shall think the good of the people may require. Thus, though authority to controul any, if not all, the alienable rights of the people ([except such as are reserved in their bill of rights] yet, until that is actually done by the legislature, the people have a clear right to exercise those rights in the way and manner they think proper; subject only to the great law of reason. And where the declaration secures a particular right, in itself alienable, or the use of a right, in the people, it does not at the same time contain, by implication, a negative of any other use of that right.")

101. George Thatcher, "Scribble Scrabble," in *The Cumberland Gazette* (Portland, ME), March 23, 1787, at 4, col. 1.

102. *See* Bailyn, *The Ideological Origins of the American Revolution* at 77. ("Liberty ... was the capacity to exercise 'natural rights' within limits set not by the mere will or desire of men in power but by non-arbitrary law—law enacted by legislatures containing within them the proper balance of forces.")

103. Israel Smith, "Charge to the Grand Jury Delivered to County of Cumberland, New Jersey," reprinted in *Gazette of the United States, and Philadelphia Daily Advertiser* (Philadelphia, PA), June 22, 1798, at 3, cols. 1–2.

104. *See* 47 *The New England Historical and Genealogical Register* 371 (1893).

105. Lot Hall, "Charge to the Grand Jury Delivered to Windham County, South Carolina," August 1797, reprinted in *Federal Galaxy* (Brattleboro, VT), August 18, 1797, at 4, col. 4. *See also* Edmund Pendleton, "Charge to the Grand Jury Delivered to Georgetown, Cheraws and Camden Districts," reprinted in *The Charleston Morning Post and Daily Advertiser* (Charleston, SC), December 13, 1786, at 2, col. 4. (The people support "no master but the laws; which we ourselves have made for our common good, in obeying those laws, and enforcing them when and where we can.").

106. Elihu Hall Bay, "Charge to the Grand Jury Delivered to the Camden District, South Carolina," April 1791, reprinted in *The City Gazette or Daily Advertiser* (Charleston, SC), May 20, 1791, at 2, col. 1. For more on Judge Bay, see Elihu Hall Bay, 1 *Reports of Cases Argued and Determined in the Superior Courts of Law in the State of South Carolina* (2d ed., New York: I. Riley, 1809).

107. John Sullivan, "Charge to the Grand Jury Delivered to Exeter, New Hampshire," July 16, 1790, reprinted in *The New Hampshire Gazetteer* (Exeter, NH), July 16, 1790, at 3, col. 1.

108. Ibid. at cols. 1–2. Sullivan was not the only late eighteenth-century jurist to view America's constitutional experience as unique in the history of mankind. *See* Edmund Pendleton, "Charge to the Grand Jury Delivered to Georgetown, Cheraws and Camden Districts," reprinted in *The Charleston Morning Post and Daily Advertiser* (Charleston, SC), December 13, 1786, at 2, col. 1 ("The political institutions of America, considered as a system, display a purity and refinement, which is without example in the annals of mankind.").

109. For more on John Sullivan, see Thomas C. Armory, *The Military Services of Major-General John Sullivan* (Boston: Wiggin and Lunt, 1868).

110. 1 *The Letters and Papers of Major General John Sullivan* 142 (Otis Hammond ed., Concord: New Hampshire Historical Society, 1930).

111. Henry St. John Bolingbroke, "Letter X: Dissertation on Parties," in 2 *The Works of Lord Bolingbroke* 88 (Philadelphia: Carey and Hart, 1841) (emphasis added).

112. *Compare* Barnett, *Restoring the Lost Constitution* (arguing for a presumption of liberty in line with the framers' understanding of constitutionalism), *with* Charles, "Restoring 'Life, Liberty, and the Pursuit of Happiness' in Our Constitutional Jurisprudence" (showing the presumption of liberty argument to be without historical merit).

113. Richard Peters, "Charge to the Grand Jury Delivered to the United States District of Pennsylvania," reprinted in *The Philadelphia Gazette and Universal Daily Advertiser* (Philadelphia, PA), August 23, 1794, at 3, col. 1.

114. Ibid. For a history of Richard Peter's life, see Royce Shingleton, *Richard Peters: Champion of the New South* (Macon, GA: Mercer University Press, 1985).

115. Edward Shippen, "Charge to the Court of Oyer and Terminer," reprinted in *Dunlap and Claypoole's American Daily Advertiser* (Philadelphia, PA), August 26, 1794, at 3, col. 4.

116. For a history of Jacob Rush's judicial career, see Louis Richards, "Honorable Jacob Rush, of the Pennsylvania Judiciary," 39 *The Pennsylvania Magazine of History and Biography* 53 (1915).

117. Jacob Rush, "Charge to the County of Berks," August 1794, reprinted in *The Philadelphia Gazette and University Daily Advertiser* (Philadelphia, PA), August 21, 1794, at 3, col. 3.

118. Ibid. at col. 4.

119. James Iredell, "Charge Delivered to the Grand

Jury for the District Court of Pennsylvania," April 11, 1797, reprinted in *American Mercury* (Hartford, CT), May 1, 1797, at 2, col. 3.

120. James Iredell, "Charge Delivered to the Grand Jury for the District Court of Massachusetts," October 12, 1792, reprinted in *Gazette of the United States* (Philadelphia, PA), November 3, 1792, at 1, col. 1 (emphasis added).

121. Jay, *The Charge of Chief Justice Jay to the Grand Juries of the Eastern Circuit* at 14 (emphasis added).

122. John Jay, "Charge to the Grand Jury," reprinted in *The City Gazette and Daily Advertiser* (Charleston, SC), August 14, 1793, at 2, col. 1.

123. *McCulloch v. Maryland*, 17 U.S. 316 (1819).

124. Ibid. at 408.

125. Ibid. at 417–18.

126. *See, e.g.*, Noah Webster, *A Collection of Essays and Fugitive Writings: On Moral, Historical, Political and Literary Subjects* 30 (Boston: I. Thomas and E.T. Andrews, 1790). ("The public good or safety requires that the powers of a Legislature should be coextensive with those of the people. That a Legislature should be competent to pass any law that the public safety and interest requires, is a position that no man will controvert.")

127. Charles, "Scribble Scrabble, the Second Amendment, and Historical Guideposts" at 1827–29.

128. Thomas McKean, "Charge Delivered to the Grand Jury for the Court of Oyer and Terminer," reprinted in *Porcupine's Gazette* (Philadelphia, PA), November 30, 1797, at 3, col. 3.

129. Alexander James Dallas, 1 *Reports of Cases Ruled and Adjudged in the Courts of Pennsylvania, Before and Since the Revolution* 325 (Philadelphia: T. Bradford, 1790).

130. William Paterson, *The Charge of Judge Paterson to the Jury in the Case of Vanhorne's Lessee Against Dorrance* 12–13 (Philadelphia: Samuel H. Smith, 1796).

131. Ibid. at 14.

132. "Liberty," *The Independent Chronicle and the Universal Advertiser* (Boston, MA), Aug. 20, 1789, at 1.

133. For an example, see *Calder v. Bull*, 3 U.S. 386 (1798) (discussing how the text of the Ex Post Facto Clause could be interpreted broadly, but once the clause was placed in context and the justices realized the consequences of a broad interpretation, the clause was read narrowly).

134. Wilson, 1 *Collected Works of James Wilson* at 432. *See also* Wilson, 1 *Collected Works of James Wilson* at 769. ("As has already been mentioned the most proper way teach and study the common law is to teach and study it as a historical science.")

135. Wilson, 2 *Collected Works of James Wilson* at 773.

136. Kames, Historical Law-Tracts at 366.

137. Wilson, 1 *Collected Works of James Wilson* at 435.

138. Ibid.

139. *See, e.g.*, Michael Dalton, *The Countrey Jus-*

tice, Containing the Practice of the Justices of the Peace Out of Their Sessions 1 (5th ed., London: John More, 1635) ("The Common Lawes of this Realme of England, receiving principally their grounds from the Lawes of God and Nature, [which Law of Nature as it pertaineth to man, is also called the Law of Reason]"). *See also* Ephraim Kirby, *Reports of Cases Adjudged in the Superior Court of the State of Connecticut* 117 (Litchfield, CT: Collier & Adam, 1789) ("The common law of England we are to pay great deference to, as being a general system of improved reason, and a source from whence our principles of jurisprudence have been mostly drawn.").

140. Wilson, 2 *Collected Works of James Wilson* at 777. *See also* Nathaniel Chipman, *Reports and Dissertations, in Two Parts* 118 (Rutland: Anthony Haswell, 1793). ("By the common law of England, exclusive of positive laws enacted by statute, are understood those rules and maxims, by which decisions are made in their courts of law, whether in relation to the mode of prosecuting a right, or to the right itself—Rules and maxims, which have been there adopted, 'time, whereof the memory of man runneth not to the contrary.'")

141. Wilson, 1 *Collected Works of James Wilson* at 508.

142. Wilson, 2 *Collected Works of James Wilson* at 774.

143. Wilson, 1 *Collected Works of James Wilson* at 467.

144. *See, e.g.*, John O. McGinnis and Michael B. Rappaport, "Originalism and Supermajoritarianism: Defending the Nexus," 102 *Northwestern Law Review Colloquy* 18, 23 (2007) (Defending originalism on the grounds that the "living Constitution variety" is only "beneficial for interpreting a bad constitution," for it continues "the traditional problems of uncertainty and partisan judicial interpretation."). For a counterpoint, see Paul Horwitz, "The Past, Tense: The History of Crisis and the Crisis of History in Constitutional Theory," 61 *Albany Law Review* 459, 507–8 (1997) (stating the acceptance of originalism "does not demand adherence to historical accuracy but accepts that there is some value to mythmaking," which is insufficient because a "nation fed a diet of myths can grow cynical and angry"). *See also* Larry Kramer, "On Finding (and Losing) Our Origins," 26 *Harvard Journal of Law and Public Policy* 95, 96 (2003) ("It does not follow that there are no problems with originalism as an approach to constitutional interpretation, but its problems, do not, in any important sense, turn on an ability to discern or understand what the Founding was all about. To put the same point another way: it is ultimately irrelevant whether there is an objective truth about what happened at the Founding [or at any other time, for that matter, including yesterday].") ; David A. Strauss, "Why Conservatives Shouldn't Be Originalists," 31 *Harvard Journal of Law and Public Policy* 969, 976 (2008) (concluding originalism "just invites manipulation and intellectual disingenuousness" of our past, not clear historical truths").

145. *See, e.g.*, Powell, "The Original Understanding of Original Intent" at 894–902 (agreeing that the intent text was important in the late eighteenth century, but different than we understand it today, with any "concern for the drafters' purpose" being "largely illusory").

146. 2 *Portrait of a Patriot* at 95 (emphasis added).

147. James Otis, "The Rights of the British Colonies Asserted and Proved," in 1 *Pamphlets of the American Revolution, 1750–1776*, at 419–82 (Bernard Bailyn ed., Cambridge, MA: Belknap Press of Harvard University Press, 1965).

148. Samuel Adams, "Natural Rights of the Colonists," in 2 *The Writings of Samuel Adams* 354–59 (Harry Alonzo Cushing ed., New York: Putnam's, 1908).

149. Continental Congress, The Declaration of Rights and Grievances (1774).

150. A Declaration of Rights, and the Constitution and Form of Government, as Agreed by the Delegates of Maryland, in Free and Full Convention 6 (1776).

151. "Constitution of Delaware Agreed Upon in Convention at New-Castle," in 1 *American Archives: Documents of the American Revolution, 1774–1776*, at 1174, 1178 (Fifth Series, Peter Force ed., Washington, D.C., n.p., 1833–46).

152. *See* New Jersey Constitution, Art. 22 (1776), reprinted in Acts of the Council and General Assembly of the State of New-Jersey, from the Establishment of the Present Government and Declaration of Independence, to the End of the First Sitting of the Eighth Session, on the 24th Day of December, 1783, at ix (1783).

153. New York Constitution, Art. 35 (1777). New York did not date legal separation to the Declaration of Independence, but to the Battles of Lexington and Concord, which occurred on April 19, 1775.

154. Georgia Constitution, Preamble (1776).

155. New Hampshire Constitution, Preamble (1776).

156. The Journal of the Proceedings of the Provincial Congress of North Carolina, Held at Halifax the 12th Day of November, 1776, at 73 (Newbern, NC: James Davis, 1776).

157. Acts and Laws of the State of Vermont, in America 1–2 (Judah-Padock and Aleden Spooner, 1779).

158. "An Ordinance to Enable the Present Magistrate and Officers to Continue the Administration of Justice, and for Settling the General Mode of Proceedings in Criminal and Other Cases Till the Same Can Be More Amply Provided For," May 1776, in 9 *Being a Collection of All the Laws of Virginia from the First Session of the Legislature, in the Year 1619*, at 127 (William Waller Hening ed., Charlottesville: University Press of Virginia, 1821) (emphasis added). A similar ordinance was passed following the ratification of the Constitution. *See* "An Act Reducing in One, the Several Acts and Parts of Acts Concerning the General Court, and Prescribing the

Manner of Proceeding Therein in Certain Cases," December 13, 1792, in 13 *Being a Collection of All the Laws of Virginia from the First Session of the Legislature, in the Year 1619*, at 424 ("The jurisdiction of the said court shall be general over all causes, matters and things at common law, as well criminal as civil, except in such cases, as by the constitution of the United States of America, or of this Commonwealth, or any statute made by the Congress of the said United States, or the General Assembly of this Commonwealth, are or shall be vested in any other tribunal; in any of which cases the jurisdiction of the general court shall cease, unless concurrent jurisdiction be thereto expressly given by this act, or some other statute.").

159. *See, e.g.*, Kunal M. Parker, "Law 'In' and 'As' History: The Common Law in the American Polity, 1790–1900," 1 *UC Irvine Law Review* 587, 594–607 (2011) (discussing the misconception that the United States distanced itself from the common law).

160. Take for instance a legal treatise written by South Carolina Judge John Grimke. Grimke traced the law from its common law origins through the Constitution of the United States, proving that former was still applicable and important. John Grimke, *The Public Laws of the State of South Carolina, from its Establishment as a British Province Down to the Year 1790, Inclusive, in Which is Comprehended Such of the Statutes of Great Britain as Were Made of Force By the Act of Assembly of 1712* (Philadelphia: R. Aitken & Son, 1790).

161. Powell, "The Original Understanding of Original Intent" at 944.

162. Toler, Cecere, and Willett, "Pre-'Originalism'" at 304.

163. *Ibid.* at 305–6. Virtually no reliance was given to the Anti-Federalist Papers during this period, yet modern day scholars find them equally, if not more, important in understanding the Constitution in context. *See, e.g.*, Rakove, *Original Meanings* at 15–17; see also Aaron Zelinsky, "Misunderstanding the *Anti-Federalist Papers*: The Dangers of Availability," 63 *Alabama Law Review* 1067 (2012). For more on the *Federalist Papers* and Supreme Court citations, see Melvyn R. Durchslag, "The Supreme Court and the *Federalist Papers*: Is There Less Here than Meets the Eye," 14 *William and Mary Bill of Rights Journal* 243 (2005); William N. Eskridge, Jr., "Should the Supreme Court Read *The Federalist* but Not Statutory Legislative History," 66 *George Washington Law Review* 1301 (1998); Ira C. Lupu, "The Most-Cited *Federalist Papers*," 15 *Constitutional Commentary* 403 (1998); Ira C. Lupu, "Time, the Supreme Court, and *The Federalist*, 66 *George Washington Law Review* 1324 (1998); Buckner F. Melton, Jr., "The Supreme Court and *The Federalist*: A Citations List and Analysis, 1789–1996," 85 *Kentucky Law Journal* 243 (1996).

164. *Debates, Resolutions and Other Proceedings, of the Convention of the Commonwealth of Massachusetts, Convened at Boston, on the 9th of January, 1788, and continued until the 7th of February Following, for the Purpose of Assenting to and Ratifying the Con-*

stitution Recommended by the Grand Federal Convention (Boston: Adams and Nourse, 1788); *Thomas Lloyd, Debates of the Convention, of the State of Pennsylvania, on the Constitution proposed for the Government of the United States* (Philadelphia: Joseph James, 1787); *Debates and the Other Proceedings of the Convention of Virginia, Convened at Richmond, On Monday the 2d Day of June, 1788, for the Purpose of Deliberating on the Constitution Recommended By the Grand Federal Convention* (Petersburg, VA: Hunter and Prentis, 1788); *Debates Which Arose in the House of Representatives of South Carolina, on the Constitution Framed for the United States* (R. Haswell ed., Charleston, SC: City Gazette Print Office, 1788); *Proceedings and Debates of the Convention of North Carolina, Convened at Hillsborough, On Monday the 21st Day of July, 1788, for the Purpose of Deliberating and Determining on the Constitution Recommended By the General Convention at Philadelphia, the 17th Day of September, 1787* (Edenton, NC: Hodge and Wills, 1789).

165. James Madison to Thomas Ritchie, September 15, 1821, in 3 *Letters and Other Writings of James Madison* 228, 228 (Philadelphia: J.B. Lippincott, 1865).

166. Ibid. For more on James Madison and his competing views on constitutional interpretation, see Kelly, "Clio and the Court" at 120–1; Powell, "The Original Understanding of Original Intent" at 936–38; Finkelman, "The Constitution and the Intentions of the Framers" at 352.

167. James Madison to Henry St. George Tucker, December 23, 1817, in 3 *Letters and Other Writings of James Madison* at 53, 54.

168. 25 *The Papers of Alexander Hamilton* 433 (Harold C. Syrett ed., New York: Columbia University Press, 1977).

169. 6 *The Papers of John Marshall* 117 (Charles F. Hobson ed., Chapel Hill: University of North Carolina Press, 1990).

170. *See* 3 *The Papers of George Washington: Retirement Series* 113–14 (Dorothy Twohig ed., Charlottesville: University of Virginia Press, 1999); 3 *The Papers of John Marshall* 507, 508 (Charles T. Cullen et al., eds., Chapel Hill: University of North Carolina Press, 1979). *See also* Lawrence B. Custer, "Bushrod Washington and John Marshall: A Preliminary Inquiry," 4 *The American Journal of Legal History* 34, 42 (1960). Bushrod Washington replaced his mentor in law, the eminent James Wilson, on the Supreme Court. *See* 6 *The Diaries of George Washington* 319 (Donald Jackson and Dorothy Twohig eds., Charlottesville: University of Virginia Press, 1979); Custer, "Bushrod Washington and John Marshall" at 38 n.18.

171. *See* Charles, "Originalism, John Marshall, and the Necessary and Proper Clause" at 563.

172. Ibid. at 558.

173. 4 *The Papers of John Marshall* 3–4 (Charles T. Cullen ed., Chapel Hill: University of North Carolina Press, 1984).

174. Furstenberg, *In the Name of the Father* at 48–50.

175. Bushrod Washington to Jared Sparks, March 3, 1826 (Historical Manuscript Collection, Morristown National Historic Park, Morristown, NJ), available at http://www.nps.gov/archive/morr/Sparks/Sparks_Letters/Sparks/Welcome.htm.

176. Articles of Agreement, Publication Contract Between Jared Sparks, Bushrod Washington, and John Marshall, March 7, 1787 (Historical Manuscript Collection, Morristown National Historic Park, Morristown, NJ), available at http://www.nps.gov/archive/morr/Sparks/Sparks_Letters/Sparks/Welcome.htm.

177. Goebel, Jr., and Naughton, Law Enforcement in Colonial New York at 325.

178. U.S. Const. Art. III, § 2 ("The judicial power shall extend to all cases, in law and equity, arising under this constitution, the laws of the United States, and treaties made, or which shall be made under their authority; to all cases affecting ambassadors, other public ministers and consuls; to all cases of admiralty and maritime jurisdiction; to controversies to which the United States shall be a party; to controversies between two or more states, between Citizens of different states, between Citizens of the same state, claiming lands under grants of different states, and between a state, or the Citizens thereof, and foreign states, Citizens or subjects."), *accord* U.S. Const. Amend. XI ("The judicial power of the United States shall not be construed to extend to any suit in law or equity, commenced or prosecuted against one of the United States by citizens of another State, or by citizens or subjects of any foreign state.").

179. *See* Pfander and Birk, "Article III and the Scottish Judiciary" at 1613–85 (tracing the Scottish influence on Anglo-American legal interpretation).

180. Frederick Pollock, "The Genius of the Common Law II: The Giants and the Gods," 12 *Columbia Law Review* 291, 291–92 (1912).

181. Harlan F. Stone, "The Common Law in the United States," 50 *Harvard Law Review* 1, 12 (1936). For Harlan F. Stone's appointment as Chief Justice, see Maurice E. Harrison, "The New Chief Justice," 29 *California Law Review* 677 (1941).

182. Stone, "The Common Law in the United States" at 13.

183. Ibid. at 23.

184. Ibid. at 6.

185. William Draper Lewis, "The Study of the Common Law," 46 *The American Law Register* 465, 478 (1898).

186. *See, e.g.,* Scalia, "Common-Law Courts in a Civil Law System," in *A Matter of Interpretation: Federal Courts and the Law* at 10 (referring to the common law of the founding generation as a "preexisting body of rules"); ibid. at 6–9 (criticizing a common law approach for today's cases and controversies).

187. Bernadette A. Meyler, "Towards a Common Law Originalism," 59 *Stanford Law Review* 551, 556 (2006).

188. Ibid. at 557.
189. "Codification of the Common Law in Massachusetts," 15 *American Jurist and Law Magazine* 111, 128 (1836).
190. "Codification of the Common Law of Massachusetts," 17 *American Jurist and Law Magazine* 17, 20–21 (1837).
191. Ibid. at 25–32.
192. Ibid. at 32.
193. Ibid. at 35.
194. Ibid. at 36.
195. *See* William E. Nelson, *Americanisation of the Common Law: The Impact of Legal Change on Massachusetts Society, 1760–1830* (Athens: University of Georgia Press, 1975); Morton J. Horwitz, *The Transformation of American Law 1780–1860* (Cambridge, MA: Harvard University Press, 1977); Clark, *The Language of Liberty 1660–1832*, at 50–52, 62–110. See also Bailyn, *The Ideological Origins of the American Revolution* at 31 (law was "a repository of experience in human dealings embodying the principles of justice, equity, and rights; above all, it was a form of history ... and, as history, it helped explain the movement of events and the meaning of the present."); J.G.A. Pocock, The Machiavellian Moment: Florentine Political Thought and the Atlantic Republican Tradition 341 (2d ed., Princeton, NJ: Princeton University Press, 2003) ("Custom ... served as the best means of explaining what made a people and its laws uniquely and autonomously themselves."); Frederick Pollock, "The Expansion of the Common Law IV: The Law of Reason," 4 *Columbia Law Review* 171, 184 (1904) (discussing how the common law "was capable of growing to the demands of new times and circumstances; its conclusions in detail were not dogmas, but flexible applications of living and still expanding principles").
196. See J.G.A. Pocock, "Time, Institutions and Action; An Essay on Traditions and Their Understanding," in *Politics, Language and Time* at 233–72; J.G.A. Pocock, Gordon Schochet, and Lois G. Schwoerer, "The History of British Political Thought: A Field and its Futures," in *British Political Thought in History, Literature and Theory, 1500–1800*, at 10, 18; Greene, *The Constitutional Origins of the American Revolution* at 50–52, 91–92.
197. See Butterfield, *The Whig Interpretation of History* at 13–33 (discussing the difference between a Whiggish or abridged history and that of the professional historian).

Chapter 4

1. *See* Reid, "The Touch of History: The Historical Method of a Common Law Judge" at 157–71.
2. George Macaulay Trevelyan, *Clio, A Muse: And Other Essays Literary and Pedestrian* 7 (London: Longmans, Green, 1914).
3. Ibid. at 9.
4. Ibid. at 12.
5. Ibid. at 8, 18–19.

6. Ibid. at 31.
7. For a recent article denouncing originalism and arguing history should have no role in constitutional interpretation, see Martin H. Redish and Matthew B. Arnold, "Judicial Review, Constitutional Interpretation, and the Democratic Dilemma: Proposing a 'Controlled Activism Alternate,'" 64 *Florida Law Review* 1485 (2012).
8. *See* Michael C. Dorf, "Dicta and Article III," 142 *University of Pennsylvania Law Review* 1997 (1994). *See also* Marc McAllister, "Dicta Redefined," 47 *Williamette Law Review* 161 (2011); Pierre N. Leval, "Judging Under the Constitution: Dicta About Dicta," 81 *New York University Law Review* 1249 (2006); Michael Abramowicz and Maxwell Stearns, "Defining Dicta," 57 *Stanford Law Review* 953 (2005); Thomas L. Fowler, "Holding, Dictum...Whatever," 25 *North Carolina Central Law Journal* 139 (2003).
9. *Cohens v. Virginia*, 19 U.S. 264, 399–400 (1821).
10. For some discussions on the problems with lawyering history, see Kramer, "When Lawyers Do History" at 387–426; Kalman, "Border Patrol" at 87–124; Flaherty, "History 'Lite' in Modern American Constitutionalism" at 523–90.
11. *See* Sutton, "The Role of History in Judging Disputes about the Meaning of the Constitution" at 1182; Powell, "Rules for Originalists" at 691–95.
12. *See* Pocock, "The Origins of Study of the Past" at 211–14.
13. This is reason enough to assume a restrained approach to history in law, and Alfred H. Kelly is one historian that advocated for such an approach. *See* Kelly, "Clio and the Court" at 157 ("The application of precedent, legal continuity, and balanced contemporary socio-political theory is almost certain to produce a more intelligent result than is the attempt to use a few scattered historical documents as though they possessed qualities of Holy Writ.... A more sophisticated and restrained approach to the use of history by the Court might well take this fact into account.").
14. To date, I have found no valid reason historical methodologies should be discarded when one applies history to interpret the law, yet some scholars have made an argument. *See, e.g.*, Bennett and Solum, *Constitutional Originalism* at 58. But a number of legal scholars see historical methodologies as the answer to objectivity. *See, e.g.*, Kramer, "When Lawyers Do History" at 396 ("since the disciplinary understanding developed by historians for historians are meant (among other things) to enhance the credibility of their interpretations, these understandings are no less applicable to lawyers who use history in legal arguments."); Festa, "Applying a Usable Past" at 512 ("And like lawyers researching political science, lawyers consulting history might be required to adopt the historian's standards of objectivity and reliability for evaluating primary and second sources, weighing historical evidence, making descriptive inferences, and for attempting to explain historical causation."); Sutton, "The Role of History in Judging Disputes about the Meaning of the Constitu-

tion" at 1185 (stating historical methodologies could help provide "a sophisticated understanding of how to use historical materials, a sophisticated understanding of the context in which those materials arise, and a commitment to follow the evidence where it leads"). *See also* Flaherty, "History 'Lite' in Modern American Constitutionalism" at 553–55 (asserting the need for [1] better use of primary and secondary sources, [2] historical context, and [3] relying on accepted historical writings or framework).

15. *See, e.g.,* Cornell, "*Heller,* New Originalism, and Law Office History" at 1095–1126.

16. *See, e.g.,* McGinnis and Rappaport, "Original Methods Originalism" at 751–802. For their view of precedent's role in this process, see John O. McGinnis and Michael Rappaport, "Reconciling Originalism and Precedent," 103 *Northwestern University Law Review* 803 (2009).

17. *See, e.g.,* Cornell, "The People's Constitution vs. The Lawyer's Constitution" at 295–338.

18. Balkin, *Living Originalism* at 21–34.

19. The historical guidepost approach to historical context is in line with Quentin Skinner's approach to intellectual history. *See* Quentin Skinner, "Hermeneutics and the Role of History," 7 *New Literary History* 214 (1975); Quentin Skinner, "The Limits of Historical Explanations," 41 *Philosophy* 199 (1966).

20. Balkin, *Living Originalism* at 229. For commentary on Balkin's view of history and framework originalism, see Neil S. Seigel, "Jack Balkin's Rich Historicism and Diet Originalism: Health Benefits and Risks for the Constitutional System," 111 *Michigan Law Review* 931 (2013); Michael C. Dorf, "The Undead Constitution," 125 *Harvard Law Review* 2011 (2012); Steven G. Calabresi and Livia Fine, "Two Cheers for Professor Balkin's Originalism," 103 *Northwestern University Law Review* 663 (2009).

21. Skinner, "The Limits of Historical Explanations" at 202.

22. Declaration of Independence (1776).

23. *See* Brandon E. Davis, "America's Immigration Crisis: Examining the Necessity of Comprehensive Immigration Reform," 54 *Loyola Law Review* 353, 354 (2008); Sarah H. Cleveland, "Powers Inherent in Sovereignty: Indians, Aliens, Territories, and the Nineteenth-Century Origins of Plenary Power Over Foreign Affairs," 81 *Texas Law Review* 1, 81 (2002); Gerald L. Neuman, "Whose Constitution?" 100 *Yale Law Journal* 909, 938 (1991).

24. *See* Charles, "Restoring 'Life, Liberty, and the Pursuit of Happiness' in Our Constitutional Jurisprudence" at 457, 491–95.

25. Ibid. at 461,469, 482, 491–502.

26. *See* David Armitage, "The Declaration of Independence and International Law," 59 *The William and Mary Quarterly* 39 (2002).

27. *See* Charles, "The Plenary Power Doctrine and the Constitutionality of Ideological Exclusion" at 67–91.

28. *See* John Jay, "Charge to the Grand Jury to the Middle Circuit in the District of Virginia, at the Capitol, in the City of Richmond, on the 22d Day of May, 1793," reprinted in *The City Gazette and Daily Advertiser* (Charleston, SC), August 14, 1793, at 2; John Jay, *The Charge of Chief Justice Jay to the Grand Juries of the Eastern Circuit* (Portsmouth, NH: George Jerry Osborne, Jr., 1790); Iredell, *Middle Circuit, 1793, Virginia* at 10; William Cushing, "A Charge Delivered to the Federal Grand Jury for the District of Virginia, on the 23d Nov. 1798: By the Honorable Judge Cushing, published by request of the Grand Jury," reprinted in *The Eastern Herald and Gazette of Maine* (District of Maine, MA), January 21, 1799, at 1; James Iredell, "Charge to the Grand Jury for the District of Pennsylvania Held in the City of Philadelphia, April 11, 1799," reprinted in *The Independent Chronicle; and the Universal Advertiser* (Boston, MA), May 27, 1799, at 1; Alexander Addison, *On the Alien Act: A Charge to the Juries of the Country Courts of the Fifth Circuit of the State of Pennsylvania* (Washington, PA: John Colerick, 1799); Alexander Addison, *Analysis of the Report of the Committee of the Virginia Assembly* (Philadelphia: Zachariah Poulson, 1800); Charles, "The Plenary Power Doctrine" at 100–1, 107, 116; 25 *The Papers of Alexander Hamilton* 491–95 (Harold C. Syrett ed., New York: Columbia University Press, 1977); Samuel Preston, *A Charge Delivered to the Grand Jury of Wayne County* (Easton, PA: Samuel Longcope, 1800).

29. An article by James E. Pfander and Theresa R. Wardon claims the congressional plenary authority over immigration was limited in that Congress did not prescribe retroactive legislation concerning naturalization and settlement to aliens who have settled lawfully. *See* James E. Pfander and Theresa R. Wardon, "Reclaiming the Immigration Constitution of the Early Republic: Prospectivity, Uniformity, and Transparency," 96 *Virginia Law Review* 359 (2010). But this interpretation of congressional power over naturalization, and its intimate relation to immigration and foreign affairs, does not comport with the historical record. The founding generation viewed these powers as important to national self-preservation. *See* Charles, "The Plenary Power Doctrine" at 92–117.

30. The legal contours of federal immigration law have perplexed legal theorists since the *Chinese Exclusion Case. Chae Chan Ping v. United States,* 130 U.S. 581 (1889).

31. *See, e.g.,* Lindsay, "Immigration, Sovereignty, and the Constitution of Foreignness" at 743–812; Motomura, "Immigration Law after a Century of Plenary Power" at 545–614; Henkin, "The Constitution and United States Sovereignty" at 853–886.

32. *See, e.g.,* Michael D. Ramsey, *The Constitution's Text in Foreign Affairs* 203–8 (Harvard University Press, 2007); Rob Natelson, "Immigration, Foreign Affairs and the Constitution," *Tenth Amendment Center,* May 2, 2010, available at http://tenthamendmentcenter.com/2010/05/03/immigration-foreign-affairs-and-the-constitution/.

33. Balkin, *Living Originalism* at 157–58.

34. James Iredell, "Charge to the Grand Jury for

the District of Pennsylvania Held in the City of
Philadelphia, April 11, 1799," reprinted in *The Inde-
pendent Chronicle; and the Universal Advertiser*
(Boston, MA), May 27, 1799, at 1, col. 2.

35. William Cushing, "A Charge Delivered to
the Federal Grand Jury for the District of Virginia,
on the 23d Nov. 1798: By the Honorable Judge
Cushing, published by request of the Grand Jury,"
reprinted in *The Eastern Herald and Gazette of
Maine* (District of Maine, MA), January 21, 1799,
at 2, col. 2.

36. Balkin, *Living Originalism* at 138–82.

37. Ariz. Rev. Stat. Ann. §11–1051 (West, 2012).

38. *Chamber of Commerce v. Whiting*, 131 S. Ct.
292 (2011).

39. *See* Kris W. Kobach, "Attrition Through Enforcement: A Rational Approach to Illegal Immigration," 15 *Tulsa Journal of Comparative and International Law* 153 (2008).

40. *Arizona v. United States*, 132 S. Ct. 2492
(2012).

41. *See, e.g.*, Cristina M. Rodriguez, "The Significance of the Local in Immigration Regulation," 106
Michigan Law Review 567 (2008).

42. *See, e.g.*, Michael M. Hethmon, "The
Chimera and the Cop: Enforcement of Federal Immigration Law," 8 *University of the District of Columbia Law Review* 83 (2004).

43. Gerald L. Neuman, "The Lost Century of
American Immigration (1776–1875)," 93 *Columbia
Law Review* 1833 (1993).

44. Ibid. at 1841–84.

45. Ibid. at 1884–95.

46. Ibid. at 1897.

47. *Arizona v. United States*, 132 S. Ct. 2492,
2513 (Scalia, J., dissenting) (emphasis added).

48. *See* Charles, "The Plenary Power Doctrine,"
at 67–91.

49. *Arizona v. United States*, 132 S. Ct. 2492
(Scalia, J., dissenting).

50. Buckner F. Melton, Jr., "Clio at the Bar: A
Guide to Historical Method for Legalists and Jurists,"
83 *Minnesota Law Review* 377, 392 (1998). ("Context
... is an element that is crucial to the understanding
of what the speaker [or writer] meant. If one ignores
the time that passed between the two occasions, and
the circumstances that changed with time, then once
cannot grasp the change in meaning.")

51. Butterfield, *The Whig Interpretation of History* at 21 ("Perhaps the greatest of all the lessons of
history is the demonstration of the complexity of
human change and the unpredictable character of
the ultimate consequences of any given act or decision of men; and on the face of it *this is a lesson that
can only be learned in detail*.") (emphasis added).

52. *See* Skinner, "The Limits of Historical Explanations" at 214 (stating the importance of providing
historical context to the "greatest detail" whenever
possible).

53. Joyce Appleby, "One Good Turn Deserves
Another: Moving Beyond the Linguistic; A Re-
sponse to David Harlan," 94 *The American Historical
Review* 1326, 1328 (1989).

54. Ibid.

55. *See* Anthony Grafton, "The History of Ideas:
Precept and Practice, 1950–2000 and Beyond," 67
The History of Ideas 1, 30 (2006).

56. Butterfield, The Whig Interpretation of History at 22–23. *See also* Pocock, Politics, Language
and Time at 105–6.

57. Pocock, *Virtue, Commerce, and History* at 10;
J.G.A. Pocock, Gordon Schochet, and Lois G.
Schwoerer, "The History of British Political
Thought: A Field and its Futures," in *British Political
Thought in History, Literature and Theory, 1500–
1800*, at 10, 11.

58. Skinner, "Hermeneutics and the Role of History" at 216.

59. Butterfield, *The Whig Interpretation of History* at 30.

60. For some dissents to using dictionaries in this
fashion, see Merkel, "*District of Columbia v. Heller*
and Antonin Scalia's Perverse Sense of Originalism"
at 379–80; Charles and O'Neill, "Saving the Press
Clause From Ruin" at 1751–52.

61. *Moore v. City of East Cleveland*, 431 U.S. 494,
503 (1977).

62. At least one Supreme Court Justice, Stephen
Breyer, seems to agree with this approach. *See* Breyer,
Making Our Democracy Work at 77. ("If there is no
historical material directly on point, what should
the Court do? Create historical 'assumptions' designed to draw answers from a historical void? Or
refuse to answer a question of practical importance
... on the basis of a skimpy, uncertain record of
eighteenth-century practice? If the Court is to decide major constitutional questions on the basis of
history, then why not ask nine historians, rather than
nine judges, to provide these answers?")

63. *See* Kates, "A Modern Historiography of the
Second Amendment" at 1211–32. The first commen-
tator to coin the term "Standard Model" was Glenn
Harlan Reynolds. *See* Glenn Harlan Reynolds, "A
Critical Guide to the Second Amendment," 62 *Ten-
nessee Law Review* 461, 467 (1995).

64. *District of Columbia v. Heller*, 554 U.S. 570,
599 (2008) ("If ... the Second Amendment right is
no more than the right to keep and use weapons as
a member of an organized militia, if, that is, the *organized* militia is the sole institutional beneficiary
of the Second Amendment's guarantee—it does not
assure the existence of a 'citizens' militia' as a safeguard against tyranny.") (citations omitted).

65. Ibid. at 592 ("Putting all of these textual elements together, we find that they guarantee the individual right to possess and carry weapons in case
of confrontation."); ibid. at 594 ("we do not read
the Second Amendment to protect the right of citizens to carry arms for *any sort* of confrontation, just
as we do not read the First Amendment to protect
the right of citizens to speak for *any purpose*.").

66. Ibid. at 595 ("In *United States v. Miller*, we
explained that 'the Militia comprised all males physically capable of acting in concert for the common
defense.' That definition comports with founding-
era sources.") (citations omitted).

67. *See, e.g.*, Charles, "The Second Amendment in Historiographical Crisis" at 1727–1866.

68. Randy E. Barnett, Op-Ed, "News Flash: The Constitution Means What is Says," *Wall Street Journal*, June 27, 2008. *See also* Randy E. Barnett, "The Gravitational Force of Originalism," 40 *Fordham Urban Law Journal* (forthcoming, 2013).

69. Lawrence Solum, "*Heller* and Originalism, Part I: An Introduction to the Series," *Legal Theory Blog*, June 28, 2008.

70. Clark M. Neily III, "The Right to Keep and Bear Arms in the States: Ambiguity, False Modesty, and (Maybe) Another Win for Originalism," 33 *Harvard Journal of Law and Public Policy* 185, 185 (2010).

71. William G. Merkel, "*Parker v. The District of Columbia* and the Hollowness of Originalist Claims to Principled Neutrality," 18 *George Mason University Civil Rights Law Journal* 251, 251 (2008).

72. *See* James Madison, Notes for a Speech in Congress, June 8, 1789, *Consource*, available at http://www.consource.org/document/notes-for-speech-in-congress/; Tucker, *View of the Constitution of the United States with Selected Writings* at 239; William Blackstone, 2 *Blackstone's Commentaries: With Notes of Reference to the Constitution and Laws of the Federal Government of the United States and of the Commonwealth of Virginia* 143 n. 40 (St. George Tucker ed., Philadelphia: W.Y. Birch and A. Small, 1803); William Rawle, *A View of the Constitution of the United States of America* 126 (2d ed., Philadelphia: Philip H. Nicklin, 1829).

73. *See* Charles, "'Arms for Their Defence?'" at 358, 365, 378–80, 383, 385–86, 396, 398–99, 402, 403, 407.

74. Charles, "The Right of Resistance and Self-Preservation" 45–52.

75. Charles, "The Second Amendment in Historiographical Crisis" at 1795–1827.

76. *See generally* Joyce Lee Malcolm, *To Keep and Bear Arms: The Origins of an Anglo-American Right* (Cambridge, MA: Harvard University Press, 1994). For Malcolm's previous writings leading up to her book, see Joyce Lee Malcolm, "The Role of the Militia in the Development of the Englishman's Right to Be Armed: Clarifying the Legacy," 5 *Journal of Firearms and Public Policy* 139 (1993); Joyce Lee Malcolm, "The Creation of a 'True Antient and Indubitable' Right: The English Bill of Rights and the Right to Be Armed," 32 *Journal of British History* 226 (1993); Joyce Lee Malcolm, "The Right of the People to Keep and Bear Arms: The Common Law Tradition," 10 *Hastings Constitutional Law Quarterly* 285 (1983).

77. Malcolm has never responded to the damaging critique of Lois G. Schwoerer, nor has Malcolm supplemented her thesis with more historical evidence. *See* Lois G. Schwoerer, "Review: To Keep and Bear Arms: The Origins of an Anglo-American Right, 61 *Journal of Southern History* 570 (1995); Lois G. Schwoerer, "To Hold and Bear Arms: The English Perspective," reprinted in *The Second Amendment in Law and History* 207–21.

78. Indeed, Standard Model writers assert Malcolm's history is the correct and true version. However, none of these Standard Model works have produced any new evidence to advance Malcolm's problematic conclusions. *See, e.g.*, David T. Hardy, "Ducking the Bullet: *District of Columbia v. Heller* and the Stevens Dissent," 2010 *Cardozo Law Review de novo* 61, 73–75 (2010).

79. *See, e.g.*, Brief for English/Early American Historians as Amici Curiae Supporting Respondents, *McDonald v. City of Chicago*, 130 S. Ct. 3020 (2010) (No. 08–1521).

80. Charles, "The Second Amendment in Historiographical Crisis" at 1795–1827.

81. Antonin Scalia, "Response," in *A Matter of Interpretation: Federal Courts and the Law* at 129, 136–37 n.13.

82. Joyce Lee Malcolm, "Remarks at Seton Hall Second Amendment Symposium: Panelist," 10 *Seton Hall Constitutional Law Journal* 829, 831 (2000).

83. Joyce Lee Malcolm, "The Supreme Court and the Uses of History: *District of Columbia v. Heller*," 56 *UCLA Law Review* 1377, 1390 (2009).

84. Malcolm, "The Right of the People to Keep and Bear Arms" at 306.

85. Ibid. at 314.

86. *See* Patrick J. Charles, "The 1792 National Militia Act, the Second Amendment, and Individual Militia Rights: A Legal and Historical Perspective," 9 *Georgetown Journal of Law and Public Policy* 323, 326–27 (2011).

87. Ibid. at 374–90.

88. Malcolm, *To Keep and Bear Arms* at 164.

89. U.S. Const. amend. II.

90. *District of Columbia v. Heller*, 554 U.S. 570, 592 (2008). *See also* Scalia and Garner, *Reading Law* at 400–1.

91. *Heller*, 554 U.S. at 592 (citations omitted).

92. For some critiques on the different standards of review employed by the lower courts, see Joseph Blocher, "Categoricalism and Balancing in First and Second Amendment Analysis," 84 *New York University Law Review* 375 (2009); Brannon P. Denning and Glenn H. Reynolds, "*Heller,* High Water (Mark)? Lower Courts and the New Right to Keep and Bear Arms," 60 *Hastings Law Journal* 1245 (2009); Darrell Miller, "Guns as Smut: Defending the Home-Bound Second Amendment," 109 *Columbia Law Review* 1278 (2009); Stacey L. Sobel, "The Tsunami of Legal Uncertainty: What's a Court to Do Post-*McDonald?*" 21 *Cornell Journal of Law and Public Policy* 489 (2012); Mark Tushnet, "Permissible Gun Regulations After *Heller*: Speculations About Method and Outcomes," 56 *UCLA Law Review* 1425 (2009).

93. A number of Circuit Courts of Appeal have adopted this approach. *See Ezell v. City of Chicago*, 651 F.3d 684 (7th Cir. 2011); *United States v. Chester*, 628 F.3d 673 (4th Cir. 2010); *United States v. Reese*, 627 F.3d 792 (10th Cir. 2010); *United States v. Marzzarella*, 614 F.3d 35 (3d Cir. 2010); *United States v. Rene*, 583 F.3d 8 (1st Cir., 2009).

94. *United States v. Williams*, 616 F.3d 685, 691 (7th Cir., 2010).

95. *See United States v. Carpio-Leon*, 701 F.3d 974 (4th Cir. 2012) (upholding firearm prohibitions on unlawful aliens based upon historical evidence); *Kachalsky v. County of Westchester*, 701 F.3d 81 (2d Cir. 2012) (upholding New York's gun licensing scheme based upon historical evidence of regulation); *NRA of Am. V. Bureau of Alcohol*, 700 F.3d 185 (5th Cir. 2012) (upholding federal prohibition on sale of firearms to persons under 21 years of age based on historical evidence). However, the majority of cases rely on "means-ends" scrutiny despite the fact that the historical test is meant to be flexible. *See United States v. Skoien*, 614 F.3d 638, 641 (7th Cir. 2010) (stating that modern gun control regulations do not need to "mirror" 1791 restrictions).

96. *See, e.g.,* Sunstein, "Applying a Useable Past" at 604; John G. Wofford, "The Blinding Light: The Uses of History and Constitutional Interpretation," 31 *University of Chicago Law Review* 502, 533 (1964).

97. *See* Gordon, "Historicism in Legal Scholarship" at 1028–36.

98. Holmes, "The Path of the Law" at 221.

99. U.S. Const. Amend. I.

100. George Hay was of this view in the midst of the 1798 Sedition Act. At the time Hay was in private practice in Richmond, Virginia, and later, in 1825, become a federal judge. His views in 1798 may not have reflected his views upon assuming the bench. *See* George Hay, "Letter III to the People of the United States," reprinted in *Aurora General Advertiser* (Philadelphia, PA), February 6, 1799, at 2, col. 3 ("The opinion that the common law of England is in force in the United States, has been demonstrated to be erroneous [and] directly repugnant to the plain meaning and words of the Constitution…. The common law is totally unnoticed."); George Hay, "Letter V to the People of the United States," reprinted in *Aurora General Advertiser* (Philadelphia, PA), February 21, 1799, at 2, col. 2 ("In Britain there is no constitution, no limitation of legislative power: but in America, there is a constitution, the power of the legislature is limited, and the object of one limitation is to secure the freedom of the press…. There can be no common law, no immemorial usage or custom concerning a thing of so modern a date. The freedom of the press, therefore, means the total exemption of the press from any kind of legislative control, and consequently the sedition bill, which is an act of legislative control, is an abridgement of its liberty, and expressly forbidden by the constitution.").

101. Charles and O'Neill, "Saving the Press Clause from Ruin" at 1702–43.

102. Pa. Const. of 1776, Declaration of Rights, § XII.

103. Thomas McKean, "Charge Delivered to the Grand Jury for the City and County of Philadelphia," undated, reprinted in *The Columbian Herald* (Charleston, SC), May 9, 1785, at 2, col. 2.

104. Ibid. at 2, col. 1. In 1790 the Pennsylvania Constitution was redrafted and expressly mentioned libels. *See* Pa. Const. of 1790, Article IX, § 7 ("That the printing presses shall be free to every person who

undertakes to examine the proceedings of the legislature, or any branch of government: And no law shall ever be made to restrain the right thereof. The free communication of thoughts and opinions is one of the invaluable rights of man; and every citizen may freely speak, write and print on any subject, being responsible for the abuse of that liberty. In prosecutions for the publication of papers, investigating the official conduct of officers, or men in a public capacity, or where the matter published is proper for public information, the truth thereof may be given in evidence: And, in all indictments for libels, the jury shall have a right to determine the law and the facts, under the direction of the court, as in other cases."). In 1800, Pennsylvania Supreme Court Judge Edward Shippen would write on this provision that the "liberty of the press … is a valuable right in every free country and ought never be unduly restrained; but when it is perverted to the purposes of private slander, it then become a most destructive engine in the hands of unprincipled men." Edward Shippen, "Charge Delivered at the Trial of William Cobbet," undated, reprinted in *Norwich Packet* (Norwich, CT), January 2, 1800, at 4, col. 3.

105. Israel Sumner, "Charge Delivered for Trial for a Libel," undated, reprinted in *Concord Herald* (Concord, NH), April 6, 1791, at 1, col. 3.

106. "Original Draft of Letter from William Cushing, Chief Justice, to John Adams" (Feb. 18, 1789), reprinted in *Massachusetts Law Quarterly*, Oct. 1942, at 12, 12.

107. Ibid. at 14–15.

108. Interpreting the Constitution through the events of the American Revolution is rare among modern legal scholars, but is useful when examining the evolution of eighteenth-century political and constitutional thought. *See generally* Greene, *The Constitutional Origins of the American Revolution* ix–xxiv, 187–90. Take for instance prominent "historical" research on the First Amendment's Free Press Clause by leading First Amendment law professors. David A. Anderson and Eugene Volokh both focus on the events contemporaneous with the Constitution or following it, yet ignore the liberty of the press as an evolving intellectual, political, and constitutional right. *See* David A. Anderson, "The Origins of the Press Clause," 30 *UCLA Law Review* 455 (1983) (providing only a glimpse of the "liberty of the press" prior to the Constitution); Eugene Volokh, "Freedom for the Press as an Industry, or for the Press as a Technology? From the Framing to Today," 160 *University of Pennsylvania Law Review* 459 (2011) (starting the historical inquiry with 1791 and ignoring any revolutionary or prerevolutionary doctrine).

109. Ibid. at 14.

110. The 1798 Sedition Act Section 2 of "An Act in addition to the act, entitled 'An Act for the punishment of certain crimes against the United States.'" 1 *United States Statutes at Large* 596 (Boston: Little, Brown, 1845).

111. William Cushing, "Charge Delivered to the Federal Grand Jury for the District of Virginia," No-

vember 23, 1798, reprinted in *J. Russell's Gazette: Commercial and Political* (Boston, MA), December 27, 1798, at 1, col. 3.

112. Ibid. at col. 4.

113. *See, e.g.*, Amar, *America's Constitution* at 103 ("In 1798, in violation of all that the Constitution's supporters had said and written in 1787–89, Congress passed a federal Sedition Act that punished Americans for criticizing Congress."); *New York Times Co. v. Sullivan*, 376 U.S. 254, 276 (1964) ("Although the Sedition Act was never tested in this Court, the attack upon its validity has carried the day in the court of history.").

114. *See* Levy, *Emergence of a Free Press* at 220–81; David Jenkins, "The Sedition Act of 1798 and the Incorporation of Seditious Libel into First Amendment Jurisprudence," 45 *The American Journal of Legal History* 154 (2001); Gordon S. Wood, *Empire of Liberty: A History of the Early Republic, 1789–1815*, at 259–60 (New York: Oxford University Press, 2009). *See also* Lawrence Rosenthal, "First Amendment Investigations and the Inescapable Pragmatism of the Common Law of Free Speech," 86 *Indiana Law Journal* 1, 19–22 (2011).

115. In 1964 the Supreme Court commented on the Sedition Act, declaring "the attack upon its validity has carried the day in the court of history." *New York Times Co.*, 376 U.S. at 276. *See also* Chafee, Jr., "Freedom of Speech in War Time" at 954 (stating the Sedition Act "surely defeated the fundamental policy of the First Amendment, the open discussion of public affairs").

116. Leonard Levy claims there is evidence to suggest Oliver Ellsworth "told federal grand juries that the federal courts had common-law jurisdiction over seditious libel." Levy, *Emergence of a Free Press* at 277. However, the case to which Levy refers had nothing to do with libel, but naturalization. *See* Wharton, *State Trials of the United States During the Administrations of Washington and Adams with References, Historical and Professional, and Preliminary Notes on the Politics of the Times* at 652–54.

117. Other late eighteenth-century jurists—not sitting on the Supreme Court—were of a similar view that the common law and custom supported the constitutionality of the Sedition Act. *See* Preston, *A Charge Delivered to the Grand Jury of Wayne County* at 9–10 (stating the Sedition Law "neither creates a new crime, nor curtails the liberties or privileges that we enjoyed before it was passed ... the greatest security and safety ... they have like men unconscious of guilt or design, voluntarily given us free liberty and privileges to publish and expose any maladministration or misconduct of their officers, with this simple restriction only, that what we publish must be the truth"); John F. Grimke, *Charge, Delivered to the Grand Juries of Beaufort and Orangeburgh Districts* 11–12 (Charleston, SC: Benjamin F. Timothy, 1798) (the Sedition Law "does not apply to the liberty of speech at all, but you may still speak what you please; if however, you exceed certain bounds you are punishable to be sure; not by this law, but by the common law of the land. As to the second

part I am certain that there is not a citizen of this country, who can be of opinion that he has a constitutional right of publishing false, scandalous, and malicious libels against any one in the community.").

118. Charles, "Originalism, John Marshall, and the Necessary and Proper Clause" at 537–45. For Alexander Addison's pamphlet, see Alexander Addison, *Liberty of Speech and the Press: A Charge to the Grand Juries of County Courts of the Fifth Circuit and the State of Pennsylvania* (Albany: Loring Andrews, 1798).

119. James Iredell, "Charge Delivered to the Grand Jury for the District Court of Pennsylvania," Part III, April 11, 1799, reprinted in *The Independent Chronicle and the Universal Advertiser* (Boston, MA), June 3, 1799, at 1, col. 2.

120. Ibid.

121. Samuel Chase, "Charge Delivered to the Grand Jury for the Case of the United States Against Thomas Cooper," undated, reprinted in *Newburyport Herald and Country Gazette* (Boston, MA), May 6, 1800, at 1, col. 4.

122. Ibid. at 2, col. 1.

123. Ibid. at 1, col. 4.

124. *Citizens United v. Federal Election Commission*, 130 S. Ct. 876 (2010). Of course, the Supreme Court is not bound to follow past precedent if the historical record proves otherwise. *See Smith v. Allwright*, 321 U.S. 649, 665–66 (1944); *City of Akron v. Akron Ctr. for Reprod. Health*, 462 U.S. 416, 458–59 (1983); *Church of Lukumi Babalu Aye v. City of Hialeah*, 508 U.S. 520, 575 (1993); *U.S. Term Limits v. Thorton*, 514 U.S. 779, 788 (1995).

125. For some prominent examples, see *Nebraska Press Ass'n v. Stuart*, 427 U.S. 539, 559 (1976); *New York Times Co.*, 376 U.S. at 256; *Gitlow v. New York*, 268 U.S. 652, 664 (1925); *Abrams v. United States*, 250 U.S. 616, 618–19 (1919).

126. For the first historical controversy concerning the Press Clause, *compare* Zechariah Chafee, *Free Speech in the United States* (Cambridge, MA: Harvard University Press, 1941), *with* Leonard Levy, *Legacy of Suppression: Freedom of Speech and Press in Early American History* (Cambridge, MA: Harvard University Press, 1960). *See also* Vikram David Amar, "From Watergate to Ken Starr: Potter Stewart's 'Or of the Press' A Quarter Century Later," 50 *Hastings Law Journal* 711, 713–14 (1999) (asserting the founding generation intended the speech and press clause to encompass the same constitutional protections); Anderson, "The Origins of the Press Clause" at 534 ("That the press clause has a distinct history does not mean, of course, that it must be given a different meaning from the speech clause today, or even that it had a different meaning in 1791.").

127. *Citizens United*, 130 S. Ct. at 951 n. 57 (Stevens, J., dissenting).

128. Ibid. at 928 n.6 (2010) (Scalia, J., concurring).

129. U.S. Const. amend I.

130. *See* Charles and O'Neill, "Saving the Press Clause from Ruin" at 1702–54.

131. *Citizens United*, 130 S. Ct. at 928 n.6 (Scalia, J., concurring).

132. Charles and O'Neill, "Saving the Press Clause from Ruin" at 1754–69.

133. Pollock, "Expansion of the Common Law III" at 109.

134. Ibid.

135. Free-men Inslaved, or, Reasons Humbly Offered to the Right Honorable the Commons of England in Parliament Assembled for the Taking off the Excise Upon Bear and Ale (1643) (stating the power of magistrates to enter one's home at "unseasonable times" is a "great disturbance, contrary to Magna Carta, which saith Everyman's House is his Castle").

136. Thomas Digges, *Englands Defence: A Treatise concerning Invasion, or A brief Discourse of what Orders were best for repulsing of Foreign Forces, if at any time they should invade us by Sea in Kent, or Elsewhere*, at preface (London: F. Haley, 1680) ("I hope neither Divine nor Lawyer will deny, seeing the end of Government is to preserve the People ... and upon an Invasion People may forthwith rise and defend themselves, for every Man's House is his Castle").

137. Patrick J. Charles, "The Statute of Northampton by the Late Eighteenth Century: Clarifying the Intellectual Legacy," 40 *Fordham Urban Law Journal City Square* (forthcoming, 2013).

138. See, e.g., Cornell and DeDino, "A Well Regulated Right" at 487–528. See also Patrick J. Charles, "The Second Amendment Standard of Review After *McDonald*: 'Historical Guideposts' and the Missing Arguments in *McDonald v. City of Chicago*," 2 *Akron Journal of Constitutional Law and Policy* 7, 23–26 (2011).

139. See, e.g., David B. Kopel and Clayton Cramer, "State Court Standards of Review for the Right to Keep and Bear Arms," 50 *Santa Clara Law Review* 1113 (2010).

140. Charles, "Scribble Scrabble, the Second Amendment, and Historical Guideposts" at 1822–23.

141. Charles, "The Second Amendment Standard of Review After *McDonald*" at 21–30.

142. *District of Columbia v. Heller*, 554 U.S. 570, 592 (2008).

143. See Garrett Epps, "Any Which Way but Loose: Interpretive Strategies and Attitudes Toward Violence in the Evolution of the Anglo-American 'Retreat Rule,'" 55 *Law and Contemporary Problems* 303, 307–8 (1992); Richard Maxwell Brown, *No Duty to Retreat: Violence and Values in American History and Society* 3–5 (New York: Oxford University Press, 1991).

144. See, e.g., Melton, "Clio at the Bar" at 385 ("Historical thinking is very different from legal thinking, and the tools of historical research are certainly much more diverse and often considerably harder to use than sources of legal authority ... the law's emphasis on an analytical approach to the subject is in many ways not just different from, but the antithesis of, a historical approach."); Powell, "Rules for Originalists" at 661 ("Using history responsibly ... is an intellectually arduous endeavor.").

145. See Wiecek, "Clio as Hostage" at 234–35; Richards, "Clio and the Court" at 891.

146. Max Lerner, "Minority Rule and Constitutional Tradition," in *The Constitution Reconsidered* 190, 191 (Conyers Read ed., revised edition, New York: Harper and Row, 1968).

147. See Powell, "Rules for Originalists" at 669–72.

148. Wiecek, "Clio as Hostage" at 267.

149. Just recently one left leaning immigration law professor was so bold to compare the status of today's unlawful immigrants to the founding fathers. See Victor C. Romero, "Our Illegal Founders," 16 *Harvard Latino Law Review* 147 (2013).

150. Horwitz, "The Past, Tense" at 505. See also Gordon, "Historicism in Legal Scholarship" at 1055 (discussing how there has never been an open dialogue about history in law and mythmaking).

151. Bernard Wolf Weinberger, 2 *An Introduction to the History of Dentistry* 291–334 (Mosby, 1948).

152. John Woodforde, *The Strange Story of False Teeth* 98–108 (Suffolk: St. Edmunsbury Press, 1968); Robert Darnton, *George Washington's False Teeth: An Unconventional Guide to the Eighteenth Century* (New York: W.W. Norton, 2003).

153. Mount Vernon Ladies Association, "Mount Vernon Exhibits George Washington's Presidential Dentures and His Last Tooth, Encased as a Souvenir by his Dentist," (October 13, 2009), available at http://www.mountvernon.org/miscellaneous/news-press/release-archive/mount-vernon-exhibits-george-washington%E2%80%99s-presidential-dent.

154. Mount Vernon Ladies Association, "Facts and Falsehoods About George Washington" (January 18, 2006), available at http://www.mountvernon.org/content/facts-falsehoods-about-george-washington-0.

155. Deborah Chandra, Madeline Comora, and Brock Cole, *George Washington's Teeth* (New York: Square Fish, 2007).

156. Edward G. Lengel, *Inventing George Washington: America's Founder, in Myth and Memory*, at xviii (New York: Harper, 2011).

157. See, e.g., Rakove, "The Origins of Judicial Review" at 1038. ("[History] is less about results than reasons, less about consequences than causes, less about carrying a story closer to our present than about pushing it further into the past. The goal of this form of historical inquiry should be to reach a prior point where we can map the conditions of uncertainty from which the development we are tracing eventually emerged.")

158. James T. Kloppenberg, "Thinking Historically: A Manifesto of Pragmatic Hermeneutics," 9 *Modern Intellectual History* 201, 204 (2012).

159. Kramer, "When Lawyers Do History" at 403 (noting how there is a "underlying assumption ... that the best way of 'finding truth' is for each of the two sides to present their [slanted] stories to an impartial umpire, a judge or jury, who can then decide which version makes more sense."); Nelson, "History and Neutrality in Constitutional Adjudi-

cation" at 1252 ("Most historical debates turn on value judgments about the desirability of looking at the past in a particular context, rather than on judgments about the probability that a particular rendition of the past is accurate.").

160. Kramer, "When Lawyers Do History" at 397.

161. Wiecek, "Clio as Hostage" at 267–68.

162. Charles and O'Neill, "Saving the Press Clause from Ruin" at 1706, 1749, 1753.

163. *See, e.g.,* Sutton, "The Role of History in Judging Disputes about the Meaning of the Constitution" at 1188 (claiming what is "true of the lawyer historian is also true of the professional historian.... No scholar wants their research second-guessed").

164. For a more thorough discussion, see generally Melton, "Clio at the Bar" at 378–96.

165. *See, e.g.,* Flaherty, "History 'Lite' in Modern American Constitutionalism" at 554. ("If historical scholarship in a given area has settled on a certain account, or more likely, on a framework for debate, historical assertions which acknowledge that account or framework will simply be more persuasive.")

166. Sutton, "The Role of History in Judging Disputes about the Meaning of the Constitution" at 1190. *See also* Tyler, Easterbrook et al., "A Dialogue with Federal Judges on the Role of History in Interpretation" at 1908. (Judge Sutton stating, "We should be skeptical of law office history, supposed historians claiming to be real historians, or history written in the context of, and for, a specific case. But sometimes that's all you have. And judges, it has been my experience, generally know how to ferret out what's worth relying on and what's not.")

167. *See* Powell, "Rules for Originalists" at 680 (discussing the impact of new historical scholarship on the fields of law and history).

168. Robert E. Shalhope, "The Ideological Origins of the Second Amendment," 69 *Journal of American History* 599 (1982).

169. Charles, "The Second Amendment in Historiographical Crisis" at 1828–29.

170. *See* Robert E. Shalhope and Lawrence Delbert Cress, "The Second Amendment and the Right to Bear Arms: An Exchange," 71 *Journal of American History* 587 (1984).

171. Robert E. Shalhope, "The Right to Bear Arms: A View From the Past," 13 *Reviews of American History* 347, 349–52 (1985). For Halbrook's book, see Stephen P. Halbrook, *That Every Man be Armed: The Evolution of a Constitutional Right* (Albuquerque: University of New Mexico Press, 1984).

172. Robert E. Shalhope, "Book Review: The Militia and the Right to Arms, or, How the Second Amendment Fell Silent," 108 *The American Historical Review* 1442 (2003).

173. *See* Brief of Amici Curiae, Jack N. Rakove, Saul Cornell, David T. Konig, William J. Novak, Lois G. Schwoerer et al. in Support of Petitioners, *District of Columbia v. Heller,* 554 U.S. 570 (2008) (No. 07–290).

174. *See, e.g.,* Kates, "A Modern Historiography of the Second Amendment" at 1213–14, 1217; Robert J. Cottrol, "Rights Protection: The Resurgent Second Amendment," 47 *Tulsa Law Review* 1, 1 n. 4 (2011).

175. *See, e.g.,* Don B. Kates, "Gun Control: Separating Reality from Symbolism," 20 *Journal of Contemporary Law* 353, 355 n. 5 (1994).

176. Levy, *Original Intent* at 341.

177. Nelson, "History and Neutrality in Constitutional Adjudication" at 1252–53.

178. There are of course exceptions. Arguably this case presented itself when more than four hundred historians signed an amicus brief in *Webster v. Reproductive Health Services,* claiming: "At the time the federal constitution was adopted, abortion was known and not illegal." *See* Brief of 281 American Historians as Amici Curiae Supporting Appellants," *Webster v. Reproductive Health Services,* 492 U.S. 490 (1989) (No. 88–605). The problem with this statement is there is some historical evidence to suggest abortions could be prohibited under the law. *See, e.g.,* Blackstone, 1 *Commentaries on the Laws of England* at 125–26 (stating how public view of abortion changed from manslaughter to a "very heinous misdemeanor"). For more on complexities of this topic, see Cornelia Hughes Dayton, "Taking the Trade: Abortion and Gender Relations in an Eighteenth-Century New England Village," 48 *The William and Mary Quarterly* 19 (1991); Sylvia A. Law, "Conversations Between Historians and the Constitution," 12 *The Public Historian* 11 (1990); Estelle B. Freedman, "Historical Interpretation and Legal Advocacy: Rethinking the *Webster* Amicus Brief," 12 *The Public Historian* 27 (1990).

179. *See* Richards, "Clio and the Court" at 888–89 (discussing how dueling histories before the court has become common).

180. Ibid. at 891 ("When history is ambiguous, the Court should use some other method to decide its cases and not try to ask questions of the past that the past cannot answer."). *See also* Wiecek, "Clio as Hostage" at 234. ("There are times when both judge and historian should recognize that history is simply beside the point. The historical data that is available is either insufficient or is hopelessly ambiguous, or simply cannot be made germane to our purposes.")

181. Nelson, "History and Neutrality in Constitutional Adjudication" at 1280.

182. *District of Columbia v. Heller,* 554 U.S. 570, 600 (2008) (citations omitted).

183. *See, e.g.,* Charles, "The Second Amendment in Historiographical Crisis" at 1773–76.

184. *See* Saikrishna B. Prakash, "Unoriginalism's Law Without Meaning," 15 *Constitutional Commentary* 529 (1998). *See also* Randy E. Barnett, "Can Lawyers Ascertain the Original Meaning of the Constitution?" *The Volokh Conspiracy* (August 19, 2013); Michael Rappaport, "Historians, Originalists, and Pauline Maier," *Liberty Law Blog* (August 17, 2013).

185. *Arizona v. United States,* 132 S. Ct. 2492, 2513 (Scalia, J., dissenting).

186. Holmes, *The Common Law* at 5.

Chapter 5

1. *District of Columbia v. Heller*, 554 U.S. 570 (2008); *McDonald v. City of Chicago*, 130 S. Ct. 3020 (2010).

2. *See, e.g., United States v. Masciandaro*, 638 F.3d 313 (4th Cir., 2011).

3. *See, e.g., Moore v. Madigan*, 702 F.3d 933 (7th Cir., 2012).

4. See *GeorgiaCarry.Org, Inc. v. Georgia*, 687 F.3d 1244 (11th Cir. 2012); *Regents of the University of Colorado v. Students for Concealed Carry on Campus*, 271 P.3d 496 (Colo. 2012); *Digiacinto v. Rector and Visitors of George Mason University*, 281 Va. 17 (Va., 2011). See also Lewis M. Wasserman, "Gun Control on College and University Campuses in the Wake of *District of Columbia v. Heller* and *McDonald v. City of Chicago*," 19 *Virginia Journal of Social Policy and Law* 1 (2011).

5. *See Woollard v. Gallagher*, 712 F.3d 865 (4th Cir. 2013); *Kachalsky v. County of Westchester*, 701 F.3d 81 (2d Cir. 2012); *Hightower v. City of Boston*, 693 F.3d 61 (1st Cir. 2012); *Powell v. Tompkins*, 2013 U.S. Dist. LEXIS 27695 (D. Mass, 2013).

6. Heller, 554 U.S. at 581–92. See also Stephen P. Halbrook, *The Founders' Second Amendment: Origins of the Right to Bear Arms* 326–27 (Chicago: Ivan R. Dee, 2008).

7. Owen McGovern, "The Responsible Gun Ownership Ordinance and Novel Textual Questions About the Second Amendment," 102 *The Journal of Criminal Law and Criminology* 471, 490 (2012).

8. Brief for Amici Curiae Illinois State Rifle Association, Inc., Congress of Racial Equality, Inc., and the Pink Pistols in Support of Defendant-Appellant, *Aguilar v. People*, No. 112116 (Illinois Supreme Court 2011) (citations omitted).

9. Eugene Volokh, "Implementing the Right to Keep and Bear Arms for Self-Defense: An Analytical Framework and Research Agenda," 56 *UCLA Law Review* 1443, 1515 (2009).

10. Eugene Volokh, "The First and Second Amendments," 109 *Columbia Law Review* 97, 102 (2009). *See also* Volokh, "Implementing the Right to Keep and Bear Arms for Self-Defense" at 1481.

11. *See, e.g.,* Robert H. Churchill, "Gun Regulation, the Police Power, and the Right to Keep and Bear Arms in Early America: The Legal Context of the Second Amendment," 25 *Law and History Review* 139 (2007); Robert J. Cottrol and Raymond T. Diamond, "The Second Amendment: Toward an Afro-Americanist Reconsideration," 80 *Georgetown Law Journal* 309 (1991).

12. *See generally* Clayton E. Cramer, *Concealed Weapon Laws of the Early Republic: Dueling, Southern Violence, and Moral Reform* (Westport, CT: Praeger, 1999).

13. *See, e.g.,* David B. Kopel, "How the British Gun Control Program Precipitated the American Revolution," 6 *Charleston Law Review* 283, 285–86 (2012).

14. Nelson Lund, "The Second Amendment, *Heller*, and Originalist Jurisprudence," 56 *UCLA Law Review* 1343, 1368 (2009). *See also* Nelson Lund, "No Conservative Consensus Yet: Douglas Ginsburg, Brett Kavanaugh, and Diane Sykes on the Second Amendment," 13 *Engage* 30 (2012).

15. *See* Richard L. Aynes, "In Blot or Not: The Meaning of Privileges and/or Immunities," 11 *University of Pennsylvania Journal of Constitutional Law* 1295 (2009); Richard L. Aynes, "Enforcing the Bill of Right Against the States: The History and the Future," 19 *Journal of Contemporary Legal Issues* 77 (2009); Michael Kent Curtis, "The Bill of Rights and the States: An Overview from One Perspective," 18 *Journal of Contemporary Legal Issues* 3 (2009); Michael Kent Curtis, "The 1859 Crisis Over Hinton Helper's Book, The Impending Crisis: Free Speech, Slavery, and Some Light on the Meaning of the First Section of the Fourteenth Amendment," 68 *Chicago-Kent Law Review* 1113 (1993); Michael Kent Curtis, *No State Shall Abridge: The Fourteenth Amendment and the Bill of Rights* (Durham: Duke University Press, 1990).

16. For some useful discussions, see Jamal Greene, "Fourteenth Amendment Originalism," 71 *Maryland Law Review* 978 (2012); Thomas B. Colby, "Originalism and the Ratification of the Fourteenth Amendment," 107 *Northwestern Law Review* (forthcoming, 2013).

17. *See* Richard L. Aynes, "*McDonald v. City of Chicago*, Self-Defense, the Right to Bear Arms, and the Future," 2 *Akron Journal of Constitutional Law and Policy* 181 (2011); Clayton E. Cramer, Nicholas J. Johnson, and George A. Mocsary, "'This Right is Not Allowed By Governments that are Afraid of the People': The Public Meaning of the Second Amendment When the Fourteenth Amendment Was Ratified," 17 *George Mason Law Review* 852 (2010); Stephen P. Halbrook, *Freedmen, the Fourteenth Amendment, and the Right to Bear Arms, 1866–1876* (Westport, CT: Praeger, 1998).

18. *See, e.g.,* Michael P. O'Shea, "Modeling the Second Amendment Right to Carry Arms (I): Judicial Tradition and the Scope of 'Bearing Arms' for Self-Defense," 61 *American University Law Review* 585 (2012). For a historian's critique, see Saul Cornell, "The Right to Carry Firearms Outside the Home: Separating Historical Myths From Historical Realities," 39 *Fordham Urban Law Journal* 1695 (2012).

19. For a discussion, see Michael C. Dorf, "Does *Heller* Protect a Right to Carry Guns Outside the Home?" 59 *Syracuse Law Review* 225 (2008).

20. Charles, "The Second Amendment in Historiographical Crisis" at 1849–51.

21. *Heller*, 554 U.S. at 594.

22. Ibid. at 626.

23. *See, e.g.,* Darrell A.H. Miller, "Text, History, and Tradition: What the Seventh Amendment Can Teach us About the Second," 122 *Yale Law Journal* 852 (2013).

24. *Heller*, 554 U.S. at 626, 635.

25. *McDonald*, 130 S. Ct. at 3057–58 (Scalia, J., concurring).

26. Dorf, "Does *Heller* Protect a Right to Carry?" at 228–29.

27. Despite Standard Model writers proclaiming the Second Amendment and its English antecedent embodied a right to armed self-defense, not one legal treatise leading up through the late eighteenth century placed such a right in their sections on homicide, manslaughter or self-defense. At the same time, there is not one legal opinion that referred to the Second Amendment or its English antecedent when discussing self-defense.

28. *See, e.g.,* Pollock, "Expansion of the Common Law III" at 109.

29. Blackstone, 4 *Commentaries on the Laws of England* at 225.

30. Ibid. at 180–201.

31. *Heller,* 554 U.S. at 592.

32. *See* Epps, "Any Which Way but Loose" at 307–8; Brown, *No Duty to Retreat* at 3–5.

33. James Davis, *The Office and Authority of a Justice of the Peace* 203 (Newbern, NC: James Davis, 1774).

34. John Haywood, *The Duty and Office of Justices of the Peace, and of the Sheriffs, Coroners, Constables, &c.* 108 (Halifax, NC: Abraham Hodge, 1800).

35. Ibid. at 107.

36. Charles, "The Second Amendment Standard of Review After *McDonald*" at 25, 29–33; Charles, "The 1792 National Militia, the Second Amendment, and Militia Rights" at 326, 344–47, 374–79.

37. Charles, "Scribble Scrabble, the Second Amendment, and Historical Guideposts" at 1822–35.

38. 2 Edw. 3, c. 3 (1328) (Eng.); 20 Rich. 2, c. 1 (1396–97) (Eng.).

39. 2 *The Perpetual Laws of the Commonwealth of Massachusetts, from the Establishment of its Constitution to the Second Session of the General Court,* in 1798, at 259 (Boston: Adams and Nourse, 1799).

40. Francois-Xavier Martin, *A Collection of Statutes of the Parliament of England in Force in the State of North Carolina* 60–61 (Newbern, NC: Editor's Press, 1792) (emphasis added).

41. *A Collection of all such acts of the General Assembly of Virginia, of Public and Permanent Nature, as are now in Force* 33 (Richmond, VA: A. Davis, 1794).

42. Brief of Academics for the Second Amendment as Amicus Curiae in Support of Petitioners, at 16–17, *Kachalsky v. County of Westchester,* 701 F.3d 81 (2d Cir. 2012) (No. 12–845).

43. The laws touching upon the discharging of firearms alone shows the emphasis the founding generation placed on preventing injury and ensuring the public safety. *See* Charles, "Scribble Scrabble, the Second Amendment, and Historical Guideposts" at 1833–35.

44. Frederick Pollock and Frederic William Maitland, 1 *The History of English Law Before the Time of Edward I,* at 583 (Cambridge, NY: Cambridge University Press, 1895).

45. Charles, "The Faces of the Second Amendment Outside the Home" at 11–13.

46. Petition of the Chancellor, Masters and Scholars of the University of Oxford to the King and King's Council (1320) (Manuscripts Division, British Library, London, UK).

47. Ibid. (emphasis added). *See also Collectanea: Third Series* 119 (Montagu Burrows ed., Oxford: Oxford Historical Society, 1896).

48. 4 *Calendar of Close Rolls, Edward II, 1323–1327,* at 559–570 (April 28, 1326, Kenilworth) (H.C. Maxwell-Lyte ed., 1898). Edward II issued a similar proclamation a month earlier. *See* ibid. at 547–52 (March 6, 1326, Leicester) (ordering the sheriff of York to arrest "any man hereafter [that] go armed on foot or horseback, within liberties or without"). *See also* 1 *Calendar of the Plea and Memoranda Rolls of the City of London, 1323–1364,* at 11–37 (November 1326) (A.H. Thomas ed., 1926) ("no man go armed by night or day, save officers and other good men of the City assigned by the Mayor and Aldermen in their wards to keep watch and preserve the peace, under penalty of forfeiture of arms and imprisonment"); ibid. ("The bearing of arms is forbidden, except to the officers of the City assigned by the Mayor and Alderman to keep watch in the Wards, and to the Hainaulters of the Queen, who are accustomed to go armed in the manner of their country.")

49. For a history discussing this, see Claire Valente, "The Deposition and Abdication of Edward II," 113 *English Historical Review* 852, 853–81 (1998).

50. 2 Edw. 3, c. 3 (1328) (Eng.).

51. Anthony Verduyn, "The Politics of Law and Order During the Early Years of Edward III," 108 *English Historical Review* 842, 850 (1993).

52. *See* Bertha Haven Putnam, "The Transformation of the Keepers of the Peace into the Justices of the Peace," 12 *Transactions of the Royal Historical Society* 19, 21–48 (1929) (discussing the legal reforms to ensure the peace at the local level as the result of the Statute of Northampton).

53. 20 Ric. 2, c. 1 (1396–97) (Eng.).

54. Charles, "The Faces of the Second Amendment Outside the Home" at 17, 21–22, 25.

55. William Lambarde, *The Duties of Constables, Borsholders, Tythingmen, and such other low and Lay Ministers of the Peace* 13–14 (London: Thomas Wight, 1602). For Lambarde's earlier restatement, see William Lambarde, *Eirenarcha: Or the Office of the Justices of the Peace, in Two Bookes* 134–35 (London: Ra. Newbery, H. Bynneman, 1582). For more on William Lambarde, see Wilfrid Prest, "William Lambarde, Elizabethan Law Reform, and Early Stuart Politics," 34 *Journal of British Studies* 464 (1995).

56. Michael Dalton, *The Countrey Justice, Containing the Practices of the Justices of the Peace Out of Their Sessions* 30 (London: n.p., 1618).

57. Ibid. at 129.

58. Lambarde, *Eirenarcha* at 134–35.

59. Dalton, *The Countrey Justice* at 129.

60. Edward Coke, *The Third Part of the Institutes of the Laws of England* 160 (London: M. Flesher, 1644).

61. Ibid.

62. *Compare* 2 Edw. 3, c. 3 (1328) (Eng.), *with* 25 Edw. 3, stat. 5, c. 2, § 13 (1350) (Eng.).

63. Coke, *The Third Part of the Institutes* at 160.

64. Ibid. at 161.

65. Ibid. at 161–62.

66. Richard Crompton, *A Manuall* 19 (London: James Flesher, 1660).

67. *See* Joseph Keble, *An Assistance to the Justices of the Peace for the Easier Performance of their Duty* 147, 224 (2d ed., London: W. Rawlins, S. Roycroft and H. Sawbridge, 1689); William Sheppard, *The Offices and Duties of the Constables, Borsholders, Tythingmen, Treasurers of the County-Stock, Overseers for the Poore, and other Lay-Ministers* 39–40 (Cambridge: Robert Daniel, 1641).

68. George Meriton, *A Guide for Constables, Churchwardens, Overseers of the Poor, Surveyors of the Highways, Treasurers of the County Stock, Masters of the House of Correction, Bayliffs of Mannours, Tolltakers in Fairs, & c.* 22–23 (London: A. Crook, 1669); Robert Gardiner, *The Compleat Constable* 18–19 (London: Richard and Edward Atkins, 1692).

69. John Layer, *The Office and Dutie of Constables, Churchwardens, and other the Overseers of the Poore* 15–16 (Cambridge: Robert Daniel, 1641).

70. Ibid. at 16.

71. *See* Charles, "The Faces of the Second Amendment Outside the Home" at 34 n. 181. *See also* Richard Burn, 2 *The Justice of the Peace and the Parish Officer* 14 (16th ed., New York: Hugh Gaine, 1788) (classifying "fire arms" as "offensive weapons"); Lord Henry Home Kames, 2 *Sketches of the History of Man* 89 (Edinburgh: W. Creech, 1774) (distinguishing between "offensive weapons" of war and "defensive weapons").

72. James Bond, *A Compleat Guide for Justices of the Peace* 42 (3d ed., London: Printed by the assigns of Richard and Edward Atkins..., 1707). *See also* ibid. at 181. ("A person going or riding with offensive Arms may be arrested by a Constable, and by him be brought before a Justice.")

73. Ibid. at 43.

74. William Forbes, *The Duty and Powers of Justices of the Peace, in This Part of Great-Britain Called Scotland* 26 (Edinburgh: Andrew Anderson, 1707).

75. William Hawkins' *Pleas of the Crown* provides citations in the margins. In terms of the section discussing the Statute of Northampton, Hawkins cites to William Lambarde, Michael Dalton, Edward Coke and Joseph Keble, all of whom read the statute according to its historical terms. *See* William Hawkins, 1 *Pleas of the Crown* 135, ch. 63, §§ 1–5 (London: Eliz. Nutt, 1716).

76. Davis, *The Office and Authority of a Justice of the Peace* at 13.

77. Haywood, *The Duty and Office of Justices of the Peace, and of Sheriffs* at 10.

78. Wilson, 2 *The Collected Works of James Wilson* at 1138.

79. *The Grants, Concessions, and Original Constitutions of the Province of New-Jersey* 289 (Philadelphia: W. Bradford, 1758).

80. Kopel and Cramer, "State Standards of Review for the Right to the Keep and Bear Arms" at 1127, 1133–34.

81. David T. Hardy, "*District of Columbia v. Heller* and *McDonald v. City of Chicago*: The Present as Interface of the Past and Future," 3 *Northeastern Law Journal* 199, 205 (2011) (emphasis added).

82. For one legal commentator that argues there is no consensus as to the scope of the right outside the home, see Miller, "Guns as Smut" at 1303–4 ("self-defense in the home, and only in the home, is the sole area in which historians and common law scholars can arrive at some historical consensus. Self-defense outside the home is so historically contested that the prudent approach is for the Court to leave these areas to political and local organs of government").

83. Malcolm's research and characterization of the statute have had far reaching implications in Standard Model scholarship. For a list of works misled by or agreeing with Malcolm's unsupported conclusions on the statute, see Lund, "The Second Amendment, *Heller*, and Originalist Jurisprudence" at 1363–64 (relying on Malcolm's research for contemporary legal analysis on the Statute of Northampton); Kevin C. Marshall, "Why Can't Martha Stewart Have a Gun?" 32 *Harvard Journal of Law and Public Policy* 695, 716–17 (2009) (same); David B. Kopel, "The Licensing of Concealed Handguns for Lawful Protection: Support from Five State Supreme Courts," 68 *Alabama Law Review* 305, 317 (2005) (same); David B. Kopel, "It Isn't About Duck Hunting: The British Origins of the Right to Arms," 93 *Michigan Law Review* 1333, 1347 (1995) (same); Hardy, "*District of Columbia v. Heller* and *McDonald v. City of Chicago*" at 205 (same); Kopel and Cramer, "*State Standards of Review for the Right to the Keep and Bear Arms*" at 1127, 1133–34 (same); Carlton F.W. Lawson, "Four Exceptions in Search of a Theory: *District of Columbia v. Heller* and Judicial Ipse Dixit," 60 *Hastings Law Journal* 1371, 1378–79 (2009) (questioning whether the Statute of Northampton was ever enforced).

84. Malcolm, *To Keep and Bear Arms* at 11.

85. Joyce Lee Malcolm, *Disarmed: The Loss of the Right to Bear Arms in Restoration England* 7 (Washington, D.C.: NRA Institute of Legislative Action 1981) (reprinted from 1980 paper delivered to the Mary Ingraham Bunting Institute of Radcliffe College). Malcolm restated this conclusion again three years later. *See* Malcolm, "The Right of the People to Keep and Bear Arms" at 293.

86. Malcolm, "The Creation of a 'True Antient and Indubitable' Right" at 242.

87. Malcolm, *To Keep and Bear Arms* at 104.

88. Ibid. 104–5.

89. *Rex v. Knight*, 87 Eng. Rep. 76 (1686).

90. The fact that the incident in question involved the participation of government officials is affirmed by the Calendar of State Papers. *See Calendar of State Papers Domestic: James II, 1687–87*, at 118 (May 1, 1686) ("The King, being informed that the *Mayor and some other magistrates* of Bristol lately

seized upon a priest, who was going to officiate privately in a house there ... and having received an account that Sir John night was not only the informer but a busy actor in the matter by going himself to search.") (emphasis added); ibid. (June 7, 1686) (Sir John Knight to Earl of Sunderland). ("But in regard the Duke of Beaufort's letter to the Mayor of Bristoll has helped me to one most considerable objection, not only against myself but against the Mayor and Aldermen, as if they acted by my influence, I think it not amiss to make a defence whilst with little trouble it may be cleared.") Knight was originally arrested for "several seditious practices." Ibid. (May 22, 1686).

91. 20 Ric. 2, c. 1 (1396–97) (Eng.).

92. Joyce Lee Malcolm contends the King's Bench was unwilling to apply the statute. Malcolm, *To Keep and Bear Arms* at 105. This interpretation is false. The King's Bench clearly acknowledged the legality of the statute, but could not inflict anymore punishment after the jury acquitted.

93. Knight, the mayor, and aldermen were all called to the Hampton Court to answer for their actions. *See* 3 *The Entering Book of Roger Morrice 1677–1691: The Reign of James II, 1685–1687*, at 134 (Tim Harris ed., Woodbridge: Boydell Press, 2007). On June 12, 1686, the mayor and aldermen requested forgiveness for "any faults," pled "ignorante of the Lawes in that Case," and were "discharged, so that [the charges] will fall upon Sir John Knight[.]" Ibid. at 136. The actions of Knight, the mayor, and aldermen were deemed favorable by those in Bristol. Ibid. at 113 (stating Sir John Knight did "disturbe and imprison a Popish Conventicle that was at Mass, but they were suddenly after set at liberty, this is very wonderfull they were disturbed once").

94. Ibid. at 307.

95. Ibid. at 307–8.

96. Ibid. at 308.

97. Ibid. at 141 (emphasis added). The indictment was presented on June 12, 1686. *See* Narcissus Luttrell, 1 *A Brief Historical Relation of State Affairs from September 1678 to April 1714*, at 380 (Oxford: Oxford University Press, 1857) ("Sir John Knight pleaded not guilty to an information exhibited against him for goeing with a blunderbuss in the streets, to the terrifyeing his majesties subjects."). Joyce Lee Malcolm does not include the indictment in her account, yet contends it occurred on June 10, 1686. *See* Malcolm, *To Keep and Bear Arms* at 104. The record to which Malcolm refers says nothing of a firearm or the Statute of Northampton. *See Calendar of State Papers Domestic: James II, 1686–87*, at 136 (June 10, 1686) ("Information is preferring against Sir John Knight for creating and encouraging fears in the hearts of his Majesty's subjects.").

98. Knight talked about his defense in a June 7, 1686, letter to the Earl of Sutherland. He defended his actions by acting in conjunction with the mayor and aldermen. *See Calendar of State Papers Domestic: James II, 1686–87*, at 136 (June 7, 1686) (Sir John Knight to Earl of Sunderland). The jury agreed with this defense, finding Knight to be "loyall." *See* Lut-

trell, 1 *A Brief Historical Relation of State Affairs* at 389 ("Sir John Knight, the loyall, was tried at the court of kings bench for a high misdemeanor, in goeing armed up and down a gun att Bristoll; who being tried by a jury of his own citty, that knew him well, he was acquitted, not thinking he did it with any ill design ... tis thought his being concerned in taking up a popish priest at Bristoll occasioned this prosecution.").

99. 3 *The Entering Book of Roger Morrice* at 307.

100. Ibid.

101. Ibid. at 142.

102. Ibid. at 307.

103. *See* Hawkins, 1 *Pleas of the Crown* at 136, ch. 63, § 9.

104. 3 *The Entering Book of Roger Morrice* at 308; *Rex v. Knight*, 90 Eng. Rep. 330 (1686).

105. 3 *The Entering Book of Roger Morrice 1677–1691* at 308. Given Knight's station, the only way he could have offended the statute is if he was outside the loyalty of the crown and had acted rebelliously in violation of government decree. It is for this reason that a brief summary of the English report claims the chief justice said Knight's crime must appear "malo animo" or with evil intent, for the legal presumption was that Knight could not offend the Statute of Northampton. It is at this point that the King's Bench acknowledged the exception for "gentlemen" or nobility to "ride armed" as not to offend the statute. *See Rex v. Knight*, 90 Eng. Rep. 330 (1686); *see also* Hawkins, 1 *Pleas of the Crown* at 136, ch. 63, § 9.

106. *The Entering Book of Roger Morrice 1677–1691* at 308.

107. *See, e.g.*, Lund, "The Second Amendment, *Heller*, and Originalist Jurisprudence" at 1368.

108. Nicholas J. Johnson, David B. Kopel, George A. Mocsary, and Michael P. O'Shea, *Firearms Law and the Second Amendment: Rights, Regulation, and Policy* 81–82 (New York: Wolters Kluwer Law and Business, 2012) (citations omitted).

109. Ibid. at 82.

110. Blackstone, 4 *Commentaries on the Laws of England* at 148–49.

111. Ibid. at 149.

112. *See* Charles, "The Faces of the Second Amendment Outside the Home" at 11–27.

113. Blackstone, 4 *Commentaries on the Laws of England* at 291.

114. Ibid. at 223.

115. Hawkins, 1 *Pleas of the Crown* at 135, ch. 63, § 5.

116. Ibid. at 136, ch. 63, § 8.

117. Ibid.

118. Ibid. at 136, ch. 63, § 9. Handguns and crossbows were prohibited to be worn and borne by any person, regardless of condition or station. *See* 25 Hen. 8, c. 17 (1533–1534) (Eng.); Keble, *An Assistant to the Justices of the Peace* at 709.

119. Hawkins, 1 *Pleas of the Crown* at 136, ch. 63, § 10.

120. *Compare* Charles, "The Faces of the Second Amendment Outside the Home" at 7–36 (providing

substantiated research on the Statute of Northampton in historical context), *with* Volokh, "The First and Second Amendments" at 101–2 (selectively quoting Hawkins and other legal treatises). *See also* Hawkins, 1 *Pleas of the Crown* at 135–36, ch. 63, §§ 5, 8, 10.

121. Charles, "The Faces of the Second Amendment Outside the Home" at 35–36.

122. *See, e.g.,* Tucker, *View of the Constitution,* at 44 (stating America was different from previous republics, like Athens and Rome, in that it consisted of "an agricultural people, dispersed over immense territory ... whose population does not amount to one able bodied militia man for each mile square").

123. *See* Saul Cornell and Nathan DeDino, "A Well Regulated Right: The Early American Origins of Gun Control," 73 *Fordham Law Review* 487, 512–15 (2004).

124. *Bliss v. Commonwealth,* 12 Ky. 90, 92 (Ky., 1822).

125. *State v. Buzzard,* 4 Ark. 18, 25–26 (Ark., 1842).

126. *See, e.g.,* Saul Cornell and Justin Florence, "The Right to Bear Arms in the Era of the Fourteenth Amendment: Gun Rights or Gun Regulation?" 50 *Santa Clara Law Review* 1043, 1052–53 (2010); Cornell, "The Right to Carry Firearms Outside the Home" at 1715–18. But not all Southern courts adopted this view. *See English v. State,* 35 Tex. 473, 474 (Tex., 1872).

127. O'Shea, "Modeling the Second Amendment Right to Arms (I)" at 671.

128. Peter Oxenbridge Thacher, *Two Charges to the Grand Jury of the County of Suffolk for the Commonwealth of Massachusetts, at the Opening Terms of the Municipal Court of the City of Boston, on Monday, December 5th, AD 1836* at 27–28 (Boston: Dutton and Wentworth, 1837).

129. For varying examples, see *The Revised Statutes of the State of Wisconsin, Passed at the Annual Session of the Legislature Commencing January 13, 1858, and Approved May 17, 1858* at 985 (Chicago: W.B. Keen, 1858) ("If any person shall go armed with a dirk, dagger, sword, pistol or pistols, or other offensive and dangerous weapon, without reasonable cause to fear an assault or other injury or violence to his person"); Edward C. Palmer, *The General Statutes of Minnesota* 629 (St. Paul, MN: Davidson and Hall, 1867). ("Whoever goes armed with a dirk, dagger, sword, pistol or pistols, or other offensive and dangerous weapon, without reasonable cause to fear an assault or other injury or violence to his person"); John Purdon, *A Digest of the Laws of Pennsylvania, from the Year One Thousand Seven Hundred to the Twenty-First Day of May, One Thousand Eight Hundred and Sixty-One* at 250 (9th ed., Philadelphia: Kay & Brother, 1862) ("If any person, not being an officer on duty in the military or naval service of the state or of the United States shall go armed with a dirk, dagger, sword or pistol, or other offensive or dangerous weapon, without reasonable cause to fear an assault or other injury or violence"); *The Revised Statutes of the State of Maine Passed October 22, 1840* at 709 (Augusta, ME: William R. Smith, 1841) ("Any person, going armed with any dirk, dagger, sword, pistol, or other offensive and dangerous weapon, without a reasonable cause to fear an assault on himself"); *The Revised Code of the District of Columbia* 570 (Washington, D.C.: A.O.P. Nicholson, 1857) ("If any person shall go armed with a dirk, dagger, sword, pistol, or other offensive and dangerous weapon, without reasonable cause to fear an assault or other injury or violence to his person"); *Revised Statutes of the State of Delaware, to the year of Our Lord One Thousand Eight Hundred and Fifty-Two* at 333 (Chicago: W.B. Keen, 1852) ("Any justice of the peace may also cause to be arrested ... all who go armed offensively to the terror of the people, or are otherwise disorderly and dangerous."); *The Statutes of Oregon Enacted and Continued in Force by the Legislative Assembly as the Session Commencing 5th December, 1853* at 220 (Salem, OR: Asahel Bush, 1854).

130. The language of these laws may have been borrowed from another source. *See, e.g.,* Elisha Hammond, *A Practical Treatise, or An Abridgement of the Law Appertaining to the Office of Justice of the Peace* 184 (West Brookfield: C.A. Mirick, 1841).

131. Cornell, "The Right to Carry Firearms Outside the Home" at 1722–25.

132. *State v. Huntly,* 25 N.C. 418 (N.C. 1842); Charles, "The Faces of the Second Amendment Outside the Home" at 36–38.

133. *Nunn v. State,* 1 Ga. 243 (Ga., 1846).

134. James Kent, 2 *Commentaries on American Law* 406 (8th ed., William Kent, 1854); James Kent, 2 *Commentaries on American Law* 442 (Oliver Wendell Holmes ed., Boston: Little, Brown, 1873).

135. Francis Wharton, *A Treatise on the Criminal Law of the United States* 527–28 (Philadelphia: James Kay, Jun., and Brother, 1846); William Oldnall Russell, *A Treatise on Crimes and Misdemeanors* 392 (5th ed., Philadelphia: T. and J. W. Johnson, 1877).

136. Charles, "The Second Amendment Standard of Review After *McDonald*" at 25, 29–33; Charles, "The 1792 National Militia, the Second Amendment, and Militia Rights" at 326, 344–47, 374–79.

137. *See* Mark Anthony Frassetto, "Firearms and Weapons Legislation Up to the Early 20th Century," at 46–51, 72–75, 90–98 (unpublished paper available on the Social Science Research Network). *See also Presser v. Illinois,* 116 U.S. 252 (1886).

138. Steven W. Kranz, "A Survey of State Conceal and Carry Statutes: Can Small Changes Help Reduce the Controversy?" 29 *Hamline Law Review* 637, 646–49 (2006); Megan Ruebsamen, "The Gun-Shy Commonwealth: Self-Defense and Concealed Carry in Post-*Heller* Massachusetts," 18 *Suffolk Journal of Trial and Appellate Advocacy* 55, 66–76 (2013).

139. Clayton E. Cramer and David B. Kopel, "'Shall Issue': The New Wave of Concealed Carry Handgun Permits," 62 *Tennessee Law Review* 679, 681–747 (1995); Kranz, "A Survey of State Conceal and Carry Statutes" at 649–58.

140. For some discussions on the implications of *Heller* and *McDonald* on politics, see Jamal Greene, "Guns, Originalism, and Cultural Cognition," 13 *University of Pennsylvania Journal of Constitutional Law* 511 (2010); Allen Rostron, "Cease Fire: A 'Win-Win' Strategy on Gun Policy for the Obama Administration," 3 *Harvard Law and Policy Review* 347 (2009); Mark V. Tushnet, "*Heller* and the Perils of Compromise," 13 *Lewis and Clark Law Review* 419 (2009); Anders Walker, "From Ballots to Bullets: *District of Columbia v. Heller* and the New Civil Rights," 69 *Louisiana Law Review* 509 (2009).

141. 25 Edw. 3, stat. 5, c. 2, § 13 (1350) (Eng.).

142. Winkler, *Gun Fight* at 166–70.

143. Cramer and Kopel, "'Shall Issue'" at 681–747.

144. In *Heller II*, the Circuit Court of Appeals for the District of Columbia was unconvinced by this line of argument. See *District of Columbia v. Heller*, 670 F.3d 1244 (D.C. Cir., 2011).

145. For some discussions, see Eugene Kontorovich, "Is the Right to Bear Arms Plural?" *The Volokh Conspiracy* (July 8, 2013); Eugene Kontorovich, "'A Good Musket' and Bearing Arms," *The Volokh Conspiracy* (July 8, 2013); Eugene Kontorovich, "Response to Professor Rosenkranz: Arms and the Man—or Arms and the People," *The Volokh Conspiracy* (July 9, 2013). For a reply to Kontorovich, see Andrew Koppelman, "'Arms' and the Man: Kontorovich on the Second Amendment," *Balkinization* (July 10, 2013).

146. Charles, "Restoring 'Life, Liberty, and the Pursuit of Happiness in Our Constitutional Jurisprudence" at 502–32.

147. Brown, *No Duty to Retreat* at 3–5.

148. "An Act to Prevent the Firing of Guns Charged with Shot or Ball in the Town of Boston," in *Boston Post-Boy and Daily Advertiser* (Boston, MA), September 5, 1768, pg. 1, col. 3.

149. "At a legal meeting of the freeholders and other inhabitants of the town of Newburyport ... held on the twenty-ninth day of March, AD 1785," in *Essex Journal, and the Massachusetts and New-Hampshire General Advertiser* (Essex, Mass.), May 11, 1785, pg. 2, col. 2 (emphasis added).

150. James E. Hicks, "United States Military Shoulder Arms, 1795–1935," 1 *The Journal of the American Military History Foundation* 22, 31 (1937). An experienced marksman with a flintlock could fire between three to four rounds per minute, but this is a high estimate. Ibid. at 30.

151. This ratio does not change should the shooter be armed with a pair of pistols. Generally, pistols took longer to reload than rifles or muskets, but could be preloaded and fire as long as the powder was not compromised. Don B. Kates and Clayton Cramer claim that eighteenth-century persons could have conceivably carried "two, four, or even six single-shot pistols on their belt," and thus fire "six bullets in about ten seconds." Kates and Cramer, "Second Amendment Limitations and Criminological Considerations" at 1356–57. This is a rather high assessment. Although the physical carrying of six un-loaded pistols may have been possible, the technology available at the time would have made it difficult to effectively carry and keep all six loaded and charged.

152. Even Standard Model writers Don B. Kates and Clayton E. Cramer agree that a "reasonably skilled wielder of a modern pistol could expect to *accurately* shoot perhaps twenty to forty bullets in about sixty to ninety seconds." Kates and Cramer, "Second Amendment Limitations and Criminological Considerations" at 1357.

153. *See* An Act to Prevent Routs, Riots, and Tumultuous Assemblies, and the Evil Consequences Thereof (Mass. 1786); An Act for the More Speedy and Effectual Suppression of Tumults and Insurrections in the Commonwealth (Mass. 1787); An Act to Prevent Routs, Riots, and Tumultuous Assemblies (N.J. 1797); An Act Against Riots and Rioters (Pa., 1705).

154. Charles, "The Faces of the Second Amendment Outside the Home" at 43–49.

Chapter 6

1. U.S. Const. amend. XIV, § 1.

2. Gerald L. Neuman, *Strangers to the Constitution: Immigrants, Borders, and Fundamental Law* 165 (Princeton, NJ: Princeton University Press, 1996).

3. Ibid.

4. Ibid. at 166.

5. Saby Ghoshray, "Rescuing the Citizenship Clause from Nativistic Distortion: A Reconstructionist Interpretation of the Fourteenth Amendment," 51 *Washburn Law Journal* 261, 263 (2012).

6. Ibid. at 264–65, 310.

7. *See* Peter H. Schuck and Rogers M. Smith, *Citizenship Without Consent: Illegal Aliens in the American Polity* 85–87 (New Haven, CT: Yale University Press, 1985); John C. Eastman, "Politics and the Court: Did the Supreme Court Really Move Left Because of Embarrassment Over *Bush v. Gore*?" 94 *Georgetown Law Journal* 1475, 1486–87 (2006); Charles Wood, "Losing Control of America's Future: The Census, Birthright Citizenship, and Illegal Aliens," 22 *Harvard Journal of Law and Public Policy* 465, 503 (1999); Brief for the Claremont Institute Center for Constitutional Jurisprudence as Amicus Curia Supporting Respondents, *Hamdi v. Rumsfield*, 542 U.S. 507 (2004) (No. 03–6696).

8. *See* William Ty Mayton, "Birthright Citizenship and the Civic Minimum," 22 *Georgetown Immigration Law Journal* 221 (2008); Lino A. Graglia, "Birthright Citizenship for Children of Illegal Aliens: An Irrational Public Policy," 14 *Texas Review of Law and Politics* 1 (2009); *Oforji v. Ashcroft*, 354 F.3d 609, 620–21 (7th Cir. 2003) (Posner, J., concurring); George F. Will, "An Argument to be Made About Immigrant Babies and Citizenship," *The Washington Post* (March 28, 2010).

9. *See* Dan Stein and John Bauer, "Automatic Citizenship for Children of Illegal Immigrants?" 7

Stanford Law and Policy Review 127 (1996). The Immigration and Nationality Act does not clarify the Fourteenth Amendment's meaning. It merely restates its text verbatim. *See* 8 U.S.C. § 1401(a) (2013).

10. Criticisms of a textualist approach to interpreting the Fourteenth Amendment are longstanding. Writing in 1938, Yale Law School professor Walton H. Hamilton argued for a broader contextual interpretation: "The bother is that language is general and abstract. The clauses are filled with verbal symbols quite receptive to a content strong enough to possess them; not one single concretion is to be found to suggest interpretation or point direction. The language is exposed to the greatest of all historical fallacies, which is to confuse event with intent and to read the exposition of a later age back into pristine statement. The men who framed and ratified the amendment had only the dimmest knowledge of events to come; they had to explore its constitutional possibilities without benefit of the labors of jurists recently seated or not yet upon the bench; they had to set down general words in terms of the problems then current. From them the clauses lived with the breath of their own age. It is only by historical reconstruction that the contemporary meaning of the Fourteenth Amendment is to be rediscovered." Walton H. Hamilton, "The Path of Due Process of Law," in *The Constitution Reconsidered* at 167, 169–70.

11. Michael D. Ramsey, "Children of Illegal Aliens as Birthright Citizens: The Original Meaning of 'Subject to the Jurisdiction Thereof,'" University of San Diego Constitution Day Debate: Birthright Citizenship (September 17, 2010). *See also* Michael D. Ramsey, "Originalism and Birthright Citizenship: Part One," *The Originalism Blog* (June 22, 2011); Michael D. Ramsey, "Originalism and Birthright Citizenship: Part Two," *The Originalism Blog* (July 1, 2011); Michael D. Ramsey, "Originalism and Birthright Citizenship: Part Three," *The Originalism Blog* (July 11, 2011).

12. Matthew Ing, "Birthright Citizenship, Illegal Aliens, and the Original Meaning of the Citizenship Clause," 45 *Akron Law Review* 719, 723 (2012).

13. Ibid. at 735–67.

14. Garrett Epps, *Wrong and Dangerous: Ten Right Wing Myths About Our Constitution* 30–31 (Lanham, MD: Rowman and Littlefield, 2012); Garrett Epps, "The Citizenship Clause: A 'Legislative History,'" 60 *American University Law Review* 331, 339 (2010) (emphasis added).

15. Ibid. at 333.

16. *See* Mark Shawhan, "'By Virtue of Being Born Here': Birthright Citizenship and the Civil Rights Act of 1866," 15 *Harvard Latino Review* 201, 209–28 (2011). *See also* Mark Shawhan, "The Significance of Domicile in Lyman Trumbull's Conception of Citizenship," 119 *Yale Law Journal* 1352 (2010).

17. 14 U.S. Stat. 27 (1866).

18. Shawhan, "'By Virtue of Being Born Here'" at 202.

19. John C. Eastman, "From *Plyer* to *Arizona*: Have the Courts Forgotten about *Corfield v.*

Coryell?" 80 University *of Chicago Law Review* 165, 195 (2013).

20. Graglia, "Birthright Citizenship for Children of Illegal Aliens" at 5–6.

21. For the importance of temporary allegiance and political rights, see Charles, "Decoding the Fourteenth Amendment's Citizenship Clause" at 215–20. *See also* Christopher R. Green, "The Original Sense of the (Equal) Protection Clause: Pre-Enactment History," 19 *George Mason University Civil Rights Law Journal* 1, 34–43 (2008) (discussing the allegiance for protection doctrine).

22. *See* Robert E. Mensel, "Jurisdiction in Nineteenth Century International Law and its Meaning in the Citizenship Clause of the Fourteenth Amendment," 32 *Saint Louis University Public Law Review* 329 (2013).

23. *See* Murphy, "Time to Reclaim" at 77.

24. Mensel, "Jurisdiction in Nineteenth Century International Law and its Meaning in the Citizenship Clause of the Fourteenth Amendment" at 386.

25. *Slaughterhouse Cases*, 83 U.S. 36, 73 (1873).

26. Indeed Justice Field's dissent states that citizenship is "dependent upon the place of their birth, and "not upon … the condition of their ancestry," but claims this in the context that the states cannot impose residence requirements for United States citizenship to vest. Field's dissent is silent as to the federal government's authority to define the terms of domicile, residence, allegiance, or personal subjection. Ibid. at 95 (Field, J., dissenting).

27. *Elk v. Wilkins*, 112 U.S. 94, 109 (1884).

28. Ibid. at 102.

29. Ibid. at 114 (Harlan, J., dissenting).

30. Ibid. at 115.

31. Charles, "Decoding the Fourteenth Amendment's Citizenship Clause" at 240–45. *See also* Bernadette A. Meyler, "The Gestation of Birthright Citizenship, 1868–1898: States' Rights, the Law of Nations and Mutual Consent," 15 *Georgetown Immigration Law Journal* 519 (2001).

32. U.S. Const. amend. XIV, § 5.

33. In terms of general application by the United States government through the late nineteenth century, citizenship claims by foreigners were handled on a case-by-case basis. In some instances, citizenship was granted to persons born of alien parents in the United States, while in others it was not. *See* Charles, "Decoding the Fourteenth Amendment's Citizenship Clause" at 237–40.

34. Marshall B. Woodworth, "Citizenship of the United States Under the Fourteenth Amendment," 30 *The American Review* 535 (1886).

35. Ibid. at 536.

36. Ibid. at 536–37.

37. Ibid. at 541.

38. Ibid. at 542.

39. Ibid. at 545.

40. Ibid. at 546. Justice John Marshall Harlan also offered some views on the case before the Supreme Court decided the case. *See* Brian L. Frye, Josh Blackman, and Michael McCloskey, "Justice John Marshall Harlan: Lectures on Constitutional

Law," 81 *George Washington Law Review Arguendo* 12, 264–68 (2013).

41. *See* Charles, "The Plenary Power Doctrine and the Constitutionality of Ideological Exclusion" at 63–118; Charles, "Decoding the Fourteenth Amendment's Citizenship Clause" at 215–47. For some commentators claiming no historical support for the plenary power doctrine, see Stephen Legomsky, *Immigration and the Judiciary: Law and Politics in Britain and America* 199–218 (New York: Oxford University Press, 1987); Henkin, "The Constitution and United States Sovereignty" at 858; Motomura, "Immigration Law after a Century of Plenary Power" at 545.

42. *See, e.g.,* Alexander Porter Morse, *A Treatise on Citizenship, by Birth and Naturalization, With References to the Law of Nations, Roman Civil Law, Law of the United States of America, and the Law of France* 159 (Boston: Little, Brown, 1881) ("temporary allegiance [which describes the obedience due by an alien to the laws of the jurisdiction in which he happens to be commorant] is everywhere recognized"); ibid. at 160 ("Certain persons may ... be under the jurisdiction of two different states.... In case of conflict, the preference will be given to the state in which the individual or family in question have their domicile.... If the oath of allegiance is the first tie which binds the citizen to the state, it is evident that the individual cannot appeal simultaneously to two sovereignties.").

43. Woodworth, "Citizenship of the United States Under the Fourteenth Amendment," at 546.

44. *Wong Kim Ark*, 169 U.S. 649, 652–53 (1898).

45. Ibid. at 653, 656, 666, 672–82, 693, 695–96 700, 704–5.

46. Ibid. at 693 (emphasis added).

47. Unknown, "Comment: *Wong Kim Ark*," 7 *Yale Law Journal* 366, 367 (1898).

48. John W. Judd, "The XIV Amendment: Its History and Evolution," 13 *The American Lawyer* 388, 399 (1905).

49. Marshall B. Woodworth, "Who Are Citizens of the United States? *Wong Kim Ark* Case Interpreted," 32 *The American Law Review* 554, 559 (1898).

50. *See* Rachel E. Rosenbloom, "Policing the Borders of Birthright Citizenship: Some Thoughts on the New (and Old) Restrictionism," 51 *Washburn Law Journal* 311, 315–16 (2012); Allison S. Hartry, "Birthright Justice: The Attack on Birthright Citizenship and Immigrant Women of Color," 36 *New York University Journal of Legislation and Public Policy* 57, 67 (2012); Matthew J. Lister, "Citizenship, In the Immigration Context," 70 *Maryland Law Review* 175, 205–6 (2010); Hiroshi Motomura, "Immigration Outside the Law," 108 *Columbia Law Review* 2037, 2091–92 (2008); Cristina M. Rodriguez, "The Citizenship Clause, Original Meaning, and the Egalitarian Unity of the Fourteenth Amendment," 11 *University of Pennsylvania Journal of Constitutional Law* 1363 (2009); James C. Ho, "Defining 'American': Birthright Citizenship and the Original Understanding of the 14th Amendment," 9 *The*

Green Bag 367 (2006); Elizabeth B. Wydra, "Birthright Citizenship: A Constitutional Guarantee," *American Constitutional Society of Law and Policy* 9 (2009).

51. *See, e.g.,* Henry Brannon, *A Treatise on the Rights and Privileges Guaranteed by the Fourteenth Amendment to the Constitution of the United States* 25 (Cincinnati: W.H. Anderson, 1901). ("Mere birth within our territory does not always make the child a citizen. He must be born under the allegiance of the United States ... within its 'jurisdiction.' Such is the case with children of aliens born here while their parents are traveling or only temporarily resident, or of foreign ministers, consuls and attaches of foreign embassies. Such children are born within our territory, and within our territorial jurisdiction, but not within the pale of allegiance to us, as when born they are not subject to our laws.") (citing *Wong Kim Ark*, 169 U.S. 682 [1898]).

52. *See, e.g.,* Schuck and Smith, *Citizenship Without Consent* at 4.

53. *See* Mensel, "Jurisdiction in Nineteenth Century International Law and its Meaning in the Citizenship Clause of the Fourteenth Amendment" at 333–40 (discussing how this dilemma applies to scholars on different sides of the issue of birthright citizenship).

54. The Congressional Research Service produced a report to answer these questions. However, the report failed to adequately address late nineteenth-century legal issues such as allegiance, domicile, residence, and personal subjections. *See* Margaret Mikyung Lee, "Birthright Citizenship Under the 14th Amendment of Persons Born in the United States to Alien Parents," *Congressional Research Service* (August 12, 2010).

55. *See, e.g.,* Eastman, "Politics and the Court" at 1486–87.

56. Epps, "The Citizenship Clause" at 350–51.

57. *See, e.g.,* Mensel, "Jurisdiction in Nineteenth Century International Law and its Meaning in the Citizenship Clause of the Fourteenth Amendment" at 355, 375; Charles, "Decoding the Citizenship Clause" at 226–28; Graglia, "Birthright Citizenship for the Children of Illegal Aliens" at 6–7; Paul Finkelman, "The *Dred Scott* Case: Slavery and the Politics of Law," 20 *Hamline Law Review* 1 (1996).

58. U.S. Const. amend. XIV, § 1.

59. Samuel T. Spear, "American Citizenship," 15 *Albany Law Journal* 484, 484–85 (1877).

60. *See, e.g.,* Ghoshray, "Rescuing the Citizenship Clause from Nativistic Distortion" at 293–94.

61. *See, e.g.,* Wood, "Losing Control of America's Future" at 512–19.

62. *See* John C. Eastman and Ediberto Roman, "Debate on Birthright Citizenship," 6 *Florida International University Law Review* 293, 302–3 (2011) ("The language of the Fourteenth Amendment makes clear that what Congress was talking about was authority over the individual, not allegiance."); Ho, "Defining 'American'" at 372 ("The text of the Citizenship Clause requires 'jurisdiction,' not allegiance.").

63. Ing, "Birthright Citizenship, Illegal Aliens, and the Original Meaning of the Citizenship Clause" at 755; Gerard N. Magliocca, "Indians as Invaders: The Citizenship Clause and Illegal Aliens," 10 *University of Pennsylvania Journal of Constitutional Law* 499, 512–13 (2008).

64. *See* Shawhan, "'By Virtue of Being Born Here'" at 204 ("Citizenship resulted from the sovereign's protection provided to an infant at birth and the corollary obligation of allegiance owed by the infant to the sovereign.").

65. Ghoshray, "Rescuing the Citizenship Clause from Nativistic Distortion" at 298.

66. *Lynch v. Clarke*, 1 Sand. Ch. 583 (1844).

67. Ibid. at 638.

68. Ibid. at 663 (emphasis added).

69. Ibid. at 641.

70. Charles, "Decoding the Fourteenth Amendment's Citizenship Clause" at 217–18. Associate Justice Samuel Chase defined allegiance as the mutual bond between the sovereign and the "subject, by which the subjects owe Duty to the [sovereign] and the [sovereign], protection to [the] subjects." Samuel Chase, *British Case Law Citations* (1800) (unpublished journal, on file with the Library of Congress Rare Books Division, Washington, D.C.).

71. *Lynch*, 1 Sand. Ch. at 645–46 (emphasis added) (the phrases "unwritten or common law" and "national law" were emphasized in the original source).

72. *See* Magliocca, "Indians and Invaders" 504–05. For a more creative and ahistorical reading of *Lynch v. Clarke*, see Berta Esperanza Hernández-Truyol, "Natives, Newcomers and Nativism: A Human Rights Model for the Twenty-First Century," 23 *Fordham Urban Law Journal* 1075, 1114 (1996) (reading *Lynch* as supporting an "open borders" policy).

73. *Lynch*, 1 Sand. Ch. at 655.

74. Ibid. at 641.

75. Webster, *A Collection of Essays and Fugitive Writings* at 319.

76. Ibid. at 318.

77. Mensel, "Jurisdiction in Nineteenth Century International Law and its Meaning in the Citizenship Clause of the Fourteenth Amendment" at 334–35.

78. The doctrine of allegiance was quite prevalent in nineteenth century immigration and citizenship law. *See* Henry Wheaton, *Elements of International Law: With a Sketch of the History of the Science* 99–101, 111–12, 122, 177–81, 230, 237–42 (Philadelphia: Carey, Lea & Blanchard, 1836) (numerous later editions were published); Daniel Gardner, *A Treatise on International Law, and a Short Explanation of the Jurisdiction and Duty of the Government of the Republic of the United States* 98, 110, 150, 157, 180, 255 (Troy, NY: N. Tuttle, 1844) (numerous later editions were published); Richard Wildman, 1 *Institutes of International Law: International Rights in Time of Peace* 6, 40–45, 82, 133 (London: W. Benning, 1849) (numerous later editions were published).

79. Henri Mercier to William H. Seward, October 31, 1862, in *United States Department of State: Message of the President of the United States to the Two Houses of Congress at the Commencement of the First Session of the Thirty Eighth Congress* 809, 810 (Washington, D.C.: Government Printing Office, 1863).

80. William H. Seward to Henri Mercier, November 4, 1862, in *United States Department of State* at 811, 812.

81. Ibid.

82. 14 Stat. 27 (1866).

83. *Congressional Globe*, 39th Congress, 1st Session 498 (1866).

84. It is unclear whether Trumbull's earlier claim was a mere slip of the tongue, given it arguably conflicts with later statements. *See* Mensel, "Jurisdiction in Nineteenth Century International Law and its Meaning in the Citizenship Clause of the Fourteenth Amendment" at 366–67.

85. *Congressional Globe*, 39th Congress, 1st Session 527 (1866) (emphasis added).

86. Ibid.

87. Ibid.

88. *See* Margaret Mikyung Lee and Erika K. Lunder, "The Constitutionality of Excluding Aliens from the Census for Apportionment and Redistricting Purposes," *Congressional Research Services* (January 20, 2010).

89. *Congressional Globe*, 39th Congress, 1st Session 572 (1866).

90. Ibid. at 1117. Ohio Representative William Lawrence agreed with Wilson's interpretation of the law. *See* ibid. at 1832.

91. Ibid. at 600, 1757.

92. Howard Jay Graham, "Our 'Declaratory' Fourteenth Amendment," 7 *Stanford Law Review* 3 (1954).

93. "Senator Trumbull's Address to the Illinois Legislature: The Civil Rights Bill," in *New York Times* (New York, NY), January 21, 1867, pg. 1.

94. Epps, "The Citizenship Clause" at 353.

95. Ibid.

96. The Fourteenth Amendment reads "subject to the jurisdiction thereof" in lieu of "not subject to any foreign power." *Compare* U.S. Const. amend. XIV, § 1, *with* 14 Stat. 27 (1866).

97. *Congressional Globe*, 39th Congress, 1st Session 2764 (1866) (known as H.R. No. 127).

98. Ibid. at 2768.

99. Ibid.

100. Ibid. at 2769.

101. Ibid.

102. Ibid.

103. Ibid.

104. Ibid. at 2869.

105. Ibid. at 2890. Senator Howard's opinion is of critical importance to understanding the scope of the Citizenship Clause. Howard was appointed to a three member committee to propose amendments to the full Senate, including Senators Fessenden and Grimes. Indeed, Senator Wade was the Senate Republicans' caucus chair and did make a proposed

amendment to the Citizenship Clause. However, it was Howard's version and view that was adopted, not Wade's. *See* Aynes, "Enforcing the Bill of Rights Against the States" at 129.

106. Mensel, "Jurisdiction in Nineteenth Century International Law and its Meaning in the Citizenship Clause of the Fourteenth Amendment" at 364.

107. *Congressional Globe*, 39th Congress, 1st Session 2890–93 (1866).

108. Ibid. at 2893.

109. Epps, "The Citizenship Clause" at 361–62.

110. *Congressional Globe*, 39th Congress, 1st Sess. 2893 (1866) (statement of Senator Trumbull). ("If [persons] are there and within the jurisdiction of Colorado, and subject to the laws of Colorado, they ought to be citizens; and that is all that is proposed. It cannot be said of any Indian who owes allegiance, partial allegiance if you please, to some other Government that he is 'subject to the jurisdiction of the United States.'")

111. Ibid.

112. Ibid.

113. Ibid.

114. Ibid. at 2768, 2896.

115. Ibid. at 2896.

116. The 1868 Louisiana Constitution provides a great example on the Fourteenth Amendment in this regard. Article 2 of the Bill of Rights declared: "All persons, without regard to race, color, or previous condition, born or naturalized in the United States, and subject to the jurisdiction thereof, and residents of this State for one year, are citizens of this State. The citizens of this State *owe allegiance* to the United States; and this *allegiance is paramount* to that which they owe to the State." La. Const. of 1868, Bill of Rights, art. II (emphasis added). States could no longer define the terms of allegiance for admittance into the political community. *See* Samuel T. Spear, "National Protection," 24 *The Independent* 1231 (1872). ("The fact that one is a citizen of the state in which he resides does not in any way release him from the higher fact that he is also a citizen of the United States. As between the two forms of citizenship the national is supreme in the responsibilities and subjection which it involves.")

117. Mensel, "Jurisdiction in Nineteenth Century International Law and its Meaning in the Citizenship Clause of the Fourteenth Amendment" at 371. ("It must be acknowledged that the evidence is not monolithic, and these conclusions cannot be made with absolute certainty.")

118. *Congressional Globe*, 39th Congress, Appendix 256 (1866).

119. Ibid. *See also Daily Evening Bulletin* (San Francisco, CA), April 19, 1870, pg. 1 col. 1 ("The Indians are not and never have been subject to our jurisdiction. That is, they are not subject to our laws, not subject to our taxes, nor to military service. Owing none of the duties of allegiance, they are not accorded any of its privileges."); ibid. ("Government is founded on the consent of the governed: and the citizen is the fundamental and only repository of

sovereignty. We want no citizens who are not fit to be sovereigns; and we can consistently have none who are not equally and freely admitted to all the rights as well as subjected to all the obligations of a common government.")

120. *Congressional Globe*, 39th Congress, 1st Session 2897 (1866).

121. Charles, "Representation Without Documentation?" at 56–60.

122. Ibid. at 61–67, 81–86.

123. The Supreme Court took this position in *Elk v. Wilkins*, 112 U.S. 94 (1884).

124. U.S. Const. amend. XIV, § 5.

125. Timothy Farrar, *Manual of the Constitution of the United States of America* 403–4 (Boston: Little, Brown, 1867).

126. Ibid. at 203.

127. U.S. Const. amend XIV, § 5.

128. 14 *The Works of Charles Sumner* 385 (Boston: Lee and Shepard, 1883).

129. Letter from Sen. Lyman Trumbull, Chairman, Senate Judiciary Comm., to President Andrew Johnson (undated), in Andrew Johnson Papers, Reel 45, Manuscript Div. Library of Congress, Washington, D.C.

130. *Boston Semi-Weekly Courier* (Boston, MA), January 1, 1852, pg. 1 col. 5.

131. *See* Epps, *Wrong and Dangerous* at 106–7; William N. Eskridge, Jr., "Destabilizing Due Process and Evolutive Equal Protection," 47 *UCLA Law Review* 1183 (2000); John Harrison, "Reconstructing the Privileges and Immunities Clause," 101 *Yale Law Journal* 1385 (1992).

132. Ghoshray, "Rescuing the Citizenship Clause from Nativistic Distortion" at 309.

133. *See, e.g.,* Emily Kendall, "Amending the Constitution to Save a Sinking Ship? The Issues Surrounding the Proposed Amendment of the Citizenship Clause and 'Anchor Babies,'" 22 *Berkeley La Raza Law Journal* 349, 353–56 (2012).

134. Ghoshray, "Rescuing the Citizenship Clause from Nativistic Distortion" at 276.

135. *See* Richard L. Aynes, "The Continuing Importance of Congressman John A. Bingham and the Fourteenth Amendment," 36 *Akron Law Review* 589, 591 (2003) ("Bingham's inseparable link with the Amendment makes him worthy of attention from both a legal and an historical view.... His words may provide meaning or context for what has been termed original intent, meaning or understanding of the Fourteenth Amendment."); Richard L. Aynes, "On Misreading John Bingham and the Fourteenth Amendment," 103 *Yale Law Journal* 57, 103 (1993) (discussing the importance of Bingham's views on contemporaries and the first federal courts to apply the Fourteenth Amendment); *McDonald v. City of Chicago*, 130 S. Ct. 3020, 3072 (2010) (Thomas, J., concurring) (finding Bingham's view to be "particularly significant" as "the principal draftsman of §1").

136. *Congressional Globe*, 35th Congress, 2nd Session 983 (1859) (emphasis added).

137. Ibid. (emphasis added). *See also* ibid. at 984

("Who, sir, are citizens of the United States? First all free persons born and domiciled within the United States—not all free white persons, but all free persons."); ibid. at 985. ("But it is not necessary to take in demonstrating that all free persons born and domiciled within the United States are citizens of the United States.")

138. *Congressional Globe*, 37th Congress, 2nd Session 1639 (1862).

139. Mensel, "Jurisdiction in Nineteenth Century International Law and its Meaning in the Citizenship Clause of the Fourteenth Amendment" at 385.

140. Interview with Margaret Stock, The Birth Right Citizenship Debate (January 26, 2011), available at http://www.cfr.org/immigration/birthright-citizenship-debate/p23900.

141. This type of "law office history" mistake was discussed in Chapter 5 where Joyce Lee Malcolm audaciously claimed the Statute of Northampton was never enforced and interpreted as maintaining a *mens rea* element. History in context, however, disproved Malcolm's claim. But not before it had far reaching implications in Second Amendment historiography, for a number of academics have restated and continue to restate this false history.

142. D.H. Heap to John P. Brown, June 12, 1861, reprinted in 1 *United States Department of State: Message of the President of the United States to the Two Houses of Congress at the Commencement of the First Session of the Thirty-Seventh Congress* 390 (Washington, D.C.: Government Printing Office, 1861).

143. *Congressional Record*, 43rd Congress, 1st Session 3279 (1874).

144. *Hartford Courant* (Hartford, CT), December 3, 1873, pg. 1 col. 6.

145. Ibid.

146. Hamilton Fish to Lawrence Washburne, June 28, 1873, reprinted in *United States Department of State: Message of the President of the United States to the Two Houses of Congress at the Commencement of the First Session of the Forty Third Congress* 256, 257 (Washington, D.C.: Government Printing Office, 1873).

147. Ibid. Secretary of State Fish confirmed this interpretation of the Fourteenth Amendment twice in this letter. *See* ibid. at 259 ("The provisions of the fourteenth amendment of the Constitution have been considered. This amendment is not only of a more recent date, but is a higher authority than the act of Congress referred to, and if there be any conflict between them, or any difference, the Constitution must control, and that makes the subjection of the person of the individual to the jurisdiction of Government a requisite of citizenship.").

148. Hamilton Fish to Ulysses S. Grant, August 25, 1873, reprinted in *Papers Relating to the Foreign Relations of the United States, Transmitted to Congress, with the Annual Message of the President, December 1, 1873* at 1186, 1189 (Washington, D.C.: Government Printing Office, 1873).

149. Ibid. at 1192.

150. *See Congressional Globe*, 39th Congress, 1st Session 607, 1809, 3042 (1866).

151. George H. Williams to Ulysses S. Grant, August 20, 1873, reprinted in *Papers Relating to the Foreign Relations of the United States* at 1216, 1219. Williams' 1873 interpretation is consistent with his 1866 statements on the scope of the Citizenship Clause. In 1874 Williams' integrity and legal experience came into question upon President Grant appointing him to fill the Supreme Court vacancy caused by the death of Chief Justice Salmon P. Chase. *See* Paul A. Freund, "Appointment of Justices: Some Historical Perspectives," 101 *Harvard Law Review* 1146, 1149–50 (1988). Williams withdrew his nomination as a result. Ibid. Certainly, one could claim that this makes Williams' opinion on the Citizenship Clause questionable, but it was quite common in the mid to late nineteenth century for Supreme Court nominees to be rejected on philosophical and political reasons, with claims of inexperience to support partisan views. *See* Grover Rees III, "Questions for Supreme Court Nominees at Confirmation Hearings: Excluding the Constitution," 17 *Georgia Law Review* 913, 944 n.94 (1983); Ruth Bader Ginsburg, "Confirming Supreme Court Justices: Thoughts on the Second Opinion Rendered by the Senate," 1988 *Illinois Law Review* 101, 107 (1988). This purpose of this article is not to weigh Williams' credentials except to say that he was a former Oregon judge, instrumental during the 1857 Oregon Constitutional Convention, and a member of Congress during the adoption of the 1866 Civil Rights Act and Fourteenth Amendment. *See* David Schuman, "The Creation of the Oregon Constitution," 74 *Oregon Law Review* 611(1995). For more on the history and life of Williams and his Supreme Court nomination, see Harvey W. Scott, "An Estimate of the Character and Services of Judge George H. Williams," 11 *The Quarterly of the Oregon Historical Society* 223 (1910); T.W. Davenport, "The Late George H. Williams," 11 *The Quarterly of the Oregon Historical Society* 279 (1910); Sidney Teiser, "Life of George H. Williams, Almost Chief-Justice, Part II," 47 *Oregon History Quarterly* 417 (1946). For the story of Williams' nomination in his own words, including that of other candidates, see George H. Williams, "Reminiscences of the Supreme Court," 8 *Yale Law Journal* 296 (1899).

152. George H. Williams to Ulysses S. Grant, August 20, 1873, reprinted in *Papers Relating to the Foreign Relations of the United States, Transmitted to Congress, with the Annual Message of the President, December 1, 1873* at 1219.

153. Ibid.

154. *See Jackson Daily Citizen* (Jackson, MI), April 2, 1874, pg. 2, col. 1.

155. *See Daily Evening Bulletin* (San Francisco, CA), December 24, 1869, pg. 1, col. 2.

156. *Congressional Record*, 43rd Congress, 1st Session 3279 (1874).

157. Ibid.

158. Ibid. at 3280.

159. *The Chicago Times* (Chicago, IL), May 3,

1874, pg. 6, col. 2 ("It is treason against the principle of American sovereignty to make any distinction between native and naturalized citizens. It is treason by implication against the constitution of the United States. The president who would presume to discriminate between a native and foreign-born citizen at home or abroad, would be unanimously and furiously impeached.").

160. *Boston Daily Globe* (Boston, MA), April 25, 1874, pg. 4.

161. *See Boston Daily Advertiser* (Boston, MA), April 23, 1874, pg. 1, col. 8; *The New York Tribune* (New York, NY), April 23, 1874, pg. 2, col. 2; *New York Times* (New York, NY), March 30 1874, pg. 5, col. 1.

162. *Congressional Record*, 43rd Congress, 1st Session 3459–60 (1874).

163. Ibid.

164. Ibid. at 3460.

165. Ibid. at 3492.

166. Ibid. at 3493.

167. Ibid. at 3597 (emphasis added).

168. Hamilton Fish to Mr. Washburne, June 28, 1873, reprinted in *Papers Relating to the Foreign Relations of the United States* at 257.

169. *Congressional Record*, 43rd Congress, 1st Session 3597 (1874).

170. Frederick Theodore Frelinghuysen to John A. Kasson, January 15, 1885, reprinted in *Papers Relating to the Foreign Relations of the United States, Transmitted to Congress, With the Annual Message of the President, December 8, 1885*, at 394, 395 (Washington, D.C.: United States Government Printing Office, 1886).

171. Ibid.

172. Ibid. (emphasis added).

173. Boyd Winchester to Thomas F. Bayard, November 4, 1885, reprinted in *Papers Relating to the Foreign Relations of the United States, Transmitted to Congress, With the Annual Message of the President, December 8, 1885* at 813.

174. Ibid. at 814.

175. Ibid.

176. Ibid.

177. Ibid.

178. Ibid.

179. Thomas F. Bayard to Boyd Winchester, November 28, 1885, reprinted in *Papers Relating to the Foreign Relations of the United States, Transmitted to Congress, With the Annual Message of the President, December 8, 1885* at 814.

180. Ibid. at 815.

181. Ibid.

182. Thomas F. Bayard to James Fenner Lee, July 24, 1886, reprinted in *Papers Relating to the Foreign Relations of the United States, Transmitted to Congress, with the Annual Message of the President, December 6, 1886*, at 12, 13 (Washington, D.C.: United States Government Printing Office, 1887).

183. Th. de Bounder de Melsbroeck to Thomas F. Bayard, March 27, 1888, reprinted in 1 *Papers Relating to the Foreign Relations of the United States, Transmitted to Congress, with the Annual Message of*

the President, December 3, 1888, at 48 (Washington, D.C.: United States Government Printing Office, 1889).

184. Thomas F. Bayard to Th. de Bounder de Melsbroeck, April 2, 1888, reprinted in 1 *Papers Relating to the Foreign Relations of the United States, Transmitted to Congress, with the Annual Message of the President, December 3, 1888* at 48, 49.

185. Ibid.

186. William F. Wharton to F.D. Grant, August 10, 1891, reprinted in *Papers Relating to the Foreign Relations of the United States, Transmitted to Congress, with the Annual Message of the President, December 8, 1891* at 48 (Washington, D.C.: United States Government Printing Office, 1892).

187. Ibid.

188. Alexander Porter Morse, *A Treatise on Citizenship, By Birth and By Naturalization, With Reference to the Law of Nations, Roman Civil Law, Law of the United States of America, and the Law of France* § 129 at 160 (Boston: Little, Brown, 1881).

189. Samuel T. Spear, "Indians Not Taxed," 32 *The Independent* 1639 (1880).

190. Ibid. at 1640 (emphasis added).

191. Samuel T. Spear, *The Law of the Federal Judiciary: A Treatise on the Provisions of the Constitution, the Laws of Congress, and the Judicial Decisions Relating to the Jurisdiction of, and Practice and Pleading in the Federal Courts* 142–43 (New York: Baker, Voorhis, 1883).

192. William L. Scruggs, "Ambiguous Citizenship," 1 *Political Science Quarterly* 3, 3–5 (1886).

193. Ibid. at 5.

194. William L. Scruggs, "The American Abroad," 23 *The Central Law Journal* 196, 198 (1886).

195. Irving Berdine Richman, "Citizenship of the United States," 5 *Political Science Quarterly* 5, 7–16 (1890).

196. Ibid. at 24.

197. Ibid. at 18, 27.

198. Ibid. at 6–7.

199. Henry C. Ide, "Citizenship by Birth—Another View," 30 *The American Law Review* 241, 249 (1896).

200. Ibid. (emphasis added).

201. Ibid. at 250.

202. Boyd Winchester to Thomas F. Bayard, November 4, 1885, reprinted in *Papers Relating to the Foreign Relations of the United States, Transmitted to Congress, With the Annual Message of the President, December 8, 1885* at 813–14.

203. Boyd Winchester, "Citizenship and its International Relation," 31 *The American Law Review* 504, 504 (1897) (emphasis added).

204. Ibid. at 505.

205. Ibid. at 507–8.

206. Ibid. at 514 (emphasis added).

207. Rosenbloom, "Policing the Borders of Birthright Citizenship" at 316–29.

208. Ibid. at 316.

209. *See* Mensel, Jurisdiction in Nineteenth Century International Law and its Meaning in the Cit-

izenship Clause of the Fourteenth Amendment" at 340–53, 376–84; William L. Scruggs, "The Evolution of American Citizenship," 1 *Southern Law Review* 182 (1901); W.W. Willoughby, "Citizenship and Allegiance in Constitutional and International Law," 1 *The American Journal of International Law* 914 (1907); Richard W. Flournoy, "Problems of Dual Nationality in Time of War," *New York Times* (New York, NY), September 12, 1915.

210. *See, e.g.*, Willoughby, "Citizenship and Allegiance in Constitutional and International Law" at 923–24, 928.

211. Ibid. at 926.

212. *See, e.g.*, Brannon, *A Treatise on the Rights and Privileges Guaranteed by the Fourteenth Amendment to the Constitution of the United States* at 25.

213. Mensel, "Jurisdiction in Nineteenth Century International Law and its Meaning in the Citizenship Clause of the Fourteenth Amendment," at 386.

214. *See* 8 U.S.C. § 1401(a) (2013).

215. This particularly holds true if Congress ever passed a federal statute restricting the citizenship of children born of one immigrant parent and one United States citizen parent. Whether the immigrant is unlawful or temporarily present is nominal, for the statute also unduly burdens a United States citizen, thus triggering equal protection considerations, among others. In such a case history would muddle rather than clarify analysis. While there is nothing in the evidentiary record concerning the Citizenship Clause to suggest Congress was prohibited from legislating on the subject, as it does with children born of one citizen parents overseas, there has been an uninterrupted tradition of affording citizenship to any child born of one citizen parents in the territorial United States. For Supreme Court precedent stipulating Congress may prescribe different rules for one citizen parents abroad, see *Nguyen v. INS*, 533 U.S. 53 (2001).

Epilogue

1. Randy E. Barnett, "Can Lawyers Ascertain the Original Meaning of the Constitution?" *The Volokh Conspiracy* (August 19, 2013).

2. *See* Michael Rappaport, "Historians, Originalists, and Pauline Maier," *Liberty Law Blog* (August 17, 2013) (asserting historians are not legally trained, commit violations of "history office law," and misunderstand the purpose of originalism); Michael Rappaport, "Tillman on Historians and Originalists," *Liberty Law Blog* (August 23, 2013) (asserting historians have a personal agenda against lawyers and originalists).

3. Randy Barnett, *The Structure of Liberty: Justice and the Rule of Law* 41–43 (New York: Oxford University Press, 1998).

4. Ibid. at 73.

5. Barnett, "Restoring the Lost Constitution," at 72.

6. Charles, "Restoring 'Life, Liberty, and the Pursuit of Happiness' in Our Constitutional Jurisprudence," at 477–517.

7. Darrin M. McMahon, *The Pursuit of Happiness: A History from the Greeks to the Present* 325 (London: Allen Lane, 2006).

8. Ibid. at 324.

9. Barnett, "Restoring the Lost Constitution" at 346.

10. Charles, "Restoring 'Life, Liberty, and the Pursuit of Happiness' in Our Constitutional Jurisprudence" at 477–517.

11. For another historian's critique, see Jack N. Rakove, "Book Review: Randy E. Barnett, Restoring the Lost Constitution: The Presumption of Liberty," 1 *N.Y.U. Journal of Law and Liberty* 660 (2005) (arguing that the main fault with Barnett's "presumption of liberty" thesis is that "the Constitution ... was much more about powers than rights").

12. *Compare* Randy Barnett, "Was the Right to Keep and Bear Arms Conditioned on Service in an Organized Militia?" 83 *Texas Law Review* 237, 237–77 (2004), *with* Charles, "The Constitutional Significance of a 'Well-Regulated' Militia Asserted and Proven With Commentary on the Future of Second Amendment Jurisprudence," at 1–101. For a historian's dissent to Randy Barnett's textual approach, see Kozuskanich, "Originalism, History, and the Second Amendment" at 413–46. For a Standard Model counter argument to Nathan Kozuskanich, see Clayton E. Cramer and Joseph Edward Olson, "What Did 'Bear Arms' Mean in the Second Amendment," 6 *Georgetown Journal of Law and Public Policy* 511 (2008).

13. For the importance of Alexander Addison on John Marshall's view of the Necessary and Proper Clause in *United States v. Fisher* and *McCulloch v. Maryland*, see Charles, "Originalism, John Marshall, and the Necessary and Proper Clause" at 545–72. For James Iredell's views on the Necessary and Proper Clause, see 4 *The Debates in the Several State Conventions on the Adoption of the Federal Constitution* at 166–67; James Iredell, "Charge Delivered to the Grand Jury for the District Court of Pennsylvania," Part II, April 11, 1799, reprinted in *The Independent Chronicle and the Universal Advertiser* (Boston, MA), May 30, 1799, at 1, col. 3; James Iredell, "Charge Delivered to the Grand Jury for the District Court of Pennsylvania," Part III, April 11, 1799, reprinted in *The Independent Chronicle and the Universal Advertiser* (Boston, MA), June 3, 1799, at 1, col. 1. For Randy Barnett's view on the Necessary and Proper Clause, see Barnett, *Restoring the Lost Constitution* at 153–90; Barnett, "The People or the State" at 1729–58; Randy E. Barnett, "Necessary and Proper," 44 *UCLA Law Review* 745 (1997).

14. Scalia and Garner, *Reading Law* at 399–402.

15. *See* Raphael, *Constitutional Myths* at 167–70.

Bibliography

Court Opinions

Abrams v. United States, 250 U.S. 616 (1919)

Arizona v. United States, 132 S. Ct. 2492 (2012)

Bliss v. Commonwealth, 12 Ky. 90 (Ky. 1822)

Brown v. Entertainment Merchants Association, 131 S. Ct. 2729 (2011)

Calder v. Bull, 3 U.S. 386 (1798)

Chae Chan Ping v. United States, 130 U.S. 581 (1889)

Chamber of Commerce v. Whiting, 131 S. Ct. 292 (2011)

Chisholm v. Georgia, 2 U.S. 419 (1793)

Church of Lukumi Babalu Aye v. City of Hialeah, 508 U.S. 520 (1993)

Citizens United v. Federal Election Commission, 130 S. Ct. 876 (2010)

City of Akron v. Akron Ctr. For Reprod. Health, 462 U.S. 416 (1983)

Cohens v. Virginia, 19 U.S. 264 (1821)

Dallas v. Commonwealth, 4 U.S. 237 (1802)

Digiacinto v. Rector and Visitors of George Mason University, 281 Va. 17 (Va. 2011)

District of Columbia v. Heller, 554 U.S. 570 (2008)

District of Columbia v. Heller, 670 F.3d 1244 (D.C. Cir. 2011)

Dred Scott v. Sandford, 60 U.S. 393 (1857)

Elk v. Wilkins, 112 U.S. 94 (1884)

English v. State, 35 Tex. 473 (Tex. 1872)

Ezell v. City of Chicago, 651 F.3d 684 (7th Cir. 2011)

First National Bank of Boston v. Bellotti, 435 U.S. 765 (1978)

GeorgiaCarry.Org, Inc. v. Georgia, 687 F.3d 1244 (11th Cir. 2012)

Gitlow v. New York, 268 U.S. 652 (1925)

Hightower v. City of Boston, 693 F.3d 61 (1st Cir. 2012)

Home Building and Loan Ass'n v. Blaisdell, 290 U.S. 398 (1934)

Kachalsky v. County of Westchester, 701 F.3d 81 (2d Cir. 2012)

Lynch v. Clarke, 1 Sand. Ch. 583 (1844)

McCulloch v. Maryland, 17 U.S. 316 (1819)

McDonald v. City of Chicago, 130 S. Ct. 3020 (2010)

McIlvaine v. Coxe's Lessee, 6 U.S. 280 (1804)

Moore v. City of East Cleveland, 431 U.S. 494 (1977)

Moore v. Madigan, 702 F.3d 933 (7th Cir. 2012)

Nebraska Press Ass'n v. Stuart, 427 U.S. 539 (1976)

New York Times Co. v. Sullivan, 376 U.S. 254 (1964)

Nguyen v. INS, 533 U.S. 53 (2001)

NRA of Am. v. Bureau of Alcohol, 700 F.3d 185 (5th Cir. 2012)

Nunn v. State, 1 Ga. 243 (Ga. 1846)

Oforji v. Ashcroft, 354 F.3d 609 (7th Cir. 2003)

Ogden v. Saunders, 25 U.S. 213 (1827)

Presser v. Illinois, 116 U.S. 252 (1886)

Respublica v. Oswald, 1 U.S. 319 (1788)

Rex v. Knight, 87 Eng. Rep. 76 (1686)

Rex v. Knight, 90 Eng. Rep. 330 (1686)

Slaughterhouse Cases, 83 U.S. 36 (1873)

Smith v. Allwright, 321 U.S. 649 (1944)

South Carolina v. United States, 199 U.S. 437 (1905)

State v. Buzzard, 4 Ark. 18 (Ark. 1842)

State v. Huntly, 25 N.C. 418 (N.C. 1842)

United States v. Carpio-Leon, 701 F.3d 974 (4th Cir. 2012)

United States v. Chester, 628 F.3d 673 (4th Cir. 2010)

United States v. Fisher, 6 U.S. 358 (1805)

United States v. Marzzarella, 614 F.3d 35 (3d Cir. 2010)

United States v. Masciandaro, 638 F.3d 313 (4th Cir. 2011)

United States v. Reese, 627 F.3d 792 (10th Cir. 2010)

United States v. Rene, 583 F.3d 8 (1st Cir. 2009)

United States v. Skoien, 614 F.3d 638 (7th Cir. 2010)

United States v. Stevens, 130 S. Ct. 1577 (2010)

United States Term Limits v. Thorton, 514 U.S. 779 (1995)

Vanhorne's Lessee v. Dorrance, 2 U.S. 304 (1795)

Ware v. Hylton, 3 U.S. 199 (1796)

Wong Kim Ark, 169 U.S. 649 (1898)

Woollard v. Gallagher, 712 F.3d 865 (4th Cir. 2013)

Manuscripts, Primary Source Material and Historical Collections

Acts and Laws of the State of Vermont, in America. Judah-Padock and Aleden Spooner, 1779.

Acts of the Council and General Assembly of the State of New-Jersey, from the Establishment of the Present Government and Declaration of Independence, to the End of the First Sitting of the Eighth Session, on the 24th Day of December, 1783 (1783).

Adams, John. *The Diary and Autobiography of John Adams: Diary 1755–1770*, 4 vols. L.H. Butterfield ed. Cambridge, MA: Harvard University Press, 1961.

Adams, John. *The Works of John Adams, Second President of the United States*, 10 vols. Charles Francis Adams, ed. Boston: Little, Brown, 1850–56.

Adams, Samuel. *The Writings of Samuel Adams*, 4 vols. Harry Alonzo Cushing, ed. New York: Putman's, 1904–8.

American Archives: Documents of the American Revolution, 1774–1776. Peter Force ed. Washington, D.C.: n.p., 1833–46.

Anonymous. "Codification of the Common Law in Massachusetts," 15 *American Jurist and Law Magazine* 111 (1836).

Anonymous. "Codification of the Common Law of Massachusetts," 17 *American Jurist and Law Magazine* 17 (1837).

Bay, Elihu Hall. *Reports of Cases Argued and Determined in the Superior Courts of Law in the State of South Carolina*. 2d ed., I. New York: Riley, 1809.

Beccaria, Cesare. *An Essay on Crimes and Punishment*. London: J. Almon, 1764.

Blackstone, William. *An Analysis of the Laws of England*. Oxford: Clarendon Press, 1756.

Blackstone, William. *Blackstone's Commentaries: With Notes of Reference to the Constitution and Laws of the Federal Government of the United States and of the Commonwealth of Virginia*. St. George Tucker, ed. Philadelphia: W.Y. Birch and A. Small, 1803.

Blackstone, William. *Commentaries on the Laws of England*, 4 vols. London: Apollo Press, 1765–69.

Bolingbroke, Henry St. John. *Letters on the Study of History*. London: W. Richardson and S. Clark, 1752.

Bolingbroke, Henry St. John. *The Works of Lord Bolingbroke*, 4 vols. Philadelphia: Carey and Hart, 1841.

Bond, James. *A Compleat Guide for Justices of the Peace*, 3d ed. London: Printed by the assigns of Richard and Edward Atkins..., 1707.

Boston Assembly. *The Votes and Proceedings of the Freeholders and Other Inhabitants of the Town of Boston*. Boston: Edes and Gill, 1772.

Brannon, Henry. *A Treatise on the Rights and Privileges Guaranteed by the Fourteenth Amendment to the Constitution of the United States*. Cincinnati: W.H. Anderson, 1901.

Burlamaqui, Jean Jacques. *The Principles of Natural and Political Law*, 2d ed. London: J. Nourse, 1763.

Chase, Samuel. *British Case Law Citations* (1800). Unpublished journal, on file with the Library of Congress Rare Books Division, Washington, D.C.

Chipman, Nathaniel. *Reports and Dissertations, in Two Parts*. Rutland: Anthony Haswell, 1793.

Coke, Edward. *The Third Part of the Institutes of the Laws of England*. London: M. Flesher, 1644.

Collectanea: Third Series. Montagu Burrows, ed. Oxford: Oxford Historical Society, 1896.

A Collection of All Such Acts of the General Assembly of Virginia, of Public and Permanent Nature, as Are Now in Force. Richmond, VA: A. Davis, 1794.

The Congressional Globe. 46 vols. Washington, D.C.: Blair and Rives, 1834–1873.

Cowell, John. *The Institutes of the Lawes of England Digested Into the Method of the Civill or Imperiall Institutions.* London: Tho. Roycroft, 1651.

Crompton, Richard. *A Manuall.* London: James Flesher, 1660.

Dallas, Alexander James. *Reports of Cases Ruled and Adjudged in the Courts of Pennsylvania, Before and Since the Revolution,* 4 vols. Philadelphia: T. Bradford, 1790.

Dalton, Michael. *The Countrey Justice, Containing the Practices of the Justices of the Peace Out of Their Sessions.* London: n.p., 1618.

Dalton, Michael. *The Countrey Justice, Containing the Practice of the Justices of the Peace Out of Their Sessions.* 5th ed. London: John More, 1635.

Davis, James. *The Office and Authority of a Justice of the Peace.* Newbern, NC: James Davis, 1774.

Debates and the Other Proceedings of the Convention of Virginia, Convened at Richmond, On Monday the 2d Day of June, 1788, for the Purpose of Deliberating on the Constitution Recommended By the Grand Federal Convention. Petersburg, VA: Hunter and Prentis, 1788).

The Debates in the Federal Convention of 1787 Which Framed the Constitution of the United States. New York: Oxford University Press, 1920.

The Debates in the Several State Conventions on the Adoption of the Federal Constitution, 5 vols., 2d ed. Jonathan Elliot, ed. Philadelphia: J.B. Lippincott, 1907.

Debates, Resolutions and Other Proceedings, of the Convention of the Commonwealth of Massachusetts, Convened at Boston, on the 9th of January, 1788, and continued until the 7th of February Following, for the Purpose of Assenting to and Ratifying the Constitution Recommended by the Grand Federal Convention. Boston: Adams and Nourse, 1788.

Debates Which Arose in the House of Representatives of South Carolina, on the Constitution Framed for the United States. Haswell, ed. Charleston, SC: City Gazette Print Office, 1788.

De Lolme, Jean Louis. *The Constitution of England; Or, An Account of the English Government.* David Lieberman, ed. Indianapolis, IN: Liberty Fund, 2007.

Digges, Thomas. *Englands Defence, A Treatise concerning Invasion, or A brief Discourse of what Orders were best for repulsing of Foreign Forces, if at any time they should invade us by Sea in Kent, or Elsewhere.* London: F. Haley, 1680.

Farrar, Timothy. *Manual of the Constitution of the United States of America.* Boston: Little, Brown, 1867.

Forbes, William. *The Duty and Powers of Justices of the Peace, in This Part of Great-Britain Called Scotland.* Edinburgh: Andrew Anderson, 1707.

Gardiner, Robert. *The Compleat Constable.* London: Richard and Edward Atkins, 1692.

Gardner, Daniel. *A Treatise on International Law, and a Short Explanation of the Jurisdiction and Duty of the Government of the Republic of the United States.* Troy, NY: N. Tuttle, 1844.

The Grants, Concessions, and Original Constitutions of the Province of New-Jersey. Aaron Learning et al., eds. Philadelphia: W. Bradford, 1758.

Grimke, John. *The Public Laws of the State of South Carolina, from its Establishment as a British Province Down to the Year 1790, Inclusive, in Which is Comprehended Such of the Statutes of Great Britain as Were Made of Force By the Act of Assembly of 1712.* Philadelphia: R. Aitken & Son, 1790.

Gross, John Daniel. *Natural Principles of Rectitude, for the Conduct of Main in All States and Situations in Life.* New York: T. and J. Swords, 1795.

Hale, Matthew. *The History and Analysis of the Common Law of England.* London: J. Nutt, Stafford, 1713.

Hamilton, Alexander. *The Papers of Alexander Hamilton,* 27 vols. Harold C. Syrett, ed. New York: Columbia University Press, 1961–87.

Hammond, Elisha. *A Practical Treatise, or An Abridgement of the Law Appertaining to the Office of Justice of the Peace.* West Brookfield: C.A. Mirick, 1841.

Hawkins, William. *Pleas of the Crown,* 2 vols. London: Eliz. Nutt, 1716.

Haywood, John. *The Duty and Office of Justices of the Peace, and of the Sheriffs, Coroners, Constables, &c.* Halifax, NC: Abraham Hodge, 1800.

Hobbes, Thomas. "A Dialogue Between a Phylosopher and a Student, of the Common-Laws of England," in *The Art of*

Rhetoric, With a Discourse of the Laws of England. London: William Crooke, 1681.

Hutcheson, Francis. *An Inquiry Into the Original of Our Ideas of Beauty and Virtue.* London: J. Darby, 1726.

Iredell, James. *Answers to Mr. Mason's Objections to the New Constitution Recommended by the Late Convention at Philadelphia.* Newbern, NC: Hodge and Wills, 1788.

Iredell, James. *Middle Circuit, 1793, Virginia* (1793). Washington, D.C.: Library of Congress Rare Books Division.

Jay, John. *John Jay Papers Digital Collection,* Columbia University Library.

Jefferson, Thomas. *The Writings of Thomas Jefferson,* 10 vols. New York: Putnam's, 1892–99.

The Journal of the Proceedings of the Provincial Congress of North Carolina, Held at Halifax the 12th Day of November, 1776. Newbern, NC: James Davis, 1776.

Kames, Henry Home. *Elucidations Respecting the Common and Statute Law of Scotland.* Edinburgh: Adam Neill, 1777.

Kames, Henry Home. *Essays and Observations: Physical and Literary,* 2 vols. Edinburgh: G. Hamilton and J. Balfour, 1754.

Kames, Henry Home. *Historical Law-Tracts,* 2 vols. Edinburgh: Bell & Bradfute, 1758.

Kames, Henry Home. *Select Decisions of the Court of Sessions, from the Year 1752 to the Year 1768.* 2d ed. Edinburgh: Bell & Bradfute, 1799.

Keble, Joseph. *An Assistance to the Justices of the Peace for the Easier Performance of their Duty.* 2d ed. London: W. Rawlins, S. Roycroft and H. Sawbridge, 1689.

Kent, James. *Commentaries on American Law,* 4 vols. 8th ed. New York: William Kent, 1854.

Kent, James. *Commentaries on American Law,* 4 vols. Oliver Wendell Holmes, ed. Boston: Little, Brown, 1873.

Kirby, Ephraim. *Reports of Cases Adjudged in the Superior Court of the State of Connecticut.* Litchfield, CT: Collier & Adam, 1789.

Lambarde, William. *The Duties of Constables, Borsholders, Tythingmen, and such other low and Lay Ministers of the Peace.* London: Thomas Wight, 1602.

Lambarde, William. *Eirenarcha: Or the Office of the Justices of the Peace, in Two Bookes.* London: Ra. Newbery, H. Bynneman, 1582.

Layer, John. *The Office and Dutie of Constables, Churchwardens, and other the Overseers of the Poore.* Cambridge: Robert Daniel, 1641.

Lloyd, Thomas. *Debates of the Convention, of the State of Pennsylvania, on the Constitution proposed for the Government of the United States.* Philadelphia: Joseph James, 1787.

Luttrell, Narcissus. *A Brief Historical Relation of State Affairs from September 1678 to April 1714,* 6 vols. Oxford: Oxford University Press, 1857.

Mackintosh, James. *A Discourse on the Study of the Law of Nature and Nations,* 2d ed. London: T. Cadell, Jun. and W. Davies, 1799.

Madison, James. *Letters and Other Writings of James Madison,* 4 vols. Philadelphia: J.B. Lippincott, 1865.

Madison, James. *Selected Writings of James Madison.* Indianapolis, IN: Hackett, 2006.

Marshall, John. *The Papers of John Marshall,* 12 vols. Chapel Hill: University of North Carolina Press, 1974–2006.

Martens, G.F. *Summary of the Law of Nations, Founded on Treaties and Customs of the Modern Nations of Europe.* William Cobbett, ed. Philadelphia: T. Bradford, 1795.

Martin, Francois-Xavier. *A Collection of Statute of the Parliament of England in Force in the State of North Carolina.* Newbern, NC: Editor's Press, 1792.

McRee, Griffith J. *Life and Correspondence of James Iredell: One of the Associate Justices of the Supreme Court.* New York: D. Appleton, 1858.

Meriton, George. *A Guide for Constables, Churchwardens, Overseers of the Poor, Surveyors of the Highways, Treasurers of the County Stock, Masters of the House of Correction, Bayliffs of Mannours, Tolltakers in Fairs, & c.* London: A. Crook, 1669.

Morrice, Roger. *The Entering Book of Roger Morrice 1677–1691: The Reign of James II, 1685–1687,* 5 vols. Woodbridge: Boydell Press, 2007.

Morse, Alexander Porter. *A Treatise on Citizenship, by Birth and Naturalization, With References to the Law of Nations, Roman Civil Law, Law of the United States of America, and the Law of France.* Boston: Little, Brown, 1881.

Palmer, Edward C. *The General Statutes of Minnesota.* St. Paul, MN: Davidson and Hall, 1867.

Pamphlets of the American Revolution, 1750–1776. Bernard Bailyn, ed. Cambridge, MA:

Belknap Press of Harvard University Press, 1965.

Papers Relating to the Foreign Relations of the United States, 62 vols. Washington, D.C.: United States Government Printing Office, 1870–1946.

The Perpetual Laws of the Commonwealth of Massachusetts, from the Establishment of its Constitution to the Second Session of the General Court, in 1798, 2 vols. Boston: Adams and Nourse, 1799.

Proceedings and Debates of the Convention of North Carolina, Convened at Hillsborough, On Monday the 21st Day of July, 1788, for the Purpose of Deliberating and Determining on the Constitution Recommended By the General Convention at Philadelphia, the 17th Day of September, 1787. Edenton, NC: Hodge and Wills, 1789.

Purdon, John. *A Digest of the Laws of Pennsylvania, from the Year One Thousand Seven Hundred to the Twenty-First Day of May, One Thousand Eight Hundred and Sixty-One*. 9th ed. Philadelphia: Kay & Brother, 1862.

Quincy, Josiah. *Portrait of a Patriot: The Major Political and Legal Papers of Josiah Quincy Junior: The Law Commonplace Book*, 3 vols. Daniel R. Coquillette and Neil Longley York, eds. Boston: Colonial Society of Massachusetts, 2007–2008.

Rawle, William. *A View of the Constitution of the United States of America*. 2d ed. Philadelphia: Philip H. Nicklin, 1829.

The Revised Code of the District of Columbia. Washington, D.C.: A.O.P. Nicholson, 1857.

Revised Statutes of the State of Delaware, to the year of Our Lord One Thousand Eight Hundred and Fifty-Two. Chicago: W.B. Keen, 1852.

The Revised Statutes of the State of Maine Passed October 22, 1840. Augusta, ME: William R. Smith, 1841.

The Revised Statutes of the State of Wisconsin, Passed at the Annual Session of the Legislature Commencing January 13, 1858, and Approved May 17, 1858. Chicago: W.B. Keen, 1858.

Russell, William Oldnall. *A Treatise on Crimes and Misdemeanors*. 5th ed. Philadelphia: T. and J.W. Johnson, 1877.

Rutherforth, Thomas. *Institutes of Natural Law: Being the Substance of a Course of Lectures on Grotius De Jure Belli et Pacis*. 3d ed. Philadelphia: William Young, 1799.

Sheppard, William. *The Offices and Duties of the Constables, Borsholders, Tythingmen, Treasurers of the County-Stock, Overseers for the Poore, and other Lay-Ministers*. Cambridge: Robert Daniel, 1641.

Spear, Samuel T. *The Law of the Federal Judiciary: A Treatise on the Provisions of the Constitution, the Laws of Congress, and the Judicial Decisions Relating to the Jurisdiction of, and Practice and Pleading in the Federal Courts*. New York: Baker, Voorhis, 1883.

The Statutes at Large: Being a Collection of All the Laws of Virginia from the First Session of the Legislature, in the Year 1619, 13 vols. William Waller Hening, ed. (1819–23). Charlottesville: University Press of Virginia.

The Statutes of Oregon Enacted and Continued in Force by the Legislative Assembly as the Session Commencing 5th December, 1853. Salem, OR: Asahel Bush, 1854.

Sullivan, John. *The Letters and Papers of Major General John Sullivan*, 3 vols. Otis Hammond, ed. Concord: New Hampshire Historical Society (1930–39).

Tucker, St. George. *View of the Constitution of the United States with Selected Writings*. Indianapolis, IN: Liberty Fund, 1999.

Van Dyke, Nicholas. *The Papers of Nicholas Van Dyke* Washington, D.C.: Library of Congress.

Vattel, Emer De. *The Law of Nations*. Knud Haakonssen ed. Indianapolis, IN: Liberty Fund, 2008.

Ward, Roberth. *An Inquiry into the Foundation and History of the Law of Nations in Europe, from the Time of the Greeks and Romans to the Age of Grotius*. London: Butterworth, 1796.

Washington, George. *The Diaries of George Washington*, 6 vols. Donald Jackson and Dorothy Twohig, eds. Charlottesville: University of Virginia Press, 1976–78.

Washington, George. *The Papers of George Washington: Retirement Series*, 4 vols. Dorothy Twohig, ed. Charlottesville: University of Virginia Press, 1998–99.

Webster, Noah. *A Collection of Essays and Fugitiv Writings: On Moral, Historical, Political and Literary Subjects*. Boston: I. Thomas and E.T. Andrews, 1790.

Wharton, Francis. *State Trials of the United States During the Administrations of Washington and Adams with References, Historical and Professional, and Preliminary Notes on the Politics of the Times*. Philadelphia: Carey and Hart, 1849.

Wharton, Francis. *A Treatise on the Criminal Law of the United States.* Philadelphia: James Kay, Jun., and Brother, 1846.

Wheaton, Henry, *Elements of International Law: With a Sketch of the History of the Science.* Philadelphia: Carey, Lea & Blanchard, 1836.

Wilson, James. *The Collected Works of James Wilson,* 2 vols. Kermit L. Hall and Mark David Hall, eds. Indianapolis, IN: Liberty Fund, 2007.

Charges to the Grand Jury

Addison, Alexander. *Analysis of the Report of the Committee of the Virginia Assembly.* Philadelphia: Zachariah Poulson, 1800.

Addison, Alexander. *Charges to the Grand Juries of the Counties of the Fifth Circuit in the State of Pennsylvania.* Washington, PA: J. Colerick, 1800.

Addison, Alexander. *Liberty of Speech and the Press: A Charge to the Grand Juries of the County Courts of the Fifth Circuit of the State of Pennsylvania.* Albany: Loring Andrews, 1798.

Addison, Alexander. *On the Alien Act: A Charge to the Juries of the Country Courts of the Fifth Circuit of the State of Pennsylvania.* Washington, PA: John Colerick, 1799.

Bay, Elihu Hall. "Charge to the Grand Jury Delivered to the Camden District, South Carolina," April 1791, reprinted in *The City Gazette or Daily Advertiser* (Charleston, SC), May 20, 1791.

Campbell, David. "Charge to the Grand Jury Delivered in the Ohio Territory," August 1791, reprinted in *The Freeman's Journal; Or, the North-American Intelligencer* (Philadelphia, PA), November 9, 1791.

Chase, Samuel. "Charge Delivered to the Grand Jury for the Case of the United States Against Thomas Cooper," undated, reprinted in *Newburyport Herald and Country Gazette* (Boston, MA), May 6, 1800.

Cushing, William. "Charge Delivered to the Federal Grand Jury for the District of Virginia," November 23, 1798, reprinted in *J. Russell's Gazette: Commercial and Political* (Boston, MA), December 27, 1798.

Cushing, William. "A Charge Delivered to the Federal Grand Jury for the District of Virginia, on the 23d November 1798: By the Honorable Judge Cushing, published

by request of the Grand Jury," reprinted in *The Eastern Herald and Gazette of Maine* (District of Maine, MA), January 21, 1799.

Ellsworth, Oliver. "Charge Delivered to the Grand Jury for the District Court of Chatham County," reprinted in *Columbian Museum and Savannah Advertiser* (Savannah, GA), May 14, 1799.

Grimke, John F. *Charge, Delivered to the Grand Juries of Beaufort and Orangeburgh Districts* (Charleston, SC), Benjamin F. Timothy, 1798.

Hall, Lot. "Charge to the Grand Jury Delivered to Windham County, South Carolina," August 1797, reprinted in *Federal Galaxy* (Brattleboro, VT), August 18, 1797.

Iredell, James. "Charge Delivered to the Grand Jury for the District Court of Massachusetts," October 12, 1792, reprinted in *Gazette of the United States* (Philadelphia, PA), November 3, 1792.

Iredell, James. "Charge Delivered to the Grand Jury for the Circuit Court of Pennsylvania," April 12, 1796, reprinted in *Federal Gazette and Baltimore Daily Advertiser* (Baltimore, MD), April 21, 1796.

Iredell, James. "Charge Delivered to the Grand Jury for the Circuit Court of Pennsylvania," April 12, 1796, reprinted in *Federal Gazette and Baltimore Daily Advertiser* (Baltimore, MD), April 22, 1796.

Iredell, James. "Charge Delivered to the Grand Jury for the District Court of Pennsylvania," April 11, 1797, reprinted in *American Mercury* (Hartford, CT), May 1, 1797.

Iredell, James. "Charge to the Grand Jury for the District of Pennsylvania Held in the City of Philadelphia, April 11, 1799," reprinted in *The Independent Chronicle; and the Universal Advertiser* (Boston, MA), May 27, 1799.

Iredell, James. "Charge Delivered to the Grand Jury for the District Court of Pennsylvania," Part II, April 11, 1799, reprinted in *The Independent Chronicle and the Universal Advertiser* (Boston, MA), May 30, 1799.

Iredell, James. "Charge Delivered to the Grand Jury for the District Court of Pennsylvania," Part III, April 11, 1799, reprinted in *The Independent Chronicle and the Universal Advertiser* (Boston, MA), June 3, 1799.

Iredell, James. "Charge Delivered to the Grand Jury for the District of South Carolina," May 12, 1794, reprinted in *Gazette of the United States and Daily Evening Advertiser* (Philadelphia, PA), June 12, 1794.

Jay, John. *The Charge of Chief Justice Jay to the Grand Juries of the Eastern Circuit* (Portsmouth, NH: George Jerry Osborne, Jr., 1790).

Jay, John. "Charge to the Grand Jury to the Middle Circuit in the District of Virginia, at the Capitol, in the City of Richmond, on the 22d Day of May, 1793," reprinted in *The City Gazette and Daily Advertiser* (Charleston, SC), August 14, 1793.

McKean, Thomas. "Charge Delivered to the Grand Jury for the City and County of Philadelphia," undated, reprinted in *The Columbian Herald* (Charleston, SC), May 9, 1785.

McKean, Thomas. "Charge Delivered to the Grand Jury for the Court of Oyer and Terminer," reprinted in *Porcupine's Gazette* (Philadelphia, PA), November 30, 1797.

Paterson, William. *The Charge of Judge Paterson to the Jury in the Case of Vanhorne's Lessee Against Dorrance.* Philadelphia: Samuel H. Smith, 1796.

Pendleton, Edmund. "Charge to the Grand Jury Delivered to Georgetown, Cheraws and Camden Districts," reprinted in *The Charleston Moring Post and Daily Advertiser* (Charleston, SC), December 13, 1786.

Peters, Richard. "Charge to the Grand Jury Delivered to the United States District of Pennsylvania," reprinted in *The Philadelphia Gazette and Universal Daily Advertiser* (Philadelphia, PA), August 23, 1794.

Preston, Samuel. *A Charge Delivered to the Grand Jury of Wayne County.* Easton, PA: Samuel Longcope, 1800.

Rush, Jacob. "Charge to the County of Berks," August 1794, reprinted in *The Philadelphia Gazette and University Daily Advertiser* (Philadelphia, PA), August 21, 1794.

Shippen, Edward. "Charge Delivered at the Trial of William Cobbet," undated, reprinted in *Norwich Packet* (Norwich, CT), January 2, 1800.

Shippen, Edward. "Charge to the Court of Oyer and Terminer," reprinted in *Dunlap and Claypoole's American Daily Advertiser* (Philadelphia, PA), August 26, 1794.

Smith, Israel. "Charge to the Grand Jury Delivered to County of Cumberland, New Jersey," reprinted in *Gazette of the United States, and Philadelphia Daily Advertiser* (Philadelphia, PA), June 22, 1798.

Sullivan, John. "Charge to the Grand Jury Delivered to Exeter, New Hampshire," July 16, 1790, reprinted in *The New Hampshire Gazetteer* (Exeter, NH), July 16, 1790.

Sumner, Israel. "Charge Delivered for Trial for a Libel," undated, reprinted in *Concord Herald* (Concord, NH), April 6, 1791.

Thacher, Peter Oxenbridge. *Two Charges to the Grand Jury of the County of Suffolk for the Commonwealth of Massachusetts, at the Opening Terms of the Municipal Court of the City of Boston, on Monday, December 5th, AD 1836.* Boston: Dutton and Wentworth, 1837.

Widcocks, Alexander. "Charge to the Grand Jury for the City of Philadelphia," September 17, 1794, reprinted in *The Oracle of the Day* (Portsmouth, NH), October 7, 1794.

Wilson, James. "Charge to the Grand Jury of the Circuit Court of Pennsylvania," July 22, 1793, reprinted in *The North-Carolina Journal* (Halifax, NC), August 21, 1793.

Books

Amar, Akhil. *America's Constitution: A Biography.* New York: Random House, 2005.

Armitage, David, ed. *British Political Thought in History, Literature and Theory, 1500–1800.* Cambridge: Cambridge University Press, 2006.

Armory, Thomas C. *The Military Services of Major-General John Sullivan.* Boston: Wiggin and Lunt, 1868.

Bailyn, Bernard. *Education in the Forming of American Society.* New York: W.W. Norton, 1972.

Bailyn, Bernard. *The Ideological Origins of the American Revolution: Enlarged Edition.* Cambridge, MA: Harvard University Press, 1992.

Balkin, Jack M. *Living Originalism.* Cambridge, MA: Harvard University Press, 2011.

Barnett, Randy E. *Restoring the Lost Constitution: The Presumption of Liberty.* Princeton, NJ: Princeton University Press, 2004.

Barnett, Randy. *The Structure of Liberty: Justice and the Rule of Law.* New York: Oxford University Press, 1998.

Bellesiles, Michael A. *Arming America: The Origins of a National Gun Culture.* New York: Alfred A. Knopf, 2000.

Bennett, Robert W. and Lawrence Solum, *Constitutional Originalism: A Debate.* Ithaca, NY: Cornell University Press, 2011.

Berger, Raoul. *Government by Judiciary: The*

Transformation of the Fourteenth Amendment. Cambridge, MA: Harvard University Press, 1977.

Bogus, Carl T., ed. *The Second Amendment in Law and History: Historians and Constitutional Scholars on the Right to Bear Arms.* New York: New Press, 2000.

Bork, Robert H. *The Tempting of America: The Political Seduction of the Law.* New York: Free Press, 1997.

Breyer, Stephen. *Making Our Democracy Work: A Judge's View.* New York: Alfred A. Knopf, 2010.

Brown, Richard Maxwell. *No Duty to Retreat: Violence and Values in American History and Society.* New York: Oxford University Press, 1991.

Butterfield, Herbert. *The Whig Interpretation of History.* London: G. Bell and Sons, 1931.

Chafee, Zechariah, Jr. *Free Speech in the United States.* Cambridge, MA: Harvard University Press, 1941.

Charles, Patrick J. *Irreconcilable Grievances: The Events That Shaped the Declaration of Independence.* Bowie, MD: Heritage, 2008.

Charles, Patrick J. *The Second Amendment: The Intent and Its Interpretation by the States and the Supreme Court.* Jefferson, NC: McFarland, 2009.

Clark, J.C.D. *The Language of Liberty 1660–1832: Political Discourse and Social Dynamics in the Anglo-American World.* Cambridge: Cambridge University Press, 1994.

Cornell, Saul. *A Well-Regulated Militia and the Origins of Gun Control in America.* New York: Oxford University Press, 2006.

Cramer, Clayton E. *Concealed Weapon Laws of the Early Republic: Dueling, Southern Violence, and Moral Reform.* Westport, CT: Praeger, 1999.

Curtis, Michael Kent. *No State Shall Abridge: The Fourteenth Amendment and the Bill of Rights.* Durham: Duke University Press, 1990.

Dabney, William M., and Marion Dargan. *William Henry Drayton and the American Revolution.* Albuquerque: University of New Mexico Press, 1962.

Darnton, Robert. *George Washington's False Teeth: An Unconventional Guide to the Eighteenth Century.* New York: W.W. Norton, 2003.

Epps, Garrett. *Wrong and Dangerous: Ten Right Wing Myths About Our Constitution.* Lanham, MD: Rowman and Littlefield, 2012.

Ferguson, Robert A. *The American Enlightenment, 1750–1820.* Cambridge, MA: Harvard University Press, 1997.

Ferguson, Robert A. *Law and Letters in American Culture.* Cambridge, MA: Harvard University Press, 1984.

Forbes, Duncan. *Hume's Philosophical Politics.* New York: Cambridge University Press, 1975.

Furstenberg, Francois. *In the Name of the Father: Washington's Legacy, Slavery, and the Making of a Nation.* New York: Penguin Press, 2006.

Goebel, Julius, Jr., and T. Raymond Naughton. *Law Enforcement in Colonial New York: A Study in Criminal Procedure (1664–1776).* Montclair, NJ: Patterson Smith, 1944.

Graber, Mark A. *Dred Scott and the Problem of Constitutional Evil.* Cambridge, NY: Cambridge University Press, 2006.

Greene, Jack P. *The Constitutional Origins of the American Revolution.* Cambridge, NY: Cambridge University Press, 2011.

Greene, Jack P. *Pursuits of Happiness: The Social Development of Early Modern British Colonies and the Formation of American Culture.* Chapel Hill: University of North Carolina Press, 1988.

Halbrook, Stephen P. *The Founders' Second Amendment: Origins of the Right to Bear Arms.* Chicago: Ivan R. Dee, 2008.

Halbrook, Stephen P. *Freedmen, the Fourteenth Amendment, and the Right to Bear Arms, 1866–1876.* Westport, CT: Praeger, 1998.

Halbrook, Stephen P. *That Every Man Be Armed: The Evolution of A Constitutional Right.* Albuquerque: University of New Mexico Press, 1984.

Haraszti, Zoltan. *John Adams and the Prophets of Progress.* Cambridge, MA: Harvard University Press, 1952.

Harding, Alan. *A Social History of English Law.* Gloucester, MA: Peter Smith, 1966.

Hill, Peter P. *French Perceptions of the Early Republic, 1783–1793.* Philadelphia: American Philosophical Society, 1988.

Holmes, Oliver Wendell. *The Common Law.* London: Macmillan, 1881.

Hont, Istvan, and Michael Ignatieff, eds. *Wealth and Virtue: The Shaping of Political Economy in the Scottish Enlightenment.* New York: Cambridge University Press, 1983.

Horwitz, Morton J. *The Transformation of*

American Law 1780–1860. Cambridge, MA: Harvard University Press, 1977.

Johnson, Nicholas J., David B. Kopel, George A. Mocsary, and Michael P. O'Shea. *Firearms Law and the Second Amendment: Rights, Regulation, and Policy*. New York: Wolters Kluwer Law and Business, 2012.

Kahn, Paul W. *Legitimacy and History: Self-Government in American Constitutional Theory*. New Haven, CT: Yale University Press, 1992.

Kalman, Laura. *The Strange Career of Legal Liberalism*. New Haven, CT: Yale University Press, 1996.

Kelly, Alfred H., and Winfred A. Harbison. *The American Constitution: An Account of the Development of the American Constitution and of American Constitutionalism from its Origins in England, Europe, and the Colonies to Our Time*. 5th ed. New York: W.W. Norton, 1976.

Kemp, Roger L. *Documents of American Democracy: A Collection of Essential Works*. Jefferson, NC: McFarland, 2010.

Krawczynski, Keith. *William Henry Drayton: South Carolina Revolutionary Patriot*. Baton Rouge: Louisiana State University Press, 2001.

Lang, Daniel G. *Foreign Policy in the Early Republic: The Law of Nations and the Balance of Power*. Baron Rouge: Louisiana State University Press, 1985.

Legomsky, Stephen. *Immigration and the Judiciary: Law and Politics in Britain and America*. New York: Oxford University Press, 1987.

Lengel, Edward G. *Inventing George Washington: America's Founder, in Myth and Memory*. New York: Harper, 2011.

Levy, Leonard W. *Emergence of a Free Press*. New York: Oxford University Press, 1985.

Levy, Leonard W. *Legacy of Suppression: Freedom of Speech and Press in Early American History*. Cambridge, MA: Harvard University Press, 1960.

Levy, Leonard W. *Original Intent and the Framers' Constitution*. New York: Macmillan, 1988.

Liggio, Leonard P., ed. *Literature of Liberty: A Review of Contemporary Legal Thought*. Menlo Park, CA: Cato Institute, 1978.

Malcolm, Joyce Lee. *To Keep and Bear Arms: The Origins of an Anglo-American Right*. Cambridge, MA: Harvard University Press, 1994.

McConnell, Michael W., Laurence H. Tribe, and Paul D. Gewirtz. *The Senate, the Courts, and the Constitution*. Washington, D.C.: Center for National Policy, 1986.

McKendrick, Nil, ed. *Historical Perspectives: Studies in English Thought and Society in Honor of J.H. Plumb*. London: Europa, 1974.

McMahon, Darrin M. *The Pursuit of Happiness: A History from the Greeks to the Present*. London: Allen Lane, 2006.

Nelson, William E. *Americanization of the Common Law: The Impact of Legal Change on Massachusetts Society, 1760–1830*. Athens: University of Georgia Press, 1975.

Neuman, Gerald L. *Strangers to the Constitution: Immigrants, Borders, and Fundamental Law*. Princeton, NJ: Princeton University Press, 1996.

Newmyer, R. Kent. *John Marshall and the Heroic Age of the Supreme Court*. Baton Rouge: Louisiana State University Press, 2001.

O'Neill, Jonathan. *Originalism in American Law and Politics: A Constitutional History*. Baltimore: Johns Hopkins University Press, 2005.

Parker, Kunal M. *Common Law, History, and Democracy in America, 1790–1900*. Cambridge, NY: Cambridge University Press, 2011.

Pocock, J.G.A. *The Ancient Constitution and the Feudal Law: A Study of English Historical Thought in the Seventeenth Century—A Reissue with a Retrospect*. Cambridge, NY: Cambridge University Press, 1987.

Pocock, J.G.A. *The Machiavellian Moment: Florentine Political Thought and the Atlantic Republican Tradition*. 2d ed. Princeton, NJ: Princeton University Press, 2003.

Pocock, J.G.A. *Political Thought and History: Essays on Theory and Method*. Cambridge, NY: Cambridge University Press, 2009.

Pocock, J.G.A. *Politics, Language and Time*. Chicago: University of Chicago Press, 1971.

Pocock, J.G.A. *Three British Revolutions: 1641, 1688, 1776*. Princeton, NJ: Princeton University Press, 1980.

Pocock, J.G.A. *Virtue, Commerce, and History: Essays on Political Thought and History, Chiefly in the Eighteenth Century*. Cambridge, NY: Cambridge University Press, 1985.

Pollock, Frederick, and Frederic William Maitland. *The History of English Law Before the Time of Edward I*, 2 vols. Cambridge, NY: Cambridge University Press, 1895.

Rakove, Jack. *Original Meanings: Politics and Ideas in the Making of the Constitution.* New York: Alfred A. Knopf, 1996.

Rakove, Jack N., ed. *Interpreting the Constitution.* Boston: Northeastern University Press, 1990.

Ramsey, Michael D. *The Constitution's Text in Foreign Affairs.* Cambridge, MA: Harvard University Press, 2007.

Raphael, Ray. *Constitutional Myths: What We Get Wrong and How to Get it Right.* New York: New Press, 2013.

Read, Conyers, ed. *The Constitution Reconsidered*, revised edition. New York: Harper and Row, 1968.

Scalia, Antonin. *A Matter of Interpretation: Federal Courts and the Law.* Princeton, NJ: Princeton University Press, 1997.

Scalia, Antonin, and Bryan A. Garner. *Reading Law: The Interpretation of Legal Texts* 89. St. Paul, MN: West, 2012.

Schuck, Peter H., and Rogers M. Smith. *Citizenship Without Consent: Illegal Aliens in the American Polity.* New Haven, CT: Yale University Press, 1985.

Schwoerer, Lois G. *No Standing Armies!: The Anti-Army Ideology in Seventeenth Century England.* Baltimore: Johns Hopkins University Press, 1974.

Sheppard, Steve, ed. *The History of Legal Education in the United States: Commentaries and Primary Sources.* Pasadena, CA: Salem Press, 1999.

Shingleton, Royce. *Richard Peters: Champion of the New South.* Macon, GA: Mercer University Press, 1985.

Skinner, Quentin. *The Foundations of Modern Political Thought*, 2 vols. Cambridge, NY: Cambridge University Press, 1978.

Spahn, Hannah. *Thomas Jefferson, Time, and History.* Charlottesville: University of Virginia Press, 2011.

Spitzer, Robert J. *Saving the Constitution from Lawyers: How Legal Training and Law Reviews Distort Constitutional Meaning.* Cambridge, NY: Cambridge University Press, 2008.

Trevelyan, George Macaulay. *Clio, A Muse: And Other Essays Literary and Pedestrian.* London: Longmans, Green, 1914.

Uviller, H. Richard, and William G. Merkel. *The Militia and the Right to Arms, or, How the Second Amendment Fell Silent.* Durham: Duke University Press, 2003.

Weinberger, Bernard Wolf. *An Introduction to the History of Dentistry*, 2 vols. Mosby, 1948.

Wilkinson, J. Harvie. *Cosmic Constitutional Theory: Why Americans are Losing Their Inalienable Right to Self-Governance.* New York: Oxford University Press, 2012.

Wiltse, Charles Maurice. *The Jeffersonian Tradition in American Democracy.* Chapel Hill: University of North Carolina Press, 1935.

Winch, Donald. *Adam Smith's Politics: An Essay in Historiographic Revision.* Cambridge, NY: Cambridge University Press, 1978.

Winkler, Adam. *Gun Fight: The Battle Over the Right to Bear Arms in America.* New York: W.W. Norton, 2011.

Wood, Gordon S. *The Creation of the American Republic 1776-1787.* 2d ed. Chapel Hill: University of North Carolina Press, 1998.

Wood, Gordon S. *Empire of Liberty: A History of the Early Republic, 1789-1815.* New York: Oxford University Press, 2009.

Wood, Gordon S. *The Purpose of the Past: Reflections on the Use of History.* New York: Penguin Press, 2008.

Articles

Abramowicz, Michael, and Maxwell Stearns. "Defining Dicta," 57 *Stanford Law Review* 953 (2005).

Amar, Vikram David. "From Watergate to Ken Starr: Potter Stewart's "Or of the Press' A Quarter Century Later," 50 *Hastings Law Journal* 711 (1999).

Anderson, David A. "The Origins of the Press Clause," 30 *UCLA Law Review* 455 (1983).

Anonymous. "Definition and History of the Law of Nations," 28 *American Jurist and Legal Magazine* 1 (1842).

Anonymous. "Definition and History of the Law of Nations," 28 *American Jurist and Legal Magazine* 249 (1843).

Appleby, Joyce. "One Good Turn Deserves Another: Moving Beyond the Linguistic; A Response to David Harlan," 94 *The American Historical Review* 1326 (1989).

Armitage, David. "The Declaration of Independence and International Law," 59 *The William and Mary Quarterly* 39 (2002).

Aynes, Richard L. "The Continuing Importance of Congressman John A. Bingham and the Fourteenth Amendment," 36 *Akron Law Review* 589 (2003).

Aynes, Richard L. "Enforcing the Bill of Right Against the States: The History and the Future," 19 *Journal of Contemporary Legal Issues* 77 (2009).

Aynes, Richard L. "Ink Blot or Not: The Meaning of Privileges and/or Immunities," 11 *University of Pennsylvania Journal of Constitutional Law* 1295 (2009).

Aynes, Richard L. "*McDonald v. City of Chicago*, Self-Defense, the Right to Bear Arms, and the Future," 2 *Akron Journal of Constitutional Law and Policy* 181 (2011).

Aynes, Richard L. "On Misreading John Bingham and the Fourteenth Amendment," 103 *Yale Law Journal* 57 (1993).

Balkin, Jack M. "Framework Originalism and the Living Constitution," 103 *Northwestern Law Review* 549 (2009).

Balkin, Jack M. "Original Meaning and Constitutional Redemption," 24 *Constitutional Commentary* 427 (2007).

Barnett, Randy E. "Necessary and Proper," 44 *UCLA Law Review* 745 (1997).

Barnett, Randy E. "The Original Meaning of the Commerce Clause," 68 *University of Chicago Law Review* 100 (2001).

Barnett, Randy E. "The People or the State? *Chisholm v. Georgia* and Popular Sovereignty," 93 *Virginia Law Review* 1729 (2007).

Barnett, Randy E. "Was the Right to Keep and Bear Arms Conditioned on Service in an Organized Militia?" 83 *Texas Law Review* 237 (2004).

Beard, Charles A. "The Act of Constitutional Interpretation," 1 *National Law Guild Quarterly* 9 (1937).

Bellia, Anthony J., Jr., and Bradford R. Clark. "The Federal Common Law of Nations," 109 *Columbia Law Review* 1 (2009).

Berger, Raoul. "Mark Tushnet's Critique of Interpretivism," 51 *George Washington Law Review* 532 (1983).

Berger, Raoul. "Original Intent and Boris Bittker," 66 *Indiana Law Journal* 723 (1991).

Blocher, Joseph. "Categoricalism and Balancing in First and Second Amendment Analysis," 84 *New York University Law Review* 375 (2009).

Brest, Paul. "The Misconceived Quest for the Original Understanding," 60 *Boston University Law Review* 204 (1980).

Bogus, Carl T. "The History and Politics of Second Amendment Scholarship: A Primer," 76 *Chicago-Kent Law Review* 3 (2000).

Brophy, Alfred L. "Introducing Applied Legal History," 31 *Law and History Review* 233 (2013).

Calabresi, Steven G., and Livia Fine. "Two Cheers for Professor Balkin's Originalism," 103 *Northwestern University Law Review* 663 (2009).

Caplan, David I. "Restoring the Balance: The Second Amendment Revisited," 5 *Fordham Urban Law Journal* 31 (1976).

Chafee, Zechariah, Jr. "Freedom of Speech in War Time," 32 *Harvard Law Review* 932 (1919).

Charles, Patrick J. "The 1792 National Militia Act, the Second Amendment, and Individual Militia Rights: A Legal and Historical Perspective," 9 *Georgetown Journal of Law and Public Policy* 323 (2011).

Charles, Patrick J. "'Arms for Their Defence?' An Historical, Legal, and Textual Analysis of the English Right to Have Arms and Whether the Second Amendment Should Be Incorporated in *McDonald v. City of Chicago*," 57 *Cleveland State Law Review* 351 (2009).

Charles, Patrick J. "The Constitutional Significance of a 'Well-Regulated' Militia Asserted and Proven with Commentary on the Future of Second Amendment Jurisprudence," 3 *Northeastern Law Journal* 1 (2011).

Charles, Patrick J. "Decoding the Fourteenth Amendment's Citizenship Clause: Unlawful Immigrants, Allegiance, Personal Subjection, and the Law," 51 *Washburn Law Journal* 211 (2012).

Charles, Patrick J. "Originalism, John Marshall, and the Necessary and Proper Clause: Resurrecting the Jurisprudence of Alexander Addison," 58 *Cleveland State Law Review* 529 (2010).

Charles, Patrick J. "The Plenary Power Doctrine and the Constitutionality of Ideological Exclusion: An Historical Perspective," 15 *Texas Review of Law and Politics* 61 (2010).

Charles, Patrick J. "Recentering Foreign Affairs Preemption in *Arizona v. United States*: Federal Plenary Power, the Spheres of Government, and the Constitutionality of S.B. 1070," 60 *Cleveland State Law Review* 133 (2012).

Charles, Patrick J. "Restoring 'Life, Liberty, and the Pursuit of Happiness' in Our Constitutional Jurisprudence," 20 *William and Mary Bill of Rights Journal* 457 (2011).

Charles, Patrick J. "The Right of Self-Preservation and Resistance: A True Legal and Historical Understanding of the Anglo-American Right to Arms," 2010 *Cardozo Law Review de novo* 18 (2010).

Charles, Patrick J. "Scribble Scrabble, the Second Amendment, and Historical Guideposts: A Short Reply to Lawrence Rosenthal and Joyce Lee Malcolm," 105 *Northwestern Law Review* 1821 (2011).

Charles, Patrick J. "The Second Amendment in Historiographical Crisis: Why the Supreme Court Must Reexamine the Embarrassing 'Standard Model' Moving Forward," 39 *Fordham Urban Law Journal* 1727 (2012).

Charles, Patrick J. "The Second Amendment Standard of Review After *McDonald*: 'Historical Guideposts' and the Missing Arguments in *McDonald v. City of Chicago*," 2 *Akron Journal of Constitutional Law and Policy* 7 (2011).

Charles, Patrick J., and Kevin Francis O'Neill. "Saving the Press Clause From Ruin: The Customary Origins of a 'Free Press' as Interface to the Present and Future," 2012 *Utah Law Review* 1691 (2012).

Churchill, Robert H. "Gun Regulation, the Police Power, and the Right to Keep and Bear Arms in Early America: The Legal Context of the Second Amendment," 25 *Law and History Review* 139 (2007).

Cleveland, Sarah H. "Powers Inherent in Sovereignty: Indians, Aliens, Territories, and the Nineteenth Century Origins of Plenary Power Over Foreign Affairs," 81 *Texas Law Review* 1 (2002).

Colby, Thomas B. "Originalism and the Ratification of the Fourteenth Amendment," 107 *Northwestern Law Review* (forthcoming 2013).

Colby, Thomas B. "The Sacrifice of the New Originalism," 99 *Georgetown Law Journal* 713 (2011).

Coleman, John M. "Thomas McKean and the Origin of an Independent Judiciary," 34 *Pennsylvania History* 111 (April 1967).

Commager, Henry Steele. "The American Enlightenment and the Ancient World: A Study in Paradox," 83 *Proceedings of the Massachusetts Historical Society* 3 (1971).

Cornell, Saul. "*Heller*, New Originalism, and Law Office History: 'Meet the New Boss, Same as the Old Boss,'" 56 *UCLA Law Review* 1095 (2009).

Cornell, Saul. "The Original Meaning of Original Understanding: A Neo-Blackstonian Critique," 67 *Maryland Law Review* 150 (2007).

Cornell, Saul. "Originalism on Trial: The Use and Abuse of History in *District of Columbia v. Heller*," 69 *Ohio State Law Journal* 625 (2008).

Cornell, Saul. "The People's Constitution vs. The Lawyer's Constitution: Popular Constitutionalism and the Original Debate Over Originalism," 23 *Yale Journal of Law and Humanities* 295 (2011).

Cornell, Saul. "The Right to Carry Firearms Outside the Home: Separating Historical Myths From Historical Realities," 39 *Fordham Urban Law Journal* 1695 (2012).

Cornell, Saul, and Nathan DeDino. "A Well Regulated Right: The Early American Origins of Gun Control," 73 *Fordham Law Review* 487 (2004).

Cornell, Saul, and Justin Florence. "The Right to Bear Arms in the Era of the Fourteenth Amendment: Gun Rights or Gun Regulation?" 50 *Santa Clara Law Review* 1043 (2010).

Cottrol, Robert J., and Raymond T. Diamond. "The Second Amendment: Toward an Afro-Americanist Reconsideration," 80 *Georgetown Law Journal* 309 (1991).

Cramer, Clayton E., and David B. Kopel. "'Shall Issue': The New Wave of Concealed Carry Handgun Permits," 62 *Tennessee Law Review* 679 (1995).

Cramer, Clayton E., and Joseph Edward Olson. "What Did 'Bear Arms' Mean in the Second Amendment," 6 *Georgetown Journal of Law and Public Policy* 511 (2008).

Cramer, Clayton E., Nicholas J. Johnson, and George A. Mocsary. "'This Right is Not Allowed By Governments that are Afraid of the People': The Public Meaning of the Second Amendment When the Fourteenth Amendment Was Ratified," 17 *George Mason Law Review* 852 (2010).

Cross, Frank B. "Originalism: The Forgotten Years," 28 *Constitutional Commentary* 37 (2012).

Curtis, Michael Kent. "The 1859 Crisis Over Hinton Helper's Book, The Impending Crisis: Free Speech, Slavery, and Some Light on the Meaning of the First Section of the Fourteenth Amendment," 68 *Chicago-Kent Law Review* 1113 (1993).

Curtis, Michael Kent. "The Bill of Rights and the States: An Overview from One Perspective," 18 *Journal of Contemporary Legal Issues* 3 (2009).

Custer, Lawrence B. "Bushrod Washington and John Marshall: A Preliminary Inquiry," 4 *The American Journal of Legal History* 34 (1960).

Davenport, T.W. "The Late George H. Williams," 11 *The Quarterly of the Oregon Historical Society* 279 (1910).

Davis, Brandon E. "America's Immigration Crisis: Examining the Necessity of Comprehensive Immigration Reform," 54 *Loyola Law Review* 353 (2008).

Dayton, Cornelia Hughes. "Taking the Trade: Abortion and Gender Relations in an Eighteenth-Century New England Village," 48 *The William and Mary Quarterly* 19 (1991).

Denning, Brannon P., and Glenn H. Reynolds. "*Heller,* High Water (Mark)? Lower Courts and the New Right to Keep and Bear Arms," 60 *Hastings Law Journal* 1245 (2009).

Dickinson, Edwin D. "The Law of Nations as Part of the National Law of the United States," 101 *Pennsylvania Law Review* 26 (1952).

Dorf, Michael C. "Dicta and Article III," 142 *University of Pennsylvania Law Review* 1997 (1994).

Dorf, Michael C. "Does *Heller* Protect a Right to Carry Guns Outside the Home?" 59 *Syracuse Law Review* 225 (2008).

Dorf, Michael C. "Integrating Normative and Descriptive Constitutional Theory: The Case of Original Meaning," 85 *Georgetown Law Journal* 1765 (1997).

Dorf, Michael C. "The Undead Constitution," 125 *Harvard Law Review* 2011 (2012).

Durchslag, Melvyn R. "The Supreme Court and the *Federalist Papers*: Is There Less Here than Meets the Eye?" 14 *William and Mary Bill of Rights Journal* 243 (2005).

Easterbrook, Frank H. "Textualism and the Dead Hand," 66 *George Washington Law Review* 1119 (1998).

Eastman, John C. "From *Plyler* to *Arizona*: Have the Courts Forgotten about *Corfield v. Coryell*?" 80 *University of Chicago Law Review* 165 (2013).

Eastman, John C. "Politics and the Court: Did the Supreme Court Really Move Left Because of Embarrassment Over *Bush v. Gore*?" 94 *Georgetown Law Journal* 1475 (2006).

Eastman, John C., and Ediberto Roman. "Debate on Birthright Citizenship," 6 *Florida International University Law Review* 293 (2011).

Ely, John Hart. "Constitutional Interpretivism: Its Allure and Impossibility," 53 *Indiana Law Journal* 399 (1977).

Epps, Garrett. "Any Which Way but Loose: Interpretive Strategies and Attitudes Toward Violence in the Evolution of the Anglo-American 'Retreat Rule,'" 55 *Law and Contemporary Problems* 303 (1992).

Epps, Garrett. "The Citizenship Clause: A 'Legislative History,'" 60 *American University Law Review* 331 (2010).

Eskridge, William N., Jr. "Destabilizing Due Process and Evolutive Equal Protection," 47 *UCLA Law Review* 1183 (2000).

Eskridge, William N., Jr. "Should the Supreme Court Read *The Federalist* but Not Statutory Legislative History?" 66 *George Washington Law Review* 1301 (1998).

Ewald, William. "James Wilson and the Scottish Enlightenment," 12 *University of Pennsylvania Journal of Constitutional Law* 1053 (2010).

Fagerstrom, Dalphy I. "Scottish Opinion and the American Revolution," 11 *The William and Mary Quarterly* 252 (1954).

Farber, Daniel A. "A Fatal Loss of Balance: *Dred Scott* Revisited," 39 *Pepperdine Law Review* 13 (2011).

Farber, Daniel A. "The Supreme Court, the Law of Nations, and Citations of Foreign Law: The Lessons of History," 95 *California Law Review* 1335 (2007).

Festa, Matthew J. "Applying a Usable Past: The Use of History in Law," 38 *Seton Hall Law Review* 479 (2008).

Festa, Matthew J. "Dueling Federalists: Supreme Court Decisions with Multiple Opinions Citing *The Federalist*," 31 *Seattle Law Review* 75 (2007).

Finkelman, Paul. "The Constitution and the Intentions of the Framers: The Limits of Historical Analysis," 50 *University of Pittsburgh Law Review* 349 (1989).

Finkelman, Paul. "The *Dred Scott* Case: Slavery and the Politics of Law," 20 *Hamline Law Review* 1 (1996).

Finkelman, Paul. "Foreign Law and American Constitutional Interpretation: A Long and Venerable Tradition," 63 *New York University Annual Survey of American Law* 29 (2007).

Finkelman, Paul. "It Really Was About a Well-Regulated Militia," 59 *Syracuse Law Review* 267 (2008).

Flaherty, Martin S. "History 'Lite' in Modern American Constitutionalism," 95 *Columbia Law Review* 523 (1995).

Fleischacker, Samuel. "Adam Smith's Reception Among the American Founders, 1776–1790," 59 *The William and Mary Quarterly* 897 (2002).

Fowler, Thomas L. "Holding, Dictum ... Whatever," 25 *North Carolina Central Law Journal* 139 (2003).

Freedman, Estelle B. "Historical Interpretation and Legal Advocacy: Rethinking the *Webster* Amicus Brief," 12 *The Public Historian* 27 (1990).

Freund, Paul A. "Appointment of Justices: Some Historical Perspectives," 101 *Harvard Law Review* 1146 (1988).

Friedman, Barry. "Discipline and Method: The Making of 'The Will of the People,'" 2010 *Michigan State Law Review* 877 (2010).

Friedman, Barry, and Scott B. Smith. "The Sedimentary Constitution," 147 *University of Pennsylvania Law Review* 1 (1998).

Ghoshray, Saby. "Rescuing the Citizenship Clause from Nativistic Distortion: A Reconstructionist Interpretation of the Fourteenth Amendment," 51 *Washburn Law Journal* 261 (2012).

Ginsburg, Ruth Bader. "Confirming Supreme Court Justices: Thoughts on the Second Opinion Rendered by the Senate," 1988 *Illinois Law Review* 101 (1988).

Goebel, Jr., Julius. "Constitutional History and Constitutional Law," 38 *Columbia Law Review* 555 (1938).

Goebel, Julius, Jr. "Ex Parte Clio," 54 *Columbia Law Review* 450 (1954).

Goebel, Julius, Jr. "Learning and Style in the Law: An Historian's Lament," 61 *Columbia Law Review* 1393 (1961).

Gordon, Robert W. "The Arrival of Critical Historicism," 49 *Stanford Law Review* 1023 (1997).

Gordon, Robert W. "Historicism in Legal Scholarship," 90 *Yale Law Journal* 1017 (1981).

Gordon, Robert W. "The Struggle Over the Past," 44 *Cleveland State Law Review* 123 (1996).

Grafton, Anthony. "The History of Ideas: Precept and Practice, 1950–2000 and Beyond," 67 *The History of Ideas* 1 (2006).

Graglia, Lino A. "Birthright Citizenship for Children of Illegal Aliens: An Irrational Public Policy," 14 *Texas Review of Law and Politics* 1 (2009).

Graham, Howard Jay. "Our 'Declaratory' Fourteenth Amendment," 7 *Stanford Law Review* 3 (1954).

Green, Christopher R. "The Original Sense of the (Equal) Protection Clause: Pre-Enactment History," 19 *George Mason University Civil Rights Law Journal* 1 (2008).

Greene, Jamal. "Fourteenth Amendment Originalism," 71 *Maryland Law Review* 978 (2012).

Greene, Jamal. "Guns, Originalism, and Cultural Cognition," 13 *University of Pennsylvania Journal of Constitutional Law* 511 (2010).

Greene, Jamal. "On the Origins of Originalism," 88 *Texas Law Review* 1 (2009).

Greene, Jamal. "Selling Originalism," 97 *Georgetown Law Journal* 647 (2009).

Greene, Jamal, Nathaniel Persily and Stephen Ansolabehere. "Profiling Originalism," 111 *Columbia Law Review* 356 (2011).

Hall, Mark David. "James Wilson's Law Lectures," 128 *The Pennsylvania Magazine of History and Biography* 65, 68 (2004).

Hamowy, Ronald. "Jefferson's Declaration of Independence," 36 *The William and Mary Quarterly* 503 (1979).

Hardy, David T. "*District of Columbia v. Heller* and *McDonald v. City of Chicago*: The Present as Interface of the Past and Future," 3 *Northeastern Law Journal* 199 (2011).

Hardy, David T. "Ducking the Bullet: *District of Columbia v. Heller* and the Stevens Dissent," 2010 *Cardozo Law Review de novo* 61 (2010).

Harrison, John. "Reconstructing the Privileges and Immunities Clause," 101 *Yale Law Journal* 1385 (1992).

Harrison, Maurice E. "The New Chief Justice," 29 *California Law Review* 677 (1941).

Hartry, Allison S. "Birthright Justice: The Attack on Birthright Citizenship and Immigrant Women of Color," 36 *New York University Journal of Legislation and Public Policy* 57 (2012).

Henkin, L. "The Constitution and United States Sovereignty: A Century of Chinese Exclusion and its Progeny," 100 *Harvard Law Review* 853 (1987).

Hernández-Truyol, Berta Esperanza. "Natives, Newcomers and Nativism: A Human

Rights Model for the Twenty-First Century," 23 *Fordham Urban Law Journal* 1075 (1996).

Hethmon, Michael M. "The Chimera and the Cop: Enforcement of Federal Immigration Law," 8 *University of the District of Columbia Law Review* 83 (2004).

Hicks, James E. "United States Military Shoulder Arms, 1795–1935," 1 *The Journal of the American Military History Foundation* 22 (1937).

Higginbothom, Don. "The Federalized Militia Debate: A Neglected Aspect of Second Amendment Scholarship," 55 *William and Mary Quarterly* 39 (1998).

Ho, James C. "Defining 'American': Birthright Citizenship and the Original Understanding of the 14th Amendment," 9 *The Green Bag* 367 (2006).

Hobson, Charles F. "The Negative on State Laws: James Madison, the Constitution, and the Crisis of Republican Government," 36 *The William and Mary Quarterly* 215 (1979).

Holmes, Oliver Wendell. "The Path of the Law," reprinted in 52 *Boston University Law Review* 212 (1972).

Horwitz, Morton J. "History and Theory," 96 *Yale Law Journal* 1825 (1987).

Horwitz, Paul. "The Past, Tense: The History of Crisis and the Crisis of History in Constitutional Theory," 61 *Albany Law Review* 459 (1997).

Howe, Daniel Walker. "Why the Scottish Enlightenment Was Useful to the Framers of the American Constitution," 31 *Comparative Studies in Society and History* 572 (1989).

Hume, Robert J. "Two Studies of the U.S. Supreme Court: The Use of Rhetorical Sources by the U.S. Supreme Court," 40 *Law and Society Review* 817 (2006).

Ide, Henry C. "Citizenship by Birth—Another View," 30 *The American Law Review* 241 (1896).

Ing, Matthew. "Birthright Citizenship, Illegal Aliens, and the Original Meaning of the Citizenship Clause," 45 *Akron Law Review* 719 (2012).

Jackson, Robert H. "Full Faith and Credit: The Lawyer's Clause of the Constitution," 45 *Columbia Law Review* 1 (1945).

Jenkins, David. "The Sedition Act of 1798 and the Incorporation of Seditious Libel into First Amendment Jurisprudence," 45 *The American Journal of Legal History* 154 (2001).

Johnson, Nicholas J. "Rights Versus Duties, History Department Lawyering, and the Incoherence of Justice Stevens *Heller* Dissent," 39 *Fordham Urban Law Journal* 1503 (2012).

Judd, John W. "The XIV Amendment—Its History and Evolution," 13 *The American Lawyer* 388 (1905).

Kalman, Laura. "Border Patrol: Reflections on the Turn to History in Legal Scholarship," 66 *Fordham Law Review* 87 (1997).

Kates, Don B. "Gun Control: Separating Reality from Symbolism," 20 *Journal of Contemporary Law* 353 (1994).

Kates, Don B. "Handgun Prohibition and the Original Meaning of the Second Amendment," 82 *Michigan Law Review* 204 (1983).

Kates, Don B. "A Modern Historiography of the Second Amendment," 56 *UCLA Law Review* 1211 (2009).

Kates, Don B. "The Second Amendment and the Ideology of Self-Protection," 9 *Constitutional Commentary* 87 (1992).

Kates, Don B. "The Value of Civilian Handgun Possession as a Deterrent to Crime or a Defense Against Crime," 18 *American Journal of Criminal Law* 113 (1991).

Kates, Don B. and Clayton E. Cramer, "Second Amendment Limitations and Criminological Considerations," 60 *Hastings Law Journal* 1339 (2009).

Kates, Don B., and Gary Mauser. "Would Banning Firearms Reduce Murder and Suicide: A Review of International and Some Domestic Evidence," 30 *Harvard Journal of Law and Public Policy* 649 (2007).

Kates, Don B., Henry E. Schaffer, John K. Lattimer, and George B. Murray. "Guns and Public Health: Epidemic of Violence or Pandemic of Propaganda," 62 *Tennessee Law Review* 513 (1995).

Kay, Richard S. "Adherence to the Original Intentions in Constitutional Adjudication: Three Objections and Responses," 82 *Northwestern University Law Review* 226 (1988).

Kelly, Alfred H. "Clio and the Court: An Illicit Love Affair," 1965 *Supreme Court Review* 119 (1965).

Kendall, Emily. "Amending the Constitution to Save a Sinking Ship? The Issues Surrounding the Proposed Amendment of the Citizenship Clause and 'Anchor Babies,'" 22 *Berkeley La Raza Law Journal* 349 (2012).

Kesavan, Vasan, and Michael Stokes Paulsen. "The Interpretive Force of the Constitution's Secret Drafting History," 68 *Georgetown Law Journal* 1113 (2003).

Kloppenberg, James T. "Thinking Historically: A Manifesto of Pragmatic Hermeneutics," 9 *Modern Intellectual History* 201 (2012).

Kobach, Kris W. "Attrition Through Enforcement: A Rational Approach to Illegal Immigration," 15 *Tulsa Journal of Comparative and International Law* 153 (2008).

Konig, David Thomas. "*Heller*, Guns, and History: The Judicial Invention of Tradition," 3 *Northeastern Law Journal* 175 (2011).

Konig, David Thomas. "Why the Second Amendment Has a Preamble: Original Public Meaning and the Political Culture of Written Constitutions in Revolutionary America," 56 *UCLA Law Review* 1295 (2009).

Kopel, David B. "How the British Gun Control Program Precipitated the American Revolution," 6 *Charleston Law Review* 283 (2012).

Kopel, David B. "It Isn't About Duck Hunting: The British Origins of the Right to Arms," 93 *Michigan Law Review* 1333 (1995).

Kopel, David B. "The Licensing of Concealed Handguns for Lawful Protection: Support from Five State Supreme Courts," 68 *Alabama Law Review* 305 (2005).

Kopel, David B., and Clayton E. Cramer. "Credentials are No Substitute for Accuracy: Nathan Kozuskanich, Stephen Halbrook, and the Role of the Historian," 19 *Widener Law Journal* 343 (2010).

Kopel, David B., and Clayton E. Cramer. "State Court Standards of Review for the Right to Keep and Bear Arms," 50 *Santa Clara Law Review* 1113 (2010).

Koppelman, Andrew. "Why Jack Balkin Is Disgusting," 27 *Constitutional Commentary* 177 (2010).

Kozuskanich, Nathan. "Originalism, History, and the Second Amendment: What Did Bearing Arms Really Mean to the Founders?" 10 *Pennsylvania Journal of Constitutional Law* 413 (2008).

Kozuskanich, Nathan. "Originalism in a Digital Age: An Inquiry into the Right to Bear Arms," 29 *Journal of the Early Republic* 585 (2009).

Kramer, Larry. "On Finding (and Losing) Our Origins," 26 *Harvard Journal of Law and Public Policy* 95 (2003).

Kramer, Larry. "Two (More) Problems with Originalism," 31 *Harvard Journal of Law and Public Policy* 907 (2008).

Kramer, Larry D. "When Lawyers Do History," 72 *George Washington Law Review* 387 (2003).

Kranz, Steven W. "A Survey of State Conceal and Carry Statutes: Can Small Changes Help Reduce the Controversy?" 29 *Hamline Law Review* 637 (2006).

LaCroix, Alison L. "Temporal Imperialism," 158 *University of Pennsylvania Law Review* 1329 (2010).

Larsen, Allison Orr. "Confronting Supreme Court Fact Finding," 98 *Virginia Law Review* 1255 (2012).

Lash, Kurt T., and Alicia Harrison. "Minority Report: John Marshall and the Defense of the Alien and Sedition Acts," 68 *Ohio State Law Journal* 435 (2007).

Law, Sylvia A. "Conversations Between Historians and the Constitution," 12 *The Public Historian* 11 (1990).

Lawson, Carlton F.W. "Four Exceptions in Search of a Theory: *District of Columbia v. Heller* and Judicial Ipse Dixit," 60 *Hastings Law Journal* 1371 (2009).

Lenner, Andrew. "Separate Spheres: Republican Constitutionalism in the Federalist Era," 41 *The American Journal of Legal History* 250 (1997).

Lenner, Andrew. "A Tale of Two Constitutions: Nationalism in the Federalist Era," 40 *The American Journal of Legal History* 72 (1996).

Leval, Pierre N. "Judging Under the Constitution: Dicta About Dicta," 81 *New York University Law Review* 1249 (2006).

Lewis, William Draper. "The Study of the Common Law," 46 *The American Law Register* 465 (1898).

Libby, O.G. "Review: An Economic Interpretation of the Constitution of the United States," 1 *The Mississippi Valley Historical Review* 113 (1914).

Lindsay, Matthew J. "Immigration as Invasion: Sovereignty, Security, and the Origins of the Federal Immigration Power," 45 *Harvard Civil Rights–Civil Liberties Law Review* 1 (2010).

Lindsay, Matthew J. "Immigration, Sovereignty, and the Constitution of Foreignness," 45 *Connecticut Law Review* 743 (2013).

Lister, Matthew J. "Citizenship, In the Immigration Context," 70 *Maryland Law Review* 175 (2010).

Lund, Nelson. "No Conservative Consensus Yet: Douglas Ginsburg, Brett Kavanaugh, and Diane Sykes on the Second Amendment," 13 *Engage* 30 (2012).

Lund, Nelson. "The Second Amendment, *Heller*, and Originalist Jurisprudence," 56 *UCLA Law Review* 1343 (2009).

Lupu, Ira C. "The Most-Cited *Federalist Papers*," 15 *Constitutional Commentary* 403 (1998).

Lupu, Ira C. "Time, the Supreme Court, and *The Federalist*, 66 *George Washington Law Review* 1324 (1998).

Lutz, Donald S. "The Relative Influence of European Writers on Late Eighteenth-Century American Political Thought," 78 *The American Political Science Review* 189 (1984).

Mackintosh, James. "A Discourse on the Study of the Law of Nature and Nations," 1 *Journal of Jurisprudence* 344 (1821).

Magliocca, Gerard N. "Indians as Invaders: The Citizenship Clause and Illegal Aliens," 10 *University of Pennsylvania Journal of Constitutional Law* 499 (2008).

Malcolm, Joyce Lee. "The Creation of a 'True Antient and Indubitable' Right: The English Bill of Rights and the Right to Be Armed," 32 *Journal of British History* 226 (1993).

Malcolm, Joyce Lee. *Disarmed: The Loss of the Right to Bear Arms in Restoration England* 7 (NRA Institute of Legislative Action 1981).

Malcolm, Joyce Lee. "Remarks at Seton Hall Second Amendment Symposium: Panelist," 10 *Seton Hall Constitutional Law Journal* 829 (2000).

Malcolm, Joyce Lee. "The Right of the People to Keep and Bear Arms: The Common Law Tradition," 10 *Hastings Constitutional Law Quarterly* 285 (1983).

Malcolm, Joyce Lee. "The Role of the Militia in the Development of the Englishman's Right to Be Armed—Clarifying the Legacy," 5 *Journal of Firearms and Public Policy* 139 (1993).

Malcolm, Joyce Lee. "The Supreme Court and the Uses of History: *District of Columbia v. Heller*," 56 *UCLA Law Review* 1377 (2009).

Marcus, Maeva. "The Effect (or Non-Effect) of Founders on the Supreme Court Bench," 80 *George Washington Law Review* 1794 (2012).

Marshall, Kevin C. "Why Can't Martha Stewart Have a Gun?" 32 *Harvard Journal of Law and Public Policy* 695 (2009).

Martin, Francisco Forrest. "Our Constitution as Federal Treaty: A New Theory of United States Constitutional Construction Based on an Originalist Understanding for Addressing a New World," 31 *Hastings Constitutional Law Quarterly* 269 (2004).

Mayton, William Ty. "Birthright Citizenship and the Civic Minimum," 22 *Georgetown Immigration Law Journal* 221 (2008).

McAfee, Thomas B. "The Constitution Based on the Consent of the Governed—Or, Should We Have an Unwritten Constitution," 80 *Oregon Law Review*, 1245 (2001).

McAllister, Marc. "Dicta Redefined," 47 *Williamette Law Review* 161 (2011).

McGinnis, John O. "Contemporary Foreign and International Law in Constitutional Construction," 69 *Albany Law Review* 801 (2006).

McGinnis, John O., and Michael Rappaport. "The Abstract Meaning Fallacy," 2012 *Illinois Law Review* 737 (2011).

McGinnis, John O., and Michael Rappaport. "Original Interpretive Principles as the Core of Originalism," 24 *Constitutional Commentary* 371 (2007).

McGinnis, John O., and Michael Rappaport. "Originalism and Supermajoritarianism: Defending the Nexus," 102 *Northwestern Law Review Colloquy* 18 (2007).

McGinnis, John O., and Michael Rappaport. "Original Methods Originalism: A New Theory of Interpretation and the Case Against Construction," 103 *Northwestern University Law Review* 751 (2009).

McGinnis, John O., and Michael Rappaport. "Reconciling Originalism and Precedent," 103 *Northwestern University Law Review* 803 (2009).

McGinnis, John O., and Ilya Somin. "Should International Law Be Part of Our Law?" 59 *Stanford Law Review* 1175 (2007).

McGovern, Owen. "The Responsible Gun Ownership Ordinance and Novel Textual Questions About the Second Amendment," 102 *The Journal of Criminal Law and Criminology* 471 (2012).

Melton, Buckner F., Jr. "Clio at the Bar: A Guide to Historical Method for Legalists and Jurists," 83 *Minnesota Law Review* 377 (1998).

Melton, Buckner F., Jr. "The Supreme Court

and *The Federalist*: A Citations List and Analysis, 1789–1996," 85 *Kentucky Law Journal* 243 (1996).

Mensel, Robert E. "Jurisdiction in Nineteenth Century International Law and its Meaning in the Citizenship Clause of the Fourteenth Amendment," 32 *Saint Louis University Public Law Review* 329 (2013).

Merkel, William G. "*District of Columbia v. Heller* and Antonin Scalia's Perverse Sense of Originalism," 13 *Lewis and Clark Law Review* 349 (2009).

Merkel, William G. "*Heller* as Hubris, and How *McDonald v. City of Chicago* May Well Change the Constitutional World as We Know It," 50 *Santa Clara Law Review* 1221 (2010).

Merkel, William G. "*Parker v. The District of Columbia* and the Hollowness of Originalist Claims to Principled Neutrality," 18 *George Mason University Civil Rights Law Journal* 251 (2008).

Merrill, Thomas W. "Originalism, Stare Decisis and the Promotion of Judicial Restraint," 22 *Constitutional Commentary* 271 (2005).

Meyler, Bernadette A. "The Gestation of Birthright Citizenship, 1868–1898: States' Rights, the Law of Nations and Mutual Consent," 15 *Georgetown Immigration Law Journal* 519 (2001).

Meyler, Bernadette A. "Towards a Common Law Originalism," 59 *Stanford Law Review* 551 (2006).

Miller, Darrell A.H. "Guns as Smut: Defending the Home-Bound Second Amendment," 109 *Columbia Law Review* 1278 (2009).

Miller, Darrell A.H. "Text, History, and Tradition: What the Seventh Amendment Can Teach us About the Second," 122 *Yale Law Journal* 852 (2013).

Mocsary, George. "Monopoly of Violence," *Claremont Review of Books* 46 (2010).

Motomura, Hiroshi. "Immigration Law after a Century of Plenary Power: Phantom Constitutional Norms and Statutory Interpretation," 100 *Yale Law Journal* 545 (1990).

Motomura, Hiroshi. "Immigration Outside the Law," 108 *Columbia Law Review* 2037 (2008).

Murphy, Paul. "Time to Reclaim: The Current Challenge of American Constitutional History," 69 *The American Historical Review* 64 (1963).

Neily III, Clark M. "The Right to Keep and Bear Arms in the States: Ambiguity, False Modesty, and (Maybe) Another Win for Originalism," 33 *Harvard Journal of Law and Public Policy* 185 (2010).

Nelson, Caleb. "Originalism and Interpretive Conventions," 70 *University of Chicago Law Review* 519 (2003).

Nelson, William E. "History and Neutrality in Constitutional Adjudication," 72 *Virginia Law Review* 1237 (1986).

Neuman, Gerald L. "International Law as a Resource in Constitutional Interpretation," 30 *Harvard Journal of Law and Public Policy* 177 (2006).

Neuman, Gerald L. "The Lost Century of American Immigration (1776–1875)," 93 *Columbia Law Review* 1833 (1993).

Neuman, Gerald L. "Whose Constitution?" 100 *Yale Law Journal* 909 (1991).

O'Shea, Michael P. "Modeling the Second Amendment Right to Carry Arms (I): Judicial Tradition and the Scope of 'Bearing Arms' for Self-Defense," 61 *American University Law Review* 585 (2012).

Parker, Kunal M. "Law 'In' and 'As' History: The Common Law in the American Polity, 1790–1900," 1 *UC Irvine Law Review* 587 (2011).

Paulsen, Michael Stokes. "Our Perfect, Perfect Constitution," 27 *Constitutional Commentary* 531 (2011).

Pfander, James E., and Daniel D. Birk. "Article III and the Scottish Judiciary," 124 *Harvard Law Review* 1613 (2011).

Pfander, James E., and Theresa R. Wardon. "Reclaiming the Immigration Constitution of the Early Republic: Prospectivity, Uniformity, and Transparency," 96 *Virginia Law Review* 359 (2010).

Pocock, J.G.A. "British History: A Plea for a New Subject," 47 *The Journal of Modern History* 601 (1975).

Pocock, J.G.A. "The Origins of Study of the Past: A Comparative Approach," 4 *Comparative Studies in Society and History* 209 (1962).

Pollock, Frederick. "The Continuity of the Common Law," 11 *Harvard Law Review* 423 (1899).

Pollock, Frederick. "The Expansion of the Common Law I: The Foundations of Justice," 3 *Columbia Law Review* 505 (1903).

Pollock, Frederick. "Expansion of the Common Law III: The Sword of Justice," 4 *Columbia Law Review* 96 (1904).

Pollock, Frederick. "The Expansion of the

Common Law IV: The Law of Reason," 4 *Columbia Law Review* 171 (1904).

Pollock, Frederick. "The Genius of the Common Law I: Our Lady and Her Knights," 12 *Columbia Law Review* 189 (1912).

Pollock, Frederick. "The Genius of the Common Law II: The Giants and the Gods," 12 *Columbia Law Review* 291 (1912).

Posner, Richard A. "Past Dependency, Pragmatism, and Critique of History in Adjudication and Legal Scholarship," 67 *University of Chicago Law Review* 573 (2000).

Post, Robert, and Reva Siegel. "Originalism as a Political Practice: The Right's Living Constitution," 75 *Fordham Law Review* 545 (2006).

Powell, H. Jefferson. "Grand Visions in an Age of Conflict," 115 *Yale Law Journal* 2067 (2006).

Powell, H. Jefferson. "The Original Understanding of Original Intent," 98 *Harvard Law Review* 885 (1988).

Powell, H. Jefferson. "Rules for Originalists," 73 *Virginia Law Review* 659 (1987).

Prest, Wilfrid. "William Lambarde, Elizabethan Law Reform, and Early Stuart Politics," 34 *Journal of British Studies* 464 (1995).

Putnam, Bertha Haven. "The Transformation of the Keepers of the Peace into the Justices of the Peace," 12 *Transactions of the Royal Historical Society* 19 (1929).

Rabban, David M. "The First Amendment in its Forgotten Years," 90 *Yale Law Journal* 514 (1981).

Rakove, Jack N. "Book Review: Randy E. Barnett, *Restoring the Lost Constitution: The Presumption of Liberty*," 1 *N.Y.U. Journal of Law and Liberty* 660 (2005).

Ramsey, Michael D. "*Missouri v. Holland* and Historical Textualism," 73 *Missouri Law Review* 969 (2008).

Redish, Martin H. "Interpretivism and the Judicial Role in a Constitutional Democracy," 19 *Harvard Journal of Law and Public Policy* 525 (1996).

Redish, Martin H., and Matthew B. Arnold. "Judicial Review, Constitutional Interpretation, and the Democratic Dilemma: Proposing a 'Controlled Activism Alternate,'" 64 *Florida Law Review* 1485 (2012).

Reed, Henry. "American Constitution in 1787 and 1866," 2 *The International Review* 604 (1875).

Rees III, Grover. "Questions for Supreme Court Nominees at Confirmation Hearings: Excluding the Constitution," 17 *Georgia Law Review* 913 (1983).

Reid, John Philip. "Law and History," 27 *Loyola Los Angeles Law Review* 193 (1993).

Reid, John Philip. "Legal History," 1966 *Annual Survey of American Law* 669 (1966).

Reid, John Philip. "The Touch of History—The Historical Method of a Common Law Judge," 27 *The American Journal of Legal History* 157 (1964).

Reynolds, Glenn Harlan. "A Critical Guide to the Second Amendment," 62 *Tennessee Law Review* 461 (1995).

Richards, Louis. "Honorable Jacob Rush, of the Pennsylvania Judiciary," 39 *The Pennsylvania Magazine of History and Biography* 53 (1915).

Richards, Neil M. "Clio and the Court: A Reassessment of the Supreme Court's Uses of History," 13 *Journal of Law and Politics* 809 (1997).

Richman, Irving Berdine. "Citizenship of the United States," 5 *Political Science Quarterly* 5 (1890).

Rodriguez, Cristina M. "The Citizenship Clause, Original Meaning, and the Egalitarian Unity of the Fourteenth Amendment," 11 *University of Pennsylvania Journal of Constitutional Law* 1363 (2009).

Rodriguez, Cristina M. "The Significance of the Local in Immigration Regulation," 106 *Michigan Law Review* 567 (2008).

Rogers III, C. Paul. "Scots Law in Post-Revolutionary and Nineteenth-Century America: The Neglected Jurisprudence," 8 *Law and History Review* 205 (1990).

Romero, Victor C. "Our Illegal Founders," 16 *Harvard Latino Law Review* 147 (2013).

Rosenbloom, Rachel E. "Policing the Borders of Birthright Citizenship: Some Thoughts on the New (and Old) Restrictionism," 51 *Washburn Law Journal* 311 (2012).

Rosenthal, Alfred. "The Marbois-Longchamps Affair," 63 *The Pennsylvania Magazine of History and Biography* 294 (July 1939).

Rosenthal, Lawrence. "First Amendment Investigations and the Inescapable Pragmatism of the Common Law of Free Speech," 86 *Indiana Law Journal* 1 (2011).

Rostron, Allen. "Cease Fire: A 'Win-Win' Strategy on Gun Policy for the Obama Administration," 3 *Harvard Law and Policy Review* 347 (2009).

Rowe, G.S. "Thomas McKean and the Coming of the Revolution," 96 *The Pennsylvania Magazine of History and Biography* 3 (1972).

Rowe, G.S. "A Valuable Acquisition in Congress: Thomas McKean, Delegate from Delaware to the Continental Congress, 1774–1783," 38 *Pennsylvania History* 225 (July 1971).

Rowe, G.S., and Alexander W. Knott. "Power, Justice, and Foreign Relations in the Confederation Period: The Marbois-Longchamps Affair, 1784–1786," 104 *The Pennsylvania Magazine of History and Biography* 275 (July 1980).

Ruebsamen, Megan. "The Gun-Shy Commonwealth: Self-Defense and Concealed Carry in Post-*Heller* Massachusetts," 18 *Suffolk Journal of Trial and Appellate Advocacy* 55 (2013).

Ruffin, Robert S. "The Constitution and the Dilemma of Historicism," 6 *San Diego Law Review* 171 (1969).

Sachs, Stephen E. "Constitutional Backdrops," 80 *George Washington Law Review* 1813 (2012).

Scalia, Antonin. "Originalism: The Lesser Evil," 57 *University of Cincinnati Law Review* 849 (1989).

Scalia, Antonin, and Stephen Breyer. "Relevance of Foreign Legal Materials in U.S. Constitutional Cases: A Conversation Between U.S. Supreme Court Justices," 3 *International Journal of Constitutional Law* 519 (2005).

Scalia, Antonin, and John F. Manning. "A Dialogue on Statutory and Constitutional Interpretation," 80 *George Washington Law Review* 1610 (2012).

Schuman, David. "The Creation of the Oregon Constitution," 74 *Oregon Law Review* 611(1995).

Schwoerer, Lois G. "Review: To Keep and Bear Arms: The Origins of an Anglo-American Right, 61 *Journal of Southern History* 570 (1995).

Scott, Harvey W. "An Estimate of the Character and Services of Judge George H. Williams," 11 *The Quarterly of the Oregon Historical Society* 223 (1910).

Scruggs, William L. "Ambiguous Citizenship," 1 *Political Science Quarterly* 3 (1886).

Scruggs, William L. "The American Abroad," 23 *The Central Law Journal* 196 (1886).

Scruggs, William L. "The Evolution of American Citizenship," 1 *Southern Law Review* 182 (1901).

Sears, Louis Martin. "Jefferson and the Law of Nations," 13 *American Political Science Review* 379 (1919).

Seigel, Neil S. "Jack Balkin's Rich Historicism and Diet Originalism: Health Benefits and Risks for the Constitutional System," 111 *Michigan Law Review* 931 (2013).

Shalhope, Robert E. "Book Review: The Militia and the Right to Arms, or, How the Second Amendment Fell Silent," 108 *The American Historical Review* 1442 (2003).

Shalhope, Robert E. "The Ideological Origins of the Second Amendment," 69 *Journal of American History* 599 (1982).

Shalhope, Robert E. "The Right to Bear Arms: A View From the Past," 13 *Reviews of American History* 347 (1985).

Shalhope, Robert E., and Lawrence Delbert Cress. "The Second Amendment and the Right to Bear Arms: An Exchange," 71 *Journal of American History* 587 (1984).

Shawhan, Mark. "'By Virtue of Being Born Here': Birthright Citizenship and the Civil Rights Act of 1866," 15 *Harvard Latino Review* 201 (2011).

Shawhan, Mark. "The Significance of Domicile in Lyman Trumbull's Conception of Citizenship," 119 *Yale Law Journal* 1352 (2010).

Siegal, Reva B. "Dead or Alive: Originalism as Popular Constitutionalism in *Heller*," 122 *Harvard Law Review* 191 (2008).

Skinner, Quentin. "Hermeneutics and the Role of History," 7 *New Literary History* 214 (1975).

Skinner, Quentin. "The Limits of Historical Explanations," 41 *Philosophy* 199 (1966).

Skinner, Quentin. "Meaning and Understanding the History of Ideas," 8 *History and Theory* 3 (1969).

Skinner, Quentin. "Motives, Intentions an Interpretation of Texts," 3 *New Literary History* 393 (1972).

Smith, Peter J. "Sources of Federalism: An Empirical Analysis of the Court's Quest for Original Meaning," 52 *UCLA Law Review* 217 (2004).

Smith, Tara. "Originalism's Misplaced Fidelity: 'Original' Meaning is Not Objective," 26 *Constitutional Commentary* 1 (2009).

Smith, Tara. "Why Originalism Won't Die— Common Mistakes in Competing Theories of Judicial Interpretation," 2 *Duke Journal of Constitutional Law and Public Policy* 159 (2007).

Snapp, J. Russell. "William Henry Drayton: The Making of a Conservative Revolutionary," 57 *The Journal of Southern History* 637 (1991).

Sobel, Stacey L. "The Tsunami of Legal Uncertainty: What's a Court to Do Post-*Mc-Donald*?" 21 *Cornell Journal of Law and Public Policy* 489 (2012).

Spear, Samuel T. "American Citizenship," 15 *Albany Law Journal* 484 (1877).

Spear, Samuel T. "National Protection," 24 *The Independent* 1231 (1872).

Spitzer, Robert J. "Historical Approach: Why History Matters: Saul Cornell's Second Amendment and the Consequences of Law Reviews," 1 *Albany Government Law Review* 312 (2008).

Stein, Dan, and John Bauer. "Automatic Citizenship for Children of Illegal Immigrants?" 7 *Stanford Law and Policy Review* 127 (1996).

Stewart, Potter. "Or of the Press," 26 *Hastings Law Journal* 631 (1975).

Stinson, J. Whitla. "The Common Law and the Law of Nations," 9 *California Law Review* 470 (1920).

Stone, Harlan F. "The Common Law in the United States," 50 *Harvard Law Review* 1 (1936).

Strauss, David A. "Can Originalism Be Saved?" 92 *Boston University Law Review* 1161 (2012).

Strauss, David A. "Common Law Constitutional Interpretation," 63 *University of Chicago Law Review* 877 (1996).

Strauss, David A. "Why Conservatives Shouldn't Be Originalists," 31 *Harvard Journal of Law and Public Policy* 969 (2008).

Sunstein, Cass. "Five Theses on Originalism," 19 *Harvard Journal of Law and Public Policy* 311 (1996).

Sunstein, Cass R. "The Idea of a Useable Past," 95 *Columbia Law Review* 601 (1995).

Sutton, Jeffrey S. "The Role of History in Judging Disputes About the Meaning of the Constitution," 41 *Texas Tech Law Review* 1173 (2009).

Teiser, Sidney. "Life of George H. Williams, Almost Chief-Justice, Part II," 47 *Oregon History Quarterly* 417 (1946).

Toler, Lorianne Updike, Joseph Carl Cecere, and Don R. Willett. "Pre-'Originalism,'" 36 *Harvard Journal of Law and Public Policy* 277 (2012).

Treanor, William Michael. "Against Textualism," 103 *Northwestern University Law Review* 983 (2009).

Treanor, William Michael. "Taking Text Too Seriously: Modern Textualism, Original Meaning, and the Case of Amar's Bill of Rights," 106 *Michigan Law Review* 487 (2007).

Tushnet, Mark V. "Constitutional Scholarship: What Next?" 5 *Constitutional Commentary* 28 (1988).

Tushnet, Mark V. "Following the Rules Laid Down: A Critique of Interpretivism and Neutral Principles," 96 *Harvard Law Review* 781 (1983).

Tushnet, Mark V. "*Heller* and the Perils of Compromise," 13 *Lewis and Clark Law Review* 419 (2009).

Tushnet, Mark V. "Interdisciplinary Legal Scholarship: The Case of History-in-Law," 71 *Chicago-Kent Law Review* 909 (1996).

Tushnet, Mark V. "Permissible Gun Regulations After *Heller*: Speculations About Method and Outcomes," 56 *UCLA Law Review* 1425 (2009).

Tyler, Amanda L., Frank H. Easterbrook, et al. "A Dialogue with Federal Judges on the Role of History in Interpretation," 80 *George Washington Law Review* 1889 (2012).

Valente, Claire. "The Deposition and Abdication of Edward II," 113 *English Historical Review* 852 (1998).

Van Der Vyver, Johan D. "Prosecuting Offenses Against the Law of Nations in the United States," 20 *Emory International Law Review* 473 (2006).

Verduyn, Anthony. "The Politics of Law and Order During the Early Years of Edward III," 108 *English Historical Review* 842 (1993).

Volokh, Eugene. "The First and Second Amendments," 109 *Columbia Law Review* 97 (2009).

Volokh, Eugene. "'The Freedom ... of the Press,' From 1791 to 1868 to Now: Freedom for the Press as an Industry or the Press as a Technology," 160 *University of Pennsylvania Law Review* 459 (2011).

Volokh, Eugene. "Implementing the Right to Keep and Bear Arms for Self-Defense: An Analytical Framework and Research Agenda," 56 *UCLA Law Review* 1443 (2009).

Walker, Anders. "From Ballots to Bullets: *District of Columbia v. Heller* and the New Civil Rights," 69 *Louisiana Law Review* 509 (2009).

Wasserman, Lewis M. "Gun Control on College and University Campuses in the Wake of *District of Columbia v. Heller* and *Mc-*

Donald v. City of Chicago," 19 *Virginia Journal of Social Policy and Law* 1 (2011).

White, G. Edward. "The Arrival of History in Constitutional Scholarship," 88 *Virginia Law Review* 485 (2002).

Whittington, Keith E. "The New Originalism," 2 *Georgetown Journal of Law and Public Policy* 599 (2004).

Wiecek, William M. "Clio as Hostage: The United States Supreme Court and the Uses of History," 24 *California Western Law Review* 227 (1987).

Williams, George H. "Reminiscences of the Supreme Court," 8 *Yale Law Journal* 296 (1899).

Willoughby, W.W. "Citizenship and Allegiance in Constitutional and International Law," 1 *The American Journal of International Law* 914 (1907).

Wilson, Douglas L. "Thomas Jefferson's Early Notebooks," 42 *The William and Mary Quarterly* 433 (1985).

Wiltse, Charles M. "Thomas Jefferson on the Law of Nations," 29 *American Journal of International Law* 66 (1935).

Winchester, Boyd. "Citizenship and its International Relation," 31 *The American Law Review* 504 (1897).

Wofford, John G. "The Blinding Light: The Uses of History and Constitutional Interpretation," 31 *University of Chicago Law Review* 502 (1964).

Wood, Charles. "Losing Control of America's Future—The Census, Birthright Citizenship, and Illegal Aliens," 22 *Harvard Journal of Law and Public Policy* 465 (1999).

Wood, Gordon. "Rhetoric and Reality in the American Revolution," 23 *William and Mary Quarterly* 3 (1966).

Woodard, Calvin. "History, Legal History, and Legal Education," 53 *Virginia Law Review* 89 (1967).

Woodworth, Marshall B. "Citizenship of the United States Under the Fourteenth Amendment," 30 *The American Review* 535 (1886).

Woodworth, Marshall B. "Who Are Citizens of the United States? *Wong Kim Ark* Case Interpreted," 32 *The American Law Review* 554 (1898).

Wydra, Elizabeth B. "Birthright Citizenship: A Constitutional Guarantee," *American Constitutional Society of Law and Policy* 9 (2009).

Zelinsky, Aaron. "Misunderstanding the *Anti-Federalist Papers*: The Dangers of Availability," 63 *Alabama Law Review* 1067 (2012).

Index